Science Fiction Confidential

OTHER WORKS BY TOM WEAVER AND FROM McFARLAND

A Sci-Fi Swarm and Horror Horde (2010)

I Talked with a Zombie (2009)

Earth vs. the Sci-Fi Filmmakers (2005)

Eye on Science Fiction
(2003; paperback 2007)

I Was a Monster Movie Maker (2001)

John Carradine
(1999; paperback 2008)

Science Fiction and Fantasy Film Flashbacks
(1998; paperback 2004)

It Came from Horrorwood
(1996; paperback 2004)

Double Feature Creature Attack
(2 vols. combined 1994/1995; paperback 2003)

Poverty Row HORRORS!
(1993; paperback 1999)

Science Fiction Stars and Horror Heroes
(1991; paperback 2006)

Interviews with B Science Fiction and Horror Movie Makers (1988; paperback 2006)

Universal Horrors: The Studio's Classic Films, 1931–1946
(and Michael Brunas and John Brunas; 2d ed., 2007)

Science Fiction Confidential

Interviews with 23 Monster Stars and Filmmakers

TOM WEAVER

McFarland & Company, Inc., Publishers
Jefferson, North Carolina, and London

Acknowledgments: Abridged versions of some of the interviews featured in this book were originally featured in the following magazines: **John Alvin:** "John Alvin: Warners Contractee," *Classic Images* #305, November 2000; **John D.F. Black:** "Unearthly Writer," *Chiller Theatre* #11, 1999; **Eve Brent:** "Hollywood & Vine," *Starlog* #275, June 2000; **Audrey Dalton:** "Snails and Smiles," *Fangoria* #189, January 2000; **Russ Doughten:** "Brother of the Blob," *Starlog* #279, October 2000; **Elaine DuPont:** "The B Girl and the Monsters," *Fangoria* #198, November 2000; **Robert Ellenstein:** "Federation President," *Starlog Yearbook* #16, August 1998; **Alex Gordon:** "*The She-Creature* Interview: Alex Gordon," *Chiller Theatre* #12, 2000; **Richard Gordon:** "Producer Richard Gordon on *Mother Riley Meets the Vampire*," *The Phantom of the Movies' VideoScope* #33, Winter 2000; **Tod Griffin:** "Tod Griffin: Capt. Neptune vs. She Demon," *Classic Images* #311, May 2001; **David Hedison:** "Lord of the Flys," *Chiller Theatre* #14, 2001; **Kathleen Hughes:** "Interview: Kathleen Hughes," *Chiller Theatre* #12, 2000; **Suzanne Kaaren:** "Devil Bat's Beauty," *Cult Movies* #33, 2000; **Dan O'Herlihy:** "The Man Alone," *Starlog* #285, April 2001; **Kate Phillips:** "Mother of the Blob," *Starlog* #278, September 2000; **Kasey Rogers:** "Kasey Rogers: *Strangers on a Train* Part I," *The Phantom of the Movies' VideoScope* #34, Spring 2000, and "Kasey Rogers Part 2," *The Phantom of the Movies' VideoScope* #35, Summer 2000; **Warren Stevens:** "Forbidden Doctor," *Starlog* #264, July 1999; **Lyn Thomas:** "Lyn Thomas," *Cult Movies* #32, 2000; **Darlene Tompkins:** "Darlene Tompkins: *Beyond the Time Barrier*," *Cult Movies* #30, 2000.

The present work is a reprint of the illustrated case bound edition of Science Fiction Confidential: Interviews with 23 Monster Stars and Filmmakers, *first published in 2002 by McFarland.*

LIBRARY OF CONGRESS CATALOGUING-IN-PUBLICATION DATA

Weaver, Tom, 1958–
    Science fiction confidential : interviews with 23 monster stars and filmmakers / Tom Weaver.
        p.   cm.
    Includes index.

    ISBN 978-0-7864-4516-5
    softcover : 50# alkaline paper

    1. Science fiction films—United States—History and criticism.
2. Horror films—United States—History and criticism.   3. Motion picture actors and actresses—United States—Interviews.   4. Motion picture producers and directors—United States—Interviews.   I. Title.
PN1995.9.S26 W4585   2010   791.43'615—dc21   2001007166

British Library cataloguing data are available

©2002 Tom Weaver. All rights reserved

No part of this book may be reproduced or transmitted in any form or by any means, electronic or mechanical, including photocopying or recording, or by any information storage and retrieval system, without permission in writing from the publisher.

On the cover: Kathleen Hughes in *It Came from Outer Space* (1953)

Manufactured in the United States of America

McFarland & Company, Inc., Publishers
  Box 611, Jefferson, North Carolina 28640
      www.mcfarlandpub.com

CONTENTS

Preface   vii

John Alvin	1
John D.F. Black	15
on *The Unearthly*	
Eve Brent	24
Anthony Cardoza	37
on *The Beast of Yucca Flats*	
Audrey Dalton	47
Phoebe Dorin	59
Russ Doughten	79
Elaine DuPont	99
Robert Ellenstein	110
Alex Gordon	122
on *The She-Creature*	
Richard Gordon	144
on *Mother Riley Meets the Vampire*	
Tod Griffin	153
David Hedison	167
Kathleen Hughes	186
Suzanne Kaaren	197
Denny Miller	207
Dan O'Herlihy	220
Kate Phillips	234
Kasey Rogers	247

Jacqueline Scott 263
Warren Stevens 277
Lyn Thomas 287
Darlene Tompkins 296

Index 305

PREFACE

A "tail end" baby boomer, I saw my first horror and sci-fi movies as a kid in the 1960s and liked them enough to work up an interest in how they were made, and in the people who made them. But those were dark days for genre movie enthusiasts; there was only a handful of books on the subject, and most of *those* were simply "appreciations" of the movies, with little or no background material on the production and personnel. The situation began to improve in the 1970s thanks in part to magazines like *Photon*, *Cinefantastique* and *Fangoria*, but even then, it was largely just the best-loved older movies and moviemakers that got the investigative treatment.

Then in the 1980s, other mag and book writers finally joined the fray, and lesser-known pictures and people were soon being spotlighted. And in the 1990s, the floodgates opened wide, particularly for fans of the '50s and '60s shockers. They opened to the point where we now know that it was the director's future wife inside the Abominable Snowman costume in *Man Beast* (1956); that the spaceship scenes in *The Brain Eaters* (1958) were actually shot in the star's Pomona garage; and that the butler in *The Maze* (1953) has an unusual, gliding walk only because the actor had just had an operation on his buttocks. We know when and how and where and why many of these movies were made—not just the basics, but in considerable detail. We know which of the producers and directors and actors were saints and which were sinners.

It borders on the obsessive for some fans: Lon Chaney's great-grandson, a swimming pool cleaner by occupation, frequently takes time out from emptying pool traps in order to be wined and dined at horror movie conventions, asked for autographs(!!), and pumped for thirteenth-hand stories about the exploits of his fabled great-grandfather—who died generations before the guy was born!

There are, perhaps, some things that Man just isn't *meant* to know—a cautionary sentiment expressed at the end of so many of these movies, it's weird that it seems to have been completely ignored by most of the genre's chroniclers! As one of the prime culprits, however, I accept full responsibility (blame?) for my contributions, and now add to the bottleneck of mind-expanding minutiae *Science Fiction Confidential*—interviews with 23 more of that era's sanguine survivors, from the Fly to a Tarzan and a Jane, from the producers of movies like *The She-Creature* and *The Blob* to an assortment of other folks from beyond the time barrier, from outer space, from Yucca Flats and from … well … somewhere in time.

As always, I've had fabulous support from a galaxy of great friends and new acquaintances, most notably John Antosiewicz, David Bailey, Buddy Barnett (*Cult Movies* magazine), Marty Baumann (*The Astounding B Monster*), Ted Bohus (*SPFX*), Robert Clarke, Kevin Clement (*Chiller Theatre*), Glenn Damato, Harlan Ellison, Michael Fitzgerald, Anne Francis, Michael Gingold (*Fangoria*), Joe Indusi, Joe Kane (*VideoScope*), Alexander Kogan, the Lincoln Center Performing Arts Library crew (Louis Paul, Christine Karatnytsky, Dan Patri, Brian O'Connell, Christopher Frith), Dave McDonnell (*Starlog*), Boyd Magers, Greg Mank, Paul Marco, Barry Murphy, Ray Nielsen, Erin Ray, Clint A.P., Rufus and Tigger Pascaretti (formerly Fresco), William Phipps, the phriendly pholks at Photofest, Oconee and Jeanne Provost, Gary Rhodes, Mary Runser, Rich Scrivani, Tony Timpone (*Fangoria*) and Wade Williams. Mark Martucci, owner of the world's coolest video collection, was always there when needed, as were research associates Mike and John Brunas. John Cocchi and Jack Dukesbery furnished invaluable assistance with the many filmographies.

For the special breed of horror film fans who feel that they *must* know how to play the Hunchback of Notre Dame while suffering with a runny nose ... what *not* to eat for lunch before wrestling a prop alligator ... how to milk a goat on TV ... the reason Dr. Caligari sits so damn much in *The Cabinet of Caligari* ... ad absurdum ... this book, with all the anecdotes and observations and trivia contained within, is appreciatively dedicated to *you*.

Tom Weaver

JOHN ALVIN

Peter Lorre was very pleasant to work with, and a practical joker of the first water. He liked to toy with Andrea King, who was the young ingenue in Beast with Five Fingers. *In the middle of one scene, Lorre pretended to throw up on the dining table in front of Andrea King!*

A Warner Brothers contractee in the 1940s, actor John Alvin played some of his best roles during that first decade of his career, appearing in major productions with stars like Errol Flynn and Cary Grant. During this same decade that he was cast in his most memorable role, as one of the five Waterloo, Iowa, brothers who lose their lives in combat in the fact-based World War II drama *The Sullivans* (1944).

Born in Chicago, the son of a doctor dad and an opera-singing mother, John Alvin Hoffstadt was introverted as a boy and got into dramatics in order to "be somebody else." After training at California's renowned Pasadena Playhouse, he acted on stage in Chicago and Detroit and then landed a berth at Warners, playing supporting parts in films like *Destination Tokyo* (1943) and *Objective, Burma!* (1945). In the horror and fantasy genres, he appeared as the arrogant wannabe-heir in the moody *The Beast With Five Fingers* (1947); guested on the TV series *Climax, One Step Beyond* and *Rocky Jones, Space Ranger* (among dozens of others); and checked Christopher Reeve into the Grand Hotel in the "time travel" tale *Somewhere in Time* (1980). Alvin here recalls these productions—and some standout moments from a lifetime of acting.

When did you decide you had to be an actor?

I guess it was in high school in Chicago. I had a very good drama teacher, and she encouraged me. I did three or four plays there, and she encouraged me to go to the Pasadena Playhouse. Even though we had the Goodman Theater right there in Chicago, she thought that the Pasadena Playhouse was the best place for me. So after I graduated from high school, I left for the Playhouse in 1939 and spent three years there. We studied voice and speech and fencing and eurythmics and makeup and set design and set building, and we even had a class where we were taught how to write plays. And we *did* many plays while I was there.

Who else was there at the Playhouse who went on to movies?

There was Victor Mature ... Gig Young ... Eleanor Parker ... Helmut Dantine ... John Ridgely ... Russell Arms, who was later on *Your Hit Parade* as a singer ... oh, so many. Also an actor named Harry Lewis, who later became a restaurateur and had a chain of Hamburger Hamlet restaurants. Another actor, Ray Montgomery, and I helped him build the first Hamburger Hamlet on the Sunset Strip, back around 1950. We were working as carpenters because there was not much work as an actor.

Also there at the Playhouse was the man who appeared in all the slasher movies ... you know, the movies that were set in London where there was a slasher who'd go out and kill people...

Laird Cregar?

Laird Cregar, right! I can tell you a little story about Laird: Laird Cregar was doing a play called *Oscar Wilde* over in Hollywood — this was after the Playhouse. He was very large, a man of about six-one or –two and he weighed 250, 300 pounds. He was playing Oscar Wilde and his mother was at the show, and she was backstage with him *after* the show. John Barrymore had seen the performance that night and he came in to talk to Laird Cregar. He had a cigarette in one hand and a cocktail in the other, and he was a little blotto. He said [*imitating Barrymore*], "Mr. Cregar, I want to tell you how much I enjoyed your performance. It was simply unbelievable, I couldn't have done better my*self*." And Laird Cregar said, "Mr. Barrymore, thank you. Coming from you, that is truly an encomium, it's one of the nicest things I've ever had said to me. Oh, pardon me, I'd like you to meet my mother..." Laird Cregar's mother was a tiny woman of about five feet, five-foot-one. Barrymore looked over at her...and then he looked over and *up* at Cregar ... and he looked back to the little lady and he said, "God, madam, what a fuck *that* must have been!" [*Laughs*] "Out of doors, no doubt!" I don't know whether that story's apocryphal or whether it's true, but that's the story!

Did you like Cregar?

Oh, he was very nice, a very charming man.

You were never swayed from your desire to be an actor?

No, I wasn't at all. While we were there [at the Playhouse], eight of us who graduated, seniors, we put our moneys together — a pittance! — and we went out to the Redwoods, near Eureka, California, up the coast, a little town called Garberville, and we built our own theater there and did plays. Then we went back to the Playhouse for our final year, which was post-graduate, and did a few more plays.

Did you ever work in radio?

I went back to Chicago in 1942 and worked in radio, and at night I appeared in plays with a company called the Actors Company. Then one day I auditioned at NBC for a job as a staff announcer at WWJ in Detroit and to have my own radio drama show. I auditioned along with 75 other guys, and I got the job. So I went to Detroit and did a show there called *Major V, the Daring Leader of the Underground* [*laughs*]. I was — and still am — fairly adept at dialects, and so Major V did all sorts of dialects — German, French, Irish, English and so on. Hugh Downs was on the staff there with me.

Your real name is John Alvin Hoffstadt. At what point did you change it?

When I was on the WWJ staff as an

Actor John Alvin looks back at his colorful career.

announcer. We were near the middle of the War and the station suggested I change my name, 'cause you don't sign off in the middle of a war with Germany with "John Hoffstadt." So I took my middle name and used it as my last.

I was there just a year: During the day, I was on the staff as an announcer, then at night I appeared in plays. A man named Henry Duffy had a stock company there and I went over and read for him and got two parts, the first one in a play with Charlotte Greenwood. The next one, which followed immediately, was *Life of the Party*, in which I played the juvenile. Passing through town was the head talent scout for Warner Brothers, Sophie Rosenstein; in Chicago, she had talked to the lady who directed the Actors Company, who said, "Be sure when you go through Detroit to see Johnny Alvin." Sophie Rosenstein did, and I read for her after the show that night. The next day she came back and she signed me to a seven-year contract at Warner Brothers. And away I went!

Was that what you were waiting for, a shot at the movies?

No, I never thought that I would ever appear in movies. I thought I was going to continue as a legitimate actor on the stage. So it came as a great surprise, actually.

Was there any hesitancy on your part at all?

Oh, not at all [*laughs*]! They give you your train ticket — in those days, it was a train, not a plane — with a return ticket if, after your screen test, they decided that they were not that interested in you. I went and did a screen test, and passed, and they signed me. There are options in a seven-year contract — at the end of six months or at the end of a year, depending on which type of contract you signed, the studio has the option of either re-signing you or letting you go. But you can't just *leave* — if there's a contract, you have to stay! And they always "up" your salary by $100, 150, whatever it was [each time the actor was re-signed].

Do you remember what movie or play your screen test was from?

No, I don't remember — it might have been from Philip Barry's *Holiday*, but I'm not sure. They usually hand you three or four pages of a movie script and they assign one of the other contract players to play the other part in it, and then you get up and you do it. I stayed there for almost six years. And not only that, but after Warners let all the contract players go in about 1947-48, I worked there, oh, in at least six or eight movies after I was dropped by the studio.

What did a Warners contract player do between pictures?

The contract players had the ability to take various classes (which I had already taken at the Pasadena Playhouse). We could study fencing, we could study singing and dancing and *boxing* — they had a guy there named Mushy Callahan, an ex-prizefighter, and he taught us how to handle ourselves if we had to fight in a film. That was one of the other good things about it.

Your film debut was in Northern Pursuit, *a small unbilled part as a German in a Canadian internment camp.*

Right, in 1943.

The Sullivans — was that on loanout to 20th Century-Fox?

Oh, yes. I was loaned out by Warner Brothers to play in *The Sullivans*, which was released in 1944. I was very surprised, and a bit upset, to learn that Warner Brothers got double my salary and I only got my regular salary [*laughs*]! But that was the way it worked!

Was there any reluctance on your part to act in a horror movie, The Beast with Five Fingers?

When you're a contract player, you damn well do it, because if you *don't*, you take a protracted leave — not at your wish! The scriptwriter was one of two brothers — was it Bob or Curt Siodmak? Yes, Curt! I really enjoyed talking to him the few times I did, on the set. I think he had an office on the studio lot.

Siodmak told me that Paul Henreid was originally cast in Beast, *and he refused it. Peter Lorre did the part instead.*

Henreid wasn't the type for that kind of role, so he was wise. He was such a smooth character, and [*imitating Lorre*] Peter Lorre was perfect to play that part. Before *Beast With Five Fingers*, Lorre and I were both in *Three Strangers* [1946] — that was with Lorre and Sydney Greenstreet.

Half a century before *Saving Private Ryan*, Alvin, Jack Campbell, Edward Ryan, George Offerman, Jr., and James Cardwell played the doomed brothers in 1944's *The Sullivans*.

Greenstreet was not too easy to work with, he was rather gruff, but I learned later that he had a son who had some illness and Greenstreet was very worried about him, and naturally he was upset. In *Three Strangers*, Dick Erdman and I were two clerks—well, "clarks," because it was supposed to be in England.

Peter Lorre was very pleasant to work with, and a practical joker of the first water. He liked to toy with Andrea King, who was the young ingenue in *Beast With Five Fingers*. One day we were rehearsing a particular scene around a big dining table—a beautiful table, with the crystal and everything. Peter Lorre set this whole gag up, he said [*imitating Lorre*], "Oh, I really don't feel too good today…" Later on: "My stomach … something is wrong…" We went ahead rehearsing, and finally the director Bob Florey said, "Okay, let's do it. Action." And in the middle of the scene, Lorre [*Alvin makes a retching sound*] pretended to throw up on the dining table in front of Andrea King! She was just shocked, she screamed and covered her face. She couldn't believe it! Lorre laughed — and then, of course, we *all* laughed. That was typical of his sense of humor.

That was with the camera rolling?

With the camera rolling. Florey said, "Well, I believe we'll have to shoot *that* again…!" [*Laughs*]

Nobody else was "in on it," you were all taken by surprise?

Yes, all of us.

Beast with Five Fingers *is such a grim movie, it's tough to imagine the cast pulling practical jokes and having fun between takes.*

Well, we tried to. Robert Alda was a very charming guy, very nice, completely relaxed, just like his son Alan. He had that same type of personality. He was a complete gentleman and *very* interested in what *you're* doing and how you do it. A very nice man — not like a lot of leading men! He wasn't struck with himself. He had done a lot of burlesque, so he was "down there with the people." Andrea King was also very nice.

And Robert Florey?

A very tall French gentleman and a very good director. Always puffing on his pipe, very calm, and very helpful. I was relatively a beginning movie actor at that time, and he was extremely helpful to people who were in that position.

Is that your mustache in the movie, or makeup?

No, that's my mustache. That's when I started wearing it, and I have it to this day. Not the same one, though [*laughs*], it's quite white now!

Your character in the movie is very arrogant and disagreeable. Is it fun to play characters like that?

Oh, much more fun than playing a straight role. You can color it, you can *do* things with it that you *can't* with a straight juvenile. At Warners, I played mostly heavies, and that's what I *wanted* to do. In fact, in *Shadow of a Woman* [1946], I was quite a heavy. I had a fight with Helmut Dantine and pushed him over a San Francisco balcony to his death down below. He was my uncle, and he had operated on me and ruined my leg — I was a cripple who walked with a cane. And finally … I *got* him [*laughs*]! *Shadow of a Woman* was from the mystery novel *He Fell Down Dead* by a famous woman writer, Virginia Perdue.

Was there any sort of "problem" with Beast with Five Fingers? *It was made in 1945 but Warners didn't release it 'til the beginning of '47.*

I didn't know about that. *I* think it was well-done. The budget was fairly good for a movie of that sort, and Bob Alda was excellent. Peter Lorre fitted his part perfectly and executed it perfectly. Having seen him do it, I can't think of anyone else who could do it better! And we also had J. Carrol Naish in it as the police chief. He was a Black Irishman but he used to do only like Italian parts or Spanish parts — oh, he was a terrific guy, *very* good, and a very nice man too. We all admired his

Conniving Charles Dingle and his arrogant son Alvin seek to usurp an inheritance in *The Beast with Five Fingers* (with J. Carrol Naish and Robert Alda, right).

acting so much, and the stories he could tell. The same way in *The Sullivans*: Our father in *The Sullivans* was Thomas Mitchell. There were a lot of breweries in the area where we shot that film, up in Northern California, and he'd sit around and tell us stories all night long whilst we were drinking pink champagne. We looked up to him and admired his acting for years and years and years.

Why did Warners drop you and the other contract players?

Because of television coming in. It scared the wits out of the studio heads; they said, "What are we gonna do? My gosh, this'll replace features in the theater!" Warners got scared and they dropped most of the contract players and a lot of the directors, who were making a heckuva lot more money than *we* were. Just as a safety measure, because they weren't sure what would happen.

And you "went over to the enemy"—you were in a lot of early TV series, and even some live TV.

Live TV gave you a bit of a stir, it made your heart pound, and you'd sweat a lot [*laughs*]. When that red light went on, *you were there*, all by yourself. There were no teleprompters then, so if you "went up" [forgot your lines], you "went up"! And if you didn't move to the spot you were *supposed* to move to—the cameraman would just have to ad lib it and follow you here and there and everywhere. One show I did was called *Climax*—*we* used to call it *Orgasm*, but it was called *Climax* [*laughs*]. It was mysteries and so on.

You were in a Climax *episode called "The Thirteenth Chair" with Ethel Barrymore.*

She was not too communicative. She was very pleasant, but mostly her conversations dealt with the Brooklyn Dodgers [*laughs*]. She was a great Dodger fan, apparently. In one of the *Climax* shows, it may have been "The Thirteenth Chair" and it may have been some other one that I did, an actor was "killed" and he dropped out of sight below the camera. The prop man came up and put a blanket over him. The camera pulled back, but the actor didn't *know* it had pulled back. So here's this blanket crawling across the stage with the camera trailing behind it [*laughs*]!

I want to bounce a few other TV series titles off of you to see if there are any anecdotes attached. Rocky Jones, Space Ranger?

Oh, yeah—the actor who played Rocky Jones, Richard Crane, died too young. Richard was the kind of guy who was always smiling and always outgoing and always happy—a typical juvenile who had a great personality. We did that over at the Hal Roach Studios.

Sheena, Queen of the Jungle *with Irish McCalla?*

Sheena I don't remember too much. We shot that out in the "jungles" nearby. Bob Shayne and I were both in that. We were *very* good friends; in fact, he and his wife Bette lived just a few miles from us out here in Thousand Oaks, and we used to socialize together. Bob, like most of us actors, had a second job: He had an insurance agency. I at one time tried to work with him, but I couldn't handle insurance [*laughs*]! But Bob was a good friend—in fact, we still see his daughter Stephanie, who was an actress and probably *still* does some modeling. I also knew his wife *before* Bette.

I didn't know there was a wife before Bette, to be honest with you.

I think Bette was his *fourth* wife—he was married several times.

It occurs to me that you probably knew him from your Warner Brothers days.

That's right, we were both at Warners at the same time. Then I did a picture for Republic called *Missing Women* [1951] and he was in that: He was the head of the heavies, and Penny Edwards and I were two car thieves [*laughs*]!

Shayne always used to talk about being blacklisted in the 1950s — but I look at the list of his movies and, whereas other "blacklisted" actors never worked, it looks to me like he never stopped *working!*

Well, he *was* blacklisted for a while—one of his four wives turned him in or gave testimony against him. And, actually, Bob *said* that he *was* a member of the Communist Party at one point. But he was 18 or 19 years old at the time, and he had no association with them after that. There were a lot of people who were just liberals, who were blacklisted as being Communists.

One Step Beyond?

That episode ["Where Are They?"] was based on a true story about a little town up north called Paradise, where stones fell out of the sky, and I played a newspaper reporter who went there to cover the story. John Newland [the series host] was under contract as an actor to Warners when I was there, so I wrote him a letter saying, "I love your series. How 'bout using *me* on it, and I'll love it even more?" [*Laughs*] And the next week I got a call to go over and pick up a script. He was very good that way.

Kolchak: The Night Stalker?

Kolchak was fun. It was nice to work with Darren McGavin. He would call us all "sweethearts": He'd say, "Okay, sweethearts, now we're gonna rehearse this one ... " I think he got that from Tallulah Bankhead or something [*laughs*]!

You had a supporting part in the suspense movie The Couch *[1962] with Grant Williams and Onslow Stevens.*

Right. Grant Williams played a character who had a mental problem, and he was working with Onslow Stevens, who was a psychiatrist. Onslow was one of our directors at the Pasadena Playhouse. He was a *very* good teacher, very well-respected. Had a terrific personality, seemed always to be smiling, very pleasant to work with. But Onslow had a rather bad drinking problem, and he disappeared in the middle of that production [*The Couch*]. I think they got him back in about a week, and he finished the movie. I also remember that Onslow, after starting out as a very young man, was blackballed in the movie business for a few years, because he had an affair with William Randolph Hearst's girlfriend Marion Davies. He didn't work for a period of time, and then he finally got back in.

How did you find out about Stevens and Marion Davies? From Stevens?

Oh, no. I'm sure he wanted to *forget* it. *I* would [*laughs*]!

What were your impressions of Alfred Hitchcock when you appeared in Marnie *[1964]?*

I played an all-purpose guy around a hotel where Sean Connery and Tippi Hedren stayed. I picked her up at the railroad station and brought her back to the hotel in a station wagon and carried her luggage in and had a few lines. And that was it. And it was "great" working with Hitchcock, who practically ignored everybody but his two stars. He didn't have a very good opinion of actors and didn't spend much time with the bit players.

Speaking of working in a hotel, talk about landing your role as the hotel manager in Somewhere in Time.

I got that role through a friend, Richard Matheson, the man who wrote it [the original novel *and* the screenplay]. He is *very* good that way — he has friends who are actors, and whenever he has a chance, he tries to get them into the film that he has written. I'd known Richard for many years, and he was instrumental in having me read for [director] Jeannot Szwarc and the producer.

How did you get to know Matheson?

My wife June and I lived in Tarzana at that time, and we had a friend down the block called Bruce Cameron. He had written several novels and belonged to some sort of a writers' clique. He was also a friend of Jerry Sohl, who was a science fiction writer — and still *is*, when he can get [work]. It's the same for writers as for actors: If you're over 40, you have to fight for every job or for every script. In fact, as I understand it, if you're over 40 now, they won't even *read* your script. Isn't that amazing? Anyway, June and I used to party with these people who were mostly writers.

Did you screen-test for the part?

No, I just went to Universal and read for them, and Jeannot Szwarc said fine. They shot it at the Grand Hotel on Mackinac Island in Michigan, and I was there for two weeks; I think I worked one week but I was there for two, just in case they needed to shoot any retakes or anything of that sort. After the first week, I called June and said, "You gotta get here. This is

Weary (time) traveler Christopher Reeve is checked in (by Alvin) at a hotel *Somewhere in Time*.

terrific!" So she flew out and joined me there on Mackinac Island — which, by the way, is spelled M-a-c-k-i-n-a-c but pronounced Mack-in-*aw*. I don't know why, but they elide the "c" and put a "w" in there! What makes Mackinac Island so terrific is the fact that there are no cars there, they don't allow any cars— you get around by bicycle or horse and buggy, or just on horseback. And the hotel itself is fabulous, just fabulous, *beautiful*. Then, of course, the Mackinac Island fudge —*that's* pretty good, too [*laughs*]!

By the way, I know that when Richard Matheson wrote his novel, he was inspired by the story of [real-life turn-of-the-century actress] Maude Adams. He thought of setting it in Virginia City, and then decided that if he did *that*, it would end up as a Western [*laughs*]! So he sort of gave up on it until he and his wife went to the Del Coronado Hotel in Coronado, which is an island the other side of the Bay from San Diego. They were having a drink there, and he thought, "This is the perfect place." It was built the same year as the Grand Hotel, 1888. In the novel, the story takes place in the Del Coronado. But when it came time to do the movie, they decided they couldn't use the Del Coronado. Because it's surrounded by so many modern buildings, it would have been very difficult to shoot it there. So the producer and Jeannot Szwarc found various hotels in a book about great old hotels in this country, they went to Mackinac Island in the dead of winter to take a look at it, and decided to shoot *Somewhere in Time* there instead.

*Had you read Matheson's novel [*Bid Time Return*]?*

Oh, yes. Why [*laughs*], we have *all* of his novels!

Szwarc once called Somewhere in Time *a very "non-Hollywood, summer stock type" movie.*

I'd go along with that completely. And some of the actors that they hired in Chicago and in Detroit were just perfect because they weren't *like* actors, they weren't acting — they seemed to be just so *real*. For instance, when they did the scene of the play, the people who were in *that* were so ... how shall I say it? They weren't actor-like, they were *natural*.

Was Universal allowed to bring cars and trucks to the island?

They were, yes. In fact, they started out from Universal City and they drove allll across the country. It was one of the few occasions that they allowed automobiles on the island. They had also allowed automobiles on the island when MGM did a film there with Jimmy Durante and Esther Williams [*This Time for Keeps*, 1947]. So they allow it on special circumstances, but *only* then.

According to Christopher Reeve, all of "his people" told him not to do the film, but he liked the story and the character and he went against their advice.

That's true, he mentioned that to us a couple of times. He said he was so glad that he had not followed their advice and had done the movie anyway.

Did the hotel continue to operate while you were all there?

Yes, they did have guests there. I remember that the set builders built a completely different front desk in the lobby — they built the desk I stood behind and did a lot of my scenes from. They put "my" new desk in a different location, and it confused the regular patrons who were used to coming there every summer [*laughs*]! The scene where Jane Seymour is in the play was shot over in another building, two or three miles away from the hotel. There was a stage there as well as a complete radio and TV setup.

At the time the movie was made, Christopher Reeve was allergic to horses and, while everybody else rode horses or rode in horse-drawn carriages from one place to another, he would have to take a bicycle.

I noticed that. I didn't know that an allergy was the reason, but I did notice that he would use his bike all the time.

The ironic part of that is, if he hadn't gotten over his allergy, he wouldn't be paralyzed today.

Yes, exactly. He was very nice, very down-to-earth and not at all the "star type." Very easy to talk to. Jane Seymour was the same way exactly.

What is the secret of Somewhere in Time*'s continuing appeal?*

In 1980 when it came out, it was a very romantic film for that time. I don't think that the box office was commensurate with the quality of the film itself. The romanticism, I think, kind of killed it! But then, later on, a man named Bill Shepard came along and rustled us all out of our homes and got us all together and we talked [about doing *Somewhere in Time* conventions]. He was the one who started this whole "rehabilitation" of the film — he brought it to the attention of many people who hadn't known of it before. They really *like* the romance of it, this group of people who got behind it. They have their conventions on Mackinac Island every October, near the end of the month, when the hotel is actually closed and there aren't any guests. The fans come, usually around 800 and sometimes 1000, and they dress in the costumes of the early 1900s and they have a costume contest. Also, the fans — in their

Alvin and "screen son" Sean Hayden in *Somewhere in Time*.

costumes of the 1900s—redo some of the scenes from *Somewhere in Time*, just for their amusement. They get their costumes on and they go out and rehearse a bit, and then they do them.

What other Somewhere in Time *veterans attend the reunions?*

On *two* occasions, I think, Christopher Reeve was there, and Jane Seymour was there twice or three times. Susan French, who plays Jane Seymour as an old lady, is there usually, and Bill Erwin, who played my son Arthur [in the modern-day scenes], is there *every* time. Jeannot Szwarc has been there a couple times.

You have to show someone one of your movies, any *one of your movies. Which one do you show?*

I would say it's a tie between *Somewhere in Time* and *The Very Thought of You* [1944]. In *The Very Thought of You*, I was Eleanor Parker's brother, a kind of a combination heavy and comic. She'd fallen in love with Dennis Morgan, who was a soldier, and I was very much against it and tried to get her to stop seeing him. I got to have a lot of corny but funny lines, and the director Delmer Daves allowed us to interject lines on our own. It was kind of fun because we could ad lib if we wanted to, and if it fit his idea.

You talked before about the fact that, early on, you saw yourself as a stage actor and you never planned to get into the movies. What regrets, if any, when you look back at your career?

Ohhhhhh ... well, I regret never

having gone to New York to work. As I mentioned earlier, the play I was in when I was signed was called *Life of the Party*, and it was Lerner and Loewe's first musical. I played the juvenile in that, and that's the one that "launched" me — I came right out to Warner Brothers when that show stopped. And then *Life of the Party* went to New York and it only lasted 13 weeks, so I was lucky on *that* score! But I still wish I had gone to New York. One other thing I want to mention is that, just after Warner Bros. left me (or *I* left Warner Bros.), I went over to a theater here in town called the Circle Theater and I read for a play called *Rain* by Somerset Maugham. It was directed, *completely*, up to the music and the performing of the music and the taping of the music and everything *else*, by Charlie Chaplin. His son Sydney was in it, playing the marine, William Schallert played the minister, and June Havoc played Sadie Thompson. That's one of my favorite stageplays that I have done. We ran for 18 or 20 weeks and everybody in town came to see it. It was a lot of fun and I got a lot of jobs out of that.

And as for the film and TV work itself — what impressions, looking back?

I'm satisfied with it. I did what I could, and you have to work according to the agent you have. If they don't build an image for you (or if *you* don't build an image for your*self*, because it all boils down to *you*), then you kind of "float around." Particularly in pictures, you have to fit a certain type the way that, say, Walter Matthau did. "The grumpy type," that was the image *he* built for himself, and those are the parts he was hired for. Unless you make a strong impression *like* that, they don't say when a part comes along, "Hey, that's a part for Walter Matthau" or "That's a part for John Alvin." I did various things, and each part was different. It sounds like I'm trying to make an excuse here, but it's true: You've got to have a set image so that, when a certain type of role is mentioned, they think of you and they say, "Get *him*." That's very important.

Overall, however, I was happy with what I did. I like what Jamie Lee Curtis said about acting: She said, "I make my living as an actress. It's what I do. It's not *who I am*."

JOHN ALVIN FILMOGRAPHY

Northern Pursuit (Warners, 1943)
Destination Tokyo (Warners, 1943)
Janie (Warners, 1944)
The Sullivans (*The Fighting Sullivans*) (20th Century–Fox, 1944)
The Very Thought of You (Warners, 1944)
The Horn Blows at Midnight (Warners, 1945)
San Antonio (Warners, 1945)
Objective, Burma! (Warners, 1945)
Roughly Speaking (Warners, 1945)
Night and Day (Warners, 1946)
Three Strangers (Warners, 1946)
One More Tomorrow (Warners, 1946)
Shadow of a Woman (Warners, 1946)
The Beast with Five Fingers (Warners, 1947)
Cheyenne (*The Wyoming Kid*) (Warners, 1947)
Dark Passage (Warners, 1947)
Stallion Road (Warners, 1947)
Deep Valley (Warners, 1947)
Love and Learn (Warners, 1947)
Under Colorado Skies (Republic, 1947)
Romance on the High Seas (Warners, 1948)
Two Guys from Texas (Warners, 1948)
The Bold Frontiersman (Republic, 1948)
The Babe Ruth Story (Monogram, 1948)
Open Secret (Eagle-Lion, 1948)
Rocky (Monogram, 1948)
Shanghai Chest (Monogram, 1948)
Train to Alcatraz (Republic, 1948)
The Fountainhead (Warners, 1949)
The Story of Seabiscuit (Warners, 1949)
The Breaking Point (Warners, 1950)
This Side of the Law (Warners, 1950)
Bright Leaf (Warners, 1950)
Dial 1119 (MGM, 1950)
Highway 301 (Warners, 1950)
Lonely Hearts Bandit (Republic, 1950)
Pretty Baby (Warners, 1950)
Photo Phonies (RKO short, 1950)
Goodbye, My Fancy (Warners, 1951)
Close to My Heart (Warners, 1951)

Come Fill the Cup (Warners, 1951)
Missing Women (Republic, 1951)
The Unknown Man (MGM, 1951)
Three Guys Named Mike (United Artists, 1953)
Carrie (Paramount, 1952)
The Iron Mistress (Warners, 1952)
April in Paris (Warners, 1952)
Torpedo Alley (Allied Artists, 1952)
Dream Wife (MGM, 1953)
Wicked Woman (United Artists, 1953)
Deep in My Heart (MGM, 1954)
The Shanghai Story (Republic, 1954)
A Bullet for Joey (United Artists, 1955)
The McConnell Story (Warners, 1955)
City of Shadows (Republic, 1955)
Illegal (Warners, 1955)
Kentucky Rifle (Howco, 1955)
The Couch (Warners, 1962)
Irma La Douce (United Artists, 1963)
Marnie (Universal, 1964)
Inside Daisy Clover (Warners, 1965)
They Call Me MISTER Tibbs! (United Artists, 1970)
Somewhere in Time (Universal, 1980)
Milk Money (Paramount, 1994)

JOHN D.F. BLACK on *The Unearthly*

To tell you the truth, I was kind of amazed that [The Unearthly] held together that well, for what it was. And I know it didn't cost four dollars!

Science fiction and *Star Trek* fans will recognize the name John D. F. Black, the space series' associate producer (and executive story consultant) during its historic first season. But horror movie fans who find the name less familiar must be forgiven, as Black's one excursion into the genre, 1957's *The Unearthly*, was written under a pen name ("Geoffrey Dennis").

A moldy, 1940s-Monogram-style chiller, *The Unearthly* starred John Carradine as a treacherous doctor who has filled his backwoods Georgia rest home with patients—and then uses them in dangerous experiments involving an artificially developed "seventeenth gland" with which he intends to halt the human aging process. There was treachery both in front of *and* behind the camera, says Black, who now tells his side of the story:

How did you land your first screenwriting job, on The Unearthly?

I was working at the *Los Angeles Times*, selling classified ads and putting myself through school at Los Angeles City College. I was just a kid, on the hustle, staying alive. I was told there was a lead, that I was supposed to go and see this person, Boris Petroff, at a place on Western Avenue as part of my work one day. The way classified ads are worked is, it's broken down into territories; the guy whose territory it *was* was on vacation and, as a temporary, I was working that area for him. So I went. The place was located near Western Avenue on Santa Monica; at that time, it was like the boondocks of Hollywood. There were a lot of little studios where people were puttin' things together; for instance, there was a guy, A. Harry Keatan, who had been in silent films and who now had a small studio where he gave children acting lessons and adults movie lessons. It was *that* kind of area.

I found the place where I was sup-

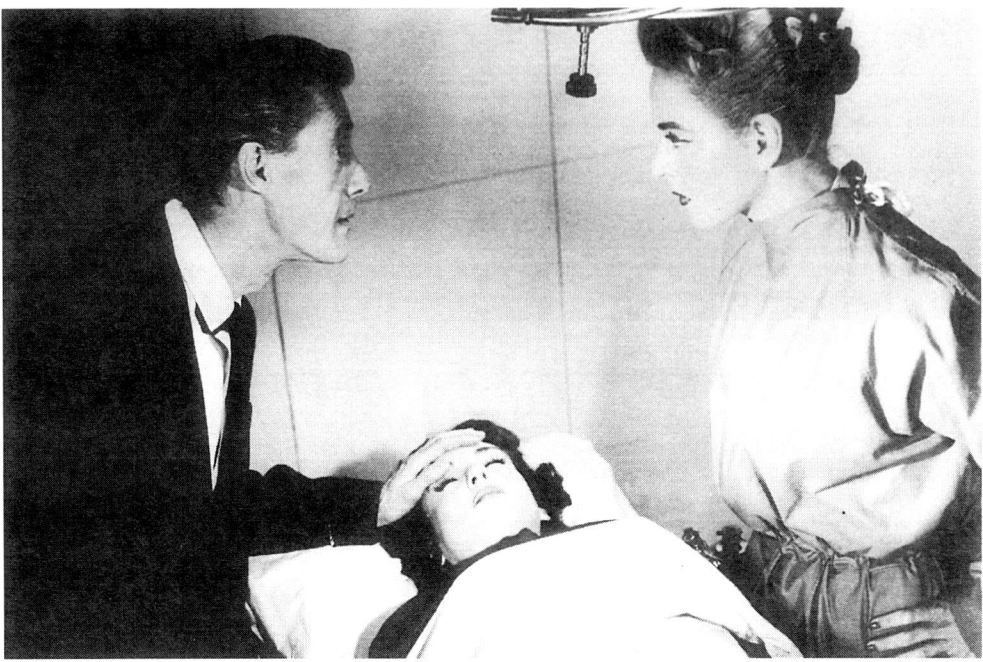

John Carradine and Marilyn Buferd (Miss America of 1946), about to lay the surgical smackdown on hapless Allison Hayes in *The Unearthly*.

posed to go; it was between a small saloon and a borax furniture store. (That's a cheap furniture store; that's what they called 'em, borax houses.) I walked down the alley and through the door of this little studio, and there behind a desk in this very dingy, small office sat Boris Petroff, who wanted me to write an ad. I said, "It's a pleasure to meet you, Mr. Petroff," and did all the bullshit that you usually do when you're trying to get as many ads out of somebody as you possibly can so that you can make a little more commission.

You had no idea what the ad was going to be about.

Correct. And I am now confronting [*Black shifts into a Russian accent*] Borrris Petrrroff, who talks like dis. He had genuine Rrrussian accent, that was his language. He was a charming man, I would guess somewhere between five-ten and six feet; on the heavy side, but not fat. And he told me what he wanted to do was to put an ad in the paper for a writer. What he was *not* saying was, he wanted a writer who was not in the union — but that was what he *meant*. He started to dictate the ad — "Want writer. Good background, intelligent, college —" I said, "That's *me*!" When you're a kid, you just go straight ahead [*laughs*]! I said, "*I* can do that job. I'm a writer." Actually, I *had* written a couple of little film things at City College — I was a direction major, and at that time I was directing *Detective Story* on the stage there. And I had done some writing in Pittsburgh, where I grew up. I told him all that and I gave him the best pitch I could — I did everything but claim I wrote *Cleopatra*. He said, "All right!" and he gave me the job. Also, this saved him nine dollars for the ad [*laughs*], which he liked a lot!

He wrote up a contract on a sheet of paper, and (though Mr. Petroff didn't want union) I took that piece of paper and I ran like a bandit to the Writers Guild. Because,

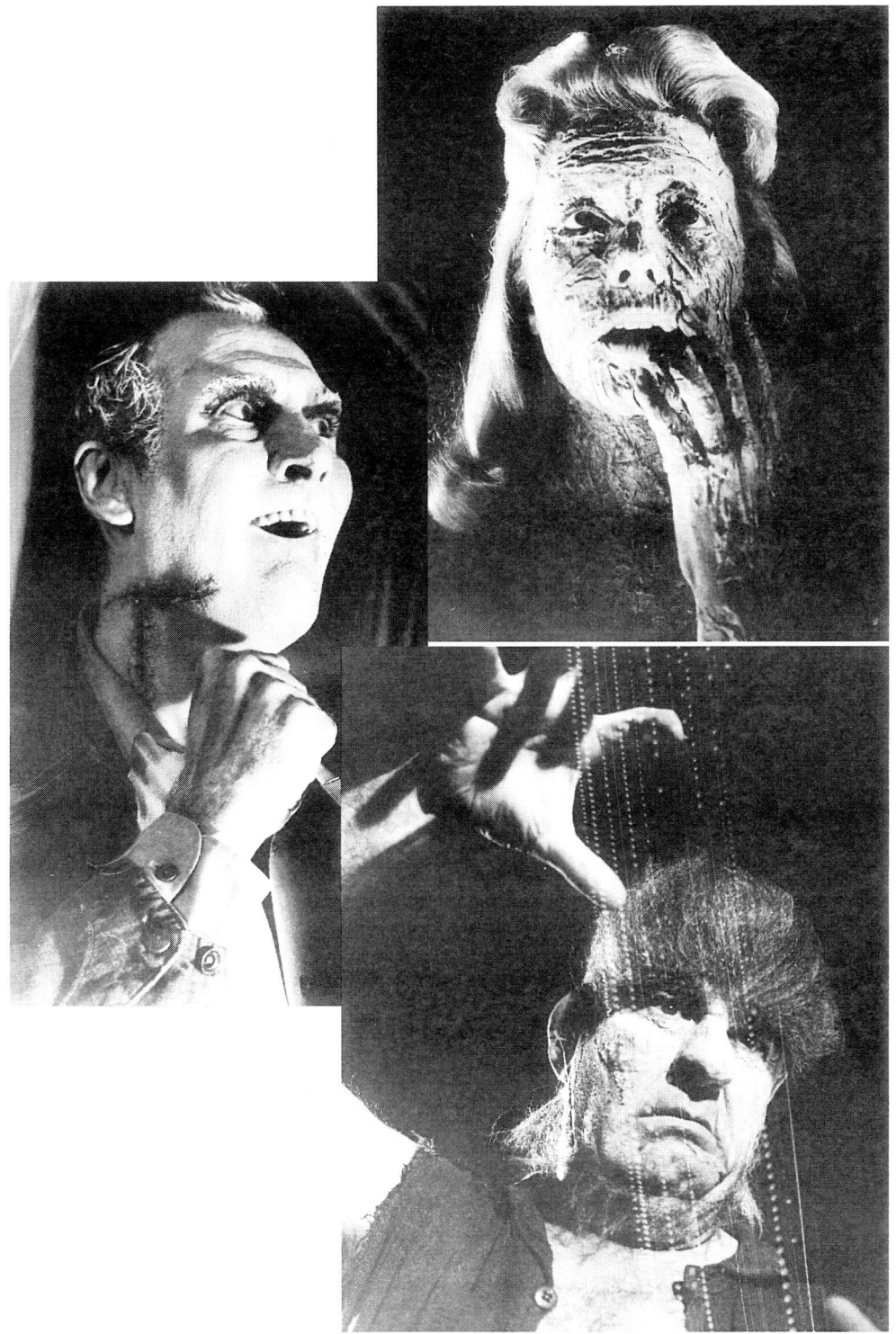

The Unearthly may have been low-budget, but its gallery of human horrors (in Harry Thomas makeup) is unmatched in the annals of '50s exploitation.

in Hollywood then as now, you can't get a job unless you're in the union and you can't get in the union unless you've got a job — and I *had* one. So I submitted the contract to the Writers Guild. I didn't have the money to pay my fee to get in, but they said, "Fine, okay." And away I went to work on what was then called *The House of Monsters*.

Why isn't your name on the movie?

I was working for the *L.A. Times* selling classified ads, and the *L.A. Times* had a rule that you could not moonlight. Going to college was one thing, but moonlighting — having another job — was forbidden. And out of that came [Black's *nom de screen*] "Geoffrey Dennis" — which was a very classy name!

Especially with the "G"!

Oh, of course! What else? I had everything but a dog named Pertwee, one of those British floppy-faced dogs [*laughs*]! So away I went to do this picture: I sat down with Boris and he told me kind-of what he wanted. The seventeenth gland was his, he wanted that.

Did he have any of the cast lined up yet?

No, except he had a connection with Myron Healey.

I'm jumping around a little, let's go back. There I was with Boris Petroff, he was gonna direct the picture and I had the writing job. He walked me through the area behind the office, which was a dressing area, and onto the stage. Now, the stage was *not* really what you would call a huge film stage. The ceiling was a little higher than your average ten-foot ceiling, it was about 14 feet. To tell you the truth, that stage was not as big as the living room in the house I bought when I started to work steady — it was a really small place, used primarily to make porno pictures. And screen tests — when some guy wanted to make a screen test of a beautiful young lady who he wanted to get next to quickly, he could (for 20 bucks or 50 bucks or whatever) get the guy who ran the place, Merle Connell, to shoot a test of the girl. It was that kind of catch-as-catch-can business.

Merle Connell photographed The Unearthly.

Right. He was a sweet man, but he wouldn't talk story with me, all he said was, "Do whatever Boris asks. And that way he'll be very happy and everything'll work fine."

Boris and I talked a little, and I wrote a little, and I wrote a lot, and I took stuff to him. Boris would say, "It should have here, 'Very clever of you, doctor!'" And I would say, "But we *had* that on the last page, Mr. Petroff." I of course called him "Mr. Petroff" every chance I got, and he liked that a lot. He was from a Russian circus family. The family got to Moscow once, and when this little bitty circus he was with *left* Moscow, the circus went one way and *he* came to the United States.

So you worked with Petroff throughout the whole writing process?

Here's what finally happened: I was working on the script, delivering pages, and then I realized it would become a nightmare if I kept doing it that way. So I just didn't show up for ten days, and finished it. I delivered it to Mr. Petroff, who gave it to Jane, his wife, who typed it. I can't type. I couldn't then, I can't now. (My wife wants me to add that I also can't spell. Or punctuate!) In any case, Mrs. Petroff typed it up; he read it; everything was fine. We needed two more "Very clever of you, doctor"s in the front and three more at the back — Boris didn't think the audience would understand that John

Carradine would be perceived as "very clever" unless we did that.

By the way, when I started the picture and he was telling me about Myron Healey, Mr. Petroff also mentioned that he had a very strong connection with Claude Rains, and wanted Claude Rains to play the doctor. And he wanted to get the script to him as soon as possible because Mr. Rains was not well. So Mr. Rains was the original thought — at least, *Boris'* thought.

If not Claude Rains'!

The truth of the matter is, I didn't care *who* played it. I wanted a movie with my name on it and all that good stuff, hooray. I wanted to be in the business. Anyway, it turned out *not* to be Mr. Rains, it turned out to be Mr. Carradine, who I'd had the opportunity to meet when he was doing *Tobacco Road* on tour in Massachusetts. I was in stock when he came through in *Tobacco Road*, and I got to play one line to Mr. Carradine: "Well, Jesus Christ, Pa, I blew the horn!" after *he* said, "You ran over Grandma!" [*Laughs*] I was not very good and he was *excellent*, quite honestly; he played the piece as well as you can play it if you're a little tight. (A *lot* tight.) But anyway, he was there a week and then he was gone, the show left, and that was my first connection with Mr. Carradine. Then I met him again when Mr. Petroff introduced me to the man who was going to be the star of the picture. Mr. Carradine shook my hand and left...and I don't whether it was *me* or whether he was actually leaving [*laughs*]! I also met Mr. Healey, when Mr. Healey was there for wardrobe. He brought his own wardrobe, of course, and they went through it with Boris picking out what he wanted him to wear. And Tor Johnson then came in — it was on the same day, I recall. He was playing Lobo...and he was sick and tired of playing characters named Lobo.

How do you know that?

He *told* me. He asked, "Why did you name me Lobo?" and I said, "I *didn't*. Boris did!" He had his "Lobo suit," which was slightly adapted, and that's what you see in the picture. That was his own wardrobe. He was a sweetheart. I don't know what house they used for the exteriors, because Boris at that point didn't want me around. Nobody *ever* wants a writer around.

By the way, did you ever collect the John Barrymore-John Carradine story? Because on *The Unearthly*, I got that.

From Carradine?

No — absolutely *not* from Carradine [*laughs*]! I trust this story, I trust the source that I got it from, but I really can't tell you who I got it from. Early in his career, John Carradine was apparently making a pest of himself with John Barrymore, wanting to get a screen test. He bugged Barrymore to death, he was all over him — Mr. Barrymore would come out of his house and Mr. Carradine would be there waiting for him, saying, "Please, I *need* a screen test, I *have* to have a screen test, please, I *need* it...!" Until, *finally*, Mr. Barrymore said, "I can arrange for a very *small* screen test, but it will be an opportunity for people to see you and for you to act. Come to the studio, and meet me at Stage Four (or whatever), at such-and-such a time — the gate guard will know you're coming."

At the appointed time, Mr. Carradine got through the gate and he raced to the stage door and went inside. The set was a country lane with a house. It was an idyllic house with picket fence — just the face of the house. Barrymore was there, and he said, "Now, John, the camera will be on the front door. This is Thanksgiving, and you will come out the front door having had the most sumptuous meal you have eaten in all your life. You *entered* the house

Double-billed with the "giant grasshopper" epic *Beginning of the End*, *The Unearthly* was one of Republic's final releases.

starving, and now you come *out* the door having had this wonderful meal. It is enough for you to lick your chops, to rub your tummy, to just *luxuriate* in what you have just had. Then you walk down to the front gate ... you come out the front gate ... you luxuriate in the meal again ... then you turn, and you go off stage left." Mr. Carradine did a walk-through, and the camera was set up, and everything was fine. No camera moves, just one camera, because it was a quick test, of course.

The camera rolled. Mr. Carradine came out the door and, *oh!*, nobody has ever played sumptuous-dinner-just-eaten like Mr. Carradine did! Licking his chops, rubbing his tummy, oh!, eyes closed, looking at Heaven — it was the best Thanksgiving dinner anybody had ever had. He came down and opened the gate and, again, luxuriated ... then exited stage left.

When the film was cut together, all of that was in, the camera not moving. Mr. Carradine exits stage left and the camera is now holding on the front door of the little house. The front door opens and out steps Mr. Barrymore — zipping up his pants [*laughs*]!

I have heard that story before, but it's a great one. I can't get you to tell me who told it to you?

No, you can't, because I got it from a man who (God rest him) is dead. He was a dear friend and told me that as a confidence. And he's dead, so I can't call him and get his permission!

Over the years I've talked to a few of the actors in The Unearthly *and they've always said it was shot in an actual house. You're the first person to mention scenes shot on a sound stage. Obviously more was shot in the house than on the stage.*

Oh, yeah, plenty — *plenty* was shot at the house. I believe the scenes in the cellars were shot on the stage. It was so chintzy, the whole operation — to build a set would cost money, and Boris wanted to save every quarter he could. And he did, apparently.

Why did Boris Petroff use the alias "Brooke L. Peters" on this picture?

He always did.

No, there are some pictures with Boris Petroff on 'em and others with Brooke L. Peters.

Well, he told me that he *always* used Brooke Peters, and I had no way of knowing. He was my boss and I was not about to argue with him. And he was being rather polite about the fact that I had joined the Writers Guild when he didn't *want* me to be in the Writers Guild. He said, "That was very clever of *you*, John, to do that," and I said, "Thank you." But I *had* to—I didn't have a lot of choice. We didn't have any major hassle about it … but that was because it was yet to come!

Before we get to the hassles, lemme ask: Have you ever heard of a 1956 movie called The Black Sleep?

No.

Petroff had to be ripping off The Black Sleep *when he concocted the story for* The Unearthly. *It's basically the same movie, except yours has a modern setting and* The Black Sleep *is nineteenth century England.*

I had no idea!

In fact, John Carradine and Tor Johnson are in both movies!

Oh, God—I never knew any of that. That kind of shocks me, because—why would *two* people wanna make that movie [*laughs*]? The rip-off doesn't make sense to me. But, then again, we're talking about Boris Petroff! Anyway … where were we?

You were hinting at hassles.

There weren't going to *be* any hassles: While the picture was being made, I worked for him and he was the boss and everything was fine. And then it was time for the picture to be edited and for credits to be discussed, and it turns out that Jane Mann [Mrs. Petroff], who was the one who typed the script last, put her name on it. And Mr. Petroff was *not* gonna pay me. He was not gonna pay me because he said he didn't *hire* me to be a writer, our one-page contract notwithstanding. Well, I was called to the Writers Guild—the man who was its president at that time was Mike Franklin. There was a board meeting held to talk to Mr. Petroff in an evening conversation. Mike Franklin called and had me come over, and I was sitting in the Guild boardroom to answer questions. Boris Petroff came in and he was explaining why I should not be paid a Guild minimum, or anything else: He said that I was hired only to be a *typist*. Mr. Franklin turned to me, serious-faced, as anybody would, and said, "John, were you hired as a typist?" And I said, "I can't *type*. I can find people who can *testify* that I can't type. I am a *terrible* typist! Get me a typewriter!" The guys who were writers at the table there started to roar. Mike Franklin said to Mr. Petroff, "The document which you gave Mr. Black says that he was to write this picture called *The House of Monsters*."

Pretty soon it was all over; Mr. Franklin said, "We will let you know, Mr. Petroff, what the decision of the Board is." And the decision was that I had to get the money, but Mrs. Petroff got the co-credit. Mr. Petroff was going to deliver the check to the Writers Guild, he *wouldn't* give it to me. I don't know whether he was angry with me or what, but he wouldn't hand me the check, he took it to the Writers Guild and the Writers Guild gave it *to me*. Handed it *to me*. And I went right to the bank and got it in cash [*laughs*], for fear that I would not be *able* to cash it subsequently, because the check would be stopped.

How much was the check for?

It was for whatever the Guild minimum was then; it was somewhere between 1200 and 1700 dollars. So I have this cashed, and I am late for a rehearsal of *Detective Story*, which as I said I was directing. We were having this afternoon rehearsal at the house of one of the kids who was in the show; I went over, and the lady who is now my wife was playing the female lead. Everybody was sitting on the floor 'cause there weren't enough chairs — nobody had enough chairs for the cast of *Detective Story*. I said to my lady, "Mary ... just sit there, one second." And I took this money, which was in fives and tens, and I *threw* it up in the air and it fluttered down around her. It was something I always wanted to do [*laughs*] — I really always wanted to do that! I have *never* done it since, *but* — you only have to do that *once*. That was my first gig, and it was absolutely thrilling.

Have you seen the movie in recent years?

I have, and to tell you the truth, I was kind of amazed that it held together that well, for what it was. And I *know* it didn't cost four dollars [*laughs*]! Frankly, I liked it better than I thought I would. It ran on one of our cable stations, and in *TV Guide* it got two stars. Two out of four. When you realize that *The Maltese Falcon* only got *three*, I think we did pretty good! Watching the picture, Tor came back into my head a great deal, because he was such a sweet man. I'm quite sure most of the reminiscences you've heard about Tor were that he was a sweetheart. And he had a marvelous laugh which he *didn't* use very often — I mean, even privately. It was just rollicking. Most large men do have a big laugh, but his was just somethin' special.

I'm from a Polish family who didn't have a whole hell of a lot of bucks. Now, when *The Unearthly* opened originally, it was at the Wiltern Theater here in Los Angeles. That theater was a *beautiful* theater that was starting to go downhill — in fact, it had been going downhill for a long time. But *The Unearthly* opened there, at Western and Wilshire, and I was there. There I was, sitting in the fifth row, watching "my" movie. And that was lovely.

Now, in Pittsburgh, where I had grown up, my aunt — my father's oldest sister — kept her family together and alive by cleaning movie theaters. She cleaned two theaters on the south side of Pittsburgh, which is where the Polish community is in Pittsburgh, and "my" *Unearthly* was going to open at one of "her" theaters. When my dad told her that *The Unearthly* was my movie, she cleaned the theater — she scrubbed the lobby on her hands and knees, so that when people walked into the theater, "my" movie *would be seen by people who'd crossed a clean floor*.

[*Pause*] I had a lot of trouble with that bit of storytelling, but I figured I owed it to you because you did call and you did want me to tell you about the environment of the picture as best I could tell it.

THE UNEARTHLY (Republic, 1957)

AB-PT Pictures Corp.; 73 minutes; Associate Producer: Robert Atroy; Produced & Directed by Brooke L. Peters [Boris Petroff]; Screenplay: Geoffrey Dennis [John D. F. Black]; Photography: W. Merle Connell; Editorial Supervisor: Richard Currier; Music Composed & Conducted by Henry Vars; Musical Supervisor: Michael Terr; Art Director: Daniel Hall; Makeup Supervisor: Harry Thomas; Sound Effects: Morton Tubor; Wardrobe Supervisor: William Zacha; Sound: Philip Mitchell; Set Decorator: Mowbray Berkeley; Production Manager: Betty Sinclair; Chief Electrician: Paul Grancell; First Grip: Art Manikin; Camera Operator: Ben Wetzler; Property Master: Tony Portoghese

John Carradine (*Dr. Charles Conway*), Myron Healy [Healey] (*Mark Houston*), Allison Hayes (*Grace Thomas*), Marilyn Buferd (*Dr. Sharon Gilchrist*), Arthur Batanides (*Danny Green*), Sally Todd (*Natalie Andries*), Tor Johnson (*Lobo*), Roy Gordon (*Dr. Loren Wright*), Guy Prescott (*Capt. George Regan*), Harry Fleer (*Harry Jedrow*), Gloria Petroff (*Girl*), Paul McWilliams (*Police Officer*), Carl Tor Johnson (*Mutant*), Raymond Guta [Guth]

EVE BRENT

*I don't think I was ever really a glamour girl—
not at heart, anyway.*

Hollywood has such a habit of putting its "seasoned citizens"—performers past a certain age—out to pasture, it requires a great deal of resiliency and adaptability to stay afloat in that youth-conscious talent pool. Eve Brent is someone who has persevered. Appearing as Jane opposite Gordon Scott's King of the Jungle in *Tarzan's Fight for Life* (1958) gave her a measure of instant fame, but cost her her reputation as a serious actress; Brent countered by branching out into stage work. And in subsequent years, the blue-eyed blonde gradually made the switch to character roles, most notably the grotesque "Aunt Stella" in the 1980 chiller *Fade to Black* and, more recently, co-starring with Dabbs Greer as nursing home residents in the opening and closing reels of the box office smash *The Green Mile* (1999).

Born in Houston, Texas, and raised in Fort Worth, Brent began her career in radio and early television and later moved on to the college and little theater stage. Arriving in Hollywood with a husband and infant son in the '50s, she landed her first movie (*Gun Girls*, *Journey into Freedom*, *The Bride and the Beast*) and episodic TV roles. Auteur director Sam Fuller changed her name from Jean Ann Lewis to Eve Brent when she appeared in his 1957 Western *Forty Guns*, the first of dozens of screen roles for the re-christened young actress. In addition to her big-screen assignments, Brent has appeared in hundreds of commercials and done more TV work (*Adventures of Superman*, *The Veil* with Boris Karloff, *The Big Valley*, *Twin Peaks*, *Tales from the Crypt*, scores of others), but she remains best-known for the jungle role she accepted merely to please her six-year-old son.

According to your publicity, you've been in show business since you were a kid.

I had a radio show in Fort Worth when I was like ten years old, *The Texas School of the Air*, and I was on television the very first night that it was introduced in Texas. I had a TV show, like a talk show, when I was around 17.

And also a great deal of work on the stage.

I caught the bug early on and just *always* acted. When my first husband came out here in early 1952, I went to work for the old *Los Angeles Examiner*, selling advertising. Broadway to Western, Pico to Slauson, which was *not* a good area, even then. At night I read for plays and I *got* in a play at the Pasadena Playhouse, and from that I got an agent. Then I got a sort of a contract at 20th Century–Fox — one of those things where they send you to school — and from *that*, Sam Fuller hired me for a part in *Forty Guns*. I had done quite a bit of television before that, over at Ziv. I must have done 20 shows there, different kinds of things — *Dr. Christian*, *West Point* and so on [acting under the name Jean Ann Lewis]. Then after Sam Fuller changed my name to Eve Brent, I did a lot *more* television shows there, *Bat Masterson* and *Highway Patrol*, *any*thing they did in those days. I did tons of shows, one right after another. It was very interesting, because at Ziv in those days, a lot of the time we had to do our makeup and wardrobe and keep track of the script — everything! It was quite an education.

Your first co-starring movie role was as Jane in Tarzan's Fight for Life.

They were testing actresses for the part of Jane in that picture, and my agent asked me if I wanted to do it. I honestly did *not* particularly want to do it although (like every *other* kid) I played Tarzan games and played like I was Jane when I was little — I jumped off roofs and whatever [*laughs*]! But my little boy Jim, who was then six years old, wanted me to be Jane, and so I went and I auditioned for it.

Was there a lot of competition for the part?

They auditioned a *lotta* lotta young women. I was talking to Gordon Scott the other day, I see him fairly often, and he told me that the lady who did *I Dream of Jeannie*, Barbara Eden, was one of the people who tested for it. And another young actress who tested for it was the girl who played the *other* part in *Tarzan's Fight for Life*, Jil Jarmyn — *she* tested for Jane, too. Jil Jarmyn was then sort-of dating Bruce Humberstone, the director of *Tarzan's Fight for Life*. He very much wanted Jil to do that part, and he was voted down by the others, [producer] Sol Lesser and different people. I ended up with the part, which did not make Bruce happy. Or *her*, although she was very nice about it. But he was difficult, he was hard for me to work with, he really was.

For instance?

For instance, he would get very upset if my feet didn't land just right when I was swinging from the tree on a vine — he said I was landing too gracefully, that I should land more on both feet. But it jarred my whole body to land on both feet, and I was trying not to injure myself, to tell you the truth [*laughs*]! It's not easy to take a big leap like that when you're a tiny little girl — and *not* particularly athletic. I played tennis and stuff, but I wasn't into stunts — for sure [*laughs*]! Anyway, that all turned out all right in the end. In fact, shortly before Bruce died I went out to dinner with him and he apologized for any discomfort he may have caused me with his temperament on that set.

What did you do in your screen test?

Scenes from the picture. I recited the poetry ("I sing with the going of the sun ... little birds fly out of my throat..."), I held my little leather sun suit up in front of myself as I looked in the mirror — it was quite extensive.

Was Gordon Scott in the screen test with you?

Yes, and I'll *never* forget the first time I saw Gordon because I almost fainted. In those days, ordinary people didn't have a lot

Brent was a child star on radio and acted on Texas TV before migrating to Hollywood in the early 1950s.

of muscles. When I saw him, I really almost fainted, he was so overpowering and so powerful-*looking*, and really very handsome.

He came onto the set in his Tarzan outfit? What there was of his outfit?

Yeah, and I had on my leather sun suit. I'm told that I wore the same outfit that Brenda Joyce had worn when *she* played Jane [in the 1940s].

Was that skimpy outfit about what you expected when you went in for that part?

It was. The first one they tried on me I refused to wear, because it was a midriff thing, and I didn't feel good in it. I just really didn't feel that "in shape." But as the picture went on, I *got* in shape really fast, because I started working out. I could have worn it toward the end of the shoot, but in the beginning I would have looked a little flabby in it [*laughs*]! So they gave me the one-piece outfit that Brenda had worn.

And you got along well with Gordon Scott?

I got along wonderfully with Gordon, we're still *very* good friends and he's friends with my husband [actor Michael Ashe]. Gordon and I didn't have any love affair, but we were naturally attracted to each other — we were two young, pretty people, vibrant and healthy. And he taught me a lot about health and health foods. The only thing I didn't give up was chocolate [*laughs*]! But he taught me how to be healthy and he taught me how to swing from the vine.

One Fight for Life *review said you "seemed to have swung into the jungle straight from the chorus line in Las Vegas."*

I never understood that review! In the first place, I was never a dancer or a showgirl, and at that point I don't think I'd ever even *been* to Las Vegas. I have always been a very serious actress. And in the movie, I had almost no makeup, except they insisted on false eyelashes. So I didn't understand that review because (in looking at the film) *I* feel I'm very natural in the part. I read it and thought, "What in the hell is *this*?"

At the time, what did Scott think of playing Tarzan?

He loved being Tarzan and he still loves being Tarzan. His life is Tarzan, and he goes all over the country to these conventions! He talked me into going to one of these "celebrity signing" things the other day, and I was just astonished at how many people are so crazy about him. And, consequently, they were very happy to meet *me*. We had a lot of fun. People are just gaga over him and he loves it. He is a fine man, someone that Tarzan and Mr. Burroughs would be proud of. He still works out and is in good shape.

When you worked with him, so early in his career, was he good about remembering his dialogue, hitting marks and so on?

Oh, no problem — he was a consummate actor in that way. He hadn't *done* any acting to speak of [before that], but *since* then he's done a lot of spaghetti Westerns and is really well-known in Europe. And well-respected. *I* really respect Gordon too — he is a fine human being. Vera Miles was married to Gordon when we did *Tarzan's Fight for Life* and she was on the set a couple of times — they had a new baby then. She was a very lovely lady.

Second-unit footage was shot in Africa. If they had asked, would you have wanted to go to Africa?

At that point, I would have *loved* to go to Africa, because I really had a spirit of adventure. But as far as going to Africa *now* ... I don't wanna go to Africa at all, because I hear that so many people have subsequently [had health problems]. Like Katharine Hepburn, who did *The African Queen* [1951] in Africa and got some kind of infection and forevermore she was really in pain with her eyes — I guess she still *is*. So I'm *glad* I didn't go to Africa!

Brent's six-year-old son wanted her to audition for the role of Jane; *she* wasn't too keen on the idea.

Any memory of your swimming scene with Tarzan?

The producers asked me if I could swim, and I said sure. But *I* couldn't swim — I could paddle around a little bit, that's all. I had a terrible fear of water, and still do. (When I was a teenager, I had a near-death experience — I almost drowned in a lake.) So before the swimming audition, I went out and took swimming lessons in a pool for about a week, and I began swimming well enough. And I guess I looked good in my swimming audition. But then when it was time to shoot the swimming scenes for the movie, we got out to the studio tank, which was on the back lot at MGM — a 75-foot tank. We got out to the tank and, with some kind of a machine, they put this *current* into the water — a *real* strong current. Well, I wasn't strong enough to swim in that thing, I just got blown away — it blew me like 20 yards every time I'd try to swim! They got so mad at me, but I just wasn't that strong a swimmer, having been swimming only about a week. So they had to get a double for my swimming, and it worked out okay.

Of the Tarzan movies you've seen, who is the best Jane?

I guess I liked Maureen O'Sullivan the best.

O'Sullivan mentioned many times in her various Tarzan interviews that she just hated her Cheetah.

I loved Cheetah the chimpanzee, I got along with him great — I love animals. But he did at one point attack me. I was walking along on the stage one day and he grabbed me by the leg and pulled me down — some people had to get him off me. He didn't mean anything by it, he wasn't mad or anything, he was just ... sexually excited [*laughs*]! I have to this day a broken vein in my leg where he grabbed me. But other than that, he and I loved each other.

Reportedly Gordon Scott had to actually fight for his life in the scene with the giant python.

We shot that scene on a stage. That thing started to wrap itself around Gordon's neck and he turned purple — and *I* didn't even notice it! I didn't know what was going on, I was sitting there acting, looking dumb. Six or seven men came in — it *took* six or seven men to get that snake off of him. He was almost killed, it was a horrible thing. A *very* close call!

Was he shaken up, or did he slough it off and go right back to work?

I don't remember, because there was such a lot of confusion. He could have gone home for the day after that happened but, knowing Gordon, we might have just kept on shooting [*laughs*]!

Was Tarzan's Fight for Life *a moneymaker?*

That's what I was told. When the picture came out, it was really a funny thing: I went to Fort Worth to visit my mother and dad and my little brother and sister, and there were people showing up outside my mother's house on Donnelly Street trying to peek in and get a glimpse of me because I was so famous in Fort Worth! It was *such* a big deal because I was a hometown girl, people were lined up around the block. I couldn't get out the door [*laughs*]! My family thought it was wonderful — they thought everything *about* Jane was wonderful. But it was kind of embarrassing to *me*!

At that point, Sol Lesser had been producing the Tarzans for many years. Was he around much?

He was around here and there. He

Brent believes that Gordon Scott was "someone that Tarzan and [Edgar Rice] Burroughs could be proud of."

was a little guy who seemed like a nice person, but I didn't really talk to him. He took me to a Boy Scout Jamboree one time [for publicity purposes], and that's about the only time I ever talked to him. That was about the time he was bowing out of the Tarzans.

You next appeared as Jane in three episodes of a Gordon Scott Tarzan TV series that never got off the ground.

The reason it didn't become a series was that was the Edgar Rice Burroughs Corp. was not ready for Tarzan to be a TV series, and the lawyers wouldn't okay it. I was disappointed, because by then I *was* enjoying being Jane. I didn't realize that playing Jane was bad for my career — but maybe it *wouldn't* have been bad for me, if the series *had* gone on television. I had really a great career starting to happen until I did Jane — which *wasn't* good for my career. Oh, God, no! I got *so* much publicity at that time, because it was *really* a big thing to be Jane. And for a number of years I really wasn't considered for anything serious. I was having *such* trouble getting any good parts, even though for a time I was with William Morris. But they just couldn't sell me, they said, "Ex-Janes are hard to sell." So I started going out and doing roadshows — I did one with George Gobel called *The Impossible Years*, Gene Raymond I went out with in *The Fifth Season*,

Sidelined with appendicitis, Jane (Brent) gets a sample of Tarzan's (Scott) bedside manner.

and Bob Cummings I toured with for over five years in *The Marriage-Go-Round*. I did a lot of theater all over, whenever I would get a call, and I did a lot of voiceover stuff. But I didn't even get *considered* for anything for a real long time, and it was really heart-breaking. Everybody *knew* me, but nobody took me seriously.

I lived that down, though. As luck would have it, now I'm very *happy* about having been Jane, because (for one thing) all the people who are involved with the Edgar Rice Burroughs Bibliophile Society have been so good to me over the years. They have conventions and I go to them when I can and we stay in touch, and whenever I've gone out on the road in shows, people's homes have always been open to me and I've been entertained royally all over this country because of the fans who are so devoted to these films. I very deeply appreciate this friendship.

Did you expect or hope to do more as Jane than they let you do in Fight for Life *and the TV episodes?*

I didn't care one way or the other.

In the older Tarzan pictures, the various Janes were always being kidnapped by natives or chased by wild animals—

And all *I* did was have appendicitis [in *Fight for Life*]!

And in the TV series, you were like a jungle housewife!

[*Laughs*] That's right! But having more action stuff to do would not have made me particularly happy. I'm not a very athletic person, basically — tennis has been about the extent of it in my life. I didn't particularly like jumping all around. But I *felt* like Jane, I felt very wholesome when I was doing it, and I loved the trees-and-jungle feeling. I was happily married at that time, married to a real estate tycoon-type person, and I didn't have any money worries. So, as I told you before, I did not do Jane for money, I mostly did it 'cause my little boy wanted me to be Jane [*laughs*]!

You later made the career transition from glamour girl to character actress.

I don't think I was ever *really* a glamour girl — not at heart, anyway. Right after I did Jane, hoping to live down that blond Jane image, I dyed my hair dark trying to prove to everybody I *wasn't* glamorous!

We'll have to agree to disagree about that.

I lived in New York a short time after I was Jane, and Walter Winchell did write in one of his columns in '61 or '62 that I was New York's most beautiful woman. I thought that was sort of an interesting quote!

You had one of your meatier character parts in Fade to Black, *as the sadistic, crippled aunt of Dennis Christopher.*

[Writer-director] Vernon Zimmerman really wanted me to do that Aunt Stella part, and I out-read a lot of people and out-tested a lot of people. Lana Turner was up for that — that's what they *told* me, anyway — and a lot of other big stars. But I got it, and I got some recognition from that. But not *enough* — it was such a total character thing, a *caricature* in a way. But I enjoyed doing it ... I enjoyed doing it a *lot*. Vernon was a lovely, lovely man, and Dennis Christopher was darling. We worked together sooo well, he was very respectful of me and I of him. He had just won some awards for *Breaking Away* [1979] and he was very big at that point, *the* most important young up-and-coming star of that year. It didn't *happen*, he didn't go on to be as big as it looked like he was going to be...and *Fade to Black* didn't do as well as hoped, although it's *become* a cult picture. Movie buffs all over the world, all ages, loved *Fade to Black*. I still get quite a bit of fan mail from it, which is wonderful.

Where were your Fade to Black *scenes shot?*

In a house over in Hollywood. The scene of Aunt Stella crashing down the stairs in the wheelchair was shot in a house in Venice. I had a double do that.

Did you have any trouble using the wheelchair throughout the movie?

They were nice enough to send a wheelchair to our apartment, and I practiced until it was second nature to me. In fact, I really *liked* doing that, because [*laughs*] — because I'm *lazy*!

You were billed Eve Brent Ashe in Fade to Black.

I told them to use Eve Brent Ashe as Mike and I had not been married that long and he's an actor and *every*body was using their husbands' names at that time — actresses were adding names right and left. So, for luck or whatever, I was going to change it. But there was a fortune teller living next door to where we shot *Fade to Black*, a seer-type woman, and she said, "Do *not* put Ashe on your name. It will be very bad luck for you." And, you know what? It *was*. People got mixed-up, they'd call for me without knowing for sure who they were talking to — I *did* run into all kinds of bad luck. Show business has a lot to do with being in the right place at the right time and making the right moves and just being lucky, and it *wasn't* lucky to have Ashe on my name. I just dropped it after that.

Your husband Michael Ashe — he's husband number three…?

[*Pause*] Number *five*, I think. [*Laughs*] Look, I'm 70 years old — a lot of this stuff, I don't even *remember*! But I've got a wonderful husband now, we've been married for the last 22 years, and I've got a wonderful dog and a lovely life in Burbank.

You had a small part as a tipsy apartment house manager in a sci-fi movie called BrainWaves *[1982] with Keir Dullea.*

[Writer-producer-director] Ulli Lommel was such a nice guy, and so was Keir. That was shot on actual locations right around town here. It was very low-budget, but a lot of caring went into that thing.

How did you land your recent role as Dabbs Greer's girlfriend in Stephen King's The Green Mile?

At that time, I didn't even have an agent for the simple reason that my agent Sid Craig had closed his offices (as a *lot* of agents have out here) and gone to work for a very big management firm that only took big stars and producers. He wasn't handling me any more, and I just wasn't really fooling with [movie work] — I was doing my stage work here and there and doing a *lot* of commercial work, which I've always been lucky enough to make a living doing. Anyway, I didn't have an agent. Well, a casting director named Mali Finn had me in to read for a *very* small part in *The Green Mile*, the part of one of the old ladies in the nursing home who had maybe one line. I did my audition on tape.

When they were looking for an actress to play Elaine, they auditioned lots and lots of women, in London and New York and here in Los Angeles. Over 50 women had gone on tape and a lot of 'em were very big stars. I'm not gonna say who, 'cause I don't wanna say who I beat out — it might be hurtful to them. In any case, there were some very big names up for the part of Elaine, because in the six books by Stephen King it's quite a big part, it's all through the books, Old Paul [Greer] talks to her off and on. (For the movie, though, they condensed the scenes of Old Paul and Elaine into two "bookends," the beginning and the end.) Well, they just couldn't [settle for] any of the people who they auditioned. One day Mali and [writer-producer-director] Frank Darabont decided to look at the tapes of the women they'd auditioned for the smaller roles. Frank saw me on the tape and said, "Let's bring Eve Brent in."

So you went in to audition again, this time for the part of Elaine.

I went in to Warner Hollywood one morning — they had faxed me the sides and I wasn't thinking too much about it one way or the other. My husband Mike came on in with me, and they bought us lunch because Frank Darabont was late getting there. We sat in the commissary and had lunch, and then I went over and talked to [co-producer] David Valdes for maybe 30, 40 minutes — a luxury you *rarely* have on auditions! Well, by the time Frank came in and I read for them on-camera, I was completely at ease. Frank and David both liked me and they liked what I did — I guess! But when I started out to the car, I said to my husband, "I don't think I did so good on that." We got to the studio gate when all of a sudden David Valdes *ran* out to the car and said, "We want you! We want you! You blew us away! We gotta *have* you! Can you go to North Carolina day after tomorrow?" I said, "*Sure!*"

Also, they said, "Can your husband go with you?" and I said, "Well, he should

"It's *privilege* and *joy*" to work with a director like *The Green Mile's* Frank Darabont, says Brent. Dabbs Greer is on the left.

probably stay here and take care of the dog." But what I was *really* thinking was that that would cost a lot of money — I didn't realize they were offering to pay his way! David Valdes said, "Let us pay for Mike going. We'd like to have him there *with* you." We all had a nice rapport in that office that day ... and forevermore!

Did you enjoy the location trip?

Oh! My husband and I got to North Carolina and, oh my God, they had a condo there for us with a Jacuzzi inside it, and it was completely stocked with anything you'd ever *dream* of eating — it was just sooo luxurious. We were there maybe ten days, then we came back here. But there were a few more days left on the picture and they sent limos for me!

It was great to see Dabbs Greer play such a good part in such a big picture, after all the years he's put into the movie business as a supporting actor and bit player.

Working with Dabbs was just such a wonderful experience. I had known him in the old days, from the Pasadena Playhouse — I didn't know him *well*, but I knew who he was 'cause he was a big shot there, he practically ran the place right under Gilmor Brown. He and I just hit it off and we had *such* a rapport. It was not an easy shoot because we had to go up a mountain together for one scene. It was quite a climb and it was raining and ... it was a rough shoot! But, because we were so supportive of each other and so "into" our roles, it was just a dream, just a wonderful time. And Frank Darabont is the most wonderful director that anyone could ever *hope* to have. I can't tell you how he pulls honesty out of people, and he's so pains-taking with every moment, and he's right there *with* you. There's a kind of a spiritual community that I can't explain exactly, except you *know* what Frank is thinking and *he* knows what the character should be thinking, and he knows his actors. You do a lot of takes— a *lot* of takes!— and it's *work*. But it's *not* work, it's *privilege* and *joy* to work for Frank. I hope one day to do something else for him, because it was a dream come true. Every actor dreams of being in a wonderful movie that is really complete, that gives you a chance to do some fine work. It doesn't matter if it's a big part. And, by the way, I didn't wear any makeup at all in *The Green Mile*, and I've never felt so free and so "just like myself." (I love being a character actress!)

I was really rooting for Dabbs Greer to get an Oscar nomination, he gave such a touching performance.

They couldn't do that. The studio puts up who they want to be nominated, and — knowing that for various reasons Michael Clarke Duncan might win a Best Supporting Actor Oscar, over and above anybody else in the picture — they had to put *him* up. It's a political thing. The studio wants to put up whoever's most likely to win, 'cause it helps their picture make more money. And Michael, of course, is the obvious choice to sponsor.

Unfortunately, you and Greer didn't get in on a lot of the Green Mile *publicity.*

Originally these parts were not scheduled to have star billing. Now we *do* have it in the front of the movie, a double-card for Dabbs and me, but they'd already made up all the publicity material. So we're not getting that much publicity, the two of us; but we're getting a lot of acknowledgment and a lot of notice here in Hollywood. I've had some offers and done a couple of things, and it's just been a wonderful experience. I even ran an *Variety* ad thanking Frank Darabont for the privilege of working with him, because I *do* appreciate what has happened to my career. I'm *again* being noticed, in the way an *actor* is noticed. Not the way a "Jane" is noticed, not the way a comic strip character, an Edgar Rice Burroughs *projection* is noticed. It was wonderful being Jane, it's wonderful *now* — as it turns out, Frank Darabont is a Tarzan fan, and he remembered seeing me as Jane when he was a little boy! So in many cases now, having played Jane turns out to be in my favor. Also all the shows I did with Jack Webb, which were quite a few. There was a *Dragnet* episode called "The LSD Story" and I had the lead in that, and people are even remembering *that* now — *TV Guide* considers it one of the best 100 shows ever done! It didn't mean much to me then to have done all those *Dragnet*s, but now it *does*.

It's mystical. Cause and effect can create value. Even though they're simultaneous, many years later they come into fruition. The causes that you make that seem like nothing, even the causes that don't seem so good, can in the end cause value in your life. I'm a Buddhist — I have been a Buddhist for 28 years — and I *live* like that. The causes you make becoming *good* causes, becoming good karma. I chant Nam Myoho Renge Kyo and I belong to the Soka Gakkai and it's had a profound meaning in my life. I've always chanted to be part of a project like this [*The Green Mile*]. Along with chanting for the happiness of other people and the health of my family, I've chanted to have my career take off. And at the age of 70, it's really starting to change!

I *love* being older. Every year I get older, I'm enjoying it more. It's wonderful getting older and it's wonderful being a character actress.

EVE BRENT FILMOGRAPHY

As Jean Lewis/Jean Ann Lewis
Female Jungle (AIP, 1956)

Gun Girls (Eros/Boots & Saddles Pictures, 1956)
The Storm Rider (20th Century–Fox, 1957)
Journey to Freedom (Republic, 1957)
The Garment Jungle (Columbia, 1957)
The Bride and the Beast (Allied Artists, 1958)

As Eve Brent
Forty Guns (20th Century–Fox, 1957)
Tarzan's Fight for Life (MGM, 1958)
The Sad Horse (20th Century–Fox, 1959)
Cage of Evil (United Artists, 1960)
Stakeout! (Crown International, 1962)
Mara of the Wilderness (Allied Artists, 1965)
A Guide for the Married Man (20th Century–Fox, 1967)
Coogan's Bluff (Universal, 1968)
For Singles Only (Columbia, 1968)
The Happy Ending (United Artists, 1969)
The Barefoot Executive (Buena Vista, 1971)
How's Your Love Life? (Cal-Tex, 1971)
The Todd Killings (National General, 1971)
The Marriage of a Young Stockbroker (20th Century–Fox, 1971)
How to Seduce a Woman (Cinerama, 1974)
Timber Tramps (Howco International, 1975)
Hustle (Paramount, 1975)
The White Buffalo (*Hunt to Kill*) (United Artists, 1977)
Date with an Angel (DeLaurentiis Entertainment, 1987)
The Experts (Paramount, 1989)
Marilyn, My Love (1994)
The Green Mile (Warners, 1999)
Waking Up in Reno (Miramax, 2001)

As Eve Brent Ashe
Fade to Black (American Cinema, 1980)
BrainWaves (Motion Picture Marketing, 1982)
Going Berserk (Universal, 1983)
Racing With the Moon (Paramount, 1984)

In 1966, the three episodes of the unaired Gordon Scott–Eve Brent Tarzan television series were compiled into the feature-length *Tarzan and the Trappers* and released to TV. Brent is "a face in the crowd" in *Beethoven's 2nd* (Universal, 1993).

ANTHONY CARDOZA on *The Beast of Yucca Flats*

I showed The Beast of Yucca Flats *to AIP — I showed it to Sam Arkoff at the Charlie Chaplin Studios on LaBrea Avenue. He got halfway through it and he said, "Oh! I forgot. I have to catch a plane." You know what* that *meant [laughs]!*

Tor Johnson as a Soviet space scientist. That right there ought to be about as much balminess as any single movie could be expected to accommodate, and yet it's only the takeoff point for even greater absurdities in the never-to-be-forgotten *The Beast of Yucca Flats*. A masterpiece in the sub-category of hypnotically bad, no-budget cinema, shot in 1959 and released in '61, *Beast* gives "Guest Star" Johnson the role of Joe Jaworsky, a defecting Russkie scientist pursued by Kremlin agents out onto the Yucca Flats A-Bomb testing ground. There, the radiation from an untimely atom blast unaccountably transforms the titanic Tor into a scarred, bellowing man-monster — "a prehistoric beast in a nuclear age" who begins prowling the desert landscape and littering it with the bodies of bit players.

There's a rare kind of perfection in *The Beast of Yucca Flats* — the perverse perfection of a piece wherein everything is as false and farcically far-out as can be imagined. The 53-minute film was produced by Anthony Cardoza, a 29-year-old Hartford, Connecticut, welder who had recently relocated to the West Coast. Cardoza's career has taken him from early collaborations with Ed Wood and *Yucca Flats* auteur Coleman Francis, to working as writer-producer-director of many of his own, more recent projects; he is currently writing his autobiography *Hartford to Hollywood*. In this interview, he looks back at the earliest — and perhaps the strangest — of his maverick movie credits.

Not long after you moved from Connecticut to California, you became part of the notorious "Ed Wood circle."

I met Ed through a kid I knew in Connecticut, a guy who had moved out here and was putting himself through college. This kid had a job as a Fuller Brush man, and that's how he met Ed. When *I* moved out here, I had him as a visitor, and he said, "I know this guy who's a producer. Jeez, you can double your money back in like a *month*." I said, "That's a good deal!" and I got sucked in [*laughs*]. They needed money [for the movie that became *Night of the Ghouls* with Tor Johnson, 1958], so I came up with some money from a house that I'd sold in Connecticut. I gave Ed all of my money, invested it in this movie — and I never got my money back. But I said, "*This isn't gonna throw me*" and I "put myself through school," learning the business from scratch [while continuing to work as a welder]. I learned everything — music and writing, how to edit music, how to edit film, *every*thing. Then I met Coleman Francis, and voila — *The Beast of Yucca Flats*.

How did you meet Coleman Francis?

He called me from nowhere, from out of the blue. I was living at the time in Van Nuys, where I'd bought a little house, and he approached me. I didn't know how he got my number — I never *did* find out. But he called me and he said, "I understand that you know Tor Johnson. Can you get him for a movie?" I knew Tor well, through Ed Wood, and I said, "Sure." I called Tor and said, "Tor, you wanna be in a movie?" and Tor said [*imitating Johnson*], "Yes, To-ny. How much do I *get*?" And I said, "Not much, Tor!" [*Laughs*]

We raised a couple of hundred — no, *I* raised it! Coleman never raised a *nickel*. I raised all the money for it: I got some welding friends, *they* all chipped in, and just…different people. It was a low budget. I was still welding, of course — I went from the day shift to nights so I could learn the movie business during the day. And I learned a lot about directing and acting through Coleman Francis. Coley was a good actor — he was in Jack Webb's TV series *Dragnet* and in other things. I picked up a lot of knowledge from Ed Wood and from Coleman. *The Beast of Yucca Flats* was Coleman's screenplay. At first it was called *The Violent Sun*.

That's not a very good title, is it?

No, it isn't! So he renamed it *The Beast of Yucca Flats*.

Where was the movie shot?

It was shot off Sierra Highway in Saugus. I was there every day. The hardest part was taking a 35mm Mitchell camera up those mountains. It took four of us to carry it up to the cave — that camera was heavy, because it was all iron. Those guys broke their backs getting it up there. Then we had to get Tor Johnson up there — we had to push him up the hill. *Literally* had to push him up the hill. We also put a rope around him and we some guys pulling him up. There were about four of us, two up above pulling and two down below pushing. It was [actor] George Principe and [actor-co-producer] Jim Oliphant and myself and … I forget who the fourth guy was. We pulled and pulled and pushed and pushed, and we finally got him up there. Really, the cliff was up there pretty high. If he ever fell, we were *all* dead! He was heavier than that camera, I'm tellin' you [*laughs*]!

This place where you shot — was it commuting distance from Hollywood? You just went back and forth?

Yeah. It was between 35 to 45 miles from Hollywood.

Was there a real cave up there?

It was an old mine that we used.

Did you ever work at night?

No, it was day-for-night shooting. Our [cinematographer], John Cagle, was a

Top: Tor Johnson as a Russian scientist? Conrad Brooks mulls over this Brobdingnagian bit of miscasting in the opening sequence of *The Beast of Yucca Flats*. *Bottom:* An atom blast sends Johnson back to his club-toting prehistoric roots in *The Beast of Yucca Flats*.

college professor at S.C. [the University of Southern California] and he taught camera.

Where did you get your cast?

They were just different people that I knew and Coley knew. Douglas Mellor, a friend of Coley's, plays the father of the two lost boys. Barbara Francis was Coleman's *ex*-wife *then*, and she plays the mother. The two boys [Ronald and Alan Francis] were Coley's sons; she had custody of 'em. Bing Stafford was a friend of Larry Aten; Bing and Larry played the two desert patrolmen. Graham Stafford, who you see as a newsboy, was Bing's younger brother. Linda Bielema was married to Larry Aten, and I think she currently works at Warner Brothers as a secretary. She was the gal that was strangled in her car and carried up the mountain by Tor Johnson and raped. (*Supposedly.* She wasn't, really [*laughs*]!) Jim Oliphant played her husband, the guy who went behind his car and was strangled by the Beast. George Principe was the passerby who discovers Oliphant's body.

And you? Who did you play?

I play one of the Kremlin agents—very badly. John Morrison was the other Kremlin agent.

Who is the FBI agent who stops to reload his gun in the middle of the gunfight, while the bad guys hold their fire and wait for him?

That was Bob Labansat. He became a wardrobe person, and I think he is to this day. Jim Miles was the black soldier who gets killed—*also* very badly! *Every*body was bad! But, you know what? This picture, everybody likes it! It's amazing!

Well, before we go on, let's you and me agree that it's a very bad picture that, for some reason, a lot of people enjoy. Is that fair enough?

That's good!

Okay—that'll save hurt feelings later! Is Coleman Francis in the picture?

Yeah, he's the guy who buys a newspaper from the news boy. He played a dual role—he also played in the scene at the service station [as the attendant]. The dog in that scene belonged to the station. Coley also narrated the movie. We shot it all M.O.S. ["Mit Out Sound," silent].

There aren't many dialogue scenes, but what few there are are obviously dubbed. When an actor talks in the movie, is that usually the same actor dubbing his or her own voice?

Yes.

Who provided the grunts and roars of Tor Johnson?

Oh, that was Coleman, too—"Rrrrraaarrr!" [*Laughs*] Later, when I made the movie *Bigfoot* [1970], *I* did all the sounds of Bigfoot and his babies and all!

What kind of shape was Tor Johnson in at this time?

He was 390 pounds, and about six-two or three, I forget.

He looks so out of condition in the movie. He can't run for more than a few seconds without pooping out. I get the impression he couldn't fight his way out of a Girl Scout meeting at that point.

That's true, that's true. At that weight, he couldn't do much.

Looks like he can hardly walk. How was he making a living in 1959?

His son Carl was a chief of police in San Fernando, and Carl used to help Tor along. Carl used to wrestle his father in the ring, but people didn't know [that they were father and son] because Carl would go under another name. His father had the

Anthony Cardoza took aim at a movie producing career starting with *The Beast of Yucca Flats*—in which he also played a gun-wielding bit part.

shaved head and Carl would have hair on his head, and they'd fight each other. Tor was also doing little bit parts in offbeat pictures.

But he made so few movies in the last 10, 12 years of his life, I have to wonder — was the son supporting him toward the end?

Yep. Although I *think* Tor had a pension, too. Tor and his wife Greta lived in a house in Sylmar, and I think his rent was paid by the son. It was a small house, a two-bedroom or something.

Did they seem to be happy, and to have enough money?

Oh, yeah. I used to go over there, and his wife Greta would fix me pickled herring and crackers and cheese and all that. We'd have a good time. And then *he'd* come to *my* house and have dinner there. It was great. We were buddies, and we ate a *lot* [*laughs*] — I almost got as heavy as *him*! I'm kidding … but I did go up to about 225 pounds from about 165. That's how much I was with Tor. Eat and eat and eat and eat. Being around Tor, you *had* to eat! His wife Greta always had the food on the table. "You gotta eat! You *must* eat!"

Tor couldn't possibly have still been wrestling when you knew him…?

Actually, no.

Besides eat, what else would the two of you do?

Well, we went out — we used to have drinks, wine and stuff like that. We didn't pal around every day, but he'd need a ride here and a ride there, so I'd pick him up. One evening we got thrown out of Jack LaRue's nightclub on Ventura Boulevard. The waitress came over and he asked her for some T.P. She asked, "What's T.P.?" and he said, "Ta-ble pus-sy…!" The waitress told Jack LaRue about that, and so Jack came up to me and asked, "Can I talk to you for a minute?" I said sure. And Jack got me off to one side and he said, "Can you get him out of here?" So I told Tor, "We gotta leave, Tor. I've got to get home." So I got him out of Jack LaRue's place — but we were actually *thrown* out [*laughs*]!

Was Tor Johnson drunk?

Well, we were *both* inebriated [*laughs*]. Not *too* bad, but…

Did he do that sort of thing often?

Uhhh … yeah [*laughs*]! Everywhere we went! But they'd get a kick out of it, the waitresses. But this one didn't, it rubbed her the wrong way.

How long did it take to shoot Beast of Yucca Flats?

We shot over a period of probably a year, or something like that. We shot weekends, 'cause I was working.

But not every weekend.

No, no, no. But for about a year, in '59. In fact, that's a funny story: Besides playing the Kremlin agent, there's another scene I'm in in the picture. At the end, when you see all the people chasing the Beast and looking for the kids, one of them is me — a big fat guy. A year went by and I was hangin' around with Tor Johnson, and I gained all that weight!

So you play the skinny Kremlin agent at the beginning of the picture —

And a big fat guy at the end [*laughs*]!

Who did Tor Johnson's makeup?

Larry Aten, who played the sheriff. The "scars" were toilet tissue that we wrinkled up and then pasted onto Tor. Then powder was put on, to make it look like he was really burned from the atomic blast. That atomic blast was, of course, the real thing — stock footage. And it was hard to get at that time — that was government footage. I forget where we acquired it, but we got it! The big flash that Tor Johnson reacts to — we did that with the lens. We just flashed it open real quick.

You only had two interiors in the movie — a bedroom scene, with the patrolman and the woman in bed…

That was shot in Saugus, in a house almost diagonally across from the cave. Marcia Knight played the wife. And, actually, *I* played her husband in that scene. The actor never showed up, so I played it. That's why the shot's so brief. So I played *three* parts in the movie.

The other interior is that … very strange pre-credits sequence of a nude girl walking around her apartment and then being killed by the Beast. Why was that shot?

Uh … Coley liked nudity. That's it [*laughs*]! Her name escapes me; she was an Italian girl from New York. I saw her that one time there, and that was it. She was choked by a guy who doubled for Tor Johnson. (That was obvious, right?) That scene was shot in an apartment in Van Nuys.

Having the Beast rape the women — didn't you worry that that was a little "much" for the time?

No. Nah. Even though I know the [Production Code people] were down on stuff like that. It was kind of mild, because we didn't really show anything.

Probably the most "ambitious" shot in the movie is the moving camera shot of the airplane chasing Douglas Mellor.

We did that at the Saugus Airport. We put a camera in the back of a little tiny Ford pickup truck.

According to Cardoza, Johnson's scar makeup was nothing but wrinkled toilet paper and powder, applied by one of his fellow cast members (Larry Aten, left).

In a 1964 interview, Coleman Francis said the picture cost $34,000.

To be honest with you, I forget how much I spent. (Remember, it was my money, and a few other people that I got involved with it.) But it *was* probably about 34,000 — that's pretty damn close. Because we had to make prints up — I had 75 or 77 prints made of it. But back then, you could buy 'em cheap.

Who taught you how to edit?

I started learning how to edit and everything through a couple of editors, Lee Strosnider and Austin McKinney — they were the two editors of *Beast of Yucca Flats*.

According to the Beast of Yucca Flats *credits, the editor was "C. Francis."*

Coleman Francis?! Why, he never edited *one bit*, he was off when I was toiling with these guys! I worked with them — every bit of time that I had, I would go right over there from my job and work with them. They edited it in a house in Hollywood, on Fountain Avenue.

We finished the picture, edited it at that house, and then we booked it ourselves in San Diego, at a couple of theaters there. The Navy guys just *loved* that thing over there — San Diego is a Navy town. We packed the house with sailors, and they just loved it. Well, I think they liked the gal in it, Marcia Knight. They just went crazy. Coley and I made personal appearances with the picture and signed autographs and everything. It went over good!

According to The Hollywood Reporter, *Tor Johnson was going to be there in person too.*

He never showed up! Tor did no touring. But Coley and I did.

So you got those bookings yourself. Did

you ever try to get an established film company to distribute it for you?

I showed it to Mr. [Spyros] Skouras at 20th Century–Fox. And his favorite scene was the scene at the end when the rabbit comes up to Tor Johnson during his death scene. And do you know that that was a wild rabbit that came up to Tor? That wasn't a trained rabbit, it was a baby jackrabbit that came out of nowhere, a *bunny*. It was like a miracle — he came over to Tor while we were shooting, while Tor was lying on the ground dying. Tor opened his eyes and saw it and kissed it. Can you imagine that? Isn't that an amazing scene? And that was Spyros Skouras' favorite scene in the movie. He said it reminded him of *All Quiet on the Western Front* [*laughs*]!

You showed him the movie in hopes of getting a Fox releasing deal?

Right. We had a lot of guts!

I wasn't gonna say that, but that's just what I was thinking!

Of course, they turned it down. Later I showed it to AIP — I showed it to Sam Arkoff at the Charlie Chaplin Studios on LaBrea Avenue. He got halfway through it and he said, "Oh! I forgot. I have to catch a plane." You know what *that* meant [*laughs*]!

Yucca Flats *got better reviews than it deserved. You really lucked out!*

A guy by the name of Tube reviewed it for *Variety*. He was a very nice guy. He used to rake the majors over, but he liked independents. He should have been an actor himself — he looked kind of like Tyrone Power. *The Hollywood Reporter* liked it too. There was something in it that they both liked. The first distributor was Cinema Associates — an old, old Jewish man. Nice person. On Wilshire Boulevard and LaBrea.

What kind of a guy was Coleman Francis?

Basically, he was a nice person. People said he drank, but I never saw him drink a drop. Not even a beer, in all our years together. He liked aspirins and Coca-Cola — he said it gave him a lift [*laughs*]! He'd take aspirin —

And then wash it down with Coke.

Yeah. He said it kept him going, kept him awake.

And you had a good partnership?

Yeah. After *Beast of Yucca Flats*, we made *The Skydivers* [1963] and then we made another one, *Night Train to Mundo Fine* [1966].

Why did you break up?

Well, it got to be a little too much. I was doing most of the work of editing and trying to sell the pictures; he just wanted to write and direct, and that's *it*. It was just too much on me. I had a *wife* and two *kids*, and still working in a *factory*. Doing pictures and working in a factory — I said, "Wait a minute! Something's *wrong* here!" So I said *that's it* and I got out of [the picture business] for about two, three years. Then I saw these biker pictures coming out in '66, '67, and I had a story treatment called *The Hellcats* that James Gordon White had written — it was about this lesbian gang on motorcycles. I changed it around and made them undercover motorcycle gals, I wrote with a couple other guys on it, and I produced it. *The Hellcats* [1967] was my first real hit after getting away from Coleman. It became a *smash* hit — it made about $12 million the first year for Crown International. And that's when tickets were a buck, buck and a quarter, buck and a half.

When did you retire as a welder?

The doctor made me quit welding in 1963. I had to get out because of my eyes. I was welding and making movies at the same time, and (from the welding) I got chalazae—little bumps under your eyelids. A doctor on Van Nuys Avenue cured it for me, but he said, "Don't go back to welding. You've had too many 'flashes.'" When somebody else is welding, and you get a flash of it in your eye—well, that takes all the fluid out of your eye. So I had to quit.

Just seeing someone welding takes the fluid out of a person's eye?

If you're welding, and you lift your hood, and then another guy's welding a booth over and you catch *his* flash in the corner of your eye, that takes the fluid out of your eye. And *that* causes chalazae.

When was your last encounter with Coleman Francis?

The last time I saw him, he was about Tor's weight. After being only like 200 pounds, he went up to about 350. He was on a bus bench with an overcoat, and he looked like he was gone … three sheets to the wind. I don't know what happened to him. I was driving by and I saw him on the bench and I couldn't believe my eyes. I felt sorry for him, but at the same time … you know … you gotta take care of yourself and *your* family.

I was told that he later died under strange circumstances.

Coleman Francis' body was found in the back of a station wagon at the Vine Street Ranch Market.

Was it natural causes, or…?

Nobody knows. *I* don't know, *he* doesn't know—he's dead [*laughs*]! Nobody seems to know. There was a plastic bag over his head and a tube going into his mouth or around his throat. I don't know if he committed suicide, or…I have no idea. Never looked it up because we were on the outs at the time.

What parting shots do you want to give me on Beast of Yucca Flats?

Well, for a cheap movie, and considering how we did it, I think it stands up. It's played on *Mystery Science Theater* and people pirate it, so *some*body's got to like it! I think it holds up pretty good. We worked hard on it. Mostly my money! I did all the raising of money and all the paying. I paid and paid and paid [*laughs*], using my welding salary.

It was a learning process, and it became a cult classic. I think it was a little bit better quality-wise than Ed Wood's movies [*laughs*]! But I don't knock Ed Wood and I don't knock Coleman. When I started, I didn't know beans about movies. So I have to praise them. If Ed Wood had the money and backing behind him, he would have been a top-notch producer-director.

And how about Coleman Francis? Would you say the same thing about him?

Yeah. If he had the money behind him and everything, sure.

THE BEAST OF YUCCA FLATS (1961)

53 minutes; Associate Producers: Laurence [Larry] Aten & Charles Stafford; Executive Producers: Roland Morin & James Oliphant; Produced by Coleman Francis & Anthony Cardoza; Written & Directed by Coleman Francis; Photography: John Cagle; Cameraman: Lee Strosnider; Music: Irwin Nafshun & Al Remington; Production Supervisor & Assistant Director: Austin McKinney; Editors: Austin McKinney, Lee Strosnider, Anthony Cardoza & [unconfirmed] C. [Coleman] Francis; Makeup: L. [Larry] Aten; Publicity: Ted

Charach; Film Effects: Ray Mercer; Sound Mixer: Titus Moody

Tor Johnson (*Joe Jaworsky/The Beast*), Douglas Mellor (*Hank Radcliffe*), Barbara Francis (*Lois Radcliffe*), Bing Stafford (*Joe Dobson*), Larry Aten (*Jim Archer*), Linda Bielema (*Vacationing Wife*), Ronald Francis, Alan Francis (*Lost Radcliffe Boys*), Tony [Anthony] Cardoza (*Kremlin Agent/Searcher*), Bob Labansat (*FBI Agent*), Jim Oliphant (*Vacationing Husband*), John Morrison (*Kremlin Agent*), Eric Tomlin (*Motorist*), Jim Miles (*Black Soldier*), George Principe (*Motorist*), Conrad Brooks (*Man at Airport*), Graham Stafford (*News Boy*), Marcia Knight (*Woman in Bed with Jim*), Coleman Francis (*Newspaper Buyer/Service Station Attendant/Narrator/Tor Johnson's Roars*), Bob Carrano (*Parachutist*), Bob Calcagni (*Pilot*)

AUDREY DALTON

It's been great fun to go back and look at [my movies]. Because now it's like looking across this great void of 30 years, 40 years at this stuff. My grandchildren think it's hilarious [laughs]—and a lot of it very boring, too!

The box office grosses of the 1997 *Titanic* may have blown those of the 1953 *Titanic* (and every other movie!) out of the water, but the old version still has its advantages—among them the lovely screen newcomer Audrey Dalton in the equivalent "Kate Winslet role" (opposite Robert Wagner as her lower-class shipboard beau).

The Dublin-born actress made her screen debut earlier that same year in Paramount's *The Girls of Pleasure Island* and seemed headed for stardom but, she once admitted, "Every time my acting career [seemed] to be on the way up, I have another baby." By putting marriage and motherhood ahead of her career, Dalton settled into B movies (among them the giant-snail shocker *The Monster That Challenged the World* and William Castle's atmospheric *Mr. Sardonicus*) and TV, where she starred three times on the classic Boris Karloff anthology series *Thriller*.

When did you first know that you wanted to be an actress?

I was probably five years old [*laughs*]—I just a-l-w-a-y-s wanted to be an actress, as long as I can remember. Probably from just being in theaters. Irish people generally are, or *used* to be, more theater-going than in a lot of places. I just wanted it *right* from the beginning. I did the usual, school plays. I played Antigone in Sophocles' play when I was 13, so I got an early start!

My family moved to London when I was 17. Later, when I finished high school in London, I applied to the Royal Academy of Dramatic Art, I auditioned there. They didn't accept anyone 'til 18, so I had a few months in a preparatory academy that they ran. I was at the Royal Academy until I came *here* [to the U.S.], which was a little under two years later.

While you were at the Royal Academy, were there any other future celebrities there?

Yeah—Joan Collins, who was "a year ahead." (It was a two-year course.) There were people of all ages there. And there were many American G.I.s there at that time, attending under the G.I. Bill.

You didn't finish your studies at RADA.

We did plays twice a year, a Shakespearean play and a modern play, and a man called Dick Nealand, a Paramount executive in London, attended these productions. He asked if I would be willing to audition for a film. And that was the beginning of *The Girls of Pleasure Island*. I did the screen test and the whole thing, along with *many* others. (The screen test was in London, at Pinewood. It was a scene from the movie.) The film is about three girls; the other two girls who were chosen were Joan Elan and Dorothy Bromiley. We were each attending the three different drama schools in London. We came [to the U.S.] in March 1952, to New York for a week or so, and then on to L.A.

Why didn't you go back to RADA after the picture?

Because I was then under contract to Paramount. Part of the deal was that you signed a contract — one of those "wonderful" seven-year contracts which actually usually lasted six months, 'cause there were six-month options. I stayed [in Hollywood] after *Pleasure Island* because I was still under contract, and then I did two pictures on loanout to Fox [*My Cousin Rachel* and *Titanic*]. Paramount renewed my contract for, I think, two years. In the meantime, I got married and so on. By the time of *Drum Beat* [1954], I had been released from my contract; *Drum Beat* was my first picture after Paramount.

Would you tell an anecdote about the making of Titanic?

On *any* movie, there's a great deal of camaraderie and fun, and you become a family for a little while. On that set, everyone knew I was a neophyte, and the grips got this gag thing going: Day after day, I would feel these funny *taps*, the feeling of something touching my body. I didn't know what it was, and finally I mentioned to the wardrobe lady that I was feel this sort of ... *twitching*. "Aaaah," I was told, "that's because you're not used to being around so much electricity on a set. Just look at all those cables, all those things. In the beginning, until you're used to it, you need to be grounded in some way." So the grips were consulted, the "problem" was explained to them, and they said, "Oh, yes!"—they understood the "problem" perfectly. They got this long leather strap and tied it around my waist so that it dragged on the floor. *That*, they said, was going to "ground" me.

Well, I *wore* it [*laughs*]—I wore it until they finally told me how they had poked fun at me: With *very* long rods or sticks or something, the grips had been touching me every time I was looking the other way. I'd look around, and of course nobody was near me or even *looking* at me. They were terribly patient, they let this thing "grow," waited 'til I *said* something to somebody, then they told me I had to wear that leather strap, which I *did*—for a *long time* [*laughs*]! I now think it was funny, but [at the time] I died with embarrassment! How could I be so dumb?

How did you like the new Titanic?

I enjoyed it. I thought it was spectacular—knowing how the ship actually broke up and all of that stuff is fascinating. I found a certain similarity in the characters in the two movies—I don't mean the historic characters but the *fictional* characters: The family that was "dysfunctional," so to speak, the love affair with the young man and so on. Even the opening sequence of the family arriving at the boat, the flurry of the passengers and everything, was just so similar to the beginning of [the 1953] *Titanic*.

Beauty Audrey Dalton met beasts both human and not-so when she ventured into genre movies.

I still prefer your Titanic.

Well ... they were just different movies. I thought the dialogue in the new one was just *inane*. But it's a fascinating picture, no question. And what a success! Of course, now people say about me, "She was in the original *Titanic*," and I have to stress the *in*, not the *on* [*laughs*]!

What was your reaction when you were offered a starring role in The Monster That Challenged the World?

Decades before Kate Winslet and Leonardo DiCaprio, Dalton and Robert Wagner starred as lovers in 1953's ***Titanic***.

This was a new team: Arthur Laven, who was the director, Jules Levy and Arthur Gardner. The three were a very hot team in Hollywood at the time, and it was presented to me at a time when I wasn't working. And I *always* like to work! I was never discriminating with a capital D, I just wanted to *work*, I *enjoyed* working. I've always felt with these science-fiction things that just that one little nugget of "well, it could be true" kind of gets you [*laughs*]! So it was fun.

A lot of the actors I've interviewed mentioned resisting when they were offered their first monster movie, because it seemed like a step down.

Of course it was. But I was also *just* pregnant, and I knew I wasn't going to be able to work much longer — in those days, once you were pregnant, you couldn't work. So I thought, "Well, let me get another one under my belt while I can!" So, yes, there was that feeling [of a step down]; it was the same way with television in the early days.

Your leading man was Tim Holt, a cowboy star who came out of semi-retirement to make it.

He was *quiet*. Professional, but *terribly* quiet. Did not have much to say at all. I had very little interaction with him. We did our stuff together, of course, but apart from that, he was quite remote. He sort of "came back" for that picture [Holt had moved back to Oklahoma], then after that, I never heard much about him again. But

Hans Conried, who played the scientist, was *great* fun. And *stories*—of course, I can't remember a one. He was one of those wonderful raconteurs, with all the accents appropriate to each story. Great, great fun!

And the Monster? Did you find it impressive?

The Monster was very impressive, let me tell you! It was *huge*. I still remember the scene in the lab, where it breaks through the door, with all the appropriate noises and whatever. *That* was done on a sound stage.

Where was Monster *shot?*

We went down to El Centro, a small town near the All-American Canal, and to the military bases. I'm remembering that some of the interiors, like the office scenes, were shot in [actual] buildings, because I have a memory of being in and out of buildings there while they shot. I also remember that Jules Levy and I had a few little go-rounds over wardrobe and costume, that kind of stuff, but other than *that*, it was great.

What was the problem with Levy?

Remember the scene on the beach, with the very sexy actress [Barbara Darrow] whose picture you see in all the ads? She was cast in that sexy part, and then Jules Levy wanted me to—oh, I don't know, go without a bra and all that stuff. Which was terribly radical at the time. Of course, I resisted—and then was asked things like, "Why? Is there something *wrong* with you?" [*Laughs*] I was very incensed. I was very young; I would have handled it differently at a later stage, I'm sure, and been more mature about it. At the time, I was incensed.

You were on Levy-Gardner-Laven's The Big Valley *a couple of times, so Jules Levy couldn't have resented your attitude* too *much.*

It wasn't [one-on-one], there was a wardrobe woman acting as intermediary. In those days, we didn't actually discuss it face to face, it was back and forth for the wardrobe lady between Levy and myself.

Was Arnold Laven a good director?

Lovely. *Absolutely.* Serious. Intent. Lovely man. And, of course, he went on and did all kinds of good things.

Did you see your own pictures when they came out?

Yes, I always did. It was always kind of fun.

How much time do you spend watching your own stuff today?

I have gone *years* without seeing it. But, since I attended the Memphis Film Festival [in 1997], people have started giving me tapes of old movies. I'm so *fortunate*—it's been grand, it's been great fun to go back and look at them. Because now it's like looking across this great void of 30 years, 40 years at this stuff. My grandchildren think it's hilarious [*laughs*]—and a lot of it very boring, too! Their attention span is ... different. So, since Memphis, I've looked at a lot of things that I haven't looked at in a long time.

What do you remember about Mr. Sardonicus?

Bill Castle. *Mr. Sardonicus* had more "prestige" somehow, because that was Columbia, shot up on Gower.

Did you know William Castle before you made that movie?

No, but I knew his *name*—he'd done a lot of television. He was such an energetic man: He just sort of "filled up a

How come there's never a giant salt shaker around when you need one? Dalton and Mimi Gibson gang up on The Monster that Challenged the World.

room" with his ideas and his thoughts. And he was particular about every detail in that picture. He was in on wardrobe, on *every*thing. Rather like the way Hitchcock worked, I think he envisioned the whole thing before it ever happened. He *knew* where he was going with everything. That, too, really was fun. We giggled and laughed all through it. Oscar Homolka was *so* much fun, with the accent and the voice and the horror and the creepy stuff. He was grand.

In the same sort of way that Hans Conried was?

Yeah. In other words, they were just so at ease on a set, so relaxed. Oscar Homolka came up with *all kinds* of wonderful things to do with the character that absolutely would break Bill Castle apart because it was just ... *funny* ... *right* ... and added so much to the scenes. The leading man was Ronald Lewis, an English actor who came over for the picture. I don't know whatever happened to him.

So you got on well with Castle.

Yes, just fine. No problems. I just did what I was told, which is what part of it is about. He was able to communicate what he wanted, and (I hope) I was able to deliver.

If you had any ideas about your character, costuming, etc., would you pipe up?

The horrific face behind her husband's (Guy Rolfe) mask was the least of Dalton's problems in *Mr. Sardonicus*.

Oh, I would pipe up. Usually that would come out in rehearsals, during a run-through. That was *your* opportunity to do it your way. Quite often that was fine; if not, they would refine that. Oftentimes you'd work out with other actors before you did a run-through for the director.

And Guy Rolfe, who played the evil baron?

He was not well, I remember. He was terribly thin, he was ill. But, again, professional. The British, they really *are* professionals when they come over. *They* always feel — or they did in those days — a little like coming to Hollywood was sort of a step down, and they were just doing it for the money.

Was it always him under the mask? It definitely sounds post-dubbed.

Yes, always, but I guess they couldn't get the sound right because of the mask. But it was always him.

I thought those skull teeth he wore were very effective.

Yes, it *was* pretty horrible [*laughs*] — it was indeed! That was part of the [mystery], "What is behind this awful mask?" I played his poor wife, trapped with him in his castle off in the mountains of Transylvania, and you just knew that all sorts of unspeakable things were going to be done to her by this creep. But it was a happy experience, and beautiful clothes. It was great!

Do you remember the "Punishment Poll" gimmick, where audiences voted on the fate of Mr. Sardonicus?

I had forgotten that until I saw it again a few years ago. My husband Rod and I were in Atlanta for several months in '91 or '92, and a museum there was showing a series of horror pictures. That was one of them, and we went to see it. And I had forgotten all about the Punishment Poll. It *was* sort of a gimmick, wasn't it? It's a terrible interruption in the picture [*laughs*]! But Bill Castle liked to do that kind of thing, it was part of the publicity.

But it wasn't on the level, since you never filmed a "happy ending" for Sardonicus.

Of course not [*laughs*]! It was just sort of silly.

Castle once mentioned the "sheer joy" of making Mr. Sardonicus.

He's right, it was great fun. And it had a lot of [horrific] *meat* to it — dreaming up that plot, and building that atmosphere of foreboding in the scenes. It was just great.

Between movies and TV, you were in a lot of things with plenty of action, like Westerns. Were you ever asked to do anything that you were a little iffy about?

Ride a horse, which I did a lot of — and didn't *like* [*laughs*]! But, again, you *have* to do it, and you *did* it. That's all.

Did you ever suspect, coming over here from London, from RADA, how many Westerns you'd end up in?

Of course not! That *really* would have been a step down, now *wouldn't* it [*laughs*]? At least, that's the way I would have felt when I was 19. But I grew to love Westerns and the characters on Western sets — the wranglers and the other people. You get to know these people, because it would be the same people almost every time. There was sort of a coterie of actors and crew who worked on them. It was very comfortable.

The Wagon Train *people must have really liked you — you did a half-dozen or more.*

I used to do one every season, and one season I think they even squeezed me into *two*. There was that [rule] that you couldn't do two in the same season, because people were going to confuse you with your other role. Ward Bond *liked* me — I mean, in the nicest way. It was because of the Irish thing. He had this thing about Ireland.

I just read the autobiography of a director named Burt Kennedy, who said Ward

The presence of a still photographer makes people (Ronald Lewis, William Castle, Dalton) act silly on the set of ***Mr. Sardonicus.***

Bond was "a real horse's ass." He said that in Westerns, whenever the horses' asses loom in the foreground of a shot, that's called a "Ward Bond shot," even to this day.

[*Laughs*] Ward Bond must have been difficult for directors. He was The Star on the set at this stage in his career, having *not* been a star for so many years— he was around for a long time prior to *Wagon*

Train. And he probably was very demanding in terms of time and rehearsing. *He knew it all.* For a director who was unsure of himself or just starting out, I think Ward Bond would probably have been intimidating. But as far as I was concerned, he was grand.

Thriller was the same thing as *Wagon Train*, I kept getting invited back. When they liked you on a series, you'd get invited back. It was like a stock company, and every year you'd come back. Alan Caillou, Abraham Sofaer, a whole bunch of people would keep showing up on *Thriller*, and you'd renew acquaintance and get to work together again. Abraham Sofaer was *great*. He was someone else who'd just sort of plunk on the set and *talk*. He knew *every*body who had *ever* worked in *any* show, in *any* movie, and he would hold court in that wonderful voice and that accent and the whole thing. He missed New York, as actors always seem to do when they have to come out here to make money!

And Thriller *was a fun show?*

Thriller was a g-r-e-a-t show — it gave me some of my *best parts*. Oh! The *Thriller*s are some of the shows I've watched recently again because I was fortunate enough to have someone send me some of those tapes. I was deeply grateful, because they're hard to find. They were grand — I enjoyed all the histrionics!

Your first episode was "The Prediction," where you played Boris Karloff's daughter.

As everyone always says, Karloff was just the perfect gentleman. A terribly British, wonderful, wonderful man. Just a very nice person. But very ill. When I worked with him in that — and I did *several* things with him — he was not in the best of health. His wife Evie always with him on the set, to take care of him.

Was he a storyteller like Hans Conried and Oscar Homolka and Abraham Sofaer?

Karloff was quiet. Very quiet. He went to his portable dressing room. Always.

You know, it's funny — everybody talks about what a perfect gentleman Karloff was and how wonderful he was. But then when I ask for details, they usually tell me he didn't talk to them and he was never around!

It had to do with his quiet voice, I think, and his demeanor. Maybe it was just in juxtaposition to the characters he played! I don't mean in "The Prediction" — *there* he was a fatherly, nice character — but Karloff played all these weird people, and you had to wonder if he was a normal, nice guy underneath.

For the last scene of "The Prediction," over director John Brahm's objections, Karloff insisted on lying on a back lot road in the rain. Was that tough on him, at his age?

It *must* have been. And the rain — Lord, when it used to rain in a film, it was *buckets*, in order for it to show up! It was hard on him at the end, because he was very frail. John Brahm had such a terrible reputation for being mean and nasty and whatever. But I never had any problems with him, and I so respected someone who was a "link to the past" like he was. He had done such big movies.

Thriller*'s "The Hollow Watcher" gave you a really good, cold-blooded role.*

That was the one I thought was *great*. Oooh, that was grand! That was a little "different" part for me, too, which was nice. Now and then I played [meanies], little spotty things, but they were the exception. I was always the nice girl, the ingenue — which was fine, which was … the

Dalton and actor Richard Devon at the 1997 Memphis Film Festival.

way I *was* [*laughs*]! So it *was* fun to have something with a little more meat to it, and to be given free rein. The director [William Claxton] let me run with it, which was fun. That hadn't happened before. Warren Oates, who played my husband, was someone I worked with quite a bit.

He often played off-center characters, and I started to wonder if there was something in his real-life personality that made people think of him for those roles.

I think that, once you start doing that, and you're good at it (and he *was* good at it), then when that kind of a part came along, they thought of you. The same writers are writing the same shows over and over again, and then you get the same kind of cast members.

Any memory of the Thriller *producers, Doug Benton or William Frye?*

Doug Benton, the associate producer, was a super guy. And William Frye was someone who [my first husband] Jim Brown used to see socially, my husband *and* I. He did a lot of stuff at Universal. Nice man. A big fan of Loretta Young's— they used to associate a lot, and he would escort her places and so on.

I also did a *Wild Wild West* with Boris Karloff ["The Night of the Golden Cobra"] and, oh, that was *great* because I got to walk two cheetahs on a leash! That was fun, and so were the exotic costumes. That was a very "different" kind of show, because it was so farout. Being a Western only remotely came into it [*laughs*]! I also remember the lovely producer [Michael Garrison] who later fell in his home and died. He was a sweetheart, a lovely man— young, energetic, great fun. He slipped on some stairs in his own home and cracked his head.

And Karloff? Was he even frailer now, six years later?

Yeah. My whole memories of him are always that his wife Evie had to hover and take care of him, and there was great solicitation of him always on the set, by everybody.

Your last movie was a Western, The Bounty Killer *[1965].*

Produced by a man named Alex Gordon, who made me feel like a *star*—even though I was over the hill by the time I did that [*laughs*]! He was *soooo* nice. That was my last picture, then I continued with TV 'til I sort of ... faded out.

Why did you drift away from acting?

It sort of drifted away from *me*—it happens. You have to *really* have staying power, and I *didn't*, I guess. I was involved with family, and I just let it drift. If I had it to do over again, I wouldn't. But I *did*. One goes on. I've been married for almost 19 years now to Rod Simmons, who is a retired engineer. My first husband was Jim Brown, who was a student when I married him; he eventually became an assistant director. We were married for 25 years, and we had four kids. I have nine grandchildren.

So far.

Oh, I think they're through—I *hope* [*laughs*]! I once got a wonderful card from someone that said, "Hell is when your children start complaining about how old they are"!

My career has just been the best. The best. I had great fun. But, like many good things, too short!

AUDREY DALTON FILMOGRAPHY

My Cousin Rachel (20th Century–Fox, 1952)
Dreamboat (20th Century–Fox, 1952)
The Girls of Pleasure Island (Paramount, 1953)
Titanic (20th Century–Fox, 1953)
Casanova's Big Night (Paramount, 1954)
Drum Beat (Warners, 1954)
The Prodigal (MGM, 1955)
The Deadliest Sin (*Confession*) (Allied Artists, 1956)
Hold Back the Night (Allied Artists, 1956)
The Monster That Challenged the World (United Artists, 1957)
Separate Tables (United Artists, 1958)
Thundering Jets (20th Century–Fox, 1958)
This Other Eden (Emmett Dalton/RF, 1959)
Lone Texan (20th Century–Fox, 1959)
Mr. Sardonicus (Columbia, 1961)
Kitten With a Whip (Universal, 1964)
The Bounty Killer (Embassy, 1965)

PHOEBE DORIN

Michael [Dunn] was like this little genius. This strange little genius, but ... this genius!

Phoebe Dorin's stage and television partner was a diminutive actor who attained full-size success via a series of towering performances in the 1960s: Michael Dunn. The three-foot-ten, 75 lb. Dunn is best known by TV fans as Dr. Miguelito Loveless on *The Wild Wild West* (1965–68), but movie buffs also recall his Oscar-nominated performance in Stanley Kramer's *Ship of Fools* (1965). New York theatergoers of a certain generation remember his work in such Broadway plays as *Ballad of the Sad Cafe*, for which he received a Tony nomination and a New York Critics Circle Award.

Even nightclub patrons remember Dunn: In the mid-60s, he and his friend and fellow actor Phoebe Dorin debuted their unique act "Michael Dunn and Phoebe." It was hailed in periodicals like *Time* and *The New York Times*, performed at night spots throughout the country, and led directly to their casting on *Wild Wild West*. (Dorin co-starred in the Loveless episodes as the mad doctor's accomplice and singing partner Antoinette.)

Manhattan-born Dorin made her living as an art director in the years before she began concentrating on her acting career. Outside of her collaborations with Dunn, she worked with an improv group and acted on- and off-Broadway; since Dunn's 1973 death (at age 39), she has worked steadily in episodic TV and done voiceovers for commercials. In this interview, Dorin candidly recounts the highs and lows of her very special friendship with Michael Dunn, the actor with whom she shared stage, nightclub and TV spotlights.

Before you got into acting, you studied at Cooper Union and worked as an art director.

Cooper Union in New York City is one of the most famous art schools in the world. It's down in the Bowery, on Third Avenue, and it's just this great, great school. You can't [just enroll], you have to win a scholarship to it, and you are never given grades, you are either asked back the next year or you're not. But it really teaches you how to think because there *are* no grades; you literally have to be very creative and learn how to put things together. It's a school of art, architecture and design, and when you enter it, you take *every*thing—the architects have to learn to paint, the painters have to learn to be architects and so on. And what happens then is, you find you have proclivities toward other things, and a lot of people *do* change what they do. Some wonderful people have come out of Cooper Union—most of the leading art directors in New York are

So you were more interested in art than singing and acting at that point?

That had always been a big conflict for me, painting and art and design [versus] theater. I always felt that the more spiritual thing was the painting and I *did* that for many years — I was an art director, I worked at CBS and at Dell Publications, at a magazine there. But I just one day thought, "I'm lying to myself" and what I did was quit cold — I quit art directing and I started waiting tables and going to acting class, until I eventually landed my first off-Broadway show. And that's where I met Michael.

In your first off-Broadway show?

Yes, *Two by Saroyan*. Alvin Ailey was in it (that was Alvin's first role), Cynthia Harris, Jimmy Broderick — an extraordinary cast. I was not only in the show in a very tiny role but I designed and painted the posters for them. One day I was on the floor mapping out this enormous poster that was supposed to go outside the theater, and I looked down and standing on the poster were these two little feet. I didn't know what they were — I'd never seen little feet like that! They were very tiny and they were in those strange little shoes that are shaped to your feet. I thought, "They don't look like *kid's* feet but they don't look like *big* feet either." And I looked up and there was Michael standing on the poster. I said to him, "You're on the poster" and he said, "Let me help you fill this in." So he grabbed a paintbrush and he helped me, and we became very, very good friends.

What parts did you and he play in the show?

He played a policeman [*laughs*]! He had to run in and he had to beat Alvin Ailey up. And *I* played a pregnant lady, and I literally gave birth on stage. (A big football.) It was very funny!

After the show every night, in order to "unwind," what Michael and I would do is go to the Plaza Hotel, one of the ritziest hotels in New York, right on Central Park where you get the hansom cabs. Across from the Plaza Hotel is the Plaza Fountain. We would go to the fountain — usually in the winter they didn't fill it with water. We were both very tiny, and we would sit in the Fountain and we would sing — he had this gorgeous singing voice, and we found out that we loved to sing together. We'd sing for hours. And we ended up with a little "following," a little coterie of people who would show up from night to night. And then of course there would be tourists and lovers taking hansom cab rides and people strolling down Fifth Avenue. They'd sit and listen and make requests for songs, and it became a "thing." In fact, if we didn't show up one night, the *next* night people would be very angry that we didn't show [*laughs*]! It was a fabulous way to release all that energy, and it was also loads of fun. Michael and I just got to be such good friends that way.

When you would sing in the fountain, what hours are we talking about here? Starting around midnight?

Well, if the show closed at around 11, we would get down there by 11:30, quarter of 12. And *every*one in New York stayed up late at night, walking the streets 'cause it was gorgeous and beautiful. That was our little following. We would sing 'til about one, two in the morning and then we would be *so* exhausted we'd go home and go to sleep [*laughs*]! That went on for quite a while.

What kind of songs did you sing in the fountain?

Phoebe Dorin today.

We sang folk songs, we sang standards, we sang show tunes—whatever people would request. And also stuff that *we* had been working on. And then of course there'd be a moment where Michael did a solo, 'cause he was *wonderful*, 'cause he was so great.

How did this turn into a nightclub act?

One day Roddy McDowall was pho-

The Plaza Hotel Fountain today. (Photograph courtesy Mary Runser.)

tographing Michael for *Life* magazine—Michael had just done *Ballad of the Sad Cafe* on Broadway and there was talk of him now doing [the movies] *Ship of Fools* and *The Tin Drum*. Roddy said, "Michael, I'm gonna follow you around, but I don't want you to do *any*thing that you don't ordinarily do. I really want to spend the day with you." So he did. And at night, we went to the Plaza Fountain and we sang, and all the people came around, and Roddy took pictures for *Life* and was so charmed by it that when we went out for a bite to eat afterwards, he said, "You guys are crazy. You have got to put this together in a club. *Why* are you giving it away?" *We* said, "Oh, no one will come," and Michael said, "No, I'm too self-conscious. When they see me, they'll freak." Roddy said, "I didn't see them freaking at the fountain. I really think you should do it." So Roddy was the one who put the little bee in our bonnet and encouraged us, and we did it.

And that was the beginning of the nightclub act.

Which of the two of you needed more encouragement?

Me! [*Laughs*] I always felt that Michael had the voice; I am primarily an actress. I can *sing*, but I wouldn't get up on Broadway and sing, it's not my thing. I'd get up on Broadway and *act* but not sing! Michael had a voice that was operatic. In fact, there were people who offered to teach him opera for *free* if he would just *do* it, but that required a great deal of stamina which Michael didn't have—physically, he was limited. But he was afraid that if he got out on stage, people would be repulsed. *Or*, he felt, by the time they could "adapt" to him on stage, it would be a half an hour into the act and the act would be over! *That's* part of the reason Roddy said, "Michael, you don't understand the dynamic. I've been watching you all night. Phoebe relates to you; she teases and laughs with you; you're both very funny; then you sing. The audience [the people around the fountain] relates to Phoebe, who is relating to you. You're *right*, Michael, they *don't* relate to you because to them you're strange, they don't know who you are or *what* you are. But in a few minutes, because of how you relate to Phoebe, they *do* know who you are and what you are." So Michael felt that if he did the act by himself, it wouldn't work—he just could not face what it would be like to do that by himself. And, as nervous as I was about singing in front of people, I knew that I was terribly funny and an awfully good actress, and if I was with Michael, I wasn't gonna have to be afraid of *any*thing. So we *both* had things that the other person didn't have, and that was the magic of the act.

Okay, finally both *of you are sold on doing the act. What was the next step, where did you go to rehearse and everything?*

You have to remember, when Roddy suggested this, we still were so poor. I was still waiting on tables and trying to be an actress, and Michael was ... well, he was sort of moving up, but we still didn't have a pot between us. Michael somehow bartered to get rehearsal space at Variety Arts, this big rehearsal studio on Broadway. We would go in three, four hours a day. We had an accompanist and we had a director, Neal Kenyon. But the act didn't work for quite a while until I came up with the idea of "library steps." We had two little units, basically little stages for ourselves: I had a little stage and he had a little stage. It was a series of spiral steps, and they would be wheeled on stage and we would run out and jump on our units and begin the act on these units, in a spotlight. What it enabled us to do was change heights. And the audience didn't realize what was going on. In other words, Michael could sit on a higher step than me

and sing to me, and they weren't aware of his height because he was taller, he was in a spotlight. It was the element that made it work. But everywhere we went to perform, we had to ship those staircase units—I can't tell you what it cost! That's what we spent most of our money on.

Most of your earnings?

Most of our earnings, yes. When we did the nightclub act in New York at Upstairs at the Duplex, I think we each earned $40 a week.

I'll never forget one day when we had a rehearsal call. Our manager John Softness was supposed to be there and I think a director named Marty Charnin, the guy who wrote *Annie*. It was the first day we were really gonna come in and "launch" this, and there were going to be a couple of really important people watching this rehearsal just to see—"*Is* this act viable or not?" We were very excited, we'd waited a long time for this. We met at one of the bars in a very exclusive hotel (I forget where), and people started showing up with shocked looks on their faces. We didn't know what was going on. And then finally we heard a woman *scream*, she was hysterical! John came in and we asked, "Why are you late?" He was weeping, and he said, "Kennedy's been shot." So that was the end of the rehearsal, that was the end of *everything* for awhile. It put everything on hold, and it took us awhile to get back into it and get the rehearsal space again.

Upstairs at the Duplex, on Grove Street in Greenwich Village—that's where you debuted?

A magical, magical place. A lot of us started there—we were working with Joanie Rivers and Dick Cavett and Jo Anne Worley, and we were *all* making 40 bucks a week. And we would be there 'til three, four in the morning. As long as there was one person left alive in that audience, Jan Wallman, the entrepreneur who ran that little club, would make us perform [*laughs*]! If they were sleeping on the table, she would say, "You're paid to do a show! The show must go on!"—and we would do the show. What it *was* for us was great training, which was fabulous. But Michael and I weren't making money until we started playing the Hungry I in San Francisco and until Michael did *Ship of Fools*. Then *his* name started to pay off and the nightclub act began being known—we were reviewed in *Time* magazine and people started coming on their own. *That's* when we started making money. Before then, we were making so little. And if they told us *we* had to pay *them* to perform, I think we would have done it [*laughs*]—that's how dumb *we* were!

How long were your gigs at places like Upstairs at the Duplex?

When we played a gig there, we played it for months.

Did he have miniature furniture in his apartment?

No. He lived on the West Side, about three doors down from the Actors Studio, in Hell's Kitchen. Hell's Kitchen was the Italian neighborhood—all the Italian Mafia. And it was one of the safest neighborhoods in New York, 'cause nobody came there to start trouble [*laughs*]! I mean, you could leave your car door open, you could leave your apartment door open—there was nobody there who was gonna dare! And everyone in the neighborhood knew Michael and adored him. His Italian friends were wonderful. I would see them a lot when I'd go down there. There was a guy named Gary and there was Nunzio [*laughs*]—oh, they all knew Michael and they loved him and they would cart him around on their shoulders! They knew Mike before he became famous. He just was a terrific guy and the neighborhood loved him. Oh, we had a great time in the beginning. I think Michael was happier when he was on the road to success. I think those were his happiest times.

What kind of songs would you sing in the act?

Very sophisticated. It would be a combination of Broadway, jazz and old standards—standards like "You Make Me Feel So Young," there'd be a lot of duets, there'd be a couple of solos that Michael would do. Very moody, beautiful solos. But it wasn't, "First we're gonna sing this," "Now we're gonna sing this," "Now we're gonna sing *this*"—the act was structured like a little play. We would start out as children on these little library steps, and it almost looked like we were in a jungle gym or a little playground. And we would keep segueing—the music kept segueing—into more and more sophisticated stuff. The act had a tremendous following. And we did it *all*—we built it with the director, we chose the songs, we even had one or two songs that were written directly for us by Charlie Smalls, a very good friend of ours. (Charlie wrote *The Wiz*, the black version of *The Wizard of Oz*, the musical.) We did blues, we did jazz, we did show tunes, we did standards. But the act was more unique than that. I *can't* explain it, you had to see the act to understand it. With Michael, it couldn't just be a singing act like Sinatra would sing or Rosemary Clooney would sing. *That* is conventional. Michael was *so* unconventional and the act was unconventional, but the music was terrific.

How long was your act?

I would say about 40 minutes. Because it not only had singing, it had a lot of comedy, a lot of patter. That was part of "the story": Before we would sing a song, there would be a little joke, a little relationship between the two of us that the audience was completely sucked into. And then we would sing. And then something else would happen and before they knew it, we were "different" people and we would sing something else. It was a combination of acting skill and the singing thing. It was almost like a miniature Broadway show. It was wonderful.

So the act was a hit.

We were like this little phenomenon. This is when nightclubs were all the rage: People didn't stay home and watch television, they went to nightclubs. Joan Rivers and Woody Allen and all these people were working out their stuff in clubs, and we were the opening act for most of 'em. We were the opening act for Dick Cavett, Bill Cosby, we went to Mr. Kelly's on Rush Street in Chicago, *Time* magazine wrote us up — it was quite a run! For nightclubs, it was really an extraordinary time, it was like a renaissance — I've never seen it that way since. The Bitter End and Upstairs at the Duplex and Julius Monk's — I don't know if these clubs mean anything to you, but they were the renaissance, they were "what was going on in New York." If you wanted to go hear a folk singer, you went and you heard Richie Havens, and then maybe you'd go watch Woody Allen do *his* nightclub act. They were *nobody* and so were *we*, *we* were nobody too.

A few minutes ago, you talked about Dunn being up for a part in a film adaptation of The Tin Drum *that was going to be made in the '60s...?*

When Gunter Grass [author of the novel *The Tin Drum*] saw Michael in *Ballad of the Sad Cafe*, he said, "Eureka! We can now bring this to the screen. *This* is the man I want to do it." But, unfortunately, Michael died before that happened. They would have done it as an American film, but they couldn't do it 'cause Michael was gone.

Dunn's real name was Gary Miller. What was the matter with that name?

I don't know why he didn't use it. I don't know the origin of "Michael Dunn." When I met him, he was Michael Dunn. By the way, kids used to follow him down the street after the nightclub act. Kids are wonderful, they just say what they're thinking and they're much more honest about how they related to Michael than older people. They'd say, "What *are* you? Are you a little man or are you a little boy?" and he would explain what he was.

He was a dwarf, correct?

He was *not* a dwarf. He had a bone disease which was a form of arthritis, the most severe form you could have. It's called achondroplasia. [Charles Proteus] Steinmetz, the electrical genius, had the same thing, and so did Toulouse-Lautrec. At a very early age there's a fall or an accident, and after *that* the bones do not grow. You can be normal 'til three or four years old, and then it will present itself. The sad thing was that Michael's parents did *not* have other children because they thought it was hereditary when in fact it was congenital. It was *very* sad. That was the disease that he had, and he was told that he would die around the same age that *those* people died, because there was nowhere for his internal organs to grow. They were cramped. And eventually they would simply give out because they didn't have the room they needed. Michael knew he was going to die very early on. He was so bright — you can't lie to someone who knows more medical research than *you* do.

Publicity photos of nightclub stars Michael Dunn and Phoebe Dorin downplayed the difference in their size.

Did you ever meet his parents?

Oh, God, I knew them very well. Fred and Jewel Miller were the most wonderful people — they did more for that kid…! I don't know if Michael would have been as adventurous and as much of a role model as he was without them. They let him do everything. They just said to themselves, "If he's gonna die, he's gonna die. He's gonna go swimming, he's gonna drive a car, he's gonna do everything. To give him less of a life would be tragic." His parents were fabulous. I wish I'd had parents as wonderful and as loving and as warm. They were in his corner the whole way.

Where did they live?

They lived in Livonia, Michigan. I went to visit them once with him. And then they moved to Florida when they retired.

How did he get to be as smart as he was? Was he self-educated?

Michael had a 185 IQ and was a college graduate. He was one of the most brilliant people you'd ever meet in your life. Very incongruous, that little body and this vast, brilliant mind. He would read three books a day. *He* wanted to be a doctor, and people would carry on about wanting him to be an opera singer — people who had heard him sing in college and ... *every*where. Michael was like this little genius. This *strange* little genius, but ... this genius! And *I* started him sculpting — he had these incredible hands. His hands were not only normal, they were almost *bigger* than normal. One day I asked him, "Have you ever worked with clay?" He said no. I said, "Well, you have such an appreciation for the arts. I want to start you sculpting." And he became quite a little sculptor [*laughs*]! That became a fabulous hobby for him, a very wonderful creative outlet.

Michael was terribly bright and terribly talented, and *could* have done anything with his life. But he wanted the attention and he wanted to be in show business, I think because it was his validation. It was his way of saying to the world, "You *see*? *Every*body has to love me, because I am really not *this* way. I am everything that everyone else is, and my fame proves it." And of course it never happens that way. Success, I think, made Michael more *lonely*, because his life didn't change in the way that he thought it would. I think he thought — as a lot of people do—"When I'm rich and famous and everyone knows who Michael Dunn is, *then* I won't be a little person anymore." I know that sounds crazy but, *some*where inside, one always feels that, once success comes, "I won't be lonely anymore," "I won't be ugly anymore," "I won't be ostracized anymore." But success can only bring you success, it's not a one-on-one relationship with any-body —*that* requires a whole different kind of work. I think that was Michael's biggest disappointment: Success didn't change *any*thing where he wanted it to change.

You talked to him about this stuff, or could you just "tell"?

Oh, he talked to me about *all* that stuff. We were best friends for *years*. We were never lovers, we were never boyfriend and girlfriend. We were just best friends. He was like a soulmate.

You're five feet tall.

Yes [*laughs*]! There was a little person and *another* little person!

In one of his interviews, Dunn said that a woman once took him into her lap and stroked him like a child — and he got so angry, he bit her!

Michael used to tell that story, but I don't know if it ever really happened. And *if* it did happen, *don't* think he bit her very hard — he might have bitten her to show her who was boss! But he was so kind, I can't imagine him biting anybody. However, I did see women relate to him like a child — that's what I meant before when I talked about children being more honest about what they felt about him. The minute he began to be famous, no one ever treated him that way because they all knew who he was. But *before* they knew who he was, I would see women treat him like a little boy — not like a child but like a little boy, even though he was ten times more bright than *they* were. He would become very offended and very hurt. He was very easily wounded by that. A couple of times, I heard him set people straight. But I never saw him do anything as mean as biting anyone. It's a terrific story [*laughs*] but I never saw any grown woman pick him up, put him on her lap and stroke him like a little kid. Because Michael was a *man*. He was not a crippled little boy, he never pretended to be a little boy. And didn't have a little voice, he had a really strong voice and he was a very strong *person*. There were women, though, that did condescend and talk to him as though he were less than [a man] or as though he had a handicap, as though he was deformed. And that used to hurt him *terribly*.

Was he really a Capuchin brother in a Detroit monastery at one point, as he claimed?

That I don't know. I know he studied religion at one time.

One old article about Dunn said that, at birth, he had dislocated hips, and they plagued him all his life.

Mm-hmm. Michael was in pain most of the time. He had a tremendous amount of pain, physically.

They also say his legs were very weak and he had steel ankle braces.

The lower half of his body was the part that was not developed. He was all chest—*alll* chest. That's why he had such a tremendous singing voice. He had a normal lung span and incredible chest cavity and upper body strength. But the lower half of his body was where this arthritic condition [affected him], it stunted his bones and stunted his legs very much like Toulouse-Lautrec. He had a lot of problems. In the nightclub act, we originally worked on two little stools, and to watch Michael try to climb up on a stool was painful! That's why it wouldn't work—people would go, "Oh, dear, is he gonna make it?" But the little library steps were easy, you never saw Michael sweat it. He did have a lot of health problems, though—a *lot* of health problems—because of the bones, which *were* very weak. And he had those special shoes made that I talked to you about, the ones he was wearing the day I first saw him, because he couldn't walk in normal shoes. He had to have them molded to his feet. I imagine he did have ankle braces from time to time, and I think he wore a back brace at one point, too. It's like someone with rheumatoid arthritis—it can get much worse and it can get better and then it can get worse again. And of course they didn't have the medicine, they didn't have the knowledge of it at that time.

Michael did something that I thought was extraordinary, that most people don't know about: When Mike became famous, he became a role model for a lot of kids who were born with the disease he had. They would write to him and tell him how lonely they were and they wanted to die and blah blah blah, and he would write to them and he would even go to *see* some of them on his own hook. And talk to them and befriend them and champion them. I really felt it was a wonderful thing. That wasn't very widely publicized, but he did do that.

Did you ever visit any of these kids with him?

No, but I knew of them. Michael would also read me the letters he got from these kids' mothers. A lot of the mothers did a lot of things wrong, and so Michael would talk to the parents too. Michael was very lucky to have had very liberal, very understanding, loving parents who knew that to shelter a child like that, to sequester the child, was the worst thing you can do for him.

One of his old magazine interviews ended rather abruptly because you showed up to take him to a tailor.

Oh, I remember that—he had to go to the tailor's because he didn't have a suit to wear for the nightclub act. He was only three-foot-whatever and he couldn't wear a little boy's suit because he *wasn't* a little boy — the chest cavity and everything. And he couldn't *look* like a little boy, he was a sophisticated man. Of course there were no men's clothes that fit him, so we had to go to a tailor and everything had to be made to order. His shirts had to be made to order, his pants, his suits.

This is a terrible story, but in retrospect it's a wonderful story: Even though we were getting famous doing our act, we were still making 40 bucks a week. I was helping out (I was working as a waitress) and we were putting all of our money into the rehearsal studio. One night after the show, we went to a party somewhere uptown and we had all the stuff from our act in Michael's car. When we got back to the car, the car had been broken into and everything we owned was gone. *Everything* we owned. I had one beautiful dress for the nightclub act — gone. His suits — gone. Now, who in God's *name* could have worn those suits?! We sat on the curb and we cried … and then we just started to *laugh*. I said, "Michael, *who* is the robber? Was it the midget robber? What in the *world* is he gonna do with your suits and your shirts?" It was really funny but it was terrible — we had no clothes! And Michael's suit at the tailor cost about $250! But Jan Wallman helped us. I think we wore black sweaters and black pants and did the nightclub act that way.

He had a car in New York?

Michael was a terrific driver. He had the pedals built up. Even the car had to be specially fitted for him! When he would open the car door and get out, people's mouths would drop open because, sitting in the seat, he looked like a tall person. And then this little guy would get out [*laughs*]!

You also appeared with Dunn on a lot of TV shows like Mike Douglas *and* The Today Show.

We appeared with the nightclub act. Then we'd sit on the panel and we'd talk. It was lots of fun.

How were you and Dunn cast on Wild Wild West *as Dr. Loveless and Antoinette?*

Michael Garrison, who conceived of *Wild Wild West*, came to see the nightclub act at the Duplex — someone took him when he was in New York. He was told, "You gotta see these kids, they'll blow you away." When Michael Garrison was watching the show, he said to himself, "Michael Dunn would make the most extraordinary villain. People have never seen anything like him before, *and* he's a fabulous little actor and he's funny as hell." And, Garrison felt, if Michael Dunn sang on every show, *with* the girl, it would be an extraordinary running villain. And so he came backstage and he told us who he was and he said he was going to do a television show called *The Wild Wild West* and we would be called. We thought, "Yeah, yeah, we've heard all *that* before" — but he did call us and the show *was* a fantastic success. And that's how it started, because he saw the nightclub act.

Did you like Garrison when you met him?

I adored Michael Garrison. He had such a wonderful vision that no one else could touch. He was creative; he wasn't bound by anything. He knew exactly what he was doing. I thought *The Wild Wild West* was way ahead of its time: It was a little sci-fi, it was a little bit of a James Bond Western, it just had *every*thing. And special effects and *stunts*. The stunts for me were the most miraculous part of it — I used to sit on the set and watch the stunts.

The fight sequences, you mean.

The fight sequences, and the way the furniture would break apart! You know, Bob Conrad was originally a stuntman, and that's where he felt most comfortable. So a lot of Jim West's stuff was *stunts*—all these fights and leaps and how-is-he-gonna-get-out-of-*this*-predicament? He would do his own stunts, he *prided* himself on that! They had the best stuntmen in the business working on our show, and I was spellbound. I came from Broadway and off-Broadway and I had never seen stunts. I mean, when I went to see movies, it was to see … you know … Ingrid Bergman [*laughs*], who the hell went to see *stunts*? So on *Wild Wild West* I just would sit there and marvel at the fight sequences. They would do it over and over again, and I just found it fascinating. I also loved the stuntmen, they were just great guys. So that was a wonderful part of *The Wild Wild West*. For me as an actress, it wasn't just "you go, you learn your lines, you weep, you laugh, everybody goes home," it was very physical. And I *loved* that, because I had never *thought* of that in terms of acting. It was very cinematic. We did a lot of location shooting, there were a lot of stunts … Michael and I did a lot of *our* own stunts, which almost killed us a couple of times! But to learn to be physical and handle all that is terribly important [in acting], and I didn't know that then. So *The Wild Wild West* was magical, just magical! Do you know anything about Mike Garrison? Do you know how he died?

I know he fell down a flight of stairs in his own home.

It was tragic. Michael was going to have a big party for everyone in the business who said that he was a bust-out failure and would never make it. It was sort of a "payback" party [*laughs*]—it was, like, to rub their noses in his success. (And the people who loved him and thought he was wonderful, the party was also for them too.) He had a big new house that he had bought with the money from the show, and that night, before the party, before the guests arrived, I guess he was coming down the stairs—but someone who had delivered flowers had gotten water on the steps. He slipped on the water and cracked his skull open. And that's how he died. I felt that the show, from that point on, was never the same, because they never understood what Michael was doing with it. They didn't really get it.

Robert Conrad and Ross Martin—how did you get along with them?

Oh, I adored them. They were both very different. Ross' daughter went to Cooper Union, so we had a lot to talk about. Ross was a real New York guy and certainly knew where I was coming from. And he was a raconteur—one of the funniest people I had ever met in my life. He did accents and jokes, and you would just sit there when we weren't working on the set and laugh 'til you fell off the seat. Bob Conrad was just the opposite, he was very insecure about his acting ability. He knew he was a good-looking guy but he felt that he was more physical.

I'm sure you've heard all the stories that they were constantly feuding. Any truth to that?

People said that they hated each other. I never saw that. Actually, what *I* saw was that they liked each other a lot. They both did totally opposite things on the show. It was very much like the nightclub act I had with Michael: Without me, you wouldn't have had the whimsy, and without Michael, you wouldn't have had the musicality. In terms of *The Wild Wild West*, without Ross, you wouldn't have had *that* part of it, and without Conrad, you wouldn't have had the physical, magical part of it with the stunts and all of *those* wonderful set pieces. So they both did different things and I think they both liked each other. They couldn't have been more different as actors, as people, but I liked them both.

Part of the reason I liked Bob Conrad was because Bob Conrad *adored* Michael. He *adored* him. So that anybody who was with Michael or working with Michael was treated in kind. He catered to us — he treated us like royalty. Ross you just simply made friends with, and I loved Ross.

And singing the occasional song on West *was Michael Garrison's idea.*

He saw the act and he said, "On every one of the shows, you're gonna sing, that's gonna be your 'thing.'" We worked with Marvin Hamlisch and a lot of the other people who worked for CBS in the music department at that time. They would research these old madrigals or old folk songs that would fit the period — I'm sure they fudged a little [*laughs*]! And then we would go in on a sound stage and pre-record them. On the set, I would play the harpsichord or I would play the lyre or I would play *some*thing — an instrument of the time — and Michael and I would sing, but basically they would loop us into what we did.

How about Richard Kiel, who played Loveless' servant Voltaire?

Oh, Richard is a doll — I adored Richard. When they got Richard and Michael together, it was really a trip. Richard was a math teacher, a very brilliant guy — just the opposite of what he looks like. Gentle, quiet, sweet and very, very astute. Michael and Richard and I would sit for hours having intellectual discussions about books we'd read and all of that stuff. Richard's wife, a darling lady, would also come to the set, and we all became very good friends. I just recently spoke to Richard, and he has the opposite of what Michael had — Richard has acromegaly, a condition where the bones grow *too* fast and *too* far. So he suffers terribly in terms of his physical walking and stuff like that. He's had that all his life, but as you get older, it's a disease that progresses.

Talk about some of your death-defying Wild Wild West *stunts.*

At the end of every show we were in, we were supposedly finished, dead ... but if you watch very carefully, you'd see the way we would have escaped death and lived on to come back on yet another episode. In "The Night of the Murderous Spring," I was in full Western regalia with all these little buttons, maybe 40 buttons up to my neck, with a bustle in the back and everything. Michael and I were escaping after some dastardly thing he did. There's a lake at CBS, at Radford Avenue, and Michael and I were going to go out onto this lake in a rowboat that was going to sink. The boat was wired to a pulley and the pulley was going to pull the boat straight down, very, very slowly, to the bottom of the lake. They wanted to get a shot of Miguelito and Antoinette going under the water, and then you would see the bubbles on top of the water and we were supposedly dead — you never saw us surface. They said to us, "Please, please, whatever you do, don't panic. Don't let go and come up to the surface very quickly. You will be soaking wet, and we do *not* have other costumes. It's the last shot of the day. Let it be the only shot." We were so dumb, we didn't request stunt doubles — we were so afraid to make them angry for one minute! God *forbid* they should have to dry out the costume!

I'm claustrophobic and Michael knew it. He was a terrific swimmer and he said to me, "You watch me. As soon as I get the signal, I'll let go, come up to the surface and you follow." I said, "Michael, I don't think I can *do* this, I'm gonna panic. The water's gonna get up to my nose, I'm gonna panic!" He said [*calmly*], "You're not gonna panic. You'll just hold on to the side of the boat. Nothing's gonna happen, it's not that deep, it's only about six feet deep. And the minute you see me let go, you will then surface and we'll be fine." "Okay, I'll do it…"

Well, we're doing the shot, I'm going down and I'm thinking, "God, please don't let me panic because they'll be angry and the costume will be wet…" We go all the way down to the bottom and I see the bubbles, and then I see Michael release. And I think, "Thank God!" and I let go … and my gown was completely caught in the pulleys. There was no zipper on this dress, it was these tiny little buttons. I could not get them open. I could not scream. I could not do anything. I thought, "My God, I'm gonna die! They don't know that I can't come up." But Michael knew I couldn't come up, 'cause he knew that if *any*one was hittin' that surface first, it was gonna be me [*laughs*]! He swam down and literally tore the dress open so that I could get out of it. He just literally tore it out of the pulleys and tore *me* out of the dress, so that I could get to the surface. So I almost died.

That's … wild!

Then there was another one ["The Night of the Green Terror"] where at the end of the show, we were in Michael's burning lab. The whole set was going to be set on fire and we had to run into a huge hollow log. At this point they knew that they could tell us *any*thing [*laughs*] — we were not gonna say, "Could I get hurt?" or "Would you mind using a double?" They knew that if they told us to do something, we'd do it and we'd make sure they didn't have any problems! This time they said to us, "You'll run into the log and then you'll hear knock-knock-knock. When you hear knock-knock-knock, you scurry out the other end of the log and Michael will follow you. And pleeeease do not panic and do not come out of that log until you hear the knock-knock-knock, because we are burning down the entire set and we are *not* gonna be rebuilding it. Do you understand?" "Oh, yeah, yeah, yeah, we understand."

So I look at Michael and I say, "Oh, God, *again*?" and he says, "Don't worry, we'll be fine. They're not gonna kill us." They start burning down the set, and it was fabulous — just to watch it was so wonderful. We get into the log, and pretty soon the log starts getting awfully smoky. I say to Michael, "Where's the knock-knock-knock?" and he says, "I — I — I dunno. Did *you* hear it?" I say, "Michael, I don't hear it! But I'm telling you, I'm startin' to choke here…" He says, "Well, I don't know what to do!" I say, "Well, I think I do. I think we're gettin' *outta* here." So I push the door on the other end of the log — but the heat from the fire has swollen it, and we can't get out of the log. And I don't know whatever happened to the knock-knock-knock [*laughs*] — we *never* heard the knock-knock-knock! They *must* have given us the knock-knock-knock, but we were so hysterical, we didn't hear it! I guess they figured out what was happening and they had to absolutely drench the set with water to get us out. But they did get the shot!

What about working with horses and all the other critters they had in the various episodes?

We worked with tarantulas, and there was one episode, "The Night of the Raven," where we had the raven — that little shitty raven. I hated that goddamn bird! In rehearsal, I was feeding the raven little bits of paper. The raven kept biting me

Wild Wild West producer Michael Garrison caught the Dunn-Dorin nitery act and cooked up the villainous team of Dr. Loveless and Antoinette for his offbeat Western-spy-sci-fi series.

because it wasn't real food — ravens eat raw meat.

So why didn't you give it real food?

If I fed it real food in the rehearsal, then it wouldn't eat on camera which is when we *needed* it to eat. This stinking bird kept biting me, so by the time I got to the camera I was shaking 'cause I *knew* what he was gonna do! I knew every time I held my fingers out, that damn bird was gonna bite! My hands were a mess — I just couldn't *wait* to get away from that awful bird! One day Michael was sleeping in a little chair, he was catching a catnap before we had to be on camera again. I think I was talking to Ross, over to the side, and the raven was on its perch with a hood over it, *very* close to Michael. Either the hood fell off the raven or the raven shook the hood off, and then someone flashed a light and the raven got frightened and tumbled off its perch. Ravens have talons that are unbelievable. It toppled right across Michael's face, and the talons strafed his face and missed his eye by millimeters! It was grabbing out to land on something, and just literally it was grabbing out at his face. It was quite something!

And you had fun on the show despite all this!

It was a marvelous show — I had so much damn fun on that show. It was great.

Robert Ellenstein, an actor who guested on one of the Wild West*s, told me he would see Dunn regularly sipping gin out of a thermos. Did he drink to dull the pain?*

Yeah. He self-medicated. And that's partly what hurt him so much. I think it hastened his death as well.

The drinking?

Mm-hmm. Mike was in physical and emotional pain. He drank because he thought he had to. Back then, alcoholism wasn't something a lot of people knew much about, and it certainly wasn't something *I* knew about. How do you tell someone who has the kind of physical handicap Michael had how to live their life? I knew that *I* wasn't dealt that hand, so I couldn't tell him what to do. It became a problem for us after a while because alcoholism hurts … everything. *Every*thing. What starts out as medicating to dull the pain, ends up where you're a slave to that medication. It's like a drug, a prescription drug — you can get hooked on *any*thing. It was very difficult for Michael. He would even stop for long periods of time, but he didn't know enough to go to AA. Who the hell knew about alcoholism at that time? Who knew liquor was really that much of a problem?

In New York, after the nightclub act, we would go out and we would go to Downey's, let's say — Downey's [an Eighth Avenue restaurant-bar] was the hangout. And there was Albert Finney and there was Richard Burton and there was Jason Robards — and they would drink Michael under the table! That's what people *did* then. No one ever looked at it and said, "Gee, those guys are alcoholics." They *were*, but *we* didn't know it. They would just drink all through the night, it was a big joke. Put a bottle of Jack Daniel's in front of them and everyone would try and drink each other under the table. Who knew that that could lead to a lot of misery for all of them? I mean, it killed Burton, and Robards almost died in a car crash with it. And Michael, who was even tinier — it did a job on his liver, I know *that*. But with Michael it was very progressive and it was very slow — he had been doing it, I guess, since he was in college. And when he was happy and he was not in pain, he *didn't* do it.

Did he ever show up tipsy for your nightclub act or for Wild West*?*

No. No. No. Mike was a true professional. And he never drove drunk. It was on his own time. But still, it does damage to your body. People told him, "Don't do this. Your liver is in a lot of trouble to begin with. Don't do this, it's poison." But I guess you don't think you can die from alcohol. Now people are so savvy about it and they know that you can. But then it was so socially acceptable, I can't tell you! People would laugh and say, "Oh, ha-ha-ha-ha-ha, did you see Michael last night? He was so drunk at Downey's! Ha-ha-ha-ha-ha-ha!" It was like a symbol of being a big man. Now we would look at them and say, "Oh, my God, what's *wrong* with them?"

Were you a drinker with him?

I had never been around liquor much and I didn't know anybody who had been around liquor, and I never drank, ever. I still don't, to this day. But [with Dunn] I went through everything that a person who loves an alcoholic goes through: The feeling of powerlessness, the loving-the-person-and-not-being-able-to-save-them, the anger at their constantly getting drunk. I went through *all* of that. I didn't know enough to go to Alanon 'cause I didn't even know that Michael *was* an alcoholic.

The nightclub act was sort of a Catch 22: People would buy us drinks. "You must have a drink"; "You must come to my table and sit with me"—they adored us. And we were there the whole night, doing three, four shows a night. I didn't drink so I'd have a ginger ale. Michael would start the Jack Daniel's. And he could really hold his liquor. *But* … it was an occupational hazard. So by the time the evening was over and Mike went out to Downey's to start drinking with all his theatrical buddies there, he'd be really drunk. I would say to him, "Michael, I can't deal with this. I just want you to know it. I don't *like* it and I can't *deal* with it." "I promise, I promise, I promise, I promise…" But promising—that doesn't *work* with alcoholism. I was never savvy enough to simply say, "This is unacceptable. You have to go to a program, or I can't be part of this with you." Toward the end, that's what caused me to pull away from him, even though I loved him. I loved him, he was my best friend. But I just couldn't take it any more.

Was Dunn much of a ladies' man?

[*Laughs*] Yeah, he was, he was a ladies' man. A raconteur and a ladies' man. He loved women—he loved them. He was hilariously funny and very bright and charismatic, and women adored him. And a lot of them were very, very beautiful women!

Was he looking to have a girlfriend or to get married?

[*Pause*] Well…he tried a couple of times, and it was very sad. I was really a good friend of his and I could read these women like a book. When he started to get famous, he started to get a lot of money … and they saw that. If you would flatter him, he'd give you the shirt off his back. It was very painful to watch. There were two women — he was engaged once to someone who didn't love him, and then he married a woman who really used him and took him for every cent that he had. She was a burlesque dancer or something and she was gorgeous, and she told him that she loved him. And Michael loved walking with her on his arm, for him it was a feat: "I'm just like you guys. I've got a beautiful woman on my arm." And when they were divorced, I was told she supposedly took *every*thing. It was terrible.

Did you try to warn him, or did you stay out of it?

I stayed out of it. I was just simply there for him, as his friends were. You couldn't really get into that with Michael.

There were ten West *episodes with Loveless, and you aren't in all of them.*

That's right.

And you're not in all of them becauuuuse…

Because … Michael married this woman I told you about. She wanted to play Antoinette, and she started working on him. And so he had me replaced, which is something I never thought he would do. It broke my heart. I heard that she couldn't act, so they replaced her immediately. Then they used different [female sidekicks for Loveless], but nobody who could ever sing with him and nobody who could ever really work with him the way I did.

How did you find out you had been replaced?

I was in California and he was in New York. I was waiting for him to call me and tell me when he was coming back out [to do another *Wild West*], and he never called. I called our manager John Softness and said, "Something's wrong. I *know* something's wrong. What's going on? I can't get him to talk to me." And John said, "Well … he asked to have you replaced, and he asked to have his wife play Antoinette."

I couldn't even speak. Finally I said, "I don't believe you," and he said, yeah, that's what happened. Then, of course, she couldn't do it. And *I* would not come back. They asked me to come back, and I wouldn't. Because of the betrayal. Being friends with him for *so* many years. I knew he loved her — I understood all of that. I understood he was trying to give her a career. But it hurt me so much that he would do that to me that I couldn't go back and work with him, I just didn't feel the trust would be the same after they had replaced me. Also, I said to myself, "You know what? I need to make my own life away from him. I have always been associated with Michael Dunn. And if *I* don't have enough talent on my own to be an actress, maybe God's kinda doing for me what I can't do for myself." I was devastated in the beginning, because not only was it *The Wild Wild West* and I felt I "owned" Antoinette, but it was also money — it was my living. But then I thought, "You know what, Pheeb? If you can't be an actress without being tied to Michael's coattails, *you're not an actress*. Go back to being an art director." So I decided I was *not* gonna go back to New York, I was not gonna go back to *Wild West*—I was gonna go ahead and be an actress on my own. And that's what I did. That's how we split up. After he divorced his wife, I saw him again and we talked and he apologized to me. I understood it — I did, I really understood it.

But he didn't speak to you again until after the divorce.

Mm-hmm. That's when he called me and asked if we could get together for dinner, and I said, "Of course we can." He told me what had happened, and … I *knew* what had happened. He told me he was so sorry, that he never wanted to do it, and that his managers begged him not to do it. (His managers had known me since we were "kids" — we'd come through *every*thing together.) But Michael *did* it because I guess *she* said, "You either do it or I'm outta here" — who *knows* what she did? I mean, this is a woman who I heard took every cent from him. I wasn't in court when this happened, but our manager John *was* and he told me what happened: Michael stood there in front of the judge and the judge said, "Michael, you don't have to pay this woman *any*thing. She's obviously an opportunist, she married you for your money. You don't have to give her alimony. You don't owe her anything. You've only been married a few years." And Michael stood there and said, "I'm as good as any man. I *want* to pay her alimony." And so he did … he *did*! You see, *those* were some of the hang-ups that he had in terms of his height. "I'm as good as any man and I can have this beautiful woman in my life" — even though she might have been out for everything he had. "I can pay her alimony just like any normal guy," he felt — and supposedly gave everything away to her. I don't know what ever happened to her, I don't even know if she obtained Michael's estate. I don't think she got that. I heard she *tried*, when he died, to get his estate, to take it away from his parents. But I have no idea what finally happened.

After your reunion, how often did you see him?

I saw him all the time — I was back in New York, and we used to go to dinner. I think things were not going that well for him. First of all, she wiped him out. And she wiped him out emotionally as well as financially. And I had never stopped caring about him, it wasn't like he wasn't my friend. I understood what he did and why he did it. Really. Michael would do something like that to keep someone in his life who he loved, knowing that she didn't love *him*. To keep her, he would do *any*thing. So I agreed to meet with him and I saw him very frequently after that. But the alcohol had taken a tremendous toll on him and I could see it, because by that time I was a lot more savvy about the alcohol and what had been going on. His skin was very yellow, so I could tell that his liver was affected. He was tiny — a *tiny* person! — and the amount of liquor that he drank! He used to put away an inordinate amount of Jack Daniel's, and that wasn't good for his liver.

So you could tell he was sick.

Yes, I could see it. He just wasn't the same Michael, he didn't have the energy and his skin was very yellow. I even said to him, "Michael, have you been to the doctor? You look very jaundiced." But it was hard to talk to him about that stuff, because Michael *knew* he was going to die. It's easy for people to say, "Well, he died of the alcoholism," but he *didn't* die of the alcoholism. The alcoholism didn't *help* him, but that's not what killed him. What killed him was the disease that he was born with, which was terribly painful for his entire life. Achondroplasia is a bone disease, and bone diseases are very painful. He knew that his organs had no place to go and that it was only a matter of time. And *if* he knew, let's say at night when things were quiet, that his heart wasn't beating right or his lungs weren't working right … he would never talk about it. *Never*. Not even with me.

A few weeks later, he left town. We were supposed to get together, but he said, "I'm going away to do [the movie] *The Abdication* [1974] with Liv Ullmann in England." And he died in his hotel room over there.

How did you hear about it?

The way I heard about it was bizarre. I was at a party and someone was talking about Michael's death. I walked over and I said, "Excuse me … what are you talking about?" "Michael Dunn died." I couldn't speak. I ran home and I called my manager, I said, "Where? What? How? What do we do?" He said Michael died in England, *in* his sleep. I guess it was his liver, but it was also his organs — he wasn't going to live much longer, Michael *knew* that. He was very young. And here's something else that happened: When they went to get his body from the hotel, it had been taken. Someone had "kidnapped" him! It might have been a maid, or the people who found his body — they also stole stuff from the hotel room. It was terrible. His poor parents — it was bizarre! I have never been through a more bizarre episode in my life! The [English authorities] finally got ahold of his body, but we were never told exactly what had happened. They shipped the body to Florida, where his parents were, and John Softness and I went to the funeral. John and Michael went to college together, the University of Miami, and had been friends for years.

I see on your résumé that you wrote and produced a 1992 TV movie called Perfect Family.

That's a movie that I wrote with my partner Christian Stoianovich. As a woman gets older in this business, there is nothing for her. And I really did not want to ever be victimized. I love writing, and I thought, "I can recreate this thing that I love to do: I can *write* the women that I want to play, but they won't *let* me play 'cause I'm past 40!" And I started writing with my partner, and it became very joyful. Christian is a director and I of course came to it from acting, so we pooled our talents in terms of writing and now I mostly write and I love it. I *love* it. It's hard, it's really hard. It takes a tremendous, tremendous amount of discipline, 'cause it's not about writing, it's about rewriting and rewriting and *re*writing. Especially if you sell something. Then *every*body wants it the way *they* see it. You can see when they're telling you how to rewrite it that it's not gonna work, but you have to do it.

Show business is a funny thing: It's a very, very unforgiving mistress. You act because you love it. You will give show business everything, *everything* that it demands of you. But later, when it's show business' turn to give you back ... it doesn't. It's very unfair that way — you can ask any actress what happens after a certain age. It's just *over* [*laughs*] — it doesn't matter how good you are, how much you've given it. But I saw it coming and I started writing waaay before the work dwindled. So I really love it and I'm not bitter in any way, because I'm lucky to still be doing "my bliss," the thing that I love the most. I don't know many people who love to get up and go to work and who are still being creative and love it so much. No one has a gun to my head saying, "You have to do this." This is my choice. I'm able to earn a living and I'm able to be very creative, which to me is everything in the world.

PHOEBE DORIN FILMOGRAPHY

Coming Apart (Kaleidoscope Films, 1969)
Rivals (Avco Embassy, 1972)
Disco Fever (Group 1, 1978)
Making Love (20th Century–Fox, 1982)
Kandyland (1987)

RUSS DOUGHTEN

We experimented a lot [with the Blob] before we came up with the things that we knew we would use in the film. It was very important to the film that that be worked out. Which it was, thanks to the combined genius of the guys who were working on it. ...I think if we had been submitted to the Oscar awards for special effects, we probably could have won *it that year.*

Movie monsters come in every size and shape — and sometimes, beginning in the 1950s, in *no* shape. Perhaps the most unusual "movie star" of that era: a few gallons of liquid silicone, mixed with a splash of red food coloring, which through the miracle of special effects was made to look large and formidable enough to engulf whole buildings. The low-budget, high-ingenuity movie was 1958's *The Blob*, Steve McQueen's first movie lead and the feature debut of producer Russ Doughten.

Born and raised in Iowa, Doughten was interested in dramatics as a boy and yet never looked upon it as a profession. But while attending Drake University on an athletic scholarship, his interest in dramatics grew and, following a World War II Navy stint, he returned to Drake to study acting and directing. Doughten later attended the Yale Graduate School of Drama, where he wrote, directed and acted.

After Yale, Doughten sent his résumé to companies that made religious movies and was invited to join Good News Productions, a filmmaking outfit operating out of the small village they owned in bucolic Chester Springs, Pennsylvania. Following his *Blob* experiences, Doughten eventually returned to Iowa and founded Heartland Productions and Mark IV Pictures, under whose banners he has produced dozens of feature-length Christian movies (including an "end of days" series based on Biblical prophecies). Later, in the mid–90s, Doughten formed Russ Doughten Films, Inc. (www.rdfilms.com), to carry on the tradition of film evangelism around the world.

Were you an actor in the Good News films at first?

No, I was hired as a producer. But I had never produced a film [*laughs*] — I had studied production on stage. I started in the editing room as an assistant for the first couple of short films, and then I was given the responsibility of editing some of the films we were doing. I was also sort of like "floor manager" of the short films that were being made at the time. After a few months I graduated to producer, and started producing some other films and some television series that we had.

Did you live in the village that the Good News people owned?

Yes. It was quite an interesting and appealing place [Chester Springs, Pennsylvania]. It had quite a history. It had been the campus of the Pennsylvania Academy of the Fine Arts at one point, and some of the buildings were there from the Revolutionary War. One of the buildings, in fact, was called Washington Building because it was thought that Washington had slept there. There was also one called Lincoln and one called Jenny Lind and three or four others. Three of the buildings had been made into studios and these were scattered around on the campus. In one building there was an auditorium and, on the second floor, a small recording studio where we shot television films and did sound recording and so on. Two of the other buildings were also made into studios—we called 'em A, B and C. We did quite a few different projects while I was working with them there. We had something built in at least one studio just about all the time, and sometimes we used more than one studio for a project.

Did Good News own the entire town of Chester Springs?

I never was 100 percent sure what the boundaries of Chester Springs were. They didn't own the post office—right in the middle of the campus was the post office, and also a home where the caretaker of the campus lived. I don't believe his home was part of the campus either. So there were two buildings right in the middle not owned by Good News; then on the outskirts of the campus, there were a few other homes not owned by Good News. Scattered along the valley there, there may have been ten other homes of some kind, but whether they were actually inside what was called Chester Springs, I'm not sure.

Jack H. Harris, who came up with the money to make The Blob, *told me that you were all "starving" when he came along … but you're making it sound like you were all very busy and productive. Were these hard times?*

In a way they were. We weren't starving, but we didn't have much. It was a missionary organization, so to speak, and we were depending on the Lord for our provision. Most of the films we made were for varied clients—missionaries, church denominations, the Salvation Army and so on. (Some of the clients we had are leaders in the Christian world today.) We had a lot of work to do, but it wasn't high-paying work. It was Christian work and everybody was working on a minimum budget … and so we had a minimum income.

We had some very skilled people working there. Tom Spalding was a cinematographer who went on to win many awards in Christian filmmaking—he worked for me and my own company much later, on several award-winning films that we made in Iowa. Vince Spangler was a lighting expert and he was very knowledgeable about all the laboratory work that was done in films. (In some cases, we processed our own film and all the stills.) We had a graphic designer who was excellent … a scene designer and builder … a couple of editors … sound recordists … and several people who were secretaries and production assistants and so on. We had a very nice team there, actually. And a very capable one.

The Doughtens at home (Russ and Gertrude Doughten with their twin sons).

What was it like living there?

At first, we lived very communal-style. The main housing building was the Jenny Lind Building, but three or four of the other buildings also had apartments in them — we fashioned them out of buildings that weren't made for that purpose. One building had been an inn, they think, at the time of the Revolutionary War. Anyway, we had several families there — each technician or creator on the campus had his own family except for two or three single people. There were quite a few children there, ranging from infant up to maybe eight or ten years of age. All three of my sons were born during the period we were there. We lived there together with all the other families.

What was the reaction when everybody found out they were going to be making a Hollywood-style science fiction movie?

Well, there was some skepticism about it, because we knew it wasn't exactly the work that we had been "called" to do [religious work]. Approximately a year before *The Blob*, we decided that we weren't making enough money with the Christian work and that we'd better find some way of doing some commercial work of some kind. So we formed a company, Valley Forge Films, a secular counterpart of Good News Productions, which was the Christian work. "Shorty" Yeaworth was the president of both of those companies, sort of the "founding father" of the group. Jack Harris was the financier behind *The Blob*— he was an independent film distributor in Philadelphia.

Who came up with the idea for The Blob?

Irv Millgate, a man who worked for the Boy Scouts of America, whose headquarters were located at New Brunswick,

New Jersey, only a few miles away from our location there. Before we met Irv, the Boy Scouts had one of their Jamborees nearby, and some of their amateur photographers filmed the Jamboree. They then brought to us a bucket load of film that they had exposed and said, "We had a bunch of photographers scattered around and they took this film and we thought it was very interesting. Can you make a film out of it?" So I was assigned the job of editing this material into something. It was a very interesting challenge and I worked at it for three or four months and came up with a pretty nice film, which became an important promotional film for the Boy Scouts of America. It was after that film was made that Irv Millgate brought to us a little two-page scenario which was called *The Molten Monster*. Millgate was very excited about it, he thought this could be a great science fiction film. Well, we looked at it and thought, "If we make it into a wholesome story — even though it's a science fiction thing — why, maybe we *could* do it."

I was not in on the direct negotiation with Jack Harris that set up the contractual arrangement which started the film, but I was assigned the job of producer. I developed the budget along with "Shorty," and "Shorty" and Jean his wife began the story. [Writer] Ted Simonson and I also worked on it, and we developed what we thought was a pretty interesting story. At that point, another writer was brought in, Kate Phillips. She was a nice lady and quite talented, and she helped appreciably with the film. But it was a kind of a group effort. "Shorty" and Jean developed some of the elements of the love story particularly, and all of us together sat around and debated on the characters that'd be in it.

Kate Phillips says she worked on the screenplay of The Blob *without ever having seen a science fiction movie.*

Well, *we* went to see a whole bunch of 'em. Jack Harris distributed a lot of the low-budget science fiction films, and he set up a bunch of screenings for us so that we could study the genre. We went to quite a few such films. I remember *The Beast With a Million Eyes* [1955] and *The Thing* [1951] and a few others. We got a lot of ideas about how Roger Corman was making his *very* low-budget films. But we wanted to make ours a little more of a dramatic story than some of those were. They had some melodramatic moments, but didn't develop a whole lot of character. So we conceived the idea of making *The Blob* with teenage stars — a teenage story, primarily. Teenagers against the town, so to speak. We bounced that around a lot and came up with several of the characters, including the Steve McQueen character and Aneta Corsaut's character. And the good cop and the "bully cop" and so on — all these things were "manufactured" as we went along. Quite a few of us, the core people there, were involved in mulling all that over and coming up with the characterizations. Kate Phillips helped greatly at that point and came up with a pretty good script. I remember I took it to my old playwriting prof at Yale to ask him to critique it before we filmed it. He was a little bit taken aback that I would have him read a film script, but he did. He read it. And he said, "Well, it'll probably be a popular story, but ... I expected *more* from you." [*Laughs*]

Who cast the movie, and how was that done?

"Shorty" and I cast it. We went to New York City and worked with an agent by the name of Arthur King. We told him that we needed a group of teenagers and asked him to help us find them. Of course, he had some "sort-of" clients that he paraded before us [*laughs*], and we did use a few of the people he brought in. We already knew *some* young people. Tony

Like the Blob itself, Doughten and others at Valley Forge Films caught some current fright flicks before embarking on their movie.

Franke, for instance, was a young man who had acted in a Good News film called *Desperate Measure,* a dramatic film that was used to recruit college students into the Salvation Army. He was a very nice young fellow and we told him we were gonna use him in *The Blob.* He thought we were going to put him in the lead role [*laughs*]! We weren't able to do *that,* but he *was* in the film, playing one of the teenagers [Al], and he did a nice job with it.

How did you get Steve McQueen involved?

We were in New York, "Shorty" and I, fretting over who was going to play the lead. We had some good-looking and nice teenagers, but they didn't really have the solid experience that we felt we had to have on the screen. "Shorty" and I were walking around, just about a block and a half or two from Central Park heading downtown, when we saw this young fellow on the street walking his dog. He saw us and he recognized us and said, "Hi! What are you guys doin' here?" Turned out to be a fellow who had come out to our studio one time, driving a little MG. I remembered it very well: I was standing on the porch of Lincoln, our administrative building, and I heard this straaaange sound going through the woods, way off, maybe three miles away [*Doughten makes the sound of a speeding car*]. It turned out to be this little MG coming up to our studio. We were then filming a short film and we had hired a young actress from New York, and *this* fellow was her boyfriend coming out to see her. His name was Steve McQueen. So we knew Steve from that experience, and when we saw him walking down the street in New York with his dog, he said, "It's great to see you. What are you guys doin'?" We said, "We're here casting a movie." He said [*excitedly*], "Casting a *movie*? Well, you know, *I'm* an actor! What *is* it? Have you got a part in it for *me*?" We said, "Well, we don't think so, Steve. The leads in this are teenagers, and you're probably a little too old for it." He said, "I tell you what: I live just around the corner. Why don't you come up to my apartment and I'll give you some coffee and you can meet my wife. Let's talk about this a little bit."

Was the wife the girl he had visited in Valley Forge?

No, the wife's name was Neile Adams — she was a dancer. Anyway, we went up to his apartment and he said, "Let me see it, let me read it." We let him see the script and he started reading it and he said, "Hey, I can *play* this part!" [*Laughs*] We said, "Well, we're sure you could probably play it, but … you'd be too old on the screen." "No, no, no," he said, "I can play pretty young. Look at this…" and he began reading parts of it and so on! He got very enthusiastic about it, and pretty soon "Shorty" and I were lookin' at each other and wondering, "Could it work?" He'd been on Broadway in a play called *A Hatful of Rain*, so he was an up-and-coming young guy. He'd only made one film — he played a minor role in *Somebody Up There Likes Me* [1956] with Paul Newman. We thought, "Well, gee, there probably is no actor in New York that *could* play this who would have any more background than this kid. Can we do it? Do we dare cast a guy this old? And can we 'cast around him' in such a way that it's going to be believable to the audience?" We debated that for a while, and finally we decided that it was right for us to cast him.

You and Yeaworth debated right there in front of McQueen, or after you left?

We debated it there, but I cannot remember exactly where we were when we made the decision. If the decision wasn't made right there in the apartment, then it wasn't long after. It was while we were in New York, on that visit, that we made the decision.

Did McQueen's wife hint around for a part?

No, she was never seriously considered. I don't know if it was even discussed that she be in it.

You also got Aneta Corsaut out of New York, correct?

Aneta Corsaut was an actress we had met in New York, and we invited her to come out to our studio to do a test. I liked her very much and "Shorty" did too, so we decided to use her. But later we came to find out she had been a former girlfriend of Steve McQueen, and was a little cool to him at that point [*laughs*]!

How did you find out? Did she tell you?

No, Steve did! They worked pretty well together — I guess it was "cooled off" enough so that it wasn't interfering with any work. But I thought it was interesting.

Did McQueen screen test?

No. We may have taken a little bit of footage with him, but we had already decided to use him. And we built all the rest of it around him [casting-wise] — we hired kids who were not teenagers. That probably is one of the weaknesses of the film, but I think by and large the audience "bought" it. The other kids were maybe 20, 21. *He* was 27 or 28 and the oldest of the bunch. Steve brought his dog along when he made the movie — I don't remember what breed it was, but it was a great big bruiser. And he also brought his *guns* along, he liked to shoot.

Real-life boyfriend-girlfriend Steve McQueen and Aneta Corsaut played *The Blob*'s romantic leads—*after* their breakup.

Did this concern you, with kids around?

There may have been some concern. He didn't go all around the property, we had him in a little building—we called it the Art Building, but it was really kind of a house, off near the edge of the property. He lived there while we were filming, and my wife was his cleaning lady [*laughs*]! There was this big hill, almost a mountain, behind his house, and that's where he did the shooting. We also had the [teenage actors] stay there in Chester Springs. We had a dormitory-like place above our administrative building, so we fixed *that* up for some of those actors. It all worked out pretty well to have them there.

Kate Phillips says that some of the policemen in The Blob *were real policemen from that area.*

Yes, some of them in the crowd scenes and so on. But the three main policemen were not actually policemen, they were actors from the Hedgerow Theater in Philadelphia. We had a lot of local people in it too, in the crowd scenes and so on. And Jack Harris is in it—he ran screaming out of the theater [*laughs*]!

The interiors of all the different houses and buildings in the movie—were those sound stages?

Those interiors were sound stages, yes. The exteriors were location. The city parts were filmed primarily in Phoenixville and Downingtown, which were about 20 miles west of Philadelphia. The doctor's house, for instance, was in Phoenixville. The drag race scene where they backed their cars through the stoplight was also shot in Phoenixville — in fact, most of it was shot right outside the doctor's house. The diner was in Downingtown. The interior of the diner was *not* a set, that scene *was* shot right inside the diner, but the scene in the basement was shot on a set. We had excellent cooperation from all the local people, the local authorities, the firemen and the policemen and so on. Everybody was really helping us.

What was "in it" for them?

Well, there wasn't a *lot* in it. We probably paid some fees, but our budget for extras and for ancillary activities was [*laughs*] — was very *low*! Most of the people were just enthusiastic *for* us. We knew a lot of the people because we attended the churches in those towns, and we had been filming out in that area for quite a while — I think "Shorty" and his group moved out there around 1950 or '51, and this was '57. We had shot dozens of films and we were known by the authorities and by many of the people. They were just enthusiastic and helpful.

Aneta Corsaut said that before work every day, there was a prayer meeting.

Yes, there was. She was a nice girl, but I don't think she was really "into" that 100 percent.

She also said, talking about you guys, "They treated us like they didn't like us. We were 'actors,' which made us the devil's folk."

[*Laughs*] That ... that's interesting. I don't think that was true.

Any idea why she said it?

Well, maybe she *felt* like that — I don't know. Although I liked her, and I was very instrumental in casting her, I didn't have a lot of time to get friendly with her. And she didn't really seem, necessarily, to want to "mix" with everybody. "The devil's folk"? Certainly there was nothing like *that* in anybody's mind. We *were* praying every day before working on a science fiction picture, and she probably didn't expect that and it may have been a little bit off-putting to her. But, gee, I don't know ... I thought we had a very friendly group that really tried to "reach out" to all those people. And, as I said before, her attitude toward Steve McQueen was pretty negative when we started. I don't know that they ever really had any kind of real reconciliation, other than just doing the job on the screen — which I felt she did very well.

You had to rent 35mm cameras because everything you'd done up to that point had been 16mm.

That's right. Tom Spalding, the cinematographer, was very good at those things, and he understood it quite well. Vince Spangler was his back-up man.

How many of the Chester Springs studios were Blob *interiors shot in?*

There were three studios, and the *Blob* interiors were filmed partially in each of those. Olin Howlin's shack and the crater were shot on an indoor set there too. We also used other areas around the campus, like for the [subjective] shot of Howlin being run into by the car. That was shot on a road that went through Chester Springs, about a quarter of a mile from our administration building. I remember that because I was hand-holding an Eymo camera out on the hood of the automobile. So I remember that sequence pretty well!

Steve McQueen — once he got down there and you got into the movie, how was he to work with?

Pretty good. He and "Shorty" got along quite well on the whole, yet from time to time they disagreed on things, like what was supposed to be in the scene. But I would say it was a pretty normal kind of relationship — two guys really trying to do the best they could on something that was "stretching" them a little bit. Steve was "a regular guy," a man's man-type of guy — he liked his guns and his dog and so on. When he wasn't on the set, he was walking around the campus or the edge of the hills doing "shooting practice" and that kind of stuff. I talked with him quite a bit because I was around him quite a bit during the shooting, but I couldn't say we got to be buddy-buddy.

The Blob effects — which of them really stand out in your mind?

The main Blob character that you see physically on the screen — the way we arrived at that was very unusual. We searched and searched for a way to bring the Blob to the screen. We were out in the area very near the national headquarters of Du Pont Company [the chemicals/plastics/synthetic fibers company], it was just across the line in Wilmington, Delaware, and somebody suggested that we look at silicone. It probably was Gottfried Buss, our sound engineer — he was an "engineering-type guy" who was creative in that area. Gottfried and [special effects man] Bart Sloane and Karl Karlson, the scenic designer, were very clever with those kinds of things, and between them they came up with the idea that we ought to go to Du Pont and look at their new discovery of silicone in liquid form. So somebody brought in from Du Pont these cans of silicone, in all viscosities. Some were just like water and some were like heavy gum — they could hardly be called a liquid at all, they were almost solid. But they were still malleable. We took all these things and started to mix them and we discovered that, yeah, it would work. We discovered that we could make something that would move like the Blob, depending upon how we used it, by mixing up a special viscosity for that particular shot. And so that's the way we got to the basic element that was used in the special effects of the monster. Then we added red coloring to it.

And the scenes of the Blob on miniature sets?

Bart was basically responsible for that. Bart and Tom and (I think) Vince worked together to develop the technique for filming [those scenes]. I thought it was really a unique thing — maybe it *wasn't* all that great, but to *me* it was, 'cause I didn't understand exactly how they figured out how to do it: They took still photographs of the sets where the Blob was supposed to have action. On the front of the still camera they used a bent bellows, like a snout that they could bend and therefore affect the refractory of the light in some way, so that what got on the film was not just a flat, straight-on shot of the set, but it was a shot that was pre-designed to have an angular look. We also developed a universal joint. A platform sat on this universal joint, I think it was an eight-by-four plywood piece mounted on this universal joint, and the camera was on one end and the photograph of the set was on the other end. These bent-bellows photographs reproduced the look of the actual set. When we tilted the plywood platform on which the photographed set and the camera were mounted, the viscous silicone would move — it would move by gravity in any direction that we tilted the platform. If we turned the platform upside down, it would look like the Blob was jumping up. But it was falling *down*, actually! We experimented until we got the right viscosity for the Blob to move, the right lighting for it, the right camera setting — sometimes the camera was slow motion, I think. We experimented a lot before we came up with

Frightened nurse Lee Payton finds that, true to the movie's publicity, nothing — not even acid — can stop *The Blob*.

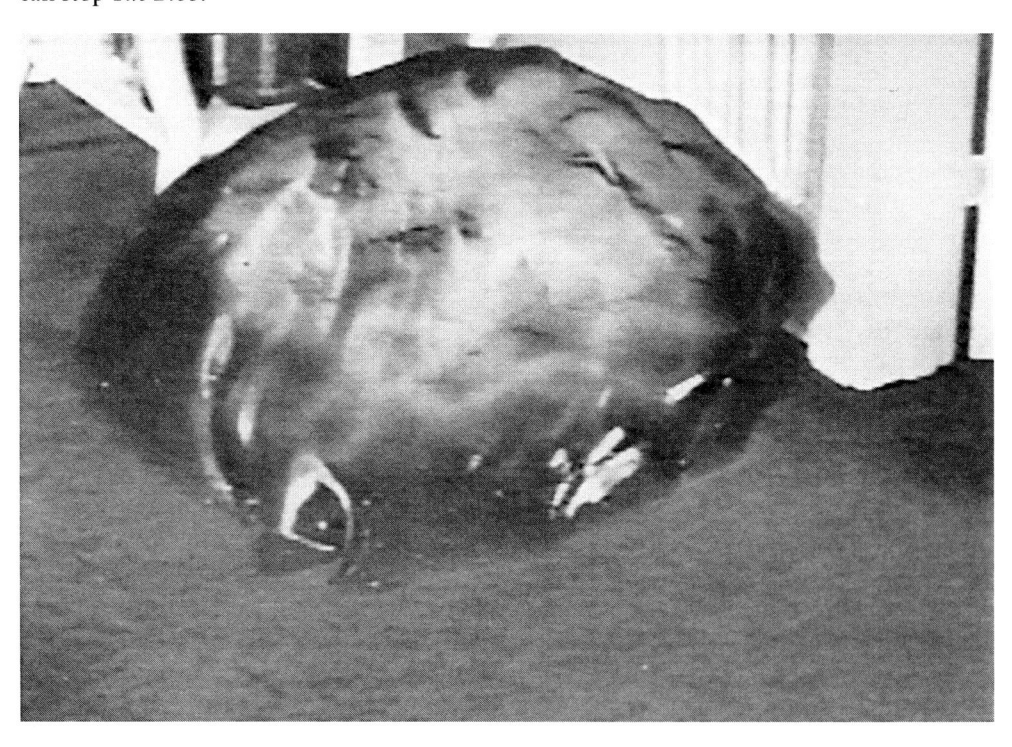

the things that we knew we would use in the film. It was very important to the film that *that* be worked out. Which it was, thanks to the combined genius of the guys who were working on it. Jack Harris got his money's worth out of that [*laughs*]! I think if we had been submitted to the Oscar awards for special effects, we probably could have *won* it that year.

There were also some other techniques that we used that these guys worked out. When Aneta and Steve were in the freezer, the Blob starts to go underneath the freezer door. In order to get the Blob to go under the door, the viscosity was a little bit thinner than it was when the Blob was on the universal joint. It seemed to work pretty well. We let it seep under the door, and to show it *recede*, to retreat back under the door, we just ran the film backwards.

In the doctor's office, we had to have the Blob a pretty good size and moving around. We couldn't use the universal joint thing in that situation, we had to have a different kind of "move-ability." So what we did was get was get [a deflated] weather balloon — if it *had* been inflated, it probably would have been five or six feet around. We took a portion of it with just a little bit of air in it — mostly it was deflated, but there *was* a little bit of air so that it wouldn't be totally flat. We put some of this colored silicone on top of this balloon and spread it out to the size that the Blob needed to be. Then, underneath the weather balloon, we manipulated it with hands. And *I* was the guy who got to do that [*laughs*]. I moved the Blob around in the doctor's office by moving my hands underneath this weather balloon. That was kind of fun, and it worked pretty well, I think.

Kate Phillips, who co-wrote the movie, told me that she was the first person to suggest that miniature sets be used in The Blob.

I doubt if she was the *first*. I can't tell you for sure who the first person was, because there was a *lot* of talking back and forth, and working through different possibilities among our own staff. But it was not an idea from "outside" [from Phillips], I'm almost positive of that.

You've told me where Steve McQueen stayed, where "The Teenagers" stayed ... where did the Blob stay?

[*Laughs*] In jars! We made the movie over a period of several weeks, and we used *some* Blob substance during the actual filming. But during the summer [after the end of principal photography], we did a lot of special effects work over a period of a few months. And we just kept the Blob in jars. The amount of Blob that we'd use in any one shot was relatively small, because the photographed backgrounds [on the plywood platform] were only about the size of a normal picture.

The size of an 8 × 10?

Maybe a little bigger than that, but not *far* off of that size. So you'd put an 8 × 10 height for the height of a room, or a wall, and the Blob within the shot would be relative to that size. Of course, the size of the Blob depended on how far along it had gotten on absorbing people [*laughs*]! When the Blob first came off of the hand of the Old Man and then ate the nurse, it was fairly small in relationship to the size of a room ... but then, as you added more and more people to it, it grew fairly fast! Considering that the "rooms" [on the plywood platform] were only eight inches high or so, it didn't take very much of the silicone. Just a handful.

A quart?

Oh, no, less than that. Less than a *pint*. We kept it in glass jars because then we could see the colors of it. We may have had eight or ten jars of it, different viscosities and different colors, from clear to deep red. Toward the end of the movie, the Blob got more and more red, and also we had to use larger amounts.

The scene that really scared me as a kid was the scene of the garage mechanic under the car, who doesn't know the Blob is coming. I thought that worked very well.

Yeah, that *did* work well, and I'm proud of that one 'cause I directed that scene. It was at the end of a long day and "Shorty" was very harassed and he hadn't fully worked out the staging of the thing. Somehow it bugged him a little bit, he didn't know exactly what he wanted to do with it. I said "Can't you do…" this and this and this? and he said, "Well, why don't *you* direct it?" So I ended up directing.

Kate Phillips marvels at the number of people who've told her that the scariest shot in the movie is the shot where you see the doctor through the Venetian blinds, covered by the Blob — but there's no such shot in the movie. Their imaginations supplied it.

That *is* interesting. It was one of the principles that we had in mind in making *The Blob*: To *not* show the Blob if we didn't absolutely have to. We felt that every scene where we showed it was obligatory from the audience point of view. We probably could have shown it maybe two or three times less, but it wasn't on the screen very much, not in actual screen time. When we had the Blob there on-screen, we wanted it to have an effect. So we did things like that Venetian blinds scene. We wanted the effect to really penetrate the audience, but not to show too much.

Aneta Corsaut said The Blob *was made by a "double crew" — after the cast had worked all day with one crew, another crew would come in and work would continue.*

Yeah, we were working day and night, but it wasn't a double crew — it was *the* crew [*laughs*]! I worked a couple weeks of 120 hours. Vince Spangler, a good friend, was one of our group. Very nice fella, very hard-working, very precise. He was 37 or 38 years old and I was just a youngster then. I was so gung ho to get this thing done on schedule and on budget — it was very important to *all* of us, for our own basic survival, that that be done. So I was really pushin' everybody. We had to work long hours and I was responsible for it because I was responsible for the schedules. One night we were inside on a set filming the crater where Olin Howlin found the Blob. We were working about two o'clock in the morning and we had just filmed part of it, and I said to one of the assistants, "Run over to the dining hall and see if you can find something to make some sandwiches out of, so that we can take a little eating break before we go on with the next sequence." Vince overheard me and he said, "Russ Doughten, *you* can work day and night if you want to, but *this* old man is tired. I am goin' home to bed, right now…!" — and he did [*laughs*]! So we didn't shoot the scene.

You had a mutiny!

Well, he was right. I had pushed them beyond the brink.

One of The Blob's *working titles was reportedly* The Glob. *Do you recall that at all?*

We were searching for a name — we had the film virtually finished and we didn't have a name for it. We were trying every title under the sun. I came up with the name *Absorbine Senior* [*laughs*], I thought that made a *great* name, but they decided, no, we can't do that. Somebody had said,

"Well, it's just this big glob. Let's call the movie *The Glob*"—I don't remember who said that. Everybody said, yeah, that describes it very well, *The Glob*. We started calling the movie *The Glob* among ourselves for a day or two, but then somebody said, "Well, you know, there's a book [by Walt Kelly] named *The Glob*. We can't use that title." We all thought, "Oh, good grief!" because that was the best possible name we could come up with and there was no way we could beat that. We even talked about whether we could get by with calling it *The Glob* anyway, and we probably *could* have, but we decided that wasn't the best idea. All of a sudden, Jack Harris said, "Why not call it *The Blob*?" Within minutes, I think, we decided that would be the name.

Ralph Carmichael, who did the music—was he part of the Good News–Valley Forge staff?

No, no. He was a friend of "Shorty," who knew him for some time before that, and Ralph was "Shorty's" automatic choice to do the music. Ralph is still living, and he has "the big band sound" now. He played last February [2000] at the National Religious Broadcasters convention. He's very well-known and has a long, long list of credits and has a tremendous reputation in Christian circles. He's recognized today as one of the outstanding composer-directors—he's had that reputation since *The Blob*, and before *The Blob*. He's not a young man, he's got long hair (sorta like me), and he likes to puff it out at the sideburns so the hair kinda goes out around his ears. He has a picturesque look!

What did you think of his Blob *music?*

I thought it was very good. He did *not* compose the title song, that was Burt Bacharach, but the rest of the music he did.

How much did the movie end up costing?

That was *my* dramatic story. Harris said, "It can only be $100,000," so that was our budget. That's what we were told before we even had the story. We had to have all the special effects and everything in it [for that amount], so we developed a story we thought we could *do* at that price. Jack raised it from one of his buddies and so on, and he mortgaged his house in Philadelphia—he went pretty heavy into it.

Yeaworth told me that Harris put up one-third of the money, a New York businessman put up a third and he, Yeaworth, put up a third.

The third that "Shorty" put up was *us*. "Shorty" didn't put up cash, he put up the production company and all the people who worked on it.

Were you able to make The Blob *for $100,000?*

We came *pretty* close, but it ended up being $110,000. That last $10,000 was basically my *blood*. Valley Forge Films was supposed to own a portion of the picture, but when Jack had to put up *another* $10,000, he said, "Well, that's coming out of *your* portion of the picture." Of course, I personally didn't own any part of the picture—in fact, I worked for $35 a week on the thing from beginning to end. I was probably paid as much or more than anybody else who worked on it [*laughs*]! We put our blood into it, the whole staff. We had a very fine group of creative people and we worked on it day and night and put our best into it. And I think we made it into something a little bit more than what Roger Corman was doing. But it cost $10,000 more than what we were told, and that was taken out of the one-third that was owed to Valley Forge Films.

The folks who made *The Blob* (including "Shorty" Yeaworth and Russ Doughten, side-by-side with glasses).

Later on, after *The Blob* was over, I left the company, partly out of being disgruntled over the film. I went to Hollywood around April 1958 — *The Blob* wasn't in release at the time that I went out there, it was in the final editing and mix stage. While I was in Hollywood, I started making the rounds [of movie companies] ... but I ended up working at a gas station on Sunset Boulevard! And one day, this guy tooled in with his roadster and it turned out to be Steve McQueen. So I got to wash his windshield and put gas in his car [*laughs*]! He was very cordial to me and asked me how I happened to be out there and so on. He was then up for the TV series *Wanted: Dead or Alive*, so things were going fairly good for him. But *I* had a considerable valley to go through at that time, and working at a gas station was part of it.

One thing that I found interesting: On the day that Steve McQueen left Good News Productions, I had been trying to "witness" to him. We were a Christian group and I had talked to him when I had a chance about the Lord and tried to help him see that the Lord was *his* savior too. He was ... fairly reluctant to talk about those things, although he did a little bit. I gave him my Bible the day that he left. It was a pretty dog-eared thing, but I thought it might be helpful to him and he might appreciate it. He *seemed* to. And later on, when he came into the gas station, he thanked me again for it. The interesting thing is, before Steve died, the story is that he *did* receive Christ, he *did* become a Christian. I never talked to Billy Graham personally about it, but I was told by one of Graham's associates that Graham had been instrumental in leading Steve to the Lord a few months before his death. To me, that was very interesting and significant.

Why were you disgruntled over The Blob?

I was disgruntled because I had

worked on the film from Day One, helping develop the script, casting, working with the scene design, working on all the special effects with Vince and the graphic man and the cinematographer for *months*. I also helped put together the design of the instruments that we used to move the Blob around. I was into it *above* my eyebrows and had managed the money (I thought) very well — I thought we gave Jack Harris a wonderful value for his $110,000. Yet when it came down to the final editing and the setting-up of the titles, I was informed that I would not be given the producer's credit for the film. I had signed all the checks, I had written all the letters, I had been the producer to *every*body all the way through it. And then, all of a sudden, I *wasn't* the producer. Maybe it was always in the plan [to cut Doughten out] and maybe "Shorty" knew about it, although he didn't say so and I doubt if he did. But Jack lowered the boom, he said, "*I* am the producer," and there was nothing I could do about it. I've read a couple of interviews that Jack has given, and 90 percent of the things he *said* that he did as far as producing was concerned was what *I* did [*laughs*]! That bugged me quite a bit. When I left, I refused to give a release to them because of the way Jack and "Shorty" put me on the outside. They *finally* said, "Well, we'll put your name on the credits," so they put me down as the associate producer on the Valley Forge film credit. Which was sort of equal to … a bucket of warm spit. That ticked me off pretty good since I had a family to take care of and I worked night and day on the film. As I told you, there were a couple of weeks when I put in over 120 hours on that film. It just [*sighs*] … it was not so good.

They were not going to put your name in the credits at all, *you're telling me?*

No, they were not. I said, "Well, then, you're not gonna release the film. And if you do, I'll sue you." A couple of my best friends from there, Tom Spalding and Ted Simonson the writer and a couple of the other guys, called me when I was out in California and just practically *cried*, telling me, "You don't know what you're doing to us. We won't get a cent from the Valley Forge percentage of *The Blob* until you sign this release."

You were already out in California and the release of The Blob *was still hung up.*

Right. I left just as the editing was completed. And I wouldn't give Jack Harris the satisfaction of telling him that he had a film [*laughs*]. But I'd been there at Valley Forge for four and a half years and I knew what things were like — I was the one in the company who had finally told 'em, "Look, we've got to work out our deal here so that people get *paid*." Before that, nobody even got a *salary*. When I first went there, I was a missionary, and so we had whatever God gave us *plus* food, a room to stay in and hospitalization insurance. That was our pay for the first two years that I was there. I lobbied all the powers-that-be, "Shorty" and others, saying, "This can't work in the long run. The company must take more responsibility for its people." So, through my efforts, we finally were charging enough fees for our work and we had a company allowance to pay our people. I got $35 a week.

So you eventually did — obviously — sign the release and let them release The Blob.

I finally signed the release and off it went. They took it to Paramount and it went on from there.

Did you see the 1972 sequel Son of Blob *that Jack Harris made?*

Yes. Just before he made that, Jack came to me when I was out in California and said, "Let's not talk about *The Blob* because there's blood on the negative [Doughten's blood, because of the budget/credit situations]. I'd like to have you consider helping me to make a sequel." I wasn't extra-eager but I thought I would like to work, so I said, "Okay, let's talk about it." And we did; I said, "If you do it, please let me have some input into the development of the story. You don't want to get stuck with a lot of things that would now be clichés, taken out of *The Blob*. Let me work on the script with you and we'll see what we can come up with." He said, basically, "Okay," but he hired another guy to work on the script, a guy who hadn't the slightest idea what it was all about. So finally we came to a parting of the ways: I said, "Don't take [the storyline] that way, Jack. It's going to be just kind of a hackneyed thing," but the other guy convinced Jack that he should do it. *Son of Blob* was just basically most of the things that we had done in *The Blob*, done over, most of them not as well. I didn't think Jack *had* anything when he got done with it.

And what about the 1988 remake?

It was better than *Son of Blob*, but I wasn't swept away by *it*, either. It may have been better technically in some ways than the original, but I didn't think it had the freshness and I didn't think it had the ability to "charm" the audience that the original *Blob* did. The first *Blob*, I think, has "the old college try" [feeling] to it, and that didn't come out in the second one, in my opinion.

You moved out to Hollywood after The Blob. *Did you make any movies out there?*

I made a couple of small independent movies. One of them was a 16mm called *Teenage Diary*, which was a Christian film that I wrote and directed. It went pretty well in the Christian marketplace, but it was a little bit too sexy for the Christian crowd. I had a scene of two teenagers out on a date on their grad night and they were on Balboa Beach in San Diego, in a little cove. I had them cuddling up to each other, and then I superimposed a big ocean wave over that scene. That was too much for the Christian audience — it became the "X-rated" Christian film of the year [*laughs*]! That was in 1961 or '62. The leading actress was Vonda Van Dyke, a young girl who later became Miss America [in 1965]. A Christian gal from Arizona.

Later you moved back to Iowa and started making movies there.

Right. I started a company called Heartland Productions — put it together in 1964 — and we made our first film, *The Hostage*, in 1965. It was released by Crown International Pictures in 1966. It was based on a book by Henry Farrell, the writer of the novel *What Ever Happened to Baby Jane?* and [the movie] *Hush ... Hush Sweet Charlotte* [1964]. We actually released it in Iowa ourselves and had a pretty nice release here, but when we turned it over to Crown, it didn't go too far. We also made *Fever Heat* [1968], which was written by Henry Felsen. Henry was a well-established writer of teenage fiction — he wrote *Hot Rod* and two or three other books that may be used to this day on junior high school required reading lists. Henry, who lived right in West Des Moines, Iowa, wrote this novel *Fever Heat* about dirt track racing — he used a pseudonym on it, Angus Vicker. I thought it had a lot going for it and that it was something we could do right here in Iowa. Henry said, "Let me write it. Please let me write it!" and he really threw himself into it and came up with a great script, I thought. I didn't know an awful lot about racing, so he took me around to the racetracks. I had a 16mm camera and I was taking pictures of the races and he introduced me to the drivers and the pit crews and the owners and the announcers and everything, so I kinda got into racing there for a while. In fact, I almost got killed on a race track with him! I was taking pictures with a 16mm camera at the track in Knoxville, Iowa, the sprint car capital of the world. I was taking some pictures of some of the crew while cars were doing hot laps [speeding around before the race]. Lo and behold, a car came around out of control — and I didn't see that it was out of control until it was within *inches* of me. Henry was standing right beside me, but *I* was a little closer to the car [*laughs*] — it went by with all of this roaring sound and fury and the smell of grease and gasoline and everything. It just about creased my hair. If I had been standing six inches over to the side, that would have been the end of my career, it was that close. That was sort of an interesting introduction to racing for me!

That was one of Nick Adams' last movies, wasn't it?

I went out to Hollywood to cast it, and a casting director set up an interview with Nick. We talked about the kind of a character we needed and he seemed to fit the bill in terms of name recognition — he had done [the TV series] *The Rebel* and he'd been nominated for an Academy Award [for *Twilight of Honor*, 1963]. I thought it'd be great if I could get somebody like him in it. Well, he *was* very interested, and we made a deal very quickly. Nick died before the picture was over.

Before the shooting was over?

No, before the editing was over. His death was called a suicide, but I really have my doubts if it was.

I've read that he was having wife trouble.

Yes, he was. His wife [actress Carol Nugent] had left him for a producer, and he was very despondent over that. But he had two children who he dearly loved and he had custody of the kids. I stayed with Nick out in California for several weeks while I was editing the film, and we got to be fairly close. It's very hard for me to think that he would take his life.

Was Fever Heat *your last "secular" film?*

Yes, it was. After that, I began working with Heartland and another company, Mark IV Pictures, which was founded in 1972 and since then has made exclusively feature-length films with a Gospel message.

In the '70s and '80s, you made a series of religious movies, "The Prophecy Films," about the end of the world.

The Prophecy Films are a series of films on the End Times which we made over a period of 11 years. They're basically about eschatology and the Tribulation period. We began with a film called *A Thief in the Night* [1972], which is still our best-known film. It's the story of an event called the Rapture of the Church — a trumpet sounds and Christ returns, and He is met in the air by the dead saints rising and by the live saints meeting him. They are then all taken up into Heaven. The rest of the world is left in a shocked state. The film starts with those events, and then the drama concerns those who have been left behind, those who did *not* meet Christ. The main character is a young lady [Patty Dunning] who has just been recently married, but who is not a believer. Her husband *was* a believer so *he's* gone, and she finds herself left there and the story follows her adventures in this new era. It's all based on the Scriptures — the elemental things happening around them are Scriptural events. It's a very interesting and exciting film and it's been shown around the world, many, many different venues and several languages. We estimate that probably 300 million people have seen it — probably as many as *The Blob* [*laughs*]!

And you've made three sequels so far, correct?

That's right. The first sequel is called *A Distant Thunder* [1978], which takes place also in the Tribulation. It starts with the Seal Judgments that are in Chapter 5 and 6 of the Bible. There are cataclysmic and geological events happening around the characters who are living through this and trying to struggle against *those* things and against the evil force of an organization called UNITE — the United Nations Imperium of Total Emergency, the world power which the Antichrist appears through. In the third film *Image of the Beast* [1980], the Antichrist becomes the ruler of the world and sets up his kingdom in Jerusalem and his image in the temple. All of this is prophesied in the Scripture, in Daniel, Ezekiel, Revelations, Thessalonians and several other prophetic books. *Image of the Beast* deals with the seven Trumpet Judgments that are in Revelations. The final film, *The Prodigal Planet* [1983], deals with the Bold Judgments, the last set of seven judgments that God's wrath brings to the world at this time of Tribulation. All these stories are very exciting dramatic stories, based on Biblical events that are yet to happen. They were made for the purpose of introducing people to Jesus Christ the Savior, who, if you confess your sins to Him and ask Him to enter your life and take charge, He brings in with Him the gift of eternal life, which we believe everybody *needs*. We tried to base the background of this series on authentic elements of prophetic scripture. The story, we say, is fiction, but the prophecy is not.

You're in all four movies, playing Reverend Matthew Turner.

Matthew Turner in *A Thief in the Night* is the pastor of a big church. We see him preaching, and he's preaching, in essence, *against* the Scripture — he teaches a totally spurious Gospel. As a result, when the Rapture happens, *he* doesn't go. Nor does the heroine of the story [Dunning], one of his parishioners. Both of them are left, and there's some interaction between them in the next two films. She is eventually beheaded in the third film, but he goes on through all four. His character changes substantially because of great guilt and remorse over the fact that many of his congregation remained with him, and he realizes that was because he didn't preach to them the true gospel. So he withdraws from society and becomes a very diligent Scriptural scholar, especially on Prophecies. He becomes an expert — he makes charts, and if people find him in his reclusive place, why, he tells 'em all about the Prophecies and explains these events that everybody is going through. He becomes a kind of sage of Prophetic elements.

These have proved to be very, very effective films — millions of the people who have seen them have become Christians afterwards. I'm *much* much more proud of these films, and the rest of 'em that we've made, than I am *The Blob*. Although *The Blob* is interesting, it has had much less impact in a *true* sense, in an *eternal* sense, than the other films. *The Blob* doesn't compare to them, or to the effect that they've had for the benefit of mankind.

Why does The Blob *hold up so well today?*

When it came out, I thought it was just basically a novelty, but I think there *is* a certain originality about the idea — it *was* an original monster. When I was making the film, I thought, "The Blob has got to be the result of the worst nightmare," and I thought about my own life when I was a kid. We lived in a small town in Iowa and my father used to get a hog every year and butcher it. When I was five or six years old,

The misguided Rev. Turner (Doughten) changes his theological tune after the Rapture of the Church. A scene from Doughten's *Image of the Beast* (1980).

I was present when they butchered this hog and took the liver out and put it in this big tub. It was in there, red and kind of shivering and so on, and I had a recurring nightmare about that — every night for months, I would dream of that thing, which in my nightmare had a life of its own. And when I was working on *The Blob*, I drew from that nightmare to characterize the Blob itself. It seemed to me to be an original idea that *did* relate to the kinds of nightmares that people have — the Blob was a tremendously powerful thing that's indefinable and a tremendous threat. Sort of like *Jaws* — you can't avoid [occasionally thinking about it] after you get the image of it. I think *that* has helped *The Blob* become very powerful in the minds of people, the fact that most people don't forget it after they see it. Our Prophecy films have a similar element — it isn't the liver [*laughs*], but the precipice between Heaven and Hell that these movies help people see in a very real way.

I also think there's a freshness to *The Blob* because it was a truly original story and the characters in it were approached as original people. Even though they were teenagers and maybe not fully developed entities, we tried very hard to give at least *some* depth to them, some purpose in their lives, that was "relate-able" to the young people who would see the film. And then the classic idea that's been done many times: Here the teenagers are, they've discovered the Blob, it is truly terrible and the audience now has experienced it — but the *other* people won't believe it because it's *too* unbelievable. The teenagers have to work hard, over and over again, to get everybody to wake up to it. That's a suspenseful element that I think also stands up. Then there's the finale, when they actually discover a way to combat this thing that has no history, nobody has any experience with it at all. The hero finally figures out from the experience that *he* had in the cold locker that, hey, there *is* a way to deal with this thing. And of course people cheer when that happens, because they want the story to come out good. So those are the three or four things about *The Blob* that help it have a "life."

THE BLOB (Paramount, 1958)

A Tonylyn Production; 85 minutes; Associate Producer: Russell Doughten; Produced by Jack H. Harris; Directed by Irvin S. Yeaworth, Jr.; Screenplay: Theodore Simonson & Kate Phillips; Original Idea: Irvine H. Millgate; Photography: Thomas Spalding (DeLuxe Color); Art Directors: William Jersey & Karl Karlson; Editor: Alfred Hillmann; Music Composed & Conducted by Ralph Carmichael; Music Supervisor: Jean Yeaworth; Title Song: Burt Bacharach & Hal David; Sound: Gottfried Buss & Robert Clement; Special Effects: Bart Sloane; Assistant Director: Bert Smith; Cameraman: Wayne Trace; Chief Set Electrician: Vincent Spangler; Assistant Editor: Floyd Ver Voorn; Makeup: Vin Kehoe; Assistant to the Producer: Frank Fuhr; Continuity: Travis Hillmann

Steven [Steve] McQueen (*Steve Andrews*), Aneta Corseaut [Corsaut] (*Jane Martin*), Earl Rowe (*Police Lt. Dave*), Olin Howlin (*Old Man*), Steven [Stephen] Chase (*Dr. T. Hallen*), John Benson (*Police Sgt. Jim Burt*), George Karas (*Officer Ritchie*), Lee Payton (*Kate, the Nurse*), Elbert Smith (*Henry Martin*), Robert Fields (*Tony Gressette*), James Bonnet (*Mooch Miller*), Anthony Franke (*Al*), Molly Ann Bourne, Diane Tabben, Pamela Curran, Josh Randolph (*Teenagers*), Vince Barbi (*George, the Diner Owner*), Audrey Metcalf (*Mrs. Martin*), Jasper Deeter (*Civil Defense Volunteer*), Tom Ogden (*Fire Chief*), Elinor Hammer (*Mrs. Porter*), Julie Cousins (*Sally, the Waitress*), Kieth Almoney (*Danny Martin*), Jack H. Harris (*Man Fleeing Theater*), Theodore Simonson (*Man in Movie Audience*), Hugh Graham, Ralph Roseman, Charlie Overdorff, David Metcalf, George Gerbereck, Eugene Sabel

ELAINE DuPONT

The topper is when your grandchildren go around singin' that little song, "There's a Monster in the Surf, yeah, yeah, yeah"—that is *a crack-up!*

Contending with movie monsters is a serious business—but not *so* serious that the occasional filmmaker can't poke a bit of fun at the genre. Actress Elaine DuPont co-starred in two low-budget flicks that combined monsters, teenagers and music: In 1959's *Ghost of Dragstrip Hollow*, she played a member of a hot rod club that throws a party in a haunted house — and meets its resident ghost. Just as way-out was director-star Jon Hall's *Beach Girls and the Monster* (1965), in which teenage beach bums and bunnies fall victim to a rather preposterous-looking man-fish (in between musical interludes, a weenie roast and a puppet show!). That right there would be enough monsters for *any*body, but DuPont was also married throughout those years to cowboy star Ray "Crash" Corrigan, who had a sideline career playing gorillas and other outlandish beasts!

A true Tinseltown "survivor," the Los Angeles-born DuPont (real name: Elaine Zazette) has gone from trick rider in live Western shows to monster mashes, and from kooky TV roles to the vice-presidency of a bank, and is still active on the Hollywood scene.

I broke into the movies quite by accident. When I was 16, I was asked to go out to Ray Corrigan's ranch, "Corriganville," which was a "movie ranch" out in the Simi Valley. Thousands of movies were made there. A lot of Westerns, but also *Around the World in 80 Days* [1956], *Ben-Hur* [1959]—it goes on and on and on. And all the big TV series of the day were made there too: *Gunsmoke, Have Gun Will Travel, Rin Tin Tin, Tales of Wells Fargo* and so on. During the week it was a movie ranch, but we were open to the public every Saturday and Sunday and all the holidays. Kids could see stuntmen in wild west gunfights and meet some stars, and there would be a musical show too—singing and dancing. A variety show, you would call it. I had been singing on some television show and I went out to Corriganville Movie Ranch and sang a classical song—*that* didn't go over too well on a

Western ranch! Ray Corrigan's manager David Miller said, "If you learn to sing one Western song, we'll put you on our show." I also learned to ride a horse and to "trick ride," and that turned into getting parts in movies. That's how it all started.

You later married "Crash" Corrigan. Do you mind me asking how much older than you he was?

About 30-some years older.

Wow.

I know [*laughs*]! I knew him four or five years before I married him.

What attracted you to him?

He was just nice, I guess, and not the typical "actor type." He was a rancher and he could ride a horse and so on. So it was kind of interesting, because he wasn't like the actors that I had been meeting.

While you were married to Corrigan, he played a Martian monster in a movie called It! The Terror from Beyond Space *[1958].*

I was on the set at KTTV and saw him dressed in that *horrible* monster suit that was *so* hot. But he was probably used to it because he did all those gorilla parts in movies with the Three Stooges and Boris Karloff and so on. He did a lot of monster things!

I recently read that Corrigan was drinking on the set of It! The Terror.

He never drank in his life. Never. I don't drink, "Crash" didn't drink and my second husband didn't drink either. And that's the truth. At the Ranch, we had this restaurant, and "Crash" *might* have had a glass of beer once a year — hey, that rhymes! — with chili. And that was it. That was the extent of his drinking. Once a year, maybe. *Maybe.* But he *was* born in Milwaukee, on [the future site of] the Schlitz Brewery [*laughs*]! Schlitz took it over and knocked the houses down. And that's where he was born — where the brewery is now!

He was a star at Republic in the '30s and '40s. What compelled him to take time out from being a star and play uncredited bits as gorillas?

He enjoyed going down to the San Diego Zoo and watching the gorillas, and he decided that's what he wanted to do [start playing gorillas]. There were three or four suits, different colors.

Did you ever go with him to the Zoo?

No, that was before my time.

Did he still have any of his ape suits when you were married to him?

The heads. I remember that one day, one of the heads was in the back seat of his '55 Cadillac convertible, and he put it on and was driving with it. With the top down, of course. It was *hysterical*. It caused all kind of pandemonium on Ventura Boulevard [*laughs*]! I was with him.

How did he cope with the heat in those get-ups? Or did he just "grin and bear it"?

I guess that's what he did, and eventually he became acclimated to it. Well, it was hot at the Ranch, too, when he performed, standing out in the sun for hours and taking pictures with people and all. I suppose your body gets "immune" to the heat.

He performed in the shows at Corriganville?

Oh, sure. He had all these reenactments of the Old West, 30 or 40 little vignettes — the O.K. Corral, Billy the Kid, it goes on and on and on. I was in all of them horse, and we'd ride out into the sunset! That's called a "flying pick-up." When he was on the Groucho Marx show *You Bet Your Life*, Groucho said to "Crash," "How did you meet your wife?" He said, "She was a pick-up." [*Laughs*] He didn't use the word "flying"! Groucho said, "Oh ... well, excuse *me*!" "Crash" said, "No, no, Groucho — a *flying* pick-up." "Oh, you met her in the airport, or on a plane or something?" So "Crash" had to explain the whole thing, and it was reeeally funny — Groucho kept joking about it, and it got worse by the minute. I was there in the audience. I wish I had a tape of it, but unfortunately I don't.

Did you ever manage Corriganville?

Yes, we both did. And when he had his heart attack, *I* had to run the ranch for about a year and a half or more.

DuPont and her cowboy star husband Ray "Crash" Corrigan flank TV Western star Nick Adams.

too. We had a lot of action-packed stuff. I was Belle Starr, I was Billy the Kid's girlfriend ... and I got shot a few times! We also had a rodeo out there, and I was the damsel in distress in the stagecoach as the Indians attacked. I would jump out of the burning stagecoach and be on the ground, and he'd be flying by on a horse. He'd grab my arm and swing me on the back of his

What's entailed in running a movie ranch like that? I can't even imagine.

[*Groan*] I know! *Every*thing, you name it. The concessions, the people, the money at the gate, the rodeo and the stunts, getting the money to the bank (without being held up!), the p.r., going on television, everything. We didn't delegate, we did it all. And we didn't have computers and all that kind of stuff.

Why did you divorce him? You make him sound like such a great guy!

[*Pause*] Gooood question…! We were still friends afterwards—he thought I was gonna remarry him, until I got married to somebody else and had another child. [DuPont had daughter Colleen by "Crash" Corrigan and daughter Heather by her second husband.] I guess we just kinda drifted apart. There was also that pretty big age gap, like 35 years, and I'm sure that had a bearing on it too. But we remained friends to the end, for sure.

Among your credits are two "monster movies," the first one a spoof—Ghost of Dragstrip Hollow.

Ghost of Dragstrip Hollow was really interesting. We all went out for an audition at an independent studio on LaBrea, a place that is now A&M Records. I call it a cattle call, because there were, like, 200 people for one part. (Now there's a *thousand* for one part.) I didn't think I was going to have to sing and dance in that picture, but I sure did.

What's the atmosphere like on the set of a goofy movie like that?

Oh, great. We were always goofin' off and trying to outdo the director [William Hole] or tease him or whatever. He was a great director—he just let us do our own thing, let us do what we wanted to do. That makes for a good film *if* you have good actors and actresses. I remember we decided to play a trick on the director: We went out to lunch just before we were going to shoot our big dance scene, and I ate some green Clorets and I came back with a green tongue and I said, "I don't think I can do the scene, I don't feel very good … !" [*Laughs*] He just couldn't believe it. But when we started laughing, he knew I was putting him on. We used to do all kinds of things like that!

Where was it shot?

It was shot all over the place. Most of it was shot in that studio on LaBrea, near Sunset. Then we went to a haunted house. *Literally*, a haunted house in the Hollywood Hills. It was old and decrepit, and I think it had a reputation for being haunted—besides *looking* haunted, it had that reputation too. The house interiors were shot in that real home. *Ghost of Dragstrip Hollow* turned out to be quite a movie, it's gone on and on and on. And it's *still* showing, I just saw it a couple weeks ago on AMC. These B movies have sure held in there!

Any memories of some of the other people in the cast?

The funny part is, I don't think any of the cast went on to do *any*thing after that, except myself. I was on *Ozzie & Harriet* for like eight and a half years, and then I did another monster picture called *Beach Girls and the Monster*, which was pretty good too, and is still playing.

You had your biggest movie part in Beach Girls and the Monster.

Jon Hall starred in that and he directed it and he *photographed* it—he did *every*thing [*laughs*]! He was also the monster in it, of course, and he did all the backgrounds [photographed the footage seen on the rear projection screen].

What about the surfing scenes?

He shot those scenes too—they call 'em stock shots. He'd shot those already, and then worked them into the movie. That's probably why the movie did so well,

Being dead doesn't mean the *Ghost of Dragstrip Hollow* (Paul Blaisdell) can't keep up with current events.

because of the great surfing footage in it. Years and years earlier, Jon Hall had been the star of *The Hurricane* [1937], and that was kind of an unusual story: Ray Corrigan was really wanted for that part because he was a physical instructor and he had a great physique and he doubled for Johnny Weissmuller as Tarzan and so on. But at the time, he was under contract to Republic, and Republic would not let him go somewhere else to do that film. So he said, "Well, I have a friend by the name of Jon Hall and he might be good for you." And Jon became a big star by being in that particular movie.

Hall was a fairly big star in his day. What was his attitude in the '60s when he was reduced to making a monster movie?

I don't think he minded, because he enjoyed directing.

Was Hall able to keep his cool doing allll these jobs?

Pretty much so. Occasionally he didn't like a shot we did and he'd pop off, but most of the time we were pretty good. We filmed a lot of it at four o'clock in the morning on Malibu Beach, which was quite a thing. We filmed right in front of a house that belonged to Jon Hall's wife, who was a big star in Mexico. Her name was Raquel Torres. I also remember that it was freezing cold because we shot it in the month of April.

Were the scenes on the beach shot silent and dubbed later?

No, we had sound men there with the overhead boom.

Did you go into the house to take breaks or to warm up?

No, actually we didn't. We didn't have the *time* to do that!

Is that where all *the beach scenes were shot?*

Right. And then other parts were shot at a beautiful home in Brentwood, up in the hills. I don't know who that house belonged to, but we took the whole crew out there, the camera and the cables and the whole bit. We shot interiors and exteriors there, and the swimming pool was right there too. The swimming pool was heated, but when you came out, the cold air got ya.

Was it a union picture?

Yes. Definitely. I was one of the four leads in it, and we got above scale — way above scale. It took about three weeks to shoot. It wasn't one of those pictures that was done in two days, that's for sure [*laughs*]! When we were making the movie, it was called *Monster from the Surf*.

What did you think of the monster suit?

It wasn't bad, actually — part of it *did* look like seaweed. I don't know who built it, but Jon was in it a *lot*.

If I was the cameraman and the director, I know I'd let somebody else get in the monster suit.

Exactly! But he wanted to do the part, so he went through it.

You have no recollection of anybody but him playing the monster?

No, I really don't. He did it all. By the way, remember the guy who played the sculptor in the movie? His name was Walker Edmiston, and [prior to *Beach Girls*] he and I were the emcees of a TV "square dance show" for about a year. We worked with puppets on it — it was similar to *The Muppets*! We had Kingsley the Lion and Ravenswood the Buzzard, and they were the size of Muppets. We were ahead of our time, we should have stayed with it! Walker Edmiston was a real talent: He sculpted the puppets for the TV show *and* the sculpture [of actress Sue Casey] that you see in *Beach Girls*. Right now I believe he's doing voiceover work.

Did Edmiston also make the puppet seen in the beach party scene in the movie?

Yes. Well, we just used one of the TV puppets, Kingsley the Lion.

Was it a coincidence that you had a TV show together and you were in Beach Girls *together?*

No, he suggested me for the part in *Beach Girls* because he happened to know the producer. So I hardly even auditioned — they went by looks and by what I had done and so on and so forth. They just wanted somebody who … well, who could *act* [*laughs*]! At that time, there weren't

DuPont wonders why all beach and pool scenes always seem to be shot in cold weather; her *Beach Girls and the Monster* co-star Arnold Lessing has other things on his mind.

that many of us around that would do B-movies *and* could act. I just more or less walked in and *did* it. That was good! And it was a pretty good part.

Edmiston must have been a very good friend of the producer — he got a part, he got you a part, and he was able to work one of his puppets and a sculpture into the plot of the movie.

Right, he did. The producer was Ed Janis, and Joan Gardner, who wrote the movie, was Ed's wife. They were great, easy to work for. My boyfriend was played by Arnold Lessing. He didn't go on to do anything else — *none* of 'em did, actually. Really strange.

Is that really Lessing singing in the beach party scene?

Yes, sure.

And is it you singing?

Yeah. Walker and I wrote that dumb little song, "There's a Monster in the Surf." We just wrote it, impromptu, on the set, and then we did it.

You wrote it right on the beach there?

Right on the beach. That was kind of unusual!

Were you paid extra for writing a song?

No, we weren't. We were given credit for it but we weren't paid extra.

The squeaky voice you sing the song in — was that the way you sang on your TV show?

Years out of her teens, DuPont filled a teenage role — and a grown-up bikini — in Beach Girls and the Monster.

Was Beach Girls *released theatrically? Did you ever see it in a theater?*

No, but I know it *was* released in theaters. It played back East, but I don't know if it played out here in California.

As you were making it, how did you think it was going to turn out?

Not as well as it did. They put it all together pretty good. Some of the spooky stuff that I thought was going to be really *bad* turned out okay. So it turned out better than I thought.

And your opinion today?

Well, when you look at yourself, you're very critical. But the topper is when your grandchildren go around singin' that little song, "There's a Monster in the Surf, yeah, yeah, yeah"—that *is* a crack-up! They like their mom to play it for them all the time.

What other movies have you been in?

I did have small parts in other movies. My first movie was *From Here to Eternity* [1953]. Just this year [2000], *Variety* put out a huge special edition and on the cover it had a picture of Elizabeth Taylor and it said, OSCAR AND THE WOMEN WHO LOVE HIM. It went clear back to the '20s, all the actresses who had won Academy Awards. And I just happened to be in a big photograph from *From Here to Eternity* with Donna Reed, Montgomery Clift and the director, Fred Zinnemann. *That* was kind of neat!

What role did you play?

I thought you'd never ask—I was a hooker! As was Donna Reed. I think I was about 16 then [*laughs*]. And the *funny* part was that my mother asked me what part I had played and I said, "Oh, just a part." She asked again, "*What* part?" and I said,

No, I just made that up and we decided it might be fun to do it that way.

You had to be a lot closer to 30 than 20 when you were playing a teenager in Beach Girls.

Oh, yeah, sure. I always photographed younger than I really was, and that helped.

Would you agree with me that Beach Girls *was probably inspired by the success of the* Beach Party *series?*

Oh, I'm sure it was, because at that time those Beach pictures were hot numbers. And *Beach Girls* also did really well.

DuPont says that *Beach Girls and the Monster* photographer director-star Jon Hall *also* played the monster in all its scenes.

"I don't *know*." I didn't want to tell her! I also did two movies with Marilyn Monroe, *How to Marry a Millionaire* [1953] and *There's No Business Like Show Business* [1954], and then two with Elvis Presley, *Loving You* and *Jailhouse Rock* [both 1957]. And I did *You're Never Too Young* [1955] with Martin and Lewis on location at Lake Arrowhead, and that was kind of fun. I got to know them pretty well.

What kind of slot did you hope to fill in Hollywood?

I didn't really think about that. I was very lucky, the parts were just given to me. Like *Ozzie & Harriet*—Ozzie used to watch *The Tom Duggan Show*, a talk show I was on. Ozzie watched the show and he liked it and he said, "I want her to be on our show too." Everything kinda fell in my lap that way, it was all laid in front of me, which was kind of nice. It doesn't happen that way any more!

The Tom Duggan Show was before my time, but I know that he was a Morton Downey-type rabble-rouser.

He was great. And it was a really good showcase for me because I got a lot of picture work off of that. I was his "telephone girl," the co-host on the show. It was kind of like "Beauty and the Beast," but he *couldn't* have been the Beast 'cause he was too good-looking. The show was on every night from 10 to 12 and it got a very good rating.

Every weeknight for two hours? Sheesh!

I know! And later on, I was engaged to him. I was married [to Ray Corrigan] at

DuPont also played a recurring role on TV's *Ozzie and Harriet* (as Sandy, girlfriend of series co-star Ricky Nelson).

the time when I went on Tom's show, but when I got a divorce, the first person who called was Tom, calling to say, "Let's have coffee." Then he was killed in an auto accident. We were on our way home from the Beverly Hills Hotel and another car hit him on the Pacific Coast Highway. I was in *my* car, behind him, luckily. I put him in my car and rushed him to the hospital — he had a big slash on his forehead. They said he was okay, so I took him home. Then I said, "You know, I think you better go back and be checked out." I took him back to Cedars. He had a ruptured spleen but nobody knew it, they didn't take x-rays in time. That's when he passed away. It was very rough.

A few years ago, I interviewed a movie producer named Aubrey Schenck who used Duggan as an actor, and he told me Duggan actually died after jumping out the window of his apartment.

Oh, no, no, no. He fell out of the apartment window on Crescent, right here in Beverly Hills, that's true, but he lived through it — isn't that amazing? Two storeys. But that didn't get him [*laughs*]! That happened about five years prior to his death.

Was that an accident or a suicide attempt?

It was an accident. He tripped over a chair and flew out the window. Luckily, he had a good doctor who saved his life.

Schenck said Duggan was always drunk.

He did have bouts with liquor, but not that night when he was driving home. The ironic thing is that the driver who hit him head-on was drinking. The drunk driver's car hit the car in *front* of Tom's, and *then* hit Tom's car. It completely demolished both cars, so you know he was coming on pretty strong. I was just lucky that I could get Tom in my car and rush him to the hospital.

At the time, did you see acting as something you'd be doing all your life?

Not really, no. I became a banker after that, and I was a banker forever. I think I was the only working actress/vice-president of a bank. I'm not doing banking now, but I *did* for many, many years. I'm doing public relations now, and still doing some voiceover work and other things here and there. And now I'm interviewing celebrities for public access TV, which is kind of fun. I just did an Academy Awards party at the Beverly Hills Hotel and interviewed celebrities — over 200 stars were there. And just this last weekend I was at La Costa, the Carl Reiner Tennis & Golf Tournament. Cliff Robertson was there, Tom Arnold, Bob Conrad — we had a pretty good turnout. So, you see, I *am* still working here and there, and I would like to do a few more parts before … well, before it's ended!

ELAINE DuPONT FILMOGRAPHY

From Here to Eternity (Columbia, 1953)
How to Marry a Millionaire (20th Century–Fox, 1953)
There's No Business Like Show Business (20th Century–Fox, 1954)
The Girl Rush (Paramount, 1955)
You're Never Too Young (Paramount, 1955)
Son of Sinbad (RKO, 1955)
Rock Around the Clock (Columbia, 1956)
Don't Knock the Rock (Columbia, 1956)
No Time to Be Young (Columbia, 1957)
Loving You (Paramount, 1957)
I Was a Teenage Werewolf (AIP, 1957)
Jailhouse Rock (MGM, 1957)
Ghost of Dragstrip Hollow (AIP, 1959)
Beach Girls and the Monster (U.S. Films, Inc., 1965)

ROBERT ELLENSTEIN

Dorothy Kilgallen saw ["The Hunchback of Notre Dame"], and in her very important syndicated newspaper column she wrote that I looked like Howdy Doody after a fight!

Veteran actor Robert Ellenstein has the attitude that he's successful because he's "still around," a formidable achievement considering he got his acting start on stage back in the 1930s. He played a policeman in his first movie and a rabbi in another, prompting him to quip that he's played "everything from cops to rabbis," but many movie and television fans probably associate him most closely with the countless "heavy" roles he's tackled on various TV series over the years. A long-time friend of Leonard Nimoy, Ellenstein played the Federation Council President in *Star Trek IV: The Voyage Home* (1986), and has also appeared on TV's *Star Trek: The Next Generation*—his latest in a long list of fantasy and sci-fi credits that dates back to the classic series *One Step Beyond*, *Thriller*, *The Wild Wild West* and, perhaps most notably, an elaborate two-part live production of "The Hunchback of Notre Dame" (1954) with Ellenstein in the title role.

The son of a Newark dentist, Ellenstein grew up in that New Jersey city and saw his father go on to become its two-term mayor. He got his feet wet acting-wise prior to serving with the Air Corps during World War II; exiting the military with a Purple Heart, he began acting, directing and teaching in Cleveland, Ohio. A veteran of the Golden Age of live TV, Ellenstein made the first of his 16 movies in 1954 (MGM's *Rogue Cop*) and is still going strong with jobs in TV and regional theater.

How early did you realize you wanted to be an actor?

I think it was in prep school. For four years I went to Mercerburg Academy in Mercerburg, Pennsylvania, a prep school that Jimmy Stewart went to, and Dick Foran. (But before me!) I did a number of plays there, five or so, playing *women's* parts—I played women until the age of 17 [*laughs*]! Well, the best actors got to play women, 'cause this was an all-male school. I did plays like *Blithe Spirit*, in which I played the leading lady, and *You Can't Take It with You*, where I played Penelope Sycamore, the mother of the family. That's when I went to the counselor and asked, "What do you think about my being an actor?" He said, "Wellll … it's a tough life."

After I graduated from there, I was an apprentice at the Ivoryton Playhouse in Ivoryton, Connecticut. The company was a good one, probably still is today. Stars like Paul Robeson came through, doing *Emperor Jones* with his troupe; they had to live other than at the Iverton Inn because of the color ban. Bill Hopper, who later played on [TV's] *Perry Mason*, was a member of their resident company, and a bunch of actors from New York. So I watched every performance and I *did* get on stage, playing a small part in *Mr. and Mrs. North*. Mostly I observed quite a bit, learned how to pull a drop curtain evenly — did a lot of things.

A few summers later, I was in a company up in Peaks Island, Maine, in the Bay of Portland. One of the actors, a guy who later became a very prominent director in New York, Arthur Penn, said to me, "You know, you're talented." (*I felt I was the best thing that ever came around* [*laughs*]!) He said, "You oughta go study with somebody like Stella Adler at the Dramatic Workshop or something." I thought, "Oh, pooey on *him*!" But I did, finally, that fall — I went to the Dramatic Workshop at the New School for Social Research on 13th Street. All the people who were going there had to get up and do a piece, and when I did mine, Erwin Piscator, a very prominent German director of the time, said to Stella, "What do you theenk of thees fellow? He eez talented, no?" She said, "Yes, I think he'd be a good character actor in about 20 years…" So, I thought, "Who's *this* bitch?" [*Laughs*] And then I got in her class, and she made me stop all that *bunk* I was doing. She was wonderful, and she's been a really big inspiration to me.

After the war, you acted and directed for the Cleveland Playhouse for five years, and then moved back to New York.

Where I couldn't get *arrested*, even though I had played all those big parts [in Cleveland]. Then I finally got a break on *Robert Montgomery Presents*. Norman Felton was one of the directors on it, and he took a shine to me. The first one I did was one in which Robert Montgomery played the lead and I played the heavy. And Montgomery wasn't crazy about me, because the part I had was one that kind of undercut *his* [*laughs*]! They were planning to do a show that was based upon a real story of a guy who played the bass fiddle at the Stork Club, who was falsely arrested for robbery in Queens and was identified as the robber by two women. This guy's story was written up in *Life*, and Montgomery wanted to do a show on that. Well, he wanted to use somebody who wasn't a star, 'cause they used stars *all* the time in the leads. So Norman Felton said, "Well, what about Ellenstein?" And Montgomery, who never remembered *any*body's name, said, "Uhn-uh. No, no, no, no. He'll be terrible, he'll ham it up." Norman pretended to look for somebody for a week or two, and finally Montgomery said, "All right. Go ahead [with Ellenstein]." And I did the episode ["Case of Identity"]. Now, Montgomery did a big "flip" where I was concerned: He arranged that I was interviewed at the end of the thing, and from then on, I could do no wrong with the *Montgomery* show. It was there that I did "Tomorrow Is Forever," playing the part that Orson Welles did in the [1946] movie, "The Hunchback of Notre Dame" and a number of other things. A few years later, Hitchcock made a movie [*The Wrong Man*, 1957] out of "Case of Identity," and for some reason he used Henry Fonda — I don't know why!

Very strange!

[*Laughs*] Well, Fonda was a *little* more

prominent than I was. But "Case of Identity" was a big hit, and my performance was written up in *Life*, two pages.

I did a lot of live television — did several shows for Sid Lumet like *You Are There* and a couple of episodes of *Omnibus*, etc., etc. A *lot* of different things. At that time, Dore Schary ran MGM — he was from my home town, Newark. His mother used to have a catering business in Newark and she knew my father. I had corresponded with Dore Schary, etc., etc., and I went to see him at the Sherry-Netherlands one time when he was in New York. He said, "Look, I could bring you out [to Hollywood] and put you under salary, but it wouldn't do you any good. What I'll do is, I'll see anything that you're in. So let me know." So I kept him informed, and when I did "Case of Identity" he had his people take a look at it and they gave him a good report. So he had me play in *Rogue Cop* as Robert Taylor's buddy, a *good* cop. From *Rogue Cop*, I started to do other things, a number of different movies, but soon I was getting to miss my wife Lois and my children, who were living in New York, out on Long Island. I decided we ought to move out, so we moved. I came out and I did more movies, a couple of them pretty well-known, like *The Young Lions* [1958], in which I had a small part that people seemed to notice.

Before we get away from the live TV days, I want to hear about "The Hunchback of Notre Dame."

These *Robert Montgomery* things were shot at Rockefeller Center, in the studio on the eighth floor where a lot of famous shows were shot. "Hunchback" was quite an undertaking. It was done in two parts [November 8 and 15, 1954]. What I had to do was kind of get into training, because Quasimodo was very athletic and very *strong*. I had to bend way over, and from that position, I had to *hop up* like four feet and land on the next platform. I had to be agile. Remember the scenes with the bell rope, where I jumped up and down to ring the bell? Even on the rope, I had to stay in that curled, crippled position, and that wasn't too easy! Well, when we got to the dress rehearsal, Norman said, "You know, I think that when we run the credits, I'm gonna have you swinging on the rope again [behind the credits]." Well, I thought those credits would never end [*laughs*]! I was holding onto the rope and jumping up and down, up and down, jumping *way* up into the air and keeping myself in that crippled position — not so easy! And not using my legs, just the arms!

Bob O'Bradovich did the makeup for that. They made some "pieces" for the cheeks and what have you, so that the head was kind of deformed and the eye drooped down. And then I had a hump, of course. They had to put all these "pieces" on, so it was two hours in makeup on each of the two days we were shooting. The second week, I had a cold, a *bad* cold, and they had to open the nose piece and *drain* me periodically, because I'd fill up with mucus! But it went fine, and a lot of people remember it.

The Variety *review said you had an acrobat doubling you.*

No, there was not. I had no stunt man.

Variety also called you "superb."

Well ... why not [*laughs*]? You know, you remember the bad reviews, you don't remember the good ones! Dorothy Kilgallen saw "Hunchback," and in her very important syndicated newspaper column she wrote that I looked like Howdy Doody after a fight [*laughs*]! You remember *those* reviews!

Above: Ellenstein as Quasimodo (in Bob O'Bradovich makeup) for the live TV production "The Hunchback of Notre Dame" in 1954.

Right: Behind the scenes on the *Robert Montgomery Presents* version of "Hunchback," Ellenstein adjusts his horrific makeup.

Before going into it, had you seen Lon Chaney and Charles Laughton's Hunchbacks? Did you draw upon them?

I had seen Laughton; I don't think I saw Lon Chaney at that point. I don't think I drew upon Laughton; I decided on what it would be, and I tried to make him as human as possible. (Which I think Laughton probably did, too.) Ever read the book, by the way? It's a *wonderful* book, it's all about the *times* and what have you, and you wonder how people *survived* in those times. And the end is very romantic: Quasimodo and Esmeralda escape, and years later people find their skeletons in an embrace. And when they're touched, they crumble to dust. It's a lovely story—he was a good writer, that guy, whatever his name is [*laughs*]!

With all the jumping-around and fighting you do, was makeup repair ever necessary?

It never fell off or anything, but (as I said) I had to open the nose and drain myself the day I had the cold.

Would you "walk me through" the preparation and production of a show like "Hunchback"?

They did a week of rehearsal. Usually on a live show, after you'd rehearse for (say) a week, they'd have a "camera day," a day when they'd bring the crew in and set the shots with the cameras—they figure out how somebody's gonna move, and they practice that. Then you'd come in the *next* day, when you were fresh, and they'd have a dress, and you'd *do* it [for broadcast].

And that was the way it was done for Robert Montgomery Presents?

No—Robert Montgomery was very *cheap*, you know! After we rehearsed all week, we'd get in early in the morning, have the run-through for the camera, then a dress, and then we were on the air. Montgomery did it all in *one day*, so he didn't have to pay people for two days' work! But it was fine—there were not too many lines for me to learn [*laughs*]!

So you did each of the two episodes three times in one day.

You're right. I slept well those nights [*laughs*]! By the way, Norman Felton, whom I'm pretty friendly with, recently sent me the notes on "Hunchback" that he got from the NBC censor, with things like, "We've got to be careful how we handle Quasimodo, because a lot of hunchbacks will take offense to it." There's a courtroom scene with a judge [Frederick Worlock] who asks Quasimodo a question, and the judge is hard of hearing, Quasimodo goes, "Eeeyyyaaawwwaaahhhooowwwaaahhh," and the judge says, "Oh, *really*? Well, in *that* case, then you'll go to prison!" There was a note from the censor about *that*: "You've got to be careful that we don't offend the deaf people." [*Laughs*] All this stuff—*pages* of this stuff! But those were the times when you couldn't say "damn" on TV. You look back and wonder how *any*thing got on!

What memories of some of the other people in the cast?

We had Hurd Hatfield—nice guy, but always worried about *some*thing—and Bram Fletcher as Frollo the priest. In the novel, the priest is the heavy. Not in ours—in ours, butter wouldn't melt in his mouth! That's the power of the Catholic Church in America, I think! Esmeralda was Celia Lipton, a British actress—and badly cast. It should have been a dark, gypsy-type, but she was blonde. But she was okay. The gal who played the villainess [Mary Sinclair] was a beautiful lady; she was married to [playwright-producer] George Abbott at one point. And Scott Forbes, who played Phoebus, I got very friendly with. Later on he had the lead in a TV series called *Jim Bowie* and he brought me out to play Johnny Appleseed in it. Lemme give you a piece of advice: Never do a part where you have to milk a goat!

I'll be sure not to. Thanks for the tip!

That was a *bitch*. I had to be crouched down with the goat's legs under my knees, and point this thing, and speak dialogue over the back of this goat [*laughs*]! Murder! I've got a copy of "Hunchback" and I looked at it and I thought, "Oh, my God…"—*I* was okay, but I thought that the thing was not what it should be. The Laughton film is much better, what with Thomas Mitchell and the rest of 'em.

When I watched it, I kept in mind all the limitations of live TV. And I was very impressed.

Well, it was okay, considering. We had crowd scenes and overhead shots and so on, even though there was nothing but pieces of sets. But they really planned it out very nicely and shot it very well. It was a big enterprise, to try to do that. It was all done on the one stage; in fact, all the commercials were live. You'd run around like mad. In fact, when we did "Tomorrow Is Forever," during the commercial (which was three minutes), I had to change from a young guy. I got my toupee off, put a beard on and changed my clothes completely. They were just putting me into the coat as I walked onto camera [*laughs*]! It was nip and tuck there! Live TV was kind of fun.

I've never acted in anything, not even a school play, but I know my limitations. I could not have taken that pressure.

Well, it's like anything else: You do it a lot, and you find it's easy.

Leonard Nimoy cast you as the Federation Council President in Star Trek IV: The Voyage Home. *Did you have to run for office or did Nimoy just elect you?*

He just elected me. Here's how I met Leonard: I was still very friendly with Scott Forbes, the British actor-playwright I met on "The Hunchback of Notre Dame." I was at his house one time for dinner and I met Leonard Nimoy and his first wife Sandy, and we became quite friendly. In fact, Leonard used to teach some acting, and I directed a couple of plays with his students. This was before he got the *Star Trek* TV series. So that's how I got *Star Trek IV: The Voyage Home*. I never read for that part, he just cast me in it. He had me come in for the movie right before, *Star Trek III* [1984], which he directed, too. But he didn't have any *power* at that time, and he even had to *tape* me for the audition—kind of "with apologies," etc., etc. And then they decided to go with somebody else. But on the next one, *Star Trek IV*, he just called me up and said, "I've got a good part for you," and that was that. It was a great job, and I made a lot of money on *that* one [*laughs*]!

What is it you like about Nimoy?

My wife Lois and I were very friendly for a long time with Leonard and Sandy. Susan, Leonard's *second* wife, the one he's married to now, was a *student* of his, and I directed her in a play when she was a student. (And she was very good in it, I must say.) She later became a director. Leonard is a bright guy, a go-getter, and he's very generous in the things that he does. He supports a lot of different projects, etc. He's come right along with me; he's made a little more money than *I* have [*laughs*] but we're still very friendly. Our kids grew up together, and he's a grandfather, too, like I am. I see him periodically and we have lunch and what have you.

I'm sure a lot of Trek *fans think he's as cerebral and "square" as some of the characters he plays.*

I'll tell you something: He never read for the part of Spock. You know how he got that part? Gene Roddenberry saw him

Ellenstein's longtime friend Leonard Nimoy gave him the role of the "Federation Council President" in the Trekkie favorite *Star Trek IV: The Voyage Home.*

sell"! Leonard *is* very bright; I've worked with him when he's directed, of course, and he knows how to handle people well. He's not the most overt, emotional person in the world. I don't mean he's mechanical or what have you, but he's really *suited* to play that part, I think. He's quite intellectual. I like him a lot.

In one of the *Star Trek* movies, Leonard had the actress who starred in [the play] *Medea* in New York, Judith Anderson. She played in *Star Trek III* and he had her to lunch, and he invited me to come. He thought to himself, "Who would really like it?" and he knows that I'm a real theater nut, so *I* had lunch with her. I was surprised to find that she was a little, *little* woman, 'cause when I saw her in *Medea*, she looked like she was seven feet tall [*laughs*]! Quite a nice, lovely lady. So those are the kind of nice things that he does for his friends—he does a *lot* of things for his friends. Recently he's been involved with "Alien Voices Productions"* and I was in two of them, H.G. Wells' *The Time Machine*

in a TV show, and he said to himself, "If I ever get this series *Star Trek* going, that's the guy I want to play Spock." So Leonard never read for the part—he walked in the office and Roddenberry said, "I want you" and that's it! It was a walk-in, an "easy

*Alien Voices *is a company co-founded by Nimoy to produce dramatized audiobook adaptations of classic sci-fi works, using actors noted for past genre roles.*

and *The Invisible Man*. In *The Time Machine* I played just one role, but in *The Invisible Man* I played four different roles, and I had to use different voices. A few weeks ago, Leonard had everybody who had worked for him in this over for dinner at his house. All the people were there, really nice people — and *that's* the kind of guy he is. He wears his success well. Not everybody does. It's hard to. A lot of people don't think their you-know-what stinks once they get a lot of money and fame, but he's not that way. He's very down-to-earth and an interesting guy.

You were also in an episode of Star Trek — The Next Generation *["Haven"].*

I did do one of those, and that was not as good for me [as the movie]. They never quite decided what the character I was playing should be. The thing was very amorphous, so I never felt really comfortable doing that one. But it reruns and I get residuals, and that's fine [*laughs*]! The theater is for art, but television (mostly) is for money. With a *few* exceptions. I did a couple of episodes of *Omnibus* and things like that back in the days of live television. Live television was much more like theater. Very *scary*, too! When they say, "All right, 30 seconds to air," you think, "Oh, boy. When I flub this line, 30 million people are gonna know it."

Are you as mystified by this whole Star Trek *phenomenon as some of us non–true believers?*

As I said, I did one of the *Next Generation*s — and I never watch it. My *wife* does — she watches *that*, and *Deep Space 9*, and *all* that stuff. To me, they all look like they're out of Gilbert and Sullivan [*laughs*]! Well, all of this stuff is really comic strips, they're not what *I'm* interested in. I like things with some depth. That's why I like the theater.

Back in the '50s and '60s, of course, you were on horror and fantasy shows like One Step Beyond *and* The Wild Wild West *constantly.*

Oh, I *enjoyed* doing *The Wild Wild West*! The guy who played Artemus, Ross Martin, was an old friend of mine; I knew him in New York *and* out here. The funny story about that show is, Bob Conrad used to do all his stunts until one day when he hurt his head doing a stunt — he's got a plate in his head now. One day, I said to Ross, "You know what I like about you? You do all your own acting!" [*Laughs*] We had a good laugh. On that show I did far-out parts like Dr. Occularis [in the two-parter "The Night of the Winged Terror"], which were fun. I also did one with Michael Dunn ["The Night Dr. Loveless Died"], who played Dr. Loveless, and he was a very nice man. Like a lot of dwarfs, he was in pain a lot. A *lot*. He used to have a thermos bottle with him and he'd drink from it periodically. Later on, I found out he was tippling gin, to kill the pain. But just the *sweetest* guy! I was out on the set with my sons one time, and he couldn't have been nicer. And he was also a very good actor. He died relatively young.

I did two *One Step Beyond*s, which is kind of like science fiction. The guy who directed them was one of the directors for *Robert Montgomery Presents*, Johnny Newland; I knew him quite well and he was a nice guy. I loved working with him because he didn't do short cuts, he did l-o-n-g takes, moving the camera a lot. This came, I think, from his training in live television. He'd shoot a five-minute scene, which was quite unusual. It'd go from a two-shot to a closeup, etc. *Now* directors pan all over the place — unmotivated panning, in my opinion, and I don't really like the way a lot of the new shows are shot. John Newland was good, and he knew about actors. A lot of the television directors don't.

Another extensive makeup session turned young Ellenstein into an old sea dog for an episode of the "supernatural" series *One Step Beyond*.

You had very good parts in both your One Step Beyond*s, and you were heavily made up in both of them.*

For the one where I played the old sea captain ["The Navigator"], Johnny called me in and said, "Here's the part I'd like you to do. We start shooting tomorrow." I had to do about eight pages the next day! So I had to quickly pull out of "my bag" my seafaring walk and a little bit of New England dialect and the "age thing" (I was still pretty young then, I was in my 30s, I think). I said, "Johnny, how come you chose me?" and he said, "Who *else* am I gonna choose?" It was because I played a lot of older people on television — he'd seen me play in "Tomorrow Is Forever," where I played a character who becomes old in the thing. The other *One Step Beyond* I did ["Message from Clara"] was very good, and the lady I worked with, Barbara Baxley, was a wonderful actress.

You were also on Thriller, *in "The Ordeal of Dr. Cordell."*

The lead character, the guy Robert Vaughn played, Dr. Cordell, was originally called something else — in fact, a *couple* of other names, but they finally settled on Dr. Cordell. Cordell, you'll find, comes up as a name in a *lot* of different shows, because that's a name that's "approved" by the front office. It's funny, the studios have certain names that they can use or *think* they can use. They can't just use, say, *your* name; I don't know what the legality is, but somewhere along the line there must have been some litigation. I did several things with Robert Vaughn, like *The Man from U.N.C.L.E.*, a series which was produced by the guy who directed me in "Case of Identity" on the *Montgomery* show, a very wonderful, fine man named Norman Felton. I owe my career to him, really, because he got behind me. I loved doing the *U.N.C.L.E.*s. You know, he's not Mr. Warmth, Bob Vaughn, but we got along fine.

Kathleen Crowley was in that Thriller *episode with Vaughn. He was supposed to choke her in one scene—and he did, hard enough that she had a mark on her neck the next day.*

Oh, that's bad news, and I don't blame her if she's still angry. When the camera comes in close, the temptation is there [to get carried away], but there are ways of doing it whereby you don't have to injure anybody. I have an actress-friend who's *still* angry at an actor who had to kiss her in a play at the Cleveland Playhouse, and he stuck his tongue down her throat [*laughs*]! And she was a young girl, too! She thought that was a little inappropriate, and I think so, too.

I've done a lot of stunts. Funny story: When I did my first film, *Rogue Cop*, I got shot in it. I said, "Suppose I spin around and fall over these ash cans and what have you?" They said [*casually*], "That'd be interesting." So I did it, and when I saw the picture, it could have been a stunt man, it could have been *any*body doing it. It was a long shot, it wasn't even close! Sometimes you take your life in your hands when you're shooting, if you're not smart enough to say no.

Probably the best movie you're in—even though you only have a small part—was North by Northwest *[1959].*

I was on *North by Northwest* for 13½ *weeks*, but you wouldn't know it from the movie! I'm the guy who was supposed to be in the crop duster shooting at Cary Grant in that famous scene. They wanted me to get up in that plane, and I said, "I'm not going up in any crop duster!" and I told them I'd be happy to do the scene in the studio. Originally, there was a shot of me burning up in the plane after the plane hits a gas tanker. They weren't gonna burn *me*, they were gonna burn a dummy (I'm happy to say), and I still have the head that they made at MGM.

By the way, Cary Grant was a *wonderful* fellow, very warm. And, boy, you talk about ["Method acting"]—in the scene where the heavies [Ellenstein, Martin Landau and Adam Williams] had to force him to drink, to get him drunk, I want to tell you, he didn't pull any punches! He struggled, and, boy, we had to fight with him. I think he was terrific at what he did—he was a great "personality actor," he was always the same in everything, like a lot of the actors in films. (Back then, they didn't want you to play different things; De Niro and the rest have changed that a lot.) He also said to me, "The thing you have to know about acting on film is that, if you raise your eyebrow in a closeup, at Radio City Music Hall it goes up 35 feet. So all you have to do is *think*." I thought that was pretty good advice!

Any anecdote about your part in Love at First Bite *[1979]?*

I had a big scene in it—which is *gone* now [*laughs*]! I was driving a car in New York, on the freeways and what have you. That was my "big scene" and it never got in the picture, I think because it was shot badly. I enjoyed doing it, because I got a trip to New York and I stayed at a real luxury hotel on 57th Street. They really treat you well when you go on location—they take you around in limousines and they give you per diems, and it's terrific. Then, after it's over, you gotta go back to unemployment [*laughs*]! I worked with [*First*

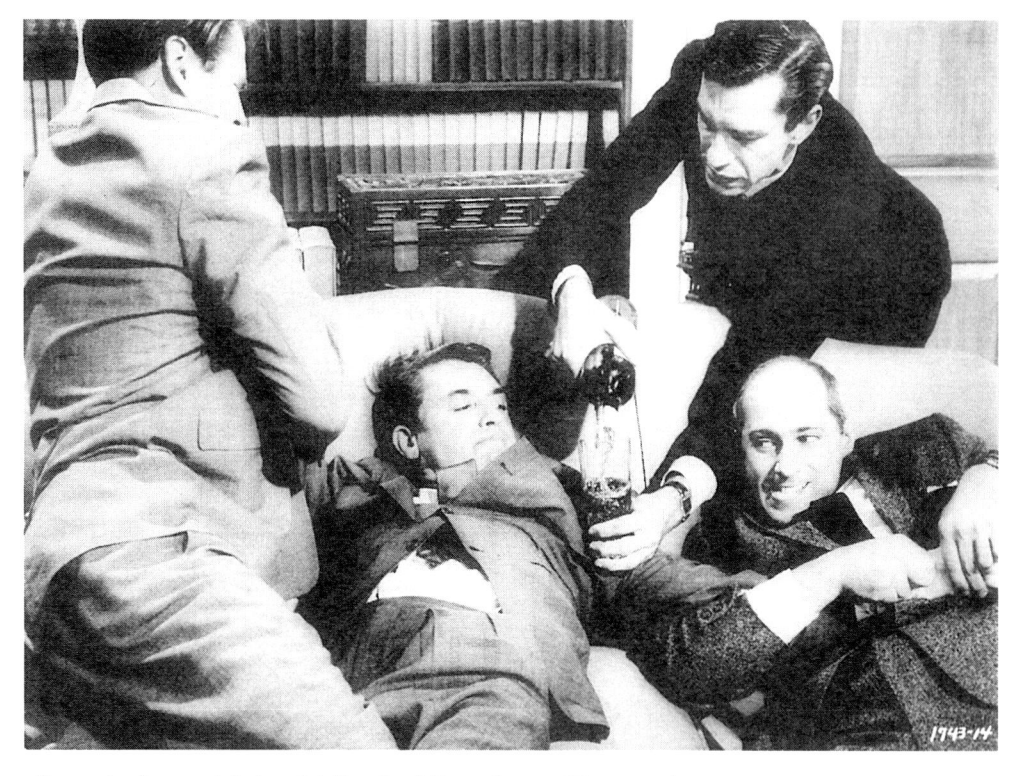

Ellenstein (lower right) and fellow buddies Adam Williams and Martin Landau get Cary Grant drunk the hard way in Alfred Hitchcock's *North by Northwest*.

Bite star] George Hamilton a couple of times on television, and he's a nice fellow.

You're still directing for the stage these days.

The last play I directed was *Back to Methuselah* by Bernard Shaw, usually done in three nights if you do the whole thing. I cut it down to two nights. It starts with Adam and Eve in the Garden of Eden and it goes as far into the future as the mind can reach. It's quite a piece. I had 33 actors in it. It finally turned out pretty well. The company that put on *Methuselah* was the Los Angeles Repertory Company, which I co-founded in 1966 and which is still going now. One of my sons is the producing director and I'm the artistic director. That keeps me out of the pool room [*laughs*]!

Have both your sons followed you in the business?

Yes, they're both actor-directors. Peter, the younger of the two, is the managing director of the repertory company, and my other son, David, has played Hamlet for me in three productions now. He's a wonderful actor. My daughter Jan lives with her husband in Evanston, Illinois. Her husband is one of the editors of the Journal of the American Bar Association [*ABA Journal*], and she's an artist and a teacher. We're a very close family.

And what advice do you offer to wannabe actors?

That you shouldn't be an actor unless you *have* to. It's tough. Unless you're *very* lucky, it's hard to survive. I feel I'm very successful, because I'm still around. I know a lot of good actors who dropped out because they couldn't support their families or even *themselves* sometimes. Stella Adler once said to me, "Bobby ... don't be an actor. You're too *nice* to be an actor."

ROBERT ELLENSTEIN FILMOGRAPHY

Rogue Cop (MGM, 1954)
Illegal (Warners, 1955)
3:10 to Yuma (Columbia, 1957)
The Garment Jungle (Columbia, 1957)
Too Much, Too Soon (Warners, 1958)
The Young Lions (20th Century–Fox, 1958)
Pork Chop Hill (United Artists, 1959)
North by Northwest (MGM, 1959)
The Gazebo (MGM, 1959)
Pay or Die (Allied Artists, 1960)
King of the Roaring 20's — The Story of Arnold Rothstein (*The Big Bankroll*) (Allied Artists, 1961)
Deathwatch (Beverly Pictures, 1966)
The Legend of Lylah Clare (MGM, 1968)
Love at First Bite (AIP, 1979)
Brewster's Millions (Universal, 1985)
Star Trek IV: The Voyage Home (Paramount, 1986)

ALEX GORDON
on *The She-Creature*

On the plane to New York after finishing The She-Creature, *Chester Morris was sitting next to Audrey Hepburn. Chester tried to describe what kind of a slimy seaweed outfit the She-Creature had on, and apparently Audrey Hepburn got a tremendous kick out of his description! … "I'd love to see that picture!" said Audrey Hepburn!*

Some monster movies can trace their inspiration back to unusual real-life occurrences. The event that spawned *The She-Creature* took place in the Pueblo, Colorado, living room of amateur hypnotist Morey Bernstein on the historic autumn 1952 evening when Bernstein placed young housewife Virginia Tighe in a deep trance. Tighe had agreed to participate in Bernstein's "age regression" experiments, and she proved an ideal subject: Regressed back beyond her moment of birth, she soon found herself "in some other scene, in some other place, in some other time" … she found herself telling the assembled listeners (her own husband, Bernstein and *his* wife) that her name was Bridey Murphy — a nineteenth-century Irish woman, and one of Tighe's "past lives."

Bernstein told the story of his 11 months of hypnotic sessions with Tighe in his book *The Search for Bridey Murphy*, an instant best-seller. In addition to the book, a now-reincarnation-conscious public could buy a $5.95 LP of the first Bernstein-Tighe session, hear Bridey Murphy songs, and (of course) go to the movies. Paramount's *The Search for Bridey Murphy* and Universal's *I've Lived Before*, both 1956, were reasonably sober treatments of the subject, but exploitation filmmakers had a very different approach: Reincarnation themes fueled the farout plots of *The Undead, I Was a Teenage Werewolf, Fright, Back from the Dead* (1957), *Curse of the Faceless Man* and *The Bride and the Beast* (1958).

The first of the reincarnation shockers was *The She-Creature*, a Golden State Production for American International release. Produced by Alex Gordon and directed by Edward L. Cahn, this 1956 chiller starred Chester Morris as an evil sideshow hypnotist who regresses his beautiful young subject (Marla English) to the dawn of time — to her life as a scaly, prehistoric she-monster which Morris can materialize out of the mists of the past and bend to his murderous will.

The Bridey Murphy fad ended with a general debunking, but the movies it inspired endure — particularly *The She-Creature*, recently remade as a Home Box Office "Creature Feature." Producer Gordon, regressed to his mid-1950s AIP heyday, recalls the production of the original *She-Creature*...

Who came up with The She-Creature? *The credits say "Original Idea by Jerry Zigmond."*

[AIP execs] Sam Arkoff, Jim Nicholson and I were invited to an annual Christmas party by "Red" Jacobs, the local distributor for American International Pictures in the Western states — he was the state's-righter. Jacobs had a company called Favorite Films and he handled not only AIP but other pictures on the West Coast. At Jacobs' home, at this Christmas party, there was a lot of exhibitors, including Jerry Zigmond, a prominent Los Angeles exhibitor. While we were talking about possible subjects to film in the future, Zigmond said, "You know, this Bridey Murphy has gotten a lot of publicity. How about making a horror picture that's somehow reminiscent of the Bridey Murphy story?" Lou Rusoff, who wrote virtually all the early American International Pictures, decided to develop a script based on this idea.

He was at the party too?

Yes. And that's how the idea of making *The She-Creature* began — the idea was to use the Bridey Murphy story as a basis of some sort and call it *The She-Creature*. Who came up with the title *The She-Creature* I don't exactly remember. I don't think it was Zigmond, I think it was James Nicholson — he usually came up with the titles.

Did you "buy into" the Bridey Murphy story at the time? Did you believe in reincarnation?

Actually, I don't remember giving it too much thought. At that time in my life, I was more interested in whatever the next project might be.

How old were you at the time of The She-Creature?

I was born September 8, 1922, so you figure that out.

So you were 33 years old and making a movie a month for AIP.

I'm not sure it was a movie a month. Maybe it worked out that way, but I don't think it was *quite* that often.

Between March and August 1956 you made Girls in Prison, The She-Creature, Flesh and the Spur, Runaway Daughters *and* Shake, Rattle and Rock. *Sounds like a crushing schedule to me!*

Really? Were there *that* many made? I would have thought there was a little more lead-in time. As I remember it, I didn't consider it a crushing schedule. Roger Corman was also making pictures for AIP at that time, and also a couple of outside companies, like the ones who made *Reform School Girl* [1957] and Elmar Rhoden, Jr., with *The Cool and the Crazy* [1958]. But the *main* companies making pictures for AIP were Golden State, which was a company that Sam Arkoff and I had, and Roger Corman's company. We were the mainstays.

How did you first get in touch with Edward L. Cahn?

The first time I was introduced to Eddie Cahn was through James Nicholson — this was at the time of *Girls in Prison* [1956], the first picture I was involved with that Eddie directed. Nicholson said that Eddie Cahn was an old-time director and producer who had made a lot of good pictures at MGM and so on. Nicholson was working out a deal with Eddie to direct a bunch of pictures for American International and he wanted me to meet him and the first picture would be *Girls in Prison*, which was then starting out in preparation and the script was being completed.

I met Eddie Cahn at lunch at the old Nickodell restaurant on Argyle in Los Angeles, a very popular Hollywood hangout at lunchtime but also after shooting at night. We got along famously right away because I was very impressed (of course) with his pictures *Law and Order* [1932] that he made with Walter Huston and Harry Carey, *Laughter in Hell* [1933] with Pat O'Brien and several others. I also knew that he had directed the "Crime Does Not Pay" shorts at MGM. (His "Our Gang" shorts I didn't care so much about — I was never too fond of those pictures!) Anyway, I was impressed with many of his pictures and with the fact that he had used players like Edward Arnold and Walter Huston and so on. Eddie seemed to be very much in tune with the oldtimers who I was always talking about and who I was trying to get into my pictures. So we had a very good rapport, and he invited me to dinner at his house and I met his wife Monya and his daughter Judith, who was also working as his script girl. Very nice people altogether.

How was The She-Creature *financed?*

Arkoff asked me to see if I could bring in some money towards the cost of *The She-Creature*, because money wasn't coming back fast enough from American International sub-distributors. My brother Dick and I had a friend in New York who was also in the film business, making documentaries. His name was Israel M. Berman, and he had his office in the same office suite that Dick had *his* Gordon Films at the time [Manhattan's old General Motors Building, 1775 Broadway]. Izzy Berman was a very nice man and he wanted to get into feature production. He knew a financier named Jack Doppelt. Izzy, reading the script and all that, said, "Okay, *She-Creature* sounds like a commercial kind of a proposition," and he said that if he could get a co-producer credit for himself, then he would bring in Doppelt. So he did. Doppelt put in $40,000; the picture cost $104,000. That's how *The She-Creature* was put together. And it came in (as usual) on time and on budget with Eddie Cahn.

By the way, my producer's fee per picture at that time was $2500 deferred, but I wasn't getting that until the picture had recouped its costs. It would take about a year, year and a half.

Who would cast pictures like Girls in Prison *and* The She-Creature, *you or Edward Cahn or both?*

I was doing *all* the casting. On *Girls in Prison*, Eddie at first wanted to throw in some suggestions and some later people, but I very soon persuaded him to let me [handle it]. Of course, I wasn't going to fight him over an actor he'd had an unpleasant experience with, or somebody he couldn't work with. There were a couple of actors like John Bleifer — Eddie had some unfortunate run-in with him on another picture years earlier, so he didn't want John Bleifer in anything. (It was for *Runaway Daughters* that I suggested Bleifer as a possibility for Mary Ellen Kaye's father. Instead we got Jay Adler, and that was fine.) So I wasn't battling him on anything like that. But when it came to all these oldtimers in *Girls in Prison* like Mae Marsh and Jane Darwell and so on … he wouldn't have *thought* of those people, but he immediately agreed that those were fine. So we had no problems at all on *Girls in Prison* with any members of the cast or anything like that.

Unlike The She-Creature, *which was a casting nightmare for you.*

My first thought was that Peter Lorre would be perfect as the hypnotist in the picture. And then I thought, well, how 'bout putting Peter Lorre and Edward Arnold together again, having Edward Arnold as the ruthless businessman? They hadn't worked together since *Crime and Punishment* [1935], so it would be a perfect combination. Eddie Cahn said, "Yeah, that's a great idea. And, you know, I directed Edward Arnold, I *know* him." I said, "I *know* you do, Eddie. You not only directed him in *Main Street After Dark* [1944] at MGM, but also in *Afraid to Talk* [1932] at Universal." Eddie Cahn had a rapport with Arnold.

I contacted the William Morris Agency and they asked how long we'd need Edward Arnold. I said, "It depends what it costs." After we kicked a few figures around, they said the best deal they could make was $3000 for one week's work. I said that was fine. Then they added, "But we better talk to Arnold, because this is a small independent picture." Apart from *Man of Conflict* [1953], a picture Arnold made for Hal Makelim, Arnold's credits were all big pictures, pretty much. Eddie Cahn said, "I'll talk to Eddie Arnold and I'm sure I can get him to do it." He tried to contact Arnold, and we got word that Arnold had died. Just then. That week. So, of course, that was a crushing blow.

Did Arnold even know that he had been committed to The She-Creature? *His* Variety *obit mentioned that that would have been his next picture.*

As he died such a very short time before the picture was due to start, he *must* have known about it.

But you were still confident about getting Peter Lorre — you even made up some She-Creature *ads with his name on them.*

Well, the Jaffe Agency had said that it was all right with Peter Lorre, that he'd do it. "We'll show him the script," they said, "but he's not doing anything right now, so we'll commit him to you." So I felt we had Peter Lorre. Well, they gave the script of *The She-Creature* to Peter Lorre and he said, "This is a piece of *junk* and I'm absolutely not gonna do it." They said, "Look, we told AIP that if they'll pay your fee, you'd do it." And he said no and he *fired* the Jaffe Agency as his agent over the picture. Absolutely refused to do it.

So now you go back to Square One again.

That's right. I thought, "My God, now I don't have Edward Arnold and I don't have Peter Lorre. What am I gonna do *now*?" I thought about who else there was in the way of horror names, and I called George Zucco's agent at the William Morris Agency asking if Zucco was available for *The She-Creature*. The agent said, "Alex, I've got to tell you quite frankly that I'm afraid George Zucco is unable to work any more. His memory is gone. But you could do me a great big favor and see him — make an appointment with him and offer him the role. He's going to turn it down, but it would be a tremendous boost to his ego to be offered a picture again after all this time." So I met George Zucco at the agent's office. Zucco was a very nice elderly man; his wife Stella was there too. Zucco said, "Actually, what I'd *like* to do is go back to England and make some prestige pictures — maybe something historical." I said, "Well, my brother Richard Gordon is working with Renown Pictures in England, representing them, and they've done pictures like *The Pickwick Papers* [1954], based on the Charles Dickens story." Zucco said, "Well, *that's* the kind of

She-Creature producer Alex Gordon poses with stars Chester Morris and Cathy Downs.

a picture I'd really be interested in doing. Maybe if another picture like that comes along, we can talk again." I said, "It would be a real pleasure to do that, Mr. Zucco. In the meantime, it was wonderful meeting you" and so on. So ... that was that. Zucco's agent also offered me Gene Lockhart to take Edward Arnold's place.

You weren't interested in Gene Lockhart?

Actually, I *loved* Gene Lockhart and I thought he was a terrific actor. But I was so disappointed in the turn of events that I felt I kinda needed to stop and *think*. I *should* have taken Gene Lockhart, but I was so busy trying to juggle the actors who were already playing other parts that I told the agent I'd get back to him on that. Which I never did.

John Carradine was my next thought as the hypnotist. We approached Carradine's agent and the agent was very interested and we arrived at a reasonable sum of money. When Carradine heard about it, he was down at Lucy's Restaurant on Melrose Avenue, after working on *The Ten Commandments* [1956]. I don't know what was the matter with Carradine, but he just went on an absolute rampage, he just went *crazy*. He started wrecking chairs and things, and screaming that he refused to work in any more of these cheap pictures and play this kind of stuff. He was a Shakespearean actor, he was working for people like Cecil B. DeMille and he refused to do any of this stuff. I never met him personally, I heard this all through his agent. And the agent was very apologetic, because he wanted Carradine to *do* it — after it, it was the *lead* in a picture. So we never got Carradine.

In the meantime, I had to get somebody to play the ruthless businessman role, since Edward Arnold was no longer available. I knew Chester Morris — I had seen him in *The Dark Tower* at the Sea Cliff Summer Theater back East, that was when I first met him. Chester and Dick and I got along extremely well. At the time when we first met him, Dick and I didn't know yet we were going to be in production of pictures, but Chester said, "Keep me in mind if you ever get any of your things off the ground." So I called Chester in New York and I offered him the role of the ruthless businessman, and he agreed. He said, "I have some time before I start summer theater touring in *The Best Man* and *Advise and Consent*, so I can certainly fly out and do your picture."

But you still didn't have anybody to play the hypnotist.

That's right, I was still stuck for the lead [the hypnotist]. I later thought to myself, "Well, Chester Morris is more than just an amateur magician, he has appeared at the Magic Castle and other places, he's friendly with Orson Welles and other people who are magicians and so on. He probably could do a very good job as the hypnotist." So I called Chester and I asked, "Could you come out a week earlier and play the lead for us, the hypnotist in the picture, instead of playing the businessman?" He said that would be fine; in fact, he said, "It's quite a challenge and I'd *like* to do it."

When you first approached Tom Conway about The She-Creature, *you offered him the part of the police lieutenant.*

That's right. Tom Conway's agent Wallace Middleton had me meet Conway over lunch or something like that, and we got on extremely well together. I said I'd love to have him in a picture at AIP and he said that would be fine, and we made a three-picture deal. I thought that Tom Conway would be very good to play the police lieutenant in *The She-Creature* and he said he would be glad to do it. Then later I thought, "I have to fill the ruthless businessman role, and we *do* have a deal with Tom Conway. So instead of the police lieutenant, let Tom Conway play the businessman." I didn't think that was perfect casting, but we were so close to the start of production by then. [Actor Ron Randell stepped in as the police lieutenant.]

And what about the female lead, Marla English?

Was that Marla's first picture with us?

Yes.

I forget now who suggested Marla English. We were considering actresses who were up-and-coming, somebody who had a few good credits. Marla had worked for Koch-Schenck in *Shield for Murder* [1954] and *Desert Sands* [1955], and her name came up. Nicholson got very excited about the idea and said, "Yes, I think she would be a good name to have at AIP. If we get along with her, maybe we can make a multiple deal with her." We met with her over lunch at the Formosa Café in Los Angeles and I got on extremely well with her, she was very, very nice, very pleasant.

Were Nicholson and Arkoff there?

No, just me and Marla English and … there was somebody else there, I think it was Eddie Cahn. We were having our lunch, and each table had a little jukebox thing of its own. She put a coin in the jukebox and this *awful* voice came on, screaming—I couldn't understand a word. I said, "Marla, my God, who on Earth is *that*?" She said, "That's Elvis." I said, "What do you mean, 'Elvis'? What's 'Elvis'?" She said, "Elvis Presley! Have you never heard of Elvis Presley?" I said, "No. Do you call this *music*?"—it was something about a hound dog, I could hardly understand *any*thing. She said, "This is rock'n'roll—where have you been? This is the hottest thing now, and you're gonna hear a lot about Elvis Presley." I said, "Well, I can do without that" [*laughs*]—I preferred a Strauss waltz, *any*thing other than this rock'n'roll! Anyway, that was my first introduction to Elvis.

Marla thought it would be fun to play in this picture and she did, and she was *very* cooperative. But, I found out later, she wasn't really all that keen on acting. She didn't object to it and it was work, and it was pretty good money at that time, but it was really her mother (who looked like an older edition of Marla, a very attractive woman) who kept pushing, pushing, pushing, thinking I'm sure that Marla should be the new Elizabeth Taylor. And that sort of "stuck," we always thought she was AIP's answer to Elizabeth Taylor. Marla was always on time and very, very nice and all that, and we had no trouble signing her for additional pictures—*Flesh and the Spur*, *Runaway Daughters* and *Voodoo Woman* [1957].

How did you find out that it was the mother who was pushing Marla English career-wise?

I heard from Marla's agent Melville Shauer that the mother was trying so hard to push her, and I think Marla felt the mother was overdoing it. Marla just didn't want to work that hard, or to be "on" all the time—she just wanted a little more privacy. The mother was *very*, very ambitious.

Was Marla English the first person you thought of for the role?

No, that was Helen Gilbert. Helen Gilbert was somebody I'd known for a long, long time. I first saw her in *Andy Hardy Gets Spring Fever* [1939], in which she played the schoolteacher Mickey Rooney has a crush on, and I thought she was really a tremendous newcomer. I met her years later, but before I was in pictures—her [then-husband] ran a restaurant, Victor's Restaurant on the Sunset Strip, and we had dinner there a few times. I thought she had a very strange career, because after she made a couple more pictures at MGM like *The Secret of Dr. Kildare* [1939] and *Florian* [1940], she then went to RKO in 1942 and she did *The Falcon Takes Over*; then she went to Paramount, and then Monogram, and then she was down to *Lippert* … ! It seemed to me a strange career, and I felt she never really got her due, never fulfilled her potential.

I was still seeing her and her sister Mari Finley socially when I got into AIP, and I certainly wanted to use Helen Gilbert in some of my pictures, I thought that would be a good opportunity to see if I could "boost" her a little bit. She did so well in *Girls in Prison*, and Eddie Cahn was so enthusiastic about her, I thought, well, maybe I could [cast her again], the next picture being *The She-Creature*. We couldn't shoot any tests or anything like that, of course, but on the last day of *Girls in Prison* I asked, "Helen, would you mind if we shot a few photographs of you looking like *The She-Creature*, which will be our next

Helen Gilbert (seen *au naturelle* on left) was briefly considered by Gordon for the role of Andrea. The producer had Gilbert don a black wig and appropriate makeup in a series of photographs.

picture? I really don't know if anything's going to come of it, and you're going to have to put on a black wig and so on ... " She said, "Fine. Anything," and we took the pictures. That was a real fast deal: There was only the cameraman and myself and Helen Gilbert in on that, because I didn't want anybody to know that I was doing it. I wanted to find out first whether there was any possibility [of Gilbert getting the role], I didn't want there to be any embarrassment.

But you decided she wouldn't be right in the part?

We *all* decided it wasn't right. Also, we really needed a "name," which Marla English was to some extent—at least for AIP. Helen Gilbert wasn't really a name—she was recognizable, but that was about it at the time. So nothing ever came of that.

So Gilbert was considered before Marla English came on the scene.

Well, *I* was considering her, I was trying to see if I could get her in there. But we *all*—Eddie Cahn, and even Helen Gilbert herself—agreed that this was not the right [part for her]. And Arkoff and Nicholson wouldn't have gone along with it anyway.

What was Marla English like on the sets of these various pictures?

She never played around. On so many sets, the crews are always playing jokes on each other or they're playing cards or this and that when things are being set up. They get bored, because it takes an hour to set *this* up, an hour to set *that* up and so on. But Marla English was very much all-business, she didn't like to have jokes played on her or on others. *I* never did it, but some others tried it. But she was very serious, and she would go to her dressing room and prepare for the next scene or read the script or whatever. She didn't kid around with people too much. She *did* have a sense of humor, but she wanted to keep her mind on her lines — she very seldom fluffed. She was very good in that respect.

A little bit later, after she took some time off from acting or did a picture [away from AIP], she was coming into town again and her agent said, "If you're still interested in Marla, why don't we talk about a multiple picture deal?" Nicholson said to me, "See if you can make a six-picture deal with her." So I met with the agent and Marla in the agent's office and pitched it at her. She said, well, she'd think about it, but she didn't really want to commit herself to that long a deal, she really didn't know whether she was going to continue acting or not. And as it turned out, she turned the deal down, and that was that.

Which movie of yours did she seem to most enjoy making?

She particularly enjoyed *Flesh and the Spur* with John Agar and Mike Connors. *Flesh and the Spur* was actually independently financed, because Mike Connors (who was Armenian) had dug up some Armenian friends and business people and *they* financed the picture. Mike Connors wanted to be the executive producer and he asked me if I would produce it, because I was bringing these things in on time and money. Of course, I loved the idea and I got John Agar and Marla English for the picture. (Marla said she *loved* making Westerns, she wished that she could make more.) I also got in Raymond Hatton in one of the biggest roles he ever had in an AIP picture, and Mike Connors chose for himself the part of the villain. The biggest problem was in the scene where the Indians have got Marla tied to a pole, and there were supposed to be ants running over her feet. We couldn't get any ants to stay on her feet — they would run off! So *I* was collecting ants and dropping 'em on her feet as she was tied up on the pole there! Finally she said, "Look, you've got six ants there, isn't that enough??" [*Laughs*] *Flesh and the Spur* was in beautiful color, although I don't think the picture was ever released on television in color or on tape in color. That's unfortunate, because Marla's Indian girl makeup was such that in black and white, it just looked very bad. In black and white, she looked dirty, as though she hadn't washed, whereas in color it was perfect, very exotic-looking.

I'll bet you had a ball filling the smaller She-Creature *parts with old-time stars and character actors.*

Oh, of course. Frank Jenks [cast as a comic relief police detective] happened to be in one of the books of an agent I was doing quite a bit of business with and I thought it would be fun to have Frank Jenks there — I always liked him. Then my usual cronies were in there, like Edmund Cobb [playing a policeman] and Luana Walters, who had already been in *Girls in Prison*. I said to her that my next picture was going to be *The She-Creature* and that I'd love to use her in it — and I knew she could use the money. "But unfortunately," I told her, "there just is not a role for you *in* this picture. We've already got Marla English in the lead and Cathy Downs playing the second girl. The only thing I can offer you is a bit part, almost an extra thing — one of the ladies at a cocktail party." She said that was fine with her. Walters also introduced me to her boyfriend, a middle-aged businessman she had known for awhile. He had been pleased with her footage in *Girls in Prison*, but when it came to a discussion of *The She-Creature*, he had big ideas. He strongly expressed his opinion that Walters should play a lead or co-lead since she had been leading lady in *The Corpse Vanishes* [1942] with Bela Lugosi and other B-type programmers. Much as I liked Walters, I had to explain to him that AIP distribution had

Mysterious Marla traded her mini-movie career for a (very) private post–1950s retirement.

to have current names heading the cast and that I could offer her only a very small bit in *The She-Creature* with a sentence or two of dialogue, hoping in a later picture to make up for that. It led to arguments and disruption. Walters insisted on doing the bit for us, but she felt it wiser to discontinue her attempt at a comeback rather than endanger the relationship with her boyfriend. I was sorry about it, but I had to agree. So *The She-Creature* was the last movie I did with her, and I think it was the last movie she ever made.

I used [in other bit parts] other actors

from old pictures, like Stuart Holmes, who was of course a villain in silent pictures like *The Four Horsemen of the Apocalypse* [1921] with Valentino, *My Pal, the King* [1932] with Tom Mix and Mickey Rooney and *many* other pictures. I met him at the Masquers Club, where Raymond Hatton took me to dinner several times—there were a lot of oldtimers there. And I always liked Jack Mulhall ever since I was a kid and saw him in *The Clutching Hand* serial [1936], so I got him in as the lawyer of Chester Morris. Jack Mulhall was a very, *very* nice guy, but somehow he was (you might say) almost *afraid* of talking pictures. In the silent days, he was playing Cary Grant-type of roles, he was playing in light romantic comedies, teamed up often with Dorothy Mackaill and so on. And when talkies came in, he was still playing leads like *Road to Paradise* [1930] with Loretta Young at Warners and in other pictures with some quite recognizable leading ladies at the various studios. But suddenly, at about 1932, he was out of the major company pictures and he was either playing supporting roles or he was into independent serials like *The Clutching Hand*, *Burn 'Em Up Barnes* [1934] at Mascot and so on. So obviously he couldn't get work at major companies any more, except in very small parts. And he even showed up in extra roles in many major company pictures. It was such a sudden change, from being this romantic light leading man to playing in action pictures or cheap independents. But you could see he was uncomfortable—it was mostly the way he was acting with his eyes. He just overdid the eye stuff in many pictures, it was a silent style of acting. It wasn't all *that* apparent, but to professionals it would be. And I could see, whenever I met him and had him in a picture, that he was uncomfortable. Even in *The She-Creature*, he was worried and uncomfortable because he had a number of lines of dialogue. Very soon after that, he became a business manager for the Screen Actors Guild and he would visit the various sets of independents, representing them. He was much happier doing that. He died at about age 90 and I went to his funeral. He was a very nice guy and everybody liked him. You could always spot him in a picture, even if he was an extra, because you'd always see his smiling face [*laughs*]—he was always smiling in the scenes!

*How much would you pay silent stars like Stuart Holmes and Creighton Hale [*The Cat and the Canary*] for playing bits and walk-ons in pictures like* The She-Creature?

They got scale. It might have been 100 a day or something like that, which at that time was not too bad. We also got in Edward Earle, who was a big romantic leading man in the silent days, the very early silents, before 1920. Edward Earle is in the same scene with Kenneth MacDonald, who I always liked when he played the villain in Charles Starrett Westerns; MacDonald had a voice very much like Boris Karloff. I got them to play the two scientists in *The She-Creature* and they were very nice on the set, a lot of fun.

Reportedly Frieda Inescort [who played Tom Conway's wife] coped with muscular dystrophy throughout her career—any memory of that?

Frieda Inescort was another person I noticed in an agent's book, and I loved her and thought she was a great actress and I asked the agent if he thought she would be interested in working just for a week. He said yes, but that she couldn't work too *much* any more because she had problems with her legs and she had great difficulty walking—she had to walk very slowly and so on. But the agent said he was sure she would love to do this because she worked

Among the extras and bit players hired by film buff Gordon were old pros Franklyn Farnum, Eva Novak, Bess Flowers and Stuart Holmes. (Man and woman on right unidentified.)

with Tom Conway on the stage many years before and they had been good friends and hadn't seen each other for years. So it was a perfect combination for her to play Tom Conway's wife. When I met with Frieda Inescort and told her about it, and then Tom Conway, oh, they were just thrilled. Even though it was just a week's work for both of 'em, they enjoyed being together again and so on.

I read somewhere, probably in something you wrote, that Conway always called her Frieda Tennis Court.

[*Laughs*] Yeah, that was his nickname for her! Now, Lance Fuller [the leading man in *The She-Creature*] is a whole story by itself. He was in *Apache Woman* [1955], my first picture at AIP. Where he came from, I don't exactly know — well, I know that he was at Universal in things like *This Island Earth* [1955]. Anyway, somebody brought him to AIP, probably Roger Corman, and told Arkoff and Nicholson that maybe Lance Fuller might be a good new leading man for 'em. We were already talking with Mike Connors, and now Lance Fuller — they were both "up-and-coming young actors." I couldn't really object too much because I was already getting my way with most of the [*Apache Woman*] casting, and Lance *seemed* like a very nice guy. But he wasn't very good on his *lines*—I mean, in *Apache Woman*, where he was playing a half-caste Indian, he was supposed to say the line, "We'll take them from the hills." And 11 times he said, "We'll take them *by* the hills" [*laughs*]. We were going crazy until finally he got it!

So on *The She-Creature* he said to me and to Eddie Cahn, "You know, I need something to *do*. All these people like Paul Muni and Edward G. Robinson, whenever they're playing a scene they're fiddling around with something or lighting a pipe. If you could give me a few things like that to do, then I'll be better on my lines and I won't be so self-conscious about what to do." Eddie Cahn said yeah, all right, okay, and gave him all this stuff to do. So when you watch the picture, you'll see him doing everything under the sun — moving things and putting bottles away and so on! But he did all right, and he was a very pleasant guy, so we used him in several pictures and at that time had no problem with him at all. And Arkoff kept asking me, "Now, which one of these two is gonna make it big, Mike Connors or Lance Fuller? Which one should we sign to a long-term contract?" I said, "Sam, I don't have any idea, I really don't know. Certainly Mike Connors strikes me as being much more in control of himself and better as an actor and all that, but who knows? Lance Fuller might catch on as well, if he gets the right kind of a role." Well, they made a multiple deal with Lance Fuller — Mike Connors wanted to be independent, because he always thought that one day he would probably "break out," and he did.

On TV, you mean.

Yes. He was also in that big picture with Bette Davis and Susan Hayward, *Where Love Has Gone* [1964] — that was his big break, but I don't think it helped him. Somehow he did not come over on that big screen, and I don't know why not. He certainly had the looks, the ability, the personality. But there was something lacking with Mike on that big screen, *apparently*. I thought he was very good and I always liked him, he was a delightful person to work with, but he never really hit it big except for television, did he? Somehow, sometimes they don't "click" on the big screen. Very strange, I think.

Lance Fuller didn't much impress me as the hero in She-Creature. *In scenes where he's staring at Marla English because he's fallen in love, he looks a little crazy, he looks like he should be playing the villain!*

Well, he *was* a weird kind of person. I sort of lost touch with him when I left AIP, but then later he called me one day when I was at Fox and he wanted to get together. I invited him to lunch and he came to the studio, and he had *makeup* on — he had a pencil mustache painted on, and his eyes were made-up and so on. He wasn't gay or anything like that, but ... he was real strange there at Fox, and I thought, "I better stay away from this guy." And *then* I read that he was arrested for walking along Beverly Drive in Beverly Hills, smashing the windscreens of cars! My God! Then he called me about a year after *that*, and I made some excuses — I said, "I'm so busy at Fox right now, I can't get together with you."

For comedy relief in The She-Creature, *you brought in El Brendel.*

We needed a little comedy stuff in there — at least Lou Rusoff thought so! — so I thought of El Brendel. Again, I saw his picture in an agent's book. I dealt mostly with six or eight agents and they always brought in their book of stills, because I don't think I would have thought of El Brendel otherwise. But when I saw his name, I thought, well, he certainly made a lot of pictures and a lot of people remember him. Not that he was any kind of "box office name," but it might be cute to have him in there. And then *he* said, "I can do my own dialogue and everything. I'll write up my scenes," and he spent *hours* telling me all this schtick he was gonna do. El

The She-Creature checks the credentials of local newspaper columnist Buddy Mason.

Brendel and his wife Flo had an act in vaudeville, and *she's* in *The She-Creature* too, playing a maid. We shot reams of stuff with them, but then it was all left on the cutting room floor — we did too much of it and it held up the picture, unfortunately. But he was a very nice guy and I just loved to talk to him because he had not the *slightest* Swedish inflection or anything [*laughs*]! It's like Erik Rhodes is always playing characters like Beddini in *Top Hat* [1935] or the Italian co-respondent in *The Gay Divorcee* [1934] and so on, but when you meet him, he's got a Midwestern accent that you don't expect at *all*!

What kind of guy was Lou Rusoff? He wrote so many of the AIP movies and yet no one ever seems to talk much about him.

Lou Rusoff was rather a strange man. He was in the business long before Sam Arkoff, and he was a fairly successful writer of radio shows — he wrote *The Adventures of Frank Merriwell* and a number of other scripts. So Arkoff relied on him to write the early AIP pictures. Also, it was under some kind of deferment arrangement and Arkoff didn't have to pay out money to Rusoff!

They were related, right?

Yes, Rusoff was Arkoff's brother-in-law — he was the brother of Arkoff's wife Hilda (known as "Slim"). He had a very nice house in North Hollywood and he had money — he wasn't wealthy or anything, but he was making a good living. And he was extremely useful to Arkoff and Nicholson, developing all these early scripts. We didn't interfere too much with his writing.

He pretty much put in [each script] what he thought should be in there, and all the "ingredients" that Nicholson wanted in there. So there wasn't an awful lot of rewriting or anything like that. Then, a little later, Rusoff wanted to be a producer as well, and so Arkoff, in order to "pay him back" for working so well all those years, let him produce a couple of pictures, *Hot Rod Gang* [1958] and so on. I got along fine with him. He was certainly hard-working and he would knock things out very quickly.

You started off by saying he was "strange."

He was a very moody person, and you never knew whether he was gonna be in a good mood or a not-so-good mood. If things weren't going right, he would worry about it and he'd kinda go off and brood about it — things like that. But *I* certainly had no problems with him, and he was nice. I was often at his house where he'd have Christmas parties, and Sam Arkoff would want me to bring along some of the players I was using in the pictures, to liven things up a bit. Rusoff died very sadly at a very young age, from a brain tumor [in 1963].

What memories of dealing with Paul Blaisdell, who made The She-Creature *costume and played it in the movie?*

I think it was Forrest Ackerman who introduced Paul to Arkoff and Nicholson. Ackerman had been friendly with Nicholson for years, before Nicholson even got involved with what became American International Pictures. Blaisdell was a very nice man, but he was short. And when it came to his first creature, in *Day the World Ended* [1956], he did insist on playing it himself. As that was dependent on the price that he wanted to make the creature and do the acting and all that, Nicholson agreed to it. There were a few problems there, like when he had to carry the girl [Lori Nelson], and he had to stand on something when he was in a scene with some other person who was much taller than he was. But it worked out fine on the whole, *Day the World Ended*. *The She-Creature* was a lot more work for him because there was a lot more to do — he had to smash through a door to kill the Paul Dubov character and other things like that, so it took a little more time. But he was a hard-working person and he took his work very, very seriously.

Did you have any input on the "look" of The She-Creature?

No, I had no input. I wasn't too much involved with Blaisdell except when he was on the set. I think we went up to his house a couple of times, but I wasn't really socially involved with him, I was more with Eddie Cahn and other people like that. Blaisdell later rehashed *The She-Creature* costume for *Voodoo Woman*. On *Voodoo Woman* it was quite apparent that he had rather a short stature in some scenes — *that* was such a fast picture that we didn't take too much time to worry about it. The costume didn't look all that good in *Voodoo Woman*, it looked better in *The She-Creature*.

And the fact that The She-Creature *was "anatomically correct"— no one worried that would cause any problems down the road?*

I don't remember hearing anything about that. I did read a few comments later about it, but at *that* time none of us worried about it or even thought about it.

I think She-Creature, *for what it was, was nicely photographed by Frederick West.*

Freddie West was *fast*, let's put it that way — that's why [production supervisor-assistant director] Bart Carré brought him

*The She-Creature just washed her plastic-tubing hair and can't do a **thing** with it....*

in. On the first AIP picture I was involved with, *Apache Woman*, Floyd Crosby did the photography. Roger Corman brought Crosby in — Crosby had worked for people like Robert Flaherty and he did many fine pictures in the silent days and early talkies. *How* Crosby got to doing such cheap independent pictures, I really never knew. But Bart Carré wanted somebody faster [than Crosby] when Golden State Productions formed — Bart said Freddie West could shoot 70 setups a day. Bart always said that some cameramen were like *painters*, they wanted to *paint* each scene and it took too long to set up, and Bart didn't want to work with painters or children or sometimes animals [*laughs*] — except for horses, he made an exception with horses! Bart went way back to the silent days as a stuntman and assistant director and bit actor and all that. Bart, with the way he laid out the pictures and everything, always came in on time and on budget, nothing ever went over-budget. Freddie West was a very nice person and did shoot fast, but the quality varied — some of his stuff was very good, but some of it was not all that great. But people weren't quibbling too much with these drive-in pictures at that time.

There's a tracking shot on the beach in She-Creature, *and some nice closeups...*

The tracking shots and all that kind of stuff were what Eddie Cahn put in. Bart Carré liked to shoot everything in straight cuts and then put it together in the cutting room once it was on film. Anything with tracking shots or overhead shots or any of *those* kind of things, that was Eddie Cahn — he tried to get in as much variety and movement as he could. Spencer Bennet was another director who was just cuts, cuts, cuts, because he was used to being a serial director. I remember on [Gordon's later movies] *The Bounty Killer* and *Requiem for a Gunfighter* [both 1965], we had a lot of trouble persuading him [to move the camera around]. He was *afraid*—he said, "If the actors fluff, then it's gonna take us two hours to catch up." My wife Ruth, who wrote the script of *The Bounty Killer*, said that actors like Dan Duryea and Audrey Dalton *knew* their lines, they were not gonna fluff, so Spence said, "Well, all right, but don't blame *me* if..." [*Laughs*] And, of course, they did it all in one take. Now, I don't altogether blame these people because very often it's on their necks if [production] does fall behind, but they must *trust* some of these better actors who *can* do it in one take. Freddie West was another one who played it safe, he usually didn't want to experiment.

Where were The She-Creature *beach scenes shot?*

All our locations were Paradise Cove, which was up the road a piece, off the Pacific Highway. It was a very nice location. There was also a little house on the beach that we used [as the house where Chester Morris discovers two dead bodies]. It was very hot there; in fact, I got a tremendous sunburn. I didn't realize how strongly the sun was beating down until the prop man Richard Rubin said to me, "You better cover up or something. You're gonna get terrible sunburn." And I *got* it, on my head and the front and back of my body, almost resulting in sun stroke. In fact, I remember that for the sneak preview of *Girls in Prison*, which took place at the Coronet Theater in Burbank one evening after the day's shooting of *The She-Creature*, I was really suffering because I was so burned. I was stupid not to put some lotion on while I was down there on the beach. I escorted Luana Walters to the theater that night. Later, the AIP crowd and the cast assembled at Burbank's Smoke House [restaurant] opposite Warner Brothers Studios. To add to my discomfort, I grabbed an oil lamp on the table to move it and did not realize my hands were black as I tried to straighten my collar. And, to make the evening's embarrassment complete, Arkoff and Nicholson left me to pick up a check for a large group of people and I had to borrow $20 from Helen Gilbert's husband Michael Bryant to help pay it — at a time when I had no credit cards!

The night scenes on the beach were all shot day-for-night, right?

Yes, all day-for-night.

Where were the interiors shot?

I can't remember the name of the studio, but it was on Sunset Boulevard between LaBrea and Western. It was a small independent studio with one sound stage that we rented for a week.

Were there any such thing as dailies in the AIP days?

Oh, yes, we would always watch the

dailies—at the end of the day, we'd watch the previous day's shooting. The lab would develop the dailies at the end of the day, and then the *next* day (after the day's shooting) the cameraman, the production manager and I would watch them. But not the actors—there were never any actors, because they would want to re-do their scenes! We never re-shot *any*thing unless there was something in the frame that *shouldn't* be in the frame or something like that.

Where were AIP dailies screened?

In a screening room at the lab—we had a deal with Pathé Lab. They gave us $30,000 in credit on each picture.

During Turner Classic Movies' recent Edward L. Cahn film festival, Robert Blake, who acted in some of Cahn's "Our Gang" shorts, said that Cahn was a great huge man; you could hear him laugh—or breathe—across a sound stage. Cahn "knew that life was supposed to be lived," he enjoyed every day in a magnificent, huge way, he loved to work, loved to laugh. And he drank beer from a quart bottle, without breathing from one bottle to the next! Do these memories match up with the Cahn you knew?

Robert Blake's comments were, I think, rather strange. When Blake says that Eddie Cahn was a great huge man—well, probably when Blake was a kid in the "Our Gang" things, Eddie *seemed* like a great big huge man to him. But actually, although Eddie was certainly at least six feet, maybe even six-one, and he was a stout and muscular man, he was no giant. And he didn't have a big laugh and he didn't *breathe* across a sound stage or anything like that [*laughs*]! And he didn't "live it up." He loved to work, yes, but I never ever saw him drink beer, either from a quart bottle or just a regular beer. He might have a glass of wine at dinner—although, frankly, I don't even remember *that*. He was certainly not a glutton or anything like that.

Incidentally, for the picture *Reform School Girl*, which I did not produce but I was helping with the casting, we had Robert Blake in as a possibility to play a role. Blake came in, and he acted out a scene for us. Well, he acted it like a *psycho*—he started to pick up chairs and throw 'em around and he was using terrible language and he was really going wild, almost out of control. Now, I know he was trying to give a performance for us [Gordon and Cahn] to see what he could do, but I was scared—quite frankly, I was scared of him! And Eddie also said, "I don't know if I can control this kid." So we got Edd Byrnes to play that role. That was my only contact with Blake.

So who was the Edward Cahn you knew?

The Eddie Cahn *I* knew was a very cultured person. My mother was invited to his house and all that, and we were really very close with him and his family. He would have very civilized conversations about whatever the subject matter would be. I usually wanted to talk about the *films*, of course, but he could talk politics, history, *any*thing. He was very educated, and so was his wife Monya. So Eddie Cahn was not the kind of person who would conjure up the image Blake described—and I knew Eddie extremely well.

And, as you mentioned, his daughter Judith Hart was his script supervisor.

Judith was a very well-educated, very nice girl. She not only worked as script girl for him on *our* pictures but also some of his other pictures. They were a very nice, very close family.

Was there a sneak preview or a premiere for The She-Creature?

Edward L. Cahn (with pipe) prepares for his next shot.

We *always* had sneak previews, yes. *She-Creature* was sneak-previewed at the Cornell Theater in Burbank, where we did most of our previews. Eddie Cahn and his daughter were there and I think Cathy Downs was there, and maybe some of the supporting players like Paul Dubov. There seemed to be a good reaction to the picture.

What was the point of a sneak preview of an AIP? What did they accomplish?

We wanted to get a reaction from the audience to see if they would laugh in the wrong places, or if they would laugh at *all* when they were *supposed* to laugh. Or whether there would be groaning or any impatience or any walk-outs. The only time I ever got a bad reaction to one of my pictures was *Jet Attack* [1958]: We previewed it at the Uptown Theater, which I didn't know was a Korean and Japanese neighborhood. Nicholson and Arkoff were out of town, they were in New York, and they had wanted a preview while they were away. I thought the Uptown was a nice theater, and they had previewed there before. What I didn't realize was, the Koreans and the Japanese being the villains in *Jet Attack*, that an American Korean audience would react badly to it. They booed and hissed and so on! The manager complained to Nicholson when he came back, and Nicholson really dressed me up and down. He said, "You know, a lot of exhibitors may not want to play the picture if they find out that it got a bad reaction from that audience." "Well, I'm *sorry*, Nick..." [*Laughs*]

Did you stay in touch with Cahn in the years after he stopped directing for you?

No, I didn't really. What happened was, when we finished *Jet Attack* in 1957, I wanted him to direct the next one, *Submarine Seahawk* [1959]. But at that time he got an offer from producer Edward Small. Eddie said [the Small offer] was a good deal for him and it meant security for quite a long time because it was going to involve a large number of pictures. With AIP, he couldn't be sure — they didn't offer him any long-term deal, it was a picture-by-picture thing. And he couldn't be sure of Arkoff and Nicholson, what would happen there or whether they would get a young man in, or what*ever*. So Eddie thought he would be better off to take the Small deal. Small had a lot of respect for Eddie Cahn; Arkoff ... well, you never knew with Arkoff whether he would suddenly have a problem with somebody and decide not to use him any more. It was an uncertain kind of situation. So Eddie Cahn took the Small offer and Spencer Bennet was suggested by Bart Carré to direct *Submarine Seahawk*. Of course I knew all about Spencer Bennet and all his credits, going back to the silent days. He was a *real* gentleman, a *very* nice person. Very muscular and athletic — he had done all kinds of athletic things in his youth. We got on *so* well with him during *Submarine Seahawk* that, after I left American International and went to Allied Artists, I asked him to direct *The Atomic Submarine* [1959], which he had to bring in in six days. (And he did.) Then I went to Columbia, and at Columbia with *The Underwater City* [1962] I suggested to Columbia to let me use either Eddie Cahn or Spencer Bennet [as director]. They said Eddie would be all right, but they thought Spencer Bennet was more of an action and serial director. Because he had directed so many serials for Sam Katzman, they would rather not go with him on *this* picture. So Orville Hampton, the writer, and I went to see Eddie Cahn at Edward Small and Eddie said he'd love to do it, but he had this Small contract and there was just no time for him in between the Small pictures to do this for us at Columbia — Eddie went from one Small picture to the next. [*The Underwater City* was ultimately directed by Frank McDonald.]

So how often were you in touch with Cahn in the years after he stopped directing for you?

We met with him a few times — not very often, because I was struggling, trying to set things up elsewhere, and Eddie was so busy at Edward Small. We probably had several lunches and maybe dinners, either at his house or we'd take them out. But we didn't really stay in touch with 'em, certainly not like we did before, and gradually sort of drifted. Each of us was busy with our own activities and all that.

Did you ever see Creature of Destruction *[1967], the Texas-made remake of* The She-Creature?

No, I didn't see *any* of the remakes of my AIP pictures.

And your opinions of The She-Creature, *looking back at it from a new millennium?*

The She-Creature (notice Styrofoam blocks for added height) closes in on Tom Conway.

The last time I saw it, I presented it at a theater in Wyoming. I was there for a lecture at the Buffalo Bill Cody Museum in Cody, Wyoming, and I was showing Westerns over a three-day weekend. And the last day, I got a call from Northwest Community College in Powell, Wyoming, and they asked me, while I was in the neighborhood, would I mind presenting *The She-Creature* to a film class there at the university? They got a 16mm print, and that was the last time I saw it. I thought it went pretty well, and the audience seemed to enjoy it. They were *laughing* a bit in some scenes, but they *seemed* to enjoy it!

And how did you like it?

I thought it stood up very well. It's a little bit on the slow side, but we couldn't figure out how to work more action into it. But I think there was enough action, between the killings and the car going over the cliff and the suspense and so on. Everybody seemed to think it moved right along; maybe it's the fact that *I've* seen it so many,

many times that I thought maybe it could have moved a little bit faster. But in retrospect I think it's okay.

An interesting side story: On the plane to New York after finishing *The She-Creature*, Chester Morris was sitting next to Audrey Hepburn. She knew Chester Morris as a stage star, and the conversation got into, "What have you been doing?" "What have *you* been doing?" Chester said, "Well, Audrey, you'll probably laugh at this, but I just finished doing a nine-day picture for an independent company, *The She-Creature*." "Oh, *that* must have been a *lot* of fun! I'd *love* to see that picture!" said Audrey Hepburn! Chester tried to describe what kind of a slimy seaweed outfit *The She-Creature* had on, and apparently Audrey Hepburn got a tremendous kick out of his description! Chester was very pleased that a prestige actress like that didn't belittle the thing, and in fact appreciated it for what it was worth!

THE SHE-CREATURE (AIP, 1956)

A Golden State Production; Released July 25, 1956; 77 minutes; Associate Producer: Israel M. Berman; Executive Producer: Samuel Z. Arkoff; Produced by Alex Gordon; Directed by Edward L. Cahn; Story & Screenplay: Lou Rusoff; Based on an Original Idea by Jerry Zigmond; Photography: Frederick E. West; Production Supervisor/Assistant Director: Bart Carré; Editor: Ronald Sinclair; Music: Ronald Stein; She-Creature Costume Created by Paul Blaisdell; Art Director: Don Ament; Set Decorator: Harry Reif; Property Master: Karl Brainard; Wardrobe: Marjorie Corso; Makeup: Jack Dusek [Dusick]; Sound: Ben Winkler; Script Supervisor: Judith Hart

Chester Morris (*Dr. Carlo Lombardi*), Marla English (*Andrea Talbott*), Tom Conway (*Timothy Chappel*), Cathy Downs (*Dorothy Chappel*), Lance Fuller (*Dr. Ted Erickson*), Ron Randell (*Police Lt. James*), Frieda Inescort (*Mrs. Chappel*), Frank Jenks (*Police Sergeant*), El Brendel (*Olaf*), Paul Dubov (*Johnny*), Bill Hudson (*Bob*), Flo Bert (*Marta*), Jeanne Evans (*Mrs. Brown*), Kenneth MacDonald (*Doctor*), Jack Mulhall (*Lombardi's Lawyer*), Edward Earle (*Prof. Anderson*), Paul Blaisdell (*The She-Creature*), Luana Walters, Stuart Holmes, Bess Flowers, Franklyn Farnum, Suzanne Ridgeway, Harold Miller (*Party Guests*), Edmund Cobb (*Pete [Police Sergeant]*), Kenner G. Kemp (*Extra*), Creighton Hale, Felice Richmond, Mari Finley

RICHARD GORDON on *Mother Riley Meets the Vampire*

Bela Lugosi of course had some trouble adjusting to Old Mother Riley. On the first day, I think he had trouble making up his mind whether he was talking to a man or a woman, because (as usual) Arthur Lucan showed up in full makeup at the studio.

In the early 1950s, horror king Bela Lugosi starred in two men-in-drag movies — one a laugh riot, the other a somewhat grimmer affair. The hilarious one, unfortunately, was the meant-to-be-serious *Glen or Glenda*, Ed Wood's heartfelt pseudo-autobiography, and the un-funny one was the English screwball comedy *Mother Riley Meets the Vampire*, with Arthur Lucan as a wacky washerwoman who runs afoul of a vampiric mad scientist!

Lugosi appeared in *Mother Riley* out of necessity: His British stage tour of *Dracula* had ended in bankruptcy for the producers, and the actor was left high and dry, without the money to return to Hollywood. Enter Lugosi fan and friend Richard Gordon, a New York-based film distributor whose solution to Bela's predicament was to persuade English producer George Minter to star Bela in a picture. The resultant movie, reminiscent of (the far superior) *Abbott and Costello Meet Frankenstein* (1948), was a comedic fizzle, and a disappointment at the box office, but it earned Bela his ticket home, and gave fans one last look at a healthy-looking Lugosi, elegantly decked out in vampire's cloak and giving a "with-it" performance that proved he still had a bit of the old magic. *Mother Riley Meets the Vampire* recently delighted an audience at England's Festival of Fantastic Films, held near the site where the movie was shot, with the convention's guest of honor Gordon in attendance.

I got Bela Lugosi the deal to go to England and do the revival tour of *Drac-

Twenty-five-year-old Richard Gordon helped arrange for his horror hero Bela Lugosi to pick up some much-needed cash by starring in *Mother Riley Meets the Vampire.*

ula. I didn't know it at the time, but the management company was badly underfinanced and was operating on a shoestring. They just about had the money to pay for Lugosi (and his wife Lillian, of course), including his fare and living expenses, but they economized in every other way — they had an amateurish supporting cast, the sets were dreadful, and it was a real cheapie. And, of course, it failed on tour before it ever got to the West End of London, and the management declared bankruptcy and left Lugosi stranded there, literally without the funds to come back to the United States. In those days in England, they didn't have a system of posting bonds to cover the actors' salaries and things like that. When the play folded, they were still owing Lugosi a considerable amount of money — which just never got paid.

How do you know the play was so bad? Did you see it?

No, I learned about it from Lillian. In her letters to me, she said it was appalling, the kind of [players] they had surrounding Lugosi. She used to complain about their amateurishness, the poverty of the sets — everything.

After the management declared bankruptcy and I got these long letters from Lillian about the predicament she and Bela were in, I felt I had to do *some*thing. I went to London and wanted to persuade [movie producer] George Minter to do a picture with Lugosi while he was there, on the theory that (first of all) he could get Lugosi cheap; (secondly) it would be something we could sell in the United States; and (of course) it would get Lugosi the money to get him back to America. Minter was then preparing a Old Mother Riley picture. I don't remember now whether it was my idea or George's to turn the Old Mother Riley picture into a vehicle that also was suitable for Lugosi; I suspect it was *his*, because I don't think it would have occurred to *me*! So that's how Lugosi came to be in *Mother Riley*

Meets the Vampire. He was paid $5000, he was contracted for four weeks, and they picked up his additional living expenses during that four-week period. And $5000, in 1951, was a lot more than it is today, and it was enough to get him and Lillian back to the United States and to Hollywood. That was how the whole thing came about.

Lugosi wasn't just "fitted" into the script for the Mother Riley *picture that Minter was preparing, was he?*

No. There *was* an existing script, but it didn't have a part for Lugosi in it. And so George, who was a very astute producer, figuring on the combination of Mother Riley and Lugosi, junked the script and had a new script written. Because of time pressure, and because neither George nor I really wanted Lugosi to be hanging around London waiting for something to happen, what they actually *did* was crib the idea from *Abbott and Costello Meet Frankenstein*—the exchange of trunks and all that stuff. That's how it happened.

Did you already know the director, John Gilling?

No, John Gilling *I* had never worked with before. Gilling was selected, or perhaps was already under contract by George Minter, for the Mother Riley picture. As far as I remember, he never made any other Riley pictures. Why Gilling got *producer-*director credit, I don't know, because George Minter effectively produced the movie. Gilling did a lot of pictures later for Hammer and other people and he was, of course, a very well-respected director in England, he was considered very proficient. He just seemed a very ordinary, down-to-earth guy to me. On *that* kind of a picture and on *that* kind of a schedule, directors don't really have time to talk much to anybody who's not actively concerned with the day-to-day shooting, so I never really got to know him.

How many days did Lugosi work?

I don't remember; he was contracted to work for four weeks, the shooting schedule was four weeks, but he didn't work every day. I wasn't there *all* of that time, I was only on the set three or four times, and I was really only there to keep an eye on Bela and keep him contented and listen to any complaints he might have and so on. Also, of course, I was "representing" George Minter—George used me to some extent [to get] trade paper publicity. He'd say his "American distributor" was there, you know, checking on the picture and all *that* kind of stuff [*laughs*]. But I really had nothing to do with the making of the picture.

Did Lugosi have any complaints?

No, Lugosi was quite happy. He of course had some trouble adjusting to Old Mother Riley. On the first day, I think he had trouble making up his mind whether he was talking to a man or a woman, because (as usual) Arthur Lucan showed up in full makeup at the studio. Arthur Lucan was known for the fact that he never appeared in public except in his Old Mother Riley garb—he would arrive at the studio fully made-up as Old Mother Riley, and when he left the studio in the evening, he would go *home* fully made-up as Mother Riley.

Reminds me a little of the stories people tell of Lugosi on the set of Dracula *[1931], stalking around in the makeup and saying "I am Dracula!" so that he'd always be in character.*

I suppose there's some analogy there [*laughs*]! But when Arthur Lucan was asked why he did that, he said he did it so that when he went out on his own and when he was socializing in between films, he could more or less be anonymous, and people wouldn't be coming up to him all the time, because they wouldn't *recognize* him without the makeup. Lugosi probably never saw him without the makeup. *I* certainly never did.

How did Lucan behave on the set?

Arthur Lucan behaved on the set exactly like he behaved in the film. He *became* Mother Riley and never stepped out of character. It was rather like Dr. Jekyll when he turned into Mr. Hyde—but with less lethal results! The only thing Lugosi complained about was an old complaint of his, one that I came across on this *and* other occasions: Arthur Lucan had this habit of ad libbing and throwing extra things into the script, extra situations. This very much confused Lugosi, because Lugosi belonged to that era of professional actors who knew their script word-by-word before they appeared on the set. And if anything happened to differentiate it, especially at *that* time of his life, Lugosi would be thrown off-balance and he'd get confused. Particularly as he was also hard of hearing. So he wasn't happy with the ad libbing. And he also felt that the Mother Riley character made him *in the film* more ridiculous than he would have liked to appear, by all the extra schtick that Arthur Lucan put into it. But apart from *that*, he was quite contented, and I think he was very relieved that he was working. And of course he also believed (as *I* did) that the picture would be salable in the United States and would help his career. I don't remember that there were *any* problems during the production.

Did you talk to Lucan?

Well, I talked to Lucan a *little* bit, but Lucan was such a crazy character. I think he looked on me as some sort of "American financier," or as the man who was going to make Old Mother Riley famous in America. And he sort of put on a big act for me, and I never really got to talk to him where I felt he was being himself. So, until I read a recent book called *The Life Stories of Lucan and McShane* [about Arthur Lucan and his actress-wife Kitty McShane], I never had any knowledge of his background or of his unhappiness and his drinking and so on.

Lucan's real-life wife Kitty McShane played his daughter Kitty in every Mother Riley movie except Meets the Vampire — *they had recently split.*

I know that George Minter, at Lucan's request, banned her from the studio during the shooting, because Lucan didn't want her around harassing him in her usual manner. Their marriage had been on the rocks for some time, and they both drank heavily. I never met her or saw her, but I heard all these stories about her. From *other people*—Lucan never said anything. But from other people, and from George Minter, I heard the stories.

She was hell on wheels, I hear.

They thought she'd come on and harass Lucan, and she'd probably either harass or *play up* to Bela, who knows? That wouldn't have worked—especially with Lillian around [*laughs*]!

Was Lillian on the set?

Lillian was not on the set on the days *I* was there, but I know that she *was* around because George Minter told me. She was there, really, to keep an eye on Lugosi. Some people tell stories about Lillian, about how tough she was and this or that, but I must say I never experienced it. As I remember her, her *main* concern was to be protective of Bela, and everything she did was in his interests. Or *intended* to be in his interests.

Do you remember what parts of the movie you saw shot? I'm assuming, since you saw Lucan and Lugosi on the set, it was the

Gordon and producer George Minter on a Nettlefold studio sound stage.

scenes at Lugosi's house from the end of the movie.

I can't recall. I was there on the first day of shooting, when everybody was introduced to everybody — that was when I met Lucan. The film was shot, incidentally, at Nettlefold Studios, one of Britain's oldest studios. It was used mostly by independent filmmakers and companies that could not afford renting space at the major studios like Pinewood, Shepperton and Elstree. Later it was renamed Walton Studios, and we shot my pictures *The Haunted Strangler* and *Fiend Without a Face* [both 1958] there.

Did you socialize in the evenings with Lugosi?

No. I think he just went back to wherever he was staying, to rest. He wasn't in the best of health already then, and I believe that the *Dracula* tour and its collapse had been a considerable strain on him. I think he just wanted to be in good shape to get through this [movie] and then come back to the United States.

Was this the only Lugosi movie you ever saw being shot?

Yes, it was. I saw him at some of his television appearances in New York — I was there when he and Romney Brent did "The Cask of Amontillado" [on TV's *Suspense*], and I was backstage with my brother Alex when Bela did *The Milton Berle Show*. And of course I saw him on the stage in *Arsenic and Old Lace* in summer stock. But *Mother Riley Meets the Vampire* was the only actual *theatrical* movie of his that I was ever on the set of.

Was there any hint of Lugosi's drug use during production?

Absolutely none. Maybe Alex and I were naïve in those days, but I have to say that as far as we were concerned, during the period we knew Lugosi, we were never aware of any drug use. Only that he was getting medication for pains that he had; Lillian, having been a nurse, used to administer the medicine, which was morphine, a pain killer. Perhaps Alex and I were not sophisticated enough to know about any other drugs.

The movie goes out of its way to point out that Lugosi's character is not *a vampire, just a crazy scientist who* thinks *he is. They really pound that point home.*

I think, more than anything else, they wanted to be sure that they were making a picture that would get a "U" Certificate from the British Board of Film Censors, and that they wouldn't have any problem selling it to the kids. A "U" Certificate meant that children were allowed to go and see the film alone; an "A" Certificate would have restricted them from seeing it unless accompanied by an adult. Mother Riley had a big "family following," and they were afraid that if they put a supernatural element into it and made Lugosi a character like Dracula, they would have trouble with the censor board and they wouldn't get the rating they wanted. *All* the Old Mother Riley pictures had "U" certificates, that was practically a pre-condition of selling them to the circuits.

As you watched the picture being made, did you think it would be salable in America?

No—in fact, I told George Minter, "I don't think I'm going to be able to sell a picture in America called *Mother Riley Meets the Vampire*, even *with* Lugosi in it," because I had *tried* releasing a couple of other Mother Rileys earlier and it was a total disaster. One, *Old Mother Riley's New Venture* [1949], I retitled *A Wild Irish Night* [*laughs*], trying to sell it as an Irish picture as there *always* was a big audience in [the U.S.] for pictures with an Irish background, because of the Irish population. We opened it in New York City at the 55th Street Playhouse (which no longer exists) and it was a disaster. So, as they were making *Mother Riley Meets the Vampire*, I came up with the title *Vampire Over London*, and George agreed that for the United States he would deliver it retitled *Vampire Over London*. That's how *that* title came about. An option for distribution in the Western Hemisphere was sold by Renown to Eliot Hyman, using the *Vampire Over London* title. When he saw the completed film, he allowed the option to lapse.

How popular were the Mother Riley movies in England?

They were originally enormously popular. They always made their major money in the north of England and in the industrial cities—not so much in London. But they were tremendously popular and financially successful. At the time when George Minter took over the series, the popularity was beginning to go down. I think if *Mother Riley Meets the Vampire* had been a bigger success, Minter might have made another Mother Riley picture. But they had pretty much come to the end of their career.

Even the Lugosi name didn't help the last one enough?

No. The fact that Kitty McShane *wasn't* in it may have been partly responsible for [the waning interest], because it was *always* Mother Riley and her daughter Kitty—they were very popular as a combination. This may be an extreme example, but it's rather like when Oliver Hardy did a couple of pictures without Stan Laurel towards the end of his career and it never worked, because people were too used to seeing them as a team. Maybe that had something to do with it.

Did you go back to the U.S. before Lugosi did?

Yes. And I didn't see him in New York when *he* got back here [by ship]. I don't remember the details, but I suspect he must have gone straight on to California and not spent any time here. Certainly we were on good terms, but I don't remember actually seeing him when he got back. Then Alex sort of "picked up" when Bela arrived in Hollywood. I never saw Bela again after that.

In that ubiquitous "Ship's Reporter" interview short, shot when Lugosi returned to the U.S. from England, Lugosi says he really enjoyed making the movie.

I think that may be possible. But I don't think it's likely that he *would* have said anything [derogatory] about Mother Riley or mentioned any of the problems. I'm sure he wanted to be very upbeat about it and put the best "face" on it, in the hope that the movie would be a success in America, and that anything he said would help to promote it.

Did you think the series was funny — and Meets the Vampire *in particular?*

I thought the series was funny for what it *was*—as kids, Alex and I used to go and see *all* the Old Mother Riley pictures, and we enjoyed seeing them. I was disappointed with the way *this* picture turned out because I had *hoped*, and I had *discussed* with George Minter, that for the sake of the American market, so that we could sell it in the United States, there would be more of an emphasis on Lugosi, and Mother Riley would be slightly toned down. I felt that Lugosi should get more play, even if it meant shooting a few extra scenes just for the American market. But Minter never followed up on those ideas. So when I got the picture, I was disappointed and I felt it would be a considerable problem to try to sell it in the United States. Alex later conceived the idea of doing a script called *King Robot*, in which we would be able to use some of the footage from *Meets the Vampire* and shoot *new* footage with Lugosi, bringing Mother Riley down to an absolute minimum. But by that time, Lugosi's health had deteriorated, and also he had become so much more aged-looking than he was when the film was made in England. It wouldn't have been possible to match the footage.

Were you able to get any U.S. bookings for Vampire Over London?

No. I eventually sold the picture to [distributor] Jack Harris, and I can't honestly say I know whether he ever tried booking it as *Vampire Over London*. He changed the title to *Carry On, Vampire*, because of the huge success of the *Carry On* series—and he was promptly sued by Anglo-Amalgamated, the producers of the *Carry On* series [laughs]! He was sued by them in California and they won the case, and he was forced to change the title. That was when it became *My Son, the Vampire*.

At a recent Festival of Fantastic Films in England, Mother Riley Meets the Vampire *was shown with you in attendance. What was the reaction? When it was over, was there an open eye in the house?*

When it was shown at that festival in Manchester, England, I have to admit that it was the big hit of the festival. They all *loved* it. Well, of course, Manchester is "home territory" for Mother Riley because the early Mother Riley films were *made* in Manchester—Mancunian Films, which produced those pictures in the early days,

Vampire Over Gordon: Bela Lugosi and Richard on a *Mother Riley Meets the Vampire* staircase.

was a Manchester film studio. It was the hit of the festival, and when I was doing my interviews, everybody wanted to talk about *Mother Riley Meets the Vampire* [*laughs*]—nobody wanted to talk about Boris Karloff or any of the other pictures that I made. I was a big hero for *Mother Riley Meets the Vampire*. So when you ask "Was there an open eye in the house?"— very much so—they applauded it wildly!

I recently watched the movie for the first time in eons, sort of expecting the pooped-out Lugosi of his other 1950s films. The movie was as bad as I remembered, but Lugosi looks good and seems "with it" and he's actually kinda funny *in it!*

I think it was the last time that he really had some scenes where he not only *looked* like he looked in better days, but was able to convey the personality of earlier days. In some of those scenes, especially when he's talking about his grandiose scheme to conquer the world, he really *was* like the Lugosi of Universal Pictures.

MOTHER RILEY MEETS THE VAMPIRE (1952)

Renown Pictures Corp. Ltd./Fernwood Films; 74 minutes; Associate Producer: Stanley Couzins; Produced & Directed by John Gilling; Story & Screenplay: Val Valentine; Photography: Stan Pavey; Art Director: Bernard Robinson; Editor: Ken Trumm; Sound Recordist: W.H. Lindop; Assistant Director: Denis O'Dell; Hair Stylist: Betty Lee; Makeup: Eric Carter; Casting Director: Maude Spector; Camera Operator: Dudley Lovell; Music Composed & Conducted by Lindo Southworth (Played by Fernwood Studio Orchestra); Produced at Nettlefold Studios, Walton-on-Thames; Released in the U.S. as *My Son, the Vampire*

Arthur Lucan (*Mother Riley*), Bela Lugosi (*Prof. Von Housen*), Dora Bryan (*Tilly*), Philip Leaver (*Anton Daschomb*), Richard Wattis (*P.C. Freddie*), Graham Moffat (*The Yokel*), Maria Mercedes (*Julia Loretti*), Roderick Lovell (*Douglas*), David Hurst (*Mugsy*), Judith Furse (*Freda*), Ian Wilson (*Hitchcock*), Hattie Jacques (*Mrs. Jenks*), George Benson (*Sergeant*), Bill Shine (*Humphrey [Drunk]*), David Hannaford (*Nasty Boy*), Charles Lloyd-Pack (*Sir Joshua Bing*), Cyril Smith (*Higgins*), Peter Bathurst (*BBC Announcer*), Dandy Nichols (*Mrs. Mott*), Arthur Brander (*Van Driver*), Tom McCauley

TOD GRIFFIN

She Demons certainly wouldn't be something I would want to show someone and say, "See what I can do?" [laughs]— I wouldn't want to do that!

A hurricane, island castaways, dancing native girls, female monsters, Nazis, a mad scientist, weird surgical experiments, a volcano— all prime ingredients for horror exploitation films. Or, in the case of *She Demons*, *one* horror exploitation film. This campy 1958 shocker from director Richard E. Cunha managed to cram all of these plot elements into its 76-minute running time, and gave statuesque Irish McCalla (TV's *Sheena, Queen of the Jungle*) the starring role as a spoiled heiress washed ashore on the island of horror. Cast as McCalla's brainy-brawny leading man was Tod Griffin, an Alabama-born actor with a long résumé of stage and television credits— including the live NBC-TV series *Operation Neptune* (1953), in which Griffin's heroic "Captain Neptune" contended with bizarre enemies from the ocean depths.

Griffin subsequently left the dicey acting profession for the even *dicier* world of industrial real estate. He has been retired since 1983 and a widower since 1997.

I was born in Birmingham, Alabama, on January 15, 1919. My dad and mom were both born on a farm in Mississippi. When they moved to Birmingham, I think they were the first of their families that ever went to "the city"— they were all farmers. My dad was the youngest of seven, my mother the youngest of 13. That was back in the days when people didn't talk too much about birth control, but also [farm couples] had a lot of kids because they needed 'em for workers on the farms. Anyway, my dad got a job with U.S. Steel in Birmingham and that's the reason they moved there. And that's where I was born.

How many brothers and sisters do you have?

None! They had a couple of things didn't go right, and then I was born and my mother couldn't have any other children. So I was an only child.

I was born in Birmingham and went to school there, and for some reason I was always interested in theatrics. In grammar school and high school and college, I in-

"One d's enough for God, it's enough for Tod"— Tod Griffin, TV and movie star of the 1950s.

dulged myself by participating in different events. When I was in college, just before World War II started, I belonged to the Air National Guard. I was thinking I'd be a year or two in that and then get out. But it was *much* later when *I* got out, 'cause World War II came along. Our whole outfit was federalized just before Pearl Harbor and then we *couldn't* get out. I went to cadet school for pilot training, graduated and ended up flying in the second World War — I was a bomber pilot.

Where did you train?

When I was accepted into cadet school, they sent us all the way out here to Santa Ana, California, because they wanted us to get as far away from home as possible. It was so funny: We were on a train and we stopped somewhere in Texas, and there was a train on the other track going in the opposite direction. *It* was taking guys from California, guys just like us, to the *East* Coast to train, and takin' *us* from the East Coast to the *West* Coast to train. Just to get us all away from home, so we could concentrate better!

I was married during the war, and after the war was over, I really didn't know what I wanted to do. The best thing that I was trained to do was to fly a four-engine plane, so I thought, "Maybe the airlines." I was 26 at the time, and they turned me down because they wanted someone 23 because he'd have three more years to fly beyond where *I* could fly. At that time, you had to retire when you were 65, so if they got someone three years younger, he could fly three years longer than I could. Which is a mistake, because you don't hire pilots for that, you hire them for their abilities. At least, I would *hope* they would when I fly with them!

Is that when you started thinking about making your living as an actor?

Well, I had to find *some*thing to do. I won't bore you with the details, but I got a coupla jobs after I got out and I wasn't really happy with any of 'em. We [former servicemen] had what they call the G.I. Bill of Rights, where you could go to school and the government would pay the tuition. I had never used that, so I told my wife Grace, "You know, I'd like to go to New York and try acting." She was always a wonderful partner, she said, "Let's *go*." So I applied for an entry into the Theater School of Dramatic Arts, located in Carnegie Hall. That's where I went to school for two years. In the meantime, I had my first paying job when I went into summer stock and became a member of the resident cast of the Red Barn Theater in Westborough, Massachusetts. I did eight, nine or ten different plays that summer, a different play every week. That's the hardest work you can find in acting. That's really where I started being a professional.

Did you also work on TV on the East Coast?

Yes, I did, I made the rounds of all the agents in New York every day — that's what actors did in those days. I'd go to the different places, CBS, ABC and NBC, and I did most of my work at NBC. If it hadn't been for my wife, I could never have done it. Grace was a wonderful person. She kept the bread on the table while I went out and tried to make the *cake*. I ended up doing just that — but not in acting!

What did your wife do for a living?

She was a top-flight "number two girl" — secretary. She might have started out as a secretary, but she always ended up in the manager's office, she was so good.

How did you land the lead in Operation Neptune?

Just a cattle call, I think, and they hired me. *Operation Neptune* was made at a time when they were just trying to put anything they could on the screen, just to get TV going. We did that for one whole summer. We took Red Skelton's time slot on NBC. Red Skelton quit for the summer — winter and fall he had an NBC show, and we replaced him for the summer. *Operation Neptune* was on TV live, Sunday evenings. But at that time, they hadn't yet built any TV studios. You know where NBC is in Man-

B-24 pilot Arthur Griffin — soon to be redubbed Tod Griffin for TV and movie roles — in front row left. Cerignola, Italy, 1944.

hattan? Well, they were using radio studios for TV studios. *Operation Neptune* was shot in one of their radio studios [*laughs*]!

I've never seen an episode, I don't even know if any still exist. What was the show like?

You could compare it to *Batman*—although, of course, *Batman* was made much later with a *lot* more money and a *lot* better equipment and everything else. I played Captain Neptune and I had a sidekick [Richard Holland as Dink Saunders] just like Batman had Robin. We had different actors, with makeup and so forth, playing the evil people. They were strange-looking people with flowing capes and so forth, and they lived underneath the sea. That was the premise of the whole show, we were the good people trying to get rid of the bad people. All of it was shot right there at NBC, except once in a while we would go outside and they would film some outside stuff to insert into an episode.

One little funny story about that: You know where Jones Beach is? One time they wanted to go out to Jones Beach early in the morning, before the crowds got there, and have me chase the bad guy down to the water and he goes into the ocean and disappears under the water. They didn't take all the actors out there, they just took me and the bad guy and the camera crew and so forth. When we got there, one of the lifeguards was setting up and he asked, "What you guys doing?" They explained to him that they were shooting *Operation Neptune* and he said, "Oh, yeah, I watch that." Well, comes time to shoot the scene and it turns out they didn't bring *my* uniform, they brought my sidekick's uniform. He had the same kind of uniform that I wore, but it was half my size! So they couldn't film *me* doing what I was supposed to do, but they filmed the bad guy running down to the water. The *next* week we went out there again, and the same lifeguard came up and he said, "What are you doin'?" Somebody said, "We filmed the bad guy, and now we got Captain Neptune chasing him." The lifeguard said, "Well, he'll never catch him, he's had a week's *start* on you!" [*Laughs*]

Did Operation Neptune *have any sort of special effects at all?*

The special effects were very simple, and it was all shot in that NBC radio studio. There were no boats shown on this show [*laughs*]. We did have a submarine [set] and I had a periscope — you never saw the top of it, of course. We went out to Jones Beach a couple times, and I remember they took us to a museum one day, a "garden" museum some place indoors. That was supposed to be a jungle [*laughs*]. The rest of it was shot right inside that little small studio. Like I said, there weren't any TV studios in those days. That's one reason that variety shows were so popular on TV at that time — for a variety show, they could use the theatrical stages that they *had* in New York. Remember DuMont [the early TV network]? There was a department store in downtown Manhattan, and they used one floor of that store as a studio. They "worked off of the walls," because there was no sound studio there. They'd set up a set on one piece of wall and then be careful that the camera didn't wander off of it, because if it got to *another* piece of the wall, that'd be the set for a different show [*laughs*]! Live TV was hectic, I'll tell you that. The directors didn't know what they were doing, either — there was no such thing as a TV director yet. We were all just trying something new.

How did the actors prepare for an Operation Neptune?

There were a lot of rehearsal halls in Manhattan that people would go out and rent. Even the legitimate theater used them for rehearsing of new plays and things like that, instead of using the whole theater. We would go to a rehearsal hall and do our lines and go through all the actions, and then go to into the studio and have a run-through with the cameras. And then the next thing we'd do was shoot it. It was live as far as New York was concerned. The shows would be kinescoped and then those kinescopes were later played for the West Coast, at the proper time.

Was the rehearsal also on Sunday, right before the show?

No, we would work on Saturday at the rehearsal hall, then go over Sunday, have a run-through for the cameramen and then shoot it. It would come on at seven o'clock on Sunday night, and that's when we would shoot it!

Were you able to "cheat"? Were some of the lines written on the walls and so forth?

No, no, no, no. All the actors that I worked with were experienced stage actors, so we memorized everything. But actors from Hollywood would come in, and they'd have to write their dialogue on tabletops, desks, chairs...! On a live show, you had to start from the beginning and

Griffin was "Captain Neptune" — an aquatic version of Captain Video — in the live sci-fi TV series *Operation Neptune* with Richard Holland (center).

go right through, no hesitation. In Hollywood, you can always say *cut* and re-do it — but on live TV, you couldn't do that. So the Hollywood actors wrote a lot of their dialogue on tables and so on, while all the New York people were stage-trained and they memorized the scripts and didn't have any problems.

How much did you get paid per episode of Operation Neptune, *if you don't mind me asking?*

If I remembered, I'd tell you, but I can't remember. I'm sure it wasn't a hell of a lot, because in those days we were all still "reaching" and trying for that break, and you would have done it for any amount they offered you.

How good a living were you making in New York, doing commercials and TV shows? Were you living in a nice apartment and so on, or were things a little tight?

Well, Grace worked, too. I made pretty good money when I worked, but like all actors, you don't *work* every day.

How long did Operation Neptune *last?*

That only ran for the summer. I would have liked for it to develop and last longer and been a better show, because it meant more work. But it didn't.

I did a lot of shows in New York, but mainly — I'd say almost 100 percent — they were all TV. To supplement our income, I also did some TV announcing. At that time, they didn't have any announcers who had experience at doing TV announcing. Radio announcers could just *read* their scripts — they weren't seen, so they could just read their speeches. Well, [TV producers] had to go to actors who were in the habit of memorizing their dialogue to work in their commercials. It was all live, and this was before they had teleprompters or anything like that. I did that for awhile, for Camel cigarettes. On Friday nights I did it for Ralph Bellamy's show *Man Against Crime*, and then on Saturday nights I did the middle commercial for a variety show with Dean Martin and Jerry Lewis. I had a commercial agent come to me one time and say, "I like your work. I'd like for you to sign with me and I'll guarantee you x-number of dollars per year." Well, at that time, if you associated yourself *too* much with a product, the other companies wouldn't hire you to play an acting part because you were too identified with that product. All the cigarette companies advertised at that point, and if I was out there all the time trying to sell Camels, well, then I couldn't act on a show that was being sponsored by Luckies, understand? I told the agent, "No, I don't wanna do that. I'm an actor." Well [*laughs*], that was the dumbest thing I ever said in my life — I'd have made a fortune the other way!

Were you a smoker?

Yeah. Oh, *yeah*! Well, back in those days, *every*body was. That's before we had any sense, and before they told us anything. By the way, do you remember William Gargan? He was a typical Irishman and I enjoyed working with him. He did one of those live early TV shows that I was on — I played an FBI guy on an episode of his series [*Martin Kane, Private Eye*]. His show was sponsored by a cigarette company, let's say it was Lucky Strikes, and a character on the show named Happy [played by Walter Kinsella] ran a tobacco store. Martin Kane was always calling on Happy in his store, and you didn't see anything *but* Lucky Strikes, all over the store! They hired an actor to act in the commercial one night, and alllll he had to do was go into the store and say, "Happy, gimme a pack of Lucky Strikes." And he got in there and just *froze*! He couldn't *see* anything but Luckies, and he ended up saying to Happy [*nervously*], " ... What's *good*?" [*Laughs*] He went dumb and blind, all at the same time!

At what point did you pick up the new name Tod Griffin?

When we were in New York. All the studios have offices in New York, so somebody from 20th Century–Fox saw me in a play and wanted to give me a screen test and they took me over to their sound stage. My birth name is Arthur Griffin, but there was already an actor in Screen Actors Guild with that name so I couldn't use it. One of the secretaries there said, "I like Tod for the first name," and I said, "*Use* it." Well, 20th Century–Fox did not sign me, but the name Tod Griffin stuck with me [*laughs*]—later on in life, nobody knew anything *but* Tod Griffin. All of my real estate, everything we ever owned, is all in the name of Tod Griffin.

Did you ever spell it with two d's? I see it spelled T-o-d-d in some of the movie reference books.

One d. A lot of people want to spell it with two d's, but I tell 'em, "Look, one d's enough for God, it's enough for Tod." [*Laughs*] They never forget that!

Why did you move out to California?

I thought the future for TV was [in Hollywood], which it was. In the early days of the motion picture industry, movies started in New York and then moved to the West Coast because of the weather and the ability to shoot outside more. TV was going that same direction, so I decided to take a trip out here to look over the field. Here's an interesting story: I was up at the Equity office in New York—Equity is the stage actors' union—and an actor came over to me and said, "Someone says you're going to the West Coast." I said, "Yeah, I'm gonna run out there, spend a week or so, look and around and come back." He said, "Look, I've got a station wagon that's loaded with my things and *I've* got to *fly* out there. I'll pay all your expenses if you'll drive my car out there." I said, "Well, if I can find somebody who'll go with me and share the driving, I'll do it." Another actor who was there said, "I'll share it with you," and I said okay. Well, the guy whose station wagon we drove out to California was Jack Palance, and the reason he was coming out was to shoot *Shane* [1953]. We drove Palance's station wagon all the way to California from Manhattan, and delivered it to his wife. Then I flew back to New York.

When did you move to California?

In 1955. When Grace and I got to California, we had no place to go, we didn't know anybody. Grace was great at finding places, and she found this one house and we went over there and met the lady who owned the place. We were in this beautiful home talking to the lady, and I thought this was where *she* lived. I said, "Would you show us the apartment?" and she said, "You're sitting in it." We were sitting in a living room with a crystal chandelier and a big, *big* window with fresh sunshine coming in. For someone coming from New York—dirty, cold Brooklyn Heights, and dreary weather and so forth—this was *beautiful*, and quite amazing!

This was a private house?

It was a private house that was divided into two apartments. It used to be Douglas Fairbanks and Mary Pickford's studio cottage on Columbia property. The landlady had been one of the switchboard operators at Columbia and she had an opportunity to buy the house at a good price. She bought it and had it moved from Columbia to this residential site. I thought it was quite proper that that's where we would live! I signed a one-year lease and we fell in love with the lady who owned it. And she wouldn't raise our rent, 'cause she was afraid we'd leave. So we were there for about another half a year and *I* raised my rent—I told her, "You're entitled to a rent raise." We signed a one-year lease and ended up staying there ten years. As a matter of fact, I made *She Demons* while we were living there.

Griffin and Victor Sen Yung narrowly escape the clawed clutches of caged *She Demons*.

She Demons was your only starring role in a movie.

Well, *She Demons* was one of the few theatrical movies I was in. And ... [*laughs*] ... it's a *terrible* movie! The reason I did it was, my agent told me he wanted some film on me. There was a casting call for *She Demons* and the agent told me, "Go check this one out. It's not much, but if they'll hire you, we'll get some film on you." Well, I couldn't be too choosy at that point, I needed work! So I saw the casting people, like, on Friday, and we started shooting *Monday*! I might have been the last one they hired.

Where we some of the different places you shot?

We used a sound stage for most of what you see in *She Demons*. The jungle scenes and all that stuff were shot on that sound stage. The beach scenes were shot out at Malibu. Remember Jim Garner? Well, where you see us on the beach in *She Demons*, years later you could spit south and hit his mobile home, it was that close. When you see the cave, that was shot at Bronson Quarry — and that's in the middle of Hollywood! You could spit on it from Sunset and Vine, it's *real* close. A lot of the studios used to use it because it was so convenient.

Was She Demons *a union picture?*

You know, I really don't know. Of course I belonged to Screen Actors Guild, but I never thought to ask, and I'm not positive one way or the other. Irish McCalla got around 1500, and I think my salary was 1000 — or it could have been 1500 too. Either way, it was not very much. Irish was a delightful gal. A wonderful person. [*Pause*] Couldn't act a dime's worth [*laughs*]. And she knew it! She was no actress.

You mean she would blow takes, or her acting wasn't very good?

No, no, she was smart, and a wonderful gal, but she'd had very little acting experience. Matter of fact, I would be very surprised if she did much of anything after *She Demons*. She was also quite a good painter and artist. I went to work on Monday and I met Irish then, and we made the movie. It took about seven days, and I never saw her again. Same for Victor Sen Yung, we never got to know each other personally very well at all. He was a nice person, but he was just doin' a job to make a buck. After the show was over, I never saw him again. It was such a short work week, and I was so busy just doing what I had to do, I didn't get to know personally *any* of those people. Rudolph Anders played the Nazi — he was in every Nazi picture ever made! And also the big guy who played his underling, Gene Roth, *he* was in every Nazi picture too! [Anders and Roth] must have been hard up because they were running out of Nazi pictures!

I assume that when they hired you on Friday, they gave you the script to look at over the weekend.

Yeah, and [*laughs*] — and it wasn't hard to read! I didn't like the script, and no picture is ever, *ever* any better than the script, I don't care *who* the actors are. And once we got to making the picture, there weren't many retakes. That shows you how quickly they wanted to get it done and get out of there.

I like the bedtime scene where you're holding up a blanket while Irish McCalla is undressing on the other side — it kinda reminds me of Clark Gable and Claudette Colbert in It Happened One Night *[1934].*

I haven't the slightest idea if they were thinking that when we did that scene. I remember holding that blanket up ... and I

Griffin in a romantic clinch with *She Demons* co-star Irish McCalla ("A wonderful person ... couldn't act a dime's worth!").

remember that, on the side, they had tried to get me to hold it lower.

So that they could get a shot of Irish McCalla undressing? Or undressed?

Yeah. I thought to myself, "You sons of guns," and I just wouldn't do it. I lowered it a *little*, but not enough to satisfy 'em. But, I tell you, it would have attracted more people if we *had* made a porno out of it!

Any memory of your scene with the snake?

That was a real snake. I didn't [hesitate], and it didn't seem to bother Irish either.

You had a very noticeable stunt double in your fight scene with Gene Roth.

I never saw the double. When I was shooting that scene, I *never* saw that part of it, and I didn't know that there would *be* a double in there. And, you're right, they *did* pick somebody that couldn't be further from me! He was half my size, blond hair [*laughs*]—it seems to me they could have gone to a *little* bit more trouble! Color his hair, or *some*thing! But they didn't even go to that trouble. It was so obvious. I know they were really on a small, small budget because, as I said before, I don't recall too many takes. If you got it half-right the first time, you'd hear, "Print it!" We did that picture in a hurry.

And they didn't even tell you they were going to extend the fight scene by bringing him in?

I thought when I left after shooting that fight scene that it was all over with. They did [the extra fighting] on the side and inserted it. If I had known they were picking *him* to do it, I think that *I* would have said something. I would have said, "I won't take *this*. Get somebody that looks *reasonably* like me." I was real shocked when I read a critic's review of *She Demons* and one of the complaints he had was that my double didn't resemble me at all. I thought, "I didn't *use* a double." But then later, when I saw the movie, I realized what he was talkin' about.

Where did you see the picture for the first time?

In a little theater on Hollywood Boulevard. My name was on the marquee and everything! I took my wife and another couple to see it, and afterwards I said, "Well, after they showed the titles, we shoulda walked out. That was the best part!" [*Laughs*] It was so dreadful. I remember one comment about *She Demons* that was made by some people who knew the business: I had a couple of producers say to me, "Look, it was a terrible script. For what you had to work with, you did pretty good. You handled it as well as it could have been handled." And they hired me in *spite* of *She Demons* [*laughs*]—they understood!

In general, what was the experience of making She Demons *like for you? Was it just hard, fast work, or did you enjoy yourself at all?*

Oh, I enjoyed it. I really *tried* to do the best I could do. I certainly didn't like the script, and I could see how they were cutting corners. *She Demons* certainly wouldn't be something I would want to show someone and say, "See what *I* can do?" [*laughs*]—I wouldn't want to do *that*! But I guess a lot of people saw it when it came out. Then it eventually went to TV and played on TV for a while.

Once you got out to Hollywood, how many theatrical features were you in, do you recall?

Look, theatrical movies, I didn't *make* those. I was 99 percent doing TV shows. I did *The Millionaire*, playing Peggie Castle's boyfriend, *How to Marry a Millionaire* playing Barbara Eden's boyfriend—those were fairly good parts. And I did a *jillion* Westerns out at Warner Brothers. I made a couple of *Maverick*s, working with Jim Garner. One of the best parts on his show was the heavy. Jim Garner had the sympathetic part, it was his show, and I always had the second best part, the heavy.

Feature-wise, you were also in She Devil *[1957] and* The Desperados Are in Town *[1956]—*

And I had a walk-on part in a movie out at 20th Century–Fox with Van Johnson, Joseph Cotten, Jack Carson, Ruth

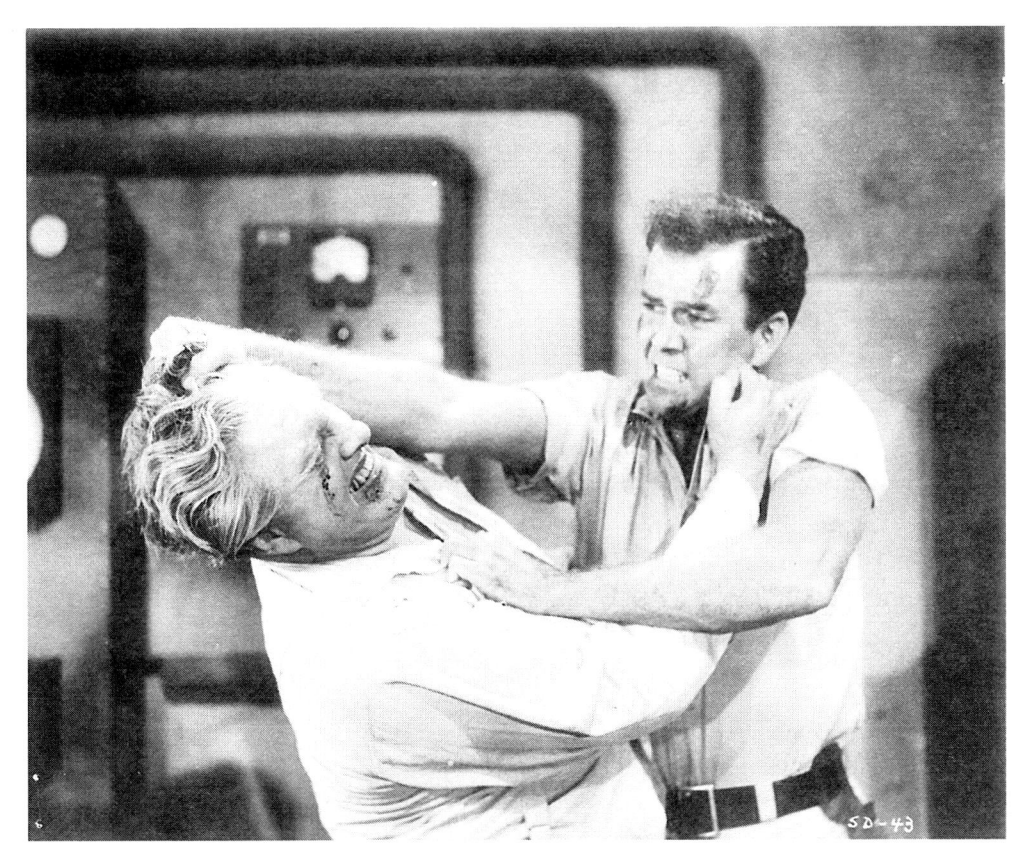

Griffin's fistic encounter with Nazi *Schweinhund* Gene Roth was spoiled by the inclusion of obvious stunt doubles in the final cut of *She Demons*.

Roman, called *The Bottom of the Bottle* [1956]. It was a terrible movie. I think they had all those high-priced actors available and said, "Let's get 'em together and make a movie." A friend of mine down in Richmond, Virginia, ran a theater there and he sent me a picture one time, a picture of the marquee of his theater when he was running *Bottom of the Bottle*. On the top was VAN JOHNSON, JOSEPH COTTEN, TOD GRIFFIN. I wrote him back, I said, "What the hell is this third billing??" [*Laughs*] Incidentally, Henry Hathaway was the director, and Henry Hathaway was *not* an easy person to get along with. I had a light stand fall and clip me across the head one day when we were in a living room set. Everyone yelled, "Tod! Watch out!" and I turned and looked, and it hit me right across the forehead. It was one of those very heavy lights that stands on the floor, with sandbags all over the footings. They didn't have enough sandbags, I guess, and it fell and clipped me across the head. It wasn't *too* bad but it brought blood, so they had to get the nurse down, and for a while everything stopped. And finally Hathaway said [*angrily*], "All right, let's go, come on! It's just a concussion!" [*Laughs*]

Why did you eventually give up on acting?

I finally realized I was not gonna be the next Harrison Ford. I was going to night school, taking adult education training in real estate because Grace and I were buying a little bit here and there and I wanted to learn more about it. Then I said,

"Why don't I go ahead and get a license? Then I can sell houses, and I can also drop it when I get a call and go do a movie." A lot of actors out here did that. But then I learned about *industrial* real estate, and I became fascinated with it and I said, "If I can get a spot there, I'll make a change in careers." And that's what I did. I ended up working with Coldwell Banker, the world's largest real estate firm, and I really found my niche and I did very, very well. I loved my work and I made a lot of friends at Coldwell and made a lot of money. Grace and I invested and so forth until we were where we could take care of ourselves. I retired in '83.

What do you look back on with more fondness, your acting days or your real estate days?

I was too serious in the real estate — I worked with some very high-class people. I was in the industrial field, I didn't sell houses and things like that. It was during the Cold War, and I dealt with mostly electronic companies, *large* companies — General Electric, Hughes Aircraft, TRW and places like that. When in my field you deal with those kinds of corporations, you're dealing with at *least* the vice-president. You establish some relationships that way. I did a lot of pro bono work with good customers like TRW and North American Aviation and Hughes Aircraft — for people like that, you do a lot of things for free, just to help them, which I did. You build up a loyalty that way. The last real estate transaction I put together, I sold a piece of real estate with a building on it, and the commission was $264,000. The company always gets half, and I got the other half of it. There's a lot of money to be made in that business, but you need more than a bucket to bring it home, you've got to know what you're doing. It can also break your heart too. I worked on projects for two years — not full-time, but off and on for two years — and if it falls through, you get *no* compensation for that. So it's tough, but it's rewarding to those people who are tough enough to *do* it.

I've had a very checkered life. I was a bomber pilot in the second World War, 40 missions, and my plane was hit every time. And it got worse and worse, each mission. But I made it through there; then came back into show business and *that* was exciting because you meet a lot of exciting people and *nothing* is guaranteed. It was a lot of fun — a tremendous amount of fun. And I'm sure it helped me throughout the rest of my life.

TOD GRIFFIN FILMOGRAPHY

The Bottom of the Bottle (20th Century–Fox, 1956)
The Desperados Are in Town (20th Century–Fox, 1956)
She Devil (20th Century–Fox, 1957)
She Demons (Astor, 1958)

DAVID HEDISON

In that final scene [of The Fly*], they cranked up the speed of the sound so my screaming "Help me!" became [in a squeaky voice] "Help me!" way up there high. Which doesn't* sound *right! You should have heard a* man's *voice screaming, "Help me!" Imagine if you actually heard Andre Delambre screeeeaming for his life. That is horror. That is horror.*

Even the staunchest foe of euthanasia would be moved by the plight of Andre Delambre, a scientist whose work in the field of matter transmission ends in tragedy when his atoms are inadvertently mixed with those of a fly. Delambre now has the head and pincer-hand — and some of the savage instincts — of an insect; he sequesters himself in his lab while entreating his wife to find the corresponding fly (with human head and hand) so that a reversal may be attempted. If this cannot be done, then he needs to destroy himself...

Based on the George Langelaan story, 1958's *The Fly* was a unique mix of science fiction and human drama that reaped millions for 20th Century–Fox and put first-time film star David Hedison in the public eye. Hailing from Rhode Island, the actor (real name: Albert David Hedison, Jr.) studied at New York's Neighborhood Playhouse and worked in stock until he got his break in the off-Broadway production *A Month in the Country*, starring his acting teacher Uta Hagen and directed by Michael Redgrave. He won a Theater World Award (Most Promising Newcomer) and, just as importantly, caught Hollywood's attention. Still using his real name Al, he film-debuted in the submarine story *The Enemy Below* (20th Century–Fox, 1957) with Robert Mitchum; placed under contract by Fox, he followed with *The Fly* and then the TV series *Five Fingers* (the studio changed his name to David Hedison at this time). Other early sci-fi credits include producer-director Irwin Allen's *The Lost World* (1960) and Allen's 1964–68 teleseries *Voyage to the Bottom of the Sea*.

According to one of your old press clippings, it was seeing Tyrone Power in Blood and Sand *[1941] that got you to wanting to be an actor.*

Oh, it did, yeah. I think I was around

12, very young, and my cousin took me to our neighborhood theater, the Palace Theater in Providence, Rhode Island, and we sat and I saw that thing. I was just overwhelmed with the beauty of Rita Hayworth, the marvelous Technicolor and the whole romance of it all—I went crazy! I begged my cousin, I said, "Let's see it *again*, let's see it again!" and we stayed over and saw it a second time. So that's what happened: It was that film that impressed me, and I wanted to be an actor from that time on.

Your father was a little dubious about you becoming an actor, he wanted you to follow him into the jewelry enameling business. Is he still alive?

No, he died when he was 83. Had a heart attack.

I was wondering if he lived long enough to see you successful, and to concede that you had done the right thing.

Oh, absolutely. He lived long enough to see me right through *Voyage to the Bottom of the Sea* and several years beyond. He died in 1977. It turned out fine.

Early on in your career, you were in New York, living in a $5-a-week room—

Absolutely. On East 50th Street.

And supporting yourself partly by selling your blood for $5 a pint.

I didn't do it that often but, yes, every now and then I would sell it for five bucks. And that was really good! Also, I would have part-time work. I worked at the Waldorf-Astoria Hotel, where what I would do was take care of the entertainment who came into the Empire Room. I would clean the silverware, I would do some bus duties, I would fix the candles on the tables—when they burned down, I would replace them. I had all kinds of odd jobs, and so on my time card, they didn't know what to call me. So what they put on my time card was "Candle Boy" [*laughs*]! So I was Albert Hedison, Candle Boy.

This was at the same time that you were taking courses at the Neighborhood Playhouse.

Oh, yeah.

Is it really true that, during your early 20th Century–Fox years, Fox was thinking of starring you in a remake of Blood and Sand?

Yes, they were. Fox was planning to make it again, this time with Sophia Loren. At first, they weren't going to give me the part, so I went to Catalina and worked with a guy who used to bullfight. He was teaching me all the passes and the rest of that stuff. I got one of those outfits that bullfighters wear, the hat and the whole thing, and I had pictures taken of me. Henry Ephron was going to produce it at Fox, so what I did was, I had several poses of myself taken in the outfit and I'd go to Henry's secretary and I'd said, "Just let me run into Henry's office for one minute"—and I would put a photograph on his desk. Then a week later, I'd put a *different* one on the desk [*laughs*]. I just kept doing that until *finally* he saw me in the commissary. He said, "David, we're gonna test you," and I said, "Great!" And the next thing I know, Fox shelved the whole project, and that was the end of it—I never even got to do the test. I think at the time they were concentrating on *The Sun Also Rises* [1957], which was basically the same idea. *The Sun Also Rises* with Tyrone Power again, and Ava Gardner, that great beauty.

Were you the first actor offered the title role in The Fly?

At first, Fox wasn't thinking of me for

The Fly at all, they offered it to one of the other contract players. I don't remember who it was, but he turned it down because he didn't want to have a cloth on his head for a third of the film, and then be *out* of the film for a third of the film.

Do you know how they came to think of you for it?

Billy Gordon, who was in casting, came to my house to bring me a script—I was supposed to screen test with Robert Evans for *The Fiend Who Walked the West* [1958]. When he came to the house, his wife was in the car, and I said, "Come on in for a drink." They came in and we all sat and talked—his wife also happened to be from Providence, Rhode Island. The next thing I knew, I guess Billy must have mentioned me to them for the *Fly* part. They sent me the script and—I gotta tell you something—I just fell in love with it. James Clavell wrote the screenplay, and I thought it was fabulous. After I read the script, I said, "*This* is going to be a winner. *This* film is gonna make money." And I thought it would be a wonderful acting challenge. So I jumped at it.

When Gordon came to your house with the Fiend Who Walked the West *script, it was just for you to be in Robert Evans' screen test, correct? You weren't "up" for that movie, were you?*

No, I was just in the test. Fox used their contract players in people's tests a lot. I tested with Ann-Margret and she got into Fox; I tested with Stella Stevens, she got in; Capucine did fine. By the way, the movie wasn't called *The Fiend Who Walked the West* at first, it had a different title [*Enough Rope* and *Rope Law* were the film's working titles]. Then when Evans played it, he played it like such a maniacal creature, I think they then changed it to *The Fiend Who Walked the West*.

You've talked in previous interviews about having some ideas of your own for The Fly— *ideas nobody seemed to want to hear!*

I went *running* to Buddy Adler, who was then head of production, and I said, "Buddy, this picture is going to make a lot of money. But we cannot use a fly mask. What we *must* have is progressive makeup. When the wife first pulls the black cloth off his head, you see part of *his* face and part of the Fly. As he gets worse and worse, as the Fly continues to take over, you can still see his eyes and his expressions and his pain." Buddy Adler felt that [the idea] was interesting, but I think Ben Nye, the makeup man, fought it. Ben Nye said they were gonna put me in a plaster cast and make sort of a mask and do it that way. "Besides, Al," he said, "you don't wanna come in at four o'clock in the *morning* [every day for makeup], do you?" I said, "Yyyyyyyyyyes! I'll come in at *three*! It'll be fan-*tas*-tic, we *must* do it that way [with progressive makeup]." Well, I was fought down, they did the mask. They put me in a plaster cast and they got the size of my face and the whole thing. And there we are.

But Buddy Adler thought that yours was an interesting idea.

He did, but it was turned down. Maybe Ben thought it would be too complicated, or whatever, for their budget. Oh, when I think of [the possibilities]! One of my favorite films was Fredric March in *Dr. Jekyll and Mr. Hyde* [1931]—do you remember that makeup?

It got scarier every transformation.

It was terrifying! Later I was so disappointed in Spencer Tracy's *Jekyll and Hyde*, because it didn't have the same effect as the Fredric March version.

Did you read the Playboy *short story "The Fly"?*

The Fly takes five.

I did. I got the script, read the script and then I went right to the short story. I thought, "My God, this is good stuff."

So, unlike the actor who didn't want the role because of the cloth, you didn't hesitate.

Not for a moment! That was my second film. The first one was *The Enemy Below* and *The Fly* was to be my first starring role. I thought, "This isn't science fiction shit, this is *wonderful* stuff." 'Cause it was believable! I *believed* it, I really believed it.

Did you get to meet James Clavell during the making of The Fly?

I did, and we became good friends. He was, naturally, a very intelligent man, and very much of an introvert. And he didn't like lots of actors! But for some reason, he and I hit it off very well. (That's because I'm such a humble person [*laughs*].) And we *did* have fun. We saw a lot of each other in England while I lived there for two years during the early '70s.

Did you ever mention to Clavell how much better The Fly *could have been if...*

I told him that, yes, and he thought that my way could have been interesting ... but he didn't care one way or the other. All he knew was that the picture made a lot of money [*laughs*], that's all he cared about! One thing he liked was what they did optically, that shot from the Fly's point of view looking at the wife. There were like eight different faces [in a honeycomb pattern]. He liked that.

How well could you see once you had the mask on?

Not too well, everything was rather blurry. In one scene toward the end, I had to tear the lab apart with an axe — I swung the axe all over the fucking place. And afterwards, one of the guys said, "Oh, David! You swung once, and I thought you were gonna go right through your leg." I had just missed my leg, because I *really* couldn't see anything. I was swinging that axe and knocking things over and — oh, God!

You were in your late twenties — how did you approach the role of a great man of science at that age?

I think they were a little afraid of me, because I was rather cute in those days [*laughs*]. They got me into makeup and they grayed the hair, they put gray on the sides, and they did everything they could to play my youthfulness down. I think it looked pretty good, I got away with it.

Did you have confidence that you *would get away with it?*

Oh, yes, I really felt good about it. I thought my best work was all the times I was under the cloth. In those scenes, I was reeeally feeling something. I felt the *pain* of the man, what he was going through. Some girls saw it once, and they said they were *crying*. Because it was basically a love story. When the Fly has the chalk in his hand and writes I LOVE YOU on the blackboard — all of that is *very* effective. The girls I mentioned were Michaela and Holly Clavell, the daughters of James Clavell. They were much too young to see it when it first came out, but then when they were about ten and 12, their father showed it to them in London and they were just in tears, watching it. The next time they saw me, they said [*blubbering*], "Oh, my *God*…!", all that stuff!

Patricia Owens told me the scene of you being killed by the hydraulic press was the first scene the two of you shot.

No, no, she's absolutely wrong. The very first thing that I did in the film with her was a garden scene. That scene, when we did it originally, was *very* effective. And then Fox decided that, since there were birds in the background, the scene had to be dubbed. I didn't understand dubbing very well, or how to go about doing it. And I had to catch a plane that day — they looped it the day I was taking a plane to go to London to do *The Son of Robin Hood* [1959]. So the scene has taken on a very sterile quality, because it's dubbed. Originally, with the original soundtrack, it was *so* much more alive. And it's a shame. When I saw it, I didn't even think it was my voice — I don't know *what* I did! That one scene is very disappointing to me.

Was Owens there that day too, dubbing her half of the scene with you?

No, she did hers at another time. I was only with Kurt Neumann. We were working on it together and we only had about an hour.

If it had been left up to Buddy Adler, The Fly *would have been an even more gruesome picture. He didn't think the horror of a man-fly was enough, he wanted you to be mixed up with fly and cat atoms and to have some of the physical characteristics of the cat as well as those of the fly.*

Oh, how stupid. I'm sure you know that when they made *Return of the Fly* [1959], they had a *huge*, stupid fly head on the guy. I thought that was disgusting, I really did. Somebody sent me a picture of the Fly in *Return of the Fly* to autograph, and I sent it right back with a little note: "Sorry, I was not in *Return of the Fly*." Why sign *that* stupid picture?

Makeup grayed the temples of 30-ish Hedison so he'd look more believable in his scientific role in *The Fly*.

Did you see rushes on The Fly?

No.

Is it you as the Fly in every shot of the movie?

Every shot, yeah. Everything the Fly did was me. Including the very end of the film, when he's in the spider web. What I did in that last scene was, I covered my teeth with my lips. They told me they didn't want

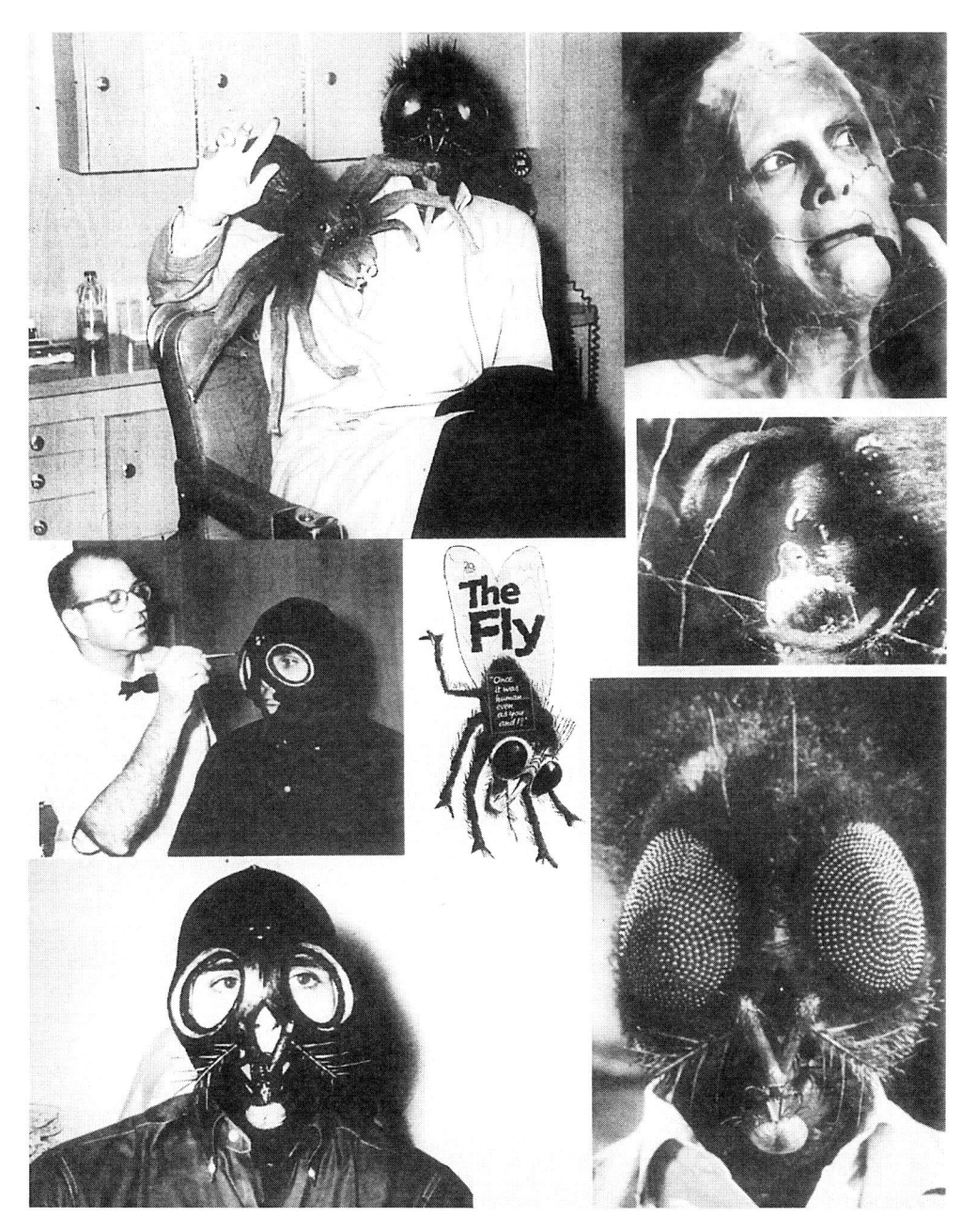

A montage of shots of Hedison in *The Fly*.

to see my teeth — they said, "Don't let us see those beautiful Hollywood teeth!" So I covered the teeth and started screaming and going, "Help me! Help me!" Now, that's *another* thing I thought could have been much more effective: In that final scene, they cranked up the speed of the sound so my screaming "Help me!" became [*in a squeaky voice*] "Help me!" way up there high. Which doesn't *sound* right! As the camera moved closer, you should have heard a *man's* voice screaming, "Help me!" Boy, I was screamin' my fuckin' *lungs* out on the set — I was screaming "Help me!" like a fuckin' *spider* was comin' at me and I was scared shitless. It was really *good*. And then when I saw the movie and I heard [*in a squeaky voice*] "Help me!" I thought, "What are they *doing*?" That's not horror—it's *funny*. Imagine if, as the camera moved in closer, you actually heard Andre Delambre *screeeeaming* for his life. That is horror. *That* is horror.

I assume you were lying in some sort of big net for that scene...?

Yes, I was, on an interior set. It was my final stuff in the film—I think. I won't swear to that, but I'm almost positive. They painted white all over my face, because people talk about the white-headed fly throughout the movie. They should have painted my tongue white too, but they left it red. There was no [prop] spider there. Lying in the web, I had to look in a certain direction and *imagine* something crawling towards me. It's called acting [*laughs*]!

What were you like at that point? That early in your career, what was your attitude on movie sets? Were you a cut-up?

At that point, I was terribly earnest. Terribly *boring*. Took it all very seriously. I remember one scene where I was going through some explanation and whatever. When the scene was over, makeup started coming over to freshen my face, and I pushed them away. "David," Patricia Owens said, "you've got dark circles under your eyes," and I said, "Patricia—*wouldn't* he? Wouldn't the scientist, at this point in his life? Of *course* he would have dark circles. He's *tired*. I don't want this powder on my face." So, you see, I was very serious, I took it *all* very seriously.

One day on the set, with Kurt Neumann, I had a huge fight. In the movie there's a scene where Andre reaches into a shot with his hand and turns a knob. Just a closeup of a hand. Well, as I walked onto the set early one morning, they had just finished shooting that. I said, "W-w-what was that?" I was told, "It was just turning a knob. Kurt did it." I said, "How could *you* do it? Why would you *do* that? That's not my hand! Kurt, you have a fat little hand—*I* don't have a hand like that! I've got long fingers! Look at my fingers, they're not like yours! That's not my hand!" And he said [*with an accent*], "It doesn't matter. It's going to be a kvik shot, nobody's going to know the difference." Well, I was furious! And what I *should* have done is say, "I'm not gonna shoot today unless we redo that scene." But I didn't, and they just kept it in. Next time you watch *The Fly*, there's a scene where Andre turns a knob—and you'll see a fat hand. And it ain't mine, kid, it's Kurt Neumann's.

Vincent Price?

When people ask me, "What was Vincent Price like to work with on *The Fly*?" I have to tell them, "I don't *know*"—because we never worked the same days. I never worked with either Herbert Marshall or Vincent, all my stuff was with Patricia and with my little boy Charlie Herbert. I did get to know Vincent Price on *Voyage to the Bottom of the Sea*, eight, nine years later. We were working on [an episode called] "The Deadly Dolls" and I was kidding around and making jokes—I was up to all kinds of nasty pranks. And Vincent looked at me in shock and he said, "David, I don't *recognize* you. You're so *funny*! When we were doing *The Fly*, you were soooo earnest!"—those are the exact words he used, "soooo earnest!" I admitted to him, as I just did to you, that I took everything so seriously in those days. So we had a lovely time on *Voyage*. In fact, I was such a cut-up and we were having *so* many laughs that he invited me to his house for dinner—Richard Basehart and Richard's

Hedison relaxes in the Fox machine shop press between takes on *The Fly*.

wife and me and my date. Anne Baxter was there, too, and some of the other Fox people. It was really nice.

When you're in the press at the end of the movie — was that an actual press?

Oh, yeah, the actual press that they used at Fox. We shot that scene in the Fox machine shop, the place where the machinists worked — that machine was really there, they used it to press metal and all that kind of stuff when they were building sets. That wasn't a set, it was an actual place. They brought in lights and the actors and the director of photography and the director and all, and we shot it.

What was Kurt Neumann like?

He was, I must say, very pleasant. He was easy to work with — he sort of let you alone. Occasionally he would say, "Why don't you try *this* instead of *that*?" or whatever. No, he was *very* easy to work with. I just had that one row with him, when he used his hand as mine.

Is your idea of a good director a director who leaves you alone?

One who leaves you alone, but realizes and appreciates what you're doing. And has the ability to *know* when you need help, and is able to make a very clean suggestion. *Not* to give you a line reading, but to give you an *idea*. Just to whisper a key phrase in your ear, like, "Why don't you try this *as if you were...*" such-and-such. The best directors, I feel, *were* actors at one point, like Syd Pollack and Mark Rydell and a lot of other wonderful directors. They know the actors and understand them.

Patricia Owens' memory of Kurt Neumann was that he was elderly and sickly.

He was in his fifties, and to us in those days, that was elderly [*laughs*]! And he was a little heavy. I know he died shortly after the film was released. What a shame. *The Fly* would have done a lot for his career.

Where did you see The Fly *for the first time?*

I came back from London after doing *Son of Robin Hood* and found that *The Fly* was a big hit. I went to see it in a theater in Westwood. I went by myself. Sat in the last row. Saw it. And left. I was disappointed in a lot of it ... disappointed that my ideas for makeup didn't work out, disappointed by that "help me, help me" [voice] — *allll* that stuff bothered me. I was disappointed in a lot of it, and thought a lot of it was quite good.

Fox opened the movie at 400 theaters simultaneously, but they had no idea the business it was going to do. After that *amazing* opening, there was a big double-page ad in *The Motion Picture Herald* that said in bold print, "THE FLY has opened — 400 theaters never saw anything so big!" [*Laughs*] Back then, that was shocking — Fox had to pull it, they couldn't use it again. That ad came out *once*, it was in *one* issue only. Today they'd leave it in!

What sets The Fly *apart from all the other monster movies of that era?*

It was in color, they were very smart to make it in color. It had a good "look" and it had a good score — the "love theme" was lovely. It was well-mounted.

And, at its heart, it was a tragic love story about a man and his wife, which no other monster movies got into back then.

Exactly. It was one of the first times that Fox had done something like that, it was one of their first science-fictions and so they were very nervous about it. They gave it an 18-day schedule and it was made for ... nothing! I got my $750 a week, or whatever it was, and that was it. And, boy, it took off.

Did you make any personal appearances with The Fly?

I don't think I did, because I was still in England making *Son of Robin Hood*. But I did on other films.

Did The Fly *help your career, or would everything else have happened the same way if* The Fly *had never been made?*

"Cake break" on the set of *The Fly*. Patricia Owens, producer-director Kurt Neumann and Hedison have first dibs over Herbert Marshall and Vincent Price (in background).

I don't think it helped it one way or the other. A lot of people enjoyed it and thought, "He's a good actor," or whatever, but I don't know if it helped it at all. In those days, I don't think being under contract helped *any*body's career. It was easygoing and you got paid every week 40–52 — you got paid 40 weeks of the year. But I think it was the worst thing I could have done in my *life*, to be put under contract to a studio. I had to turn down so much good stuff. I remember — this was like 1958 — Joe Papp wrote me a letter, he thought it would be wonderful if I came back to New York and did *Henry V* in the Park. I went to the studio head, it was Buddy again, and they wouldn't let me do it, they had a picture in mind for me. When *that* sort of thing came up, I wished I had waited a while, done more theater in New York, and *then* done a two-picture-a-year deal like Joanne Woodward and Paul Newman and those people did. They were wise, they stayed longer in New York. I just did that one play with Uta Hagen [*A Month in the Country*] and, next thing I knew, whoosh, I was off to Hollywood. Which was not a good career choice.

In the late '50s, you told an interviewer that you didn't star in the upcoming Return of the Fly — *you said, "Thank the Lord, no."*

I said "Thank the Lord, no" because I knew what they would do. In those days, when they made sequels, they were pretty awful. Not like today — today they get better and better. I just didn't want to do two Fly pictures. My career was just getting started, and I wanted to do something totally different.

A lot of your early publicity says your real name is Ara Heditsian.

And that's not true. When my grandfather came to this country, his name was Heditsian. For business purposes, he changed the name. In Armenian, -sian means "son of" and, because he was in the jewelry business, he thought it would be much easier to use -son. So he made it Hedison. Therefore my father was Albert Hedison Sr., and then when I was born, I was Albert David Hedison Jr.— that's what's on my birth certificate. And there we are!

And the first name, Ara?

Ara is an Armenian name that my grandmother used to call me. But it's not on the birth certificate, it's just an Armenian name ... named after an Armenian king who was called Ara the Beautiful.

I know from some of your earlier interviews that The Lost World *is no favorite of yours.*

I had met with Irwin Allen, and he liked me a lot. I read the script, and I thought, "I don't want to do *this*." Jill St. John in pink tights and that silly little dog and ... [*sighs*]. There was no reality to any of it. It sort of started out interestingly enough, but when we got into the dinosaurs and all that ... Jesus! A friend of mine told me, "Al, don't do this. You don't have to do this film." And I said, "Yeah, but, you know ... this one talked to me and the *other* one talked to me, and I don't really want to go on suspension, and..."

Who was it told you not to do it?

It was a woman named Else Schreiber. She was a wonderful [acting] coach who worked with Gregory Peck on all the films that he did — they would sit down and talk about them and read the scenes and all that sort of thing. She had her own house up on Doheny Drive and she worked with certain actors at Fox and all over Hollywood. You would go there with a script and you'd work on it together and run certain scenes and so on. She was marvelous. Before I started *Five Fingers* [Hedison's 1959–60 TV series], I worked with her on a couple of the episodes, just to get a feel for the character and what have you. Then *The Lost World* came up, and I couldn't figure out *any*thing on *that* script. So I brought it to *her*, to work on it. "Oh," she said, "don't do this. Don't do this. You don't *have* to do this."

But you did it, to avoid suspension.

Also, I felt they had a very good cast. They did have good people in it, like Claude Rains and Michael Rennie. Come on, if *they* were going to do it, I figured, what the hell, I'll join the team. I was stupid. I should have gone on suspension. But I did it. And I was *very* unhappy making the film.

Had you read Arthur Conan Doyle's novel The Lost World?

I had read that in school. It was certainly changed a lot in the script!

If Fox had done The Lost World *with a period setting, do you think the movie might have been better?*

I think it would have been. It could have been charming and wonderful. But maybe they didn't have it in the budget to do that.

Where did you shoot the picture?

Lost World was shot on the Fox lot, which was then a huge lot. The jungle was

Hedison (with cave girl Vitina Marcus) avoided getting caught a second time in a giant spider's web in *The Lost World*.

all on the back lot — in fact, the whole film was shot on the lot. The cave was a set which I think was used in an earlier film, *Journey to the Center of the Earth* [1959]. Fox would always recycle their sets and redress them so it looked like another set.

What memories of working with Claude Rains?

I remember going into his dressing room and bombarding him with questions, because I knew he did a lot of films at Warner Brothers. As a kid growing up, Warner Brothers was my favorite studio. James Cagney, I *loved* his work, and Humphrey Bogart and Peter Lorre and Sydney Greenstreet and *The Maltese Falcon* [1941], and Bette Davis and Ida Lupino, and Max Steiner and Franz Waxman, who wrote the music — that whole *group* of people. I just was *thrilled* with Warner Brothers pictures. In fact, when I did my play [*A Month in the Country*] in New York and I was getting all kinds of offers from studios, for tests and whatnot, I was terribly disappointed when it was zeroed down to 20th Century–Fox — I wanted to be with Warner Brothers! But it just didn't work out.

Anyway, back to Claude Rains: I would be asking him all kinds of questions: "What was *he* like? What was *she* like? What was it like working with Bette Davis in *Mr. Skeffington* [1944]?" He told me, "After she saw a rough cut, she called me on the phone and she said, 'Why, Claude, you bastard, you stole the picture!'" He was telling me all these lovely little stories about people so I just hounded him, I was talking to him all the time. Thrilling fellow, wwwonderful actor.

Top: A breakaway "Hollywood airplane" provides background for Irwin Allen, Jill St. John and Hedison in this *Lost World* behind-the-scenes shot. *Bottom:* Sunny modern-day California can be seen behind Hedison and Jill St. John as they act in a scene from *The Lost World*.

And he didn't mind.

Didn't mind at *all*.

Did he mind being in The Lost World?

[*Pause*] I don't know. Now that I'm older, I know why a lot of these actors did what they did: Because there were bills to pay, rents and mortgages. That's what it's like. When you're a young actor, you don't think of those things. You say no [to one offer], you say yeah [to another] ... and, when you're young, the world wants you anyway. As you get older, the parts are fewer and farther between. So I can now understand why a lot of these actors did what they did. I remember being on a segment of *Voyage* ["The Traitor"]—a particularly shitty script—and there was George Sanders playing a guest role. This was toward the end of his time. A wonderful man, very sweet, very shy ... did his part very well ... and I thought, "Why the *fuck* is he doing this thing??" What were they paying then, $2500 an episode? I thought it was strange; I thought, "Maybe he *knows* Irwin and he's doing it as a favor." But, it's obvious to me now, the guy just needed the money. And that's the reality of life, my friend.

It must be tough to give a good performance in movies and TV shows that are that *far-out ... but you guys managed to do it. And not a lot of you have gotten enough recognition.*

Well, the thing is, [people] never recognize science fiction performances. Ever. As good as they are. Jeff Goldblum in *The Fly* [1986] gave an extraordinary performance, and he wasn't even nominated for an award. And I thought he should have been. Also, there were some marvelous performances in [David] Cronenberg's *Dead Ringers* [1988]—the English actor Jeremy Irons played two parts, and he was wonderful. And no one recognizes that.

Because it's science fiction.

What they will recognize is an actor who's like the guy next door and who plays a real emotion. Lost his child and starts to cry. *That* they will recognize.

You were a young actor with, I can tell, the proper respect for the older movies and the older stars. How did it feel to find yourself billed above Claude Rains in The Lost World?

Oh, it was embarrassing! Also on *The Fly*: It was Al Hedison, Patricia Owens, Vincent Price and Herbert Marshall. I thought, "Boy, talk about chutzpah!" [*Laughs*] But it was nothing *I* did, it was the studio, building up their new stars. I just was embarrassed to even look at the credits because, my God, Vincent Price had been around, and Herbert Marshall—jeez, the stuff *he'd* done. And there was my name, up above theirs. It just didn't seem fair.

The big 1960 actors' strike hit while The Lost World *was in production. Was there an effort to make up for lost time when you finally did get back to work?*

When the strike was over, we worked long hours to get the picture over with so they could release it by a certain date. Financially, the strike didn't affect me at all because I was under contract, but some of the other actors, of course, weren't being paid during the strike. When there's a strike, you stop work and there were no salaries [for freelance actors]. I was on what in those days was called a 40–52: They paid you for 40 weeks of the year whether you worked or not, so my salary didn't stop. But the other actors, the ones who were not under contract, were getting no salary until they resumed production.

You made some personal appearances with

The Lost World when it was new—in New York, for one place.

I made a couple of appearances for Irwin, to push that film. They sent me on a little tour, a little junket. Then, about a year later, Irwin sent me the script of the movie *Voyage to the Bottom of the Sea* [1961] because he wanted me to play the Capt. Crane part. I thought, "I will no more work for this guy on this kind of filming again—" [*laughs*]. "Never!" I just thanked him for it and I said I couldn't, I was working on something else, I wouldn't be able to do it and so forth and so on. I got out of it—and I *wasn't* put on suspension. I got out of it, it was fine, and that was the *end* of it. Bob Sterling got the part.

Then the TV series [of *Voyage*] came up. This sounds like I'm bragging, but I don't mean to brag, I'm just trying to tell you the truth of the situation: Irwin just *insisted* that I play that part. And again I turned it down. I went back East, and Irwin called me back East and he said, "It'll be wonderful for your career! All the people will see you on television!" blah blah, so forth and so on. I said, "It's not the kind of thing I want to do, Irwin. I want to do, like, a doctor show, or a *this*, or a *that* … something with a little character. I don't want to work with photo effects and all that stuff." So I turned it down again. Then I went to Egypt for an international television festival, because *Five Fingers* was very successful there. Also there were other stars like Terry Moore and Bob Conrad and so on and so forth. Roger Moore was doing *The Saint*, so he flew in from London; that's when we first met, 1963. On my way back home, I stopped off in London and my agent Jean Diamond called and she said, "Roger Moore is doing a *Saint*, and there's a part in it he thinks you're very right for." So I stayed in London and did it—it was called "Luella." Anyway, while I'm there, my phone rings—it's Irwin Allen. He *didn't* give up! I said, "Irwin, I told you, *I don't want to do it.*" And that was it—finished. I thought!

Two days later, four o'clock in the morning, he calls again … wakes me up in the middle of the night. He tells me he's got Richard Basehart to play the Admiral. So now I start thinking, "Jesus Christ, if he's got Richard Basehart to do this shit…" I talked to Roger Moore about it, and Roger said, "What the hell. Might be a lot of fun, it might be successful, you'll make a little money…." He kind of talked me into it. I called Irwin and I said, "Okay, we're on." And that was the beginning of it—I was on *Voyage* for four years. But for *years* I wondered, "*Why* the hell did Irwin insist? *Why* did he want me for it so much?" I figured it was because he liked me. And he *did* like me. We used to *fight*, but he *liked* me! Then, one day just about two years ago [1998], taking a nap, it finally hits me: "God *damn* it, I know why he wanted me so badly. Because he had all this stock footage on me!" [*Laughs*] Irwin could use stock footage of me from *The Lost World*, he could use stock footage of me from *The Enemy Below*, he had that foolish [electronic] board from *The Fly*, he had all these things, "pieces" of Al Hedison, all over the place! And he used them—he did a *Lost World*–type segment, you remember ["Turn Back the Clock," 1964]? A lot of my stuff from the original picture was in that. So these days I'm thinking maybe *that's* why he was so insistent! As I say, this dawned on me maybe two years ago—the fact that Irwin Allen kept insisting on me crossed my mind, and suddenly the light bulb came on: "Hey, *wait* a minute. It *wasn't* because he loved me so much…!" [*Laughs*]

You mentioned that you and Irwin Allen used to fight. About what?

About more characterization [on *Voyage to the Bottom of the Sea*], and not just effects and acting like a robot. Richard

Basehart and I, our parts were interchangeable. The characters weren't all that specific, so if Richard were out sick, they would just give me his lines! And there was none of this "Oh, come on, I can't. Those are Richard's lines, that's *his* character, those lines shouldn't be coming from me"—because *it made no difference*. They could have given me *Kowalski's* lines and it would have made no difference [*laughs*]. We were all playing the same kind of character and saying the same kind of words. You just had to bring as much of yourself into the part as you possibly could. Those are the kinds of things Irwin and I would be arguing about. I was at a recent convention with Bob May, the guy who played the Robot on *Lost in Space*, and he came to me and told me that he used to see Irwin and me arguing. Finally he went to Irwin one day and he asked, "Irwin, why do you and David shout at each other? Why are you always arguing?" And Irwin said [*shouting, with a Brooklyn accent*], "Because I *love* him!" [*Laughs*]

Did you get along with Allen better on Lost World, *or did you find things to fight with him about then too?*

He more or less left me alone on *The Lost World*. But *Voyage to the Bottom of the Sea* was really much more personal, because in a way it was my show and it was Richard's show. It meant more to me, and I wanted to get everything right, on target. Anyway, it didn't work that way!

Funny thing: Irwin would have these lovely dinner parties at his house, and I'd be invited. I would go to his house, and I'd be the only actor there from any of his shows. I remember I went to, like, a New Year's Eve party there—these were important parties with wonderful people. He might have some of the oldtimers like Peter Lorre and Groucho Marx, but he would never have any of the younger people, and I'd think, "Jeez, I'm the only [young actor] here...!" I thought it was quite an honor. For some reason, he liked me.

Did you ever fight with him about money?

I remember, about the third season of *Voyage*, going to Irwin because Richard Basehart was making a hell of a lot of money and I was getting piddle-dee-dee next to what Richard was making. And I was getting a lot of fan mail at Fox, and they were writing [episodes] for me, and whatever. So I went to Irwin and I said, "Listen, I really think I should get some more money." And there we went again, a shouting match. Finally he said to me [*in a loud, whiny Brooklyn accent*], "There *is* no mawww, Basehart's *got* it awwwll!" [*Laughs*] The deal on *Voyage*, the ownership of the show, was: 25 percent went to Fox, 25 percent to ABC, 25 percent to Irwin and 25 percent to Richard.

Good grief!

And about a month before Richard died [in 1984], I had lunch with him, and he *still* hadn't seen any part of that 25 percent!

Do you ever watch The Fly *or* Lost World *these days? Or any of your old movies?*

No, I don't. It's strange; I don't like to look at them, I don't know why. There was something quite good on American Movie Classics the other day, a documentary called *The Fly Papers* [a 2000 documentary about the five *Fly* films]. It was *very* interesting. And then *right* after that, they showed *The Fly* ... and that's when I flicked off the TV. I just didn't want to go home again. I saw it once, and that's enough.

And The Lost World—*obviously!*—*falls into the same category.*

Oh, obviously! In fact, I don't think I

Anatomy of a mermaid: Hedison and Diane Webber in a 1967 *Voyage to the Bottom of the Sea* episode.

ever saw that whole picture. Not from beginning to end. I've seen parts of it — I'd put the TV on and there'd be *The Lost World*, and I'd stand there and watch it for about five minutes. And then I'd ... flick it off.

Have you done any movies lately?

I just finished a film in Italy with Michael York and Franco Nero and Diane Venora. It's a sequel to a very successful film made a year or two ago, *Omega Code*—this one is called *Omega Code 2*. It'll be out in August of 2001. I play Michael York's father and I age three times in the film. I start at 40, then I'm in my 60s, and I end up in the early 80s. It's very interesting.

So no thoughts yet of retiring?

Oh, cut it out! No way. I'm much too young [*laughs*]! Good Lord...!

DAVID HEDISON FILMOGRAPHY

As Al Hedison
The Enemy Below (20th Century–Fox, 1957)
The Fly (20th Century–Fox, 1958)
Rally 'Round the Flag, Boys! (voice only; 1958)
The Son of Robin Hood (20th Century–Fox, 1959)

As David Hedison
The Lost World (20th Century–Fox, 1960)
Marines, Let's Go! (20th Century–Fox, 1961)
The Greatest Story Ever Told (United Artists, 1965)
Kemek (*For Love or Murder*) (GHM Productions, 1970)
Live and Let Die (United Artists, 1973)
ffolkes (*Assault Force*) (Universal, 1980)
The Naked Face (MGM/United Artists/Cannon Group, 1984)
Hollywood Dreaming (*Smart Alec*) (1986)
License to Kill (United Artists, 1989)
Undeclared War (1990)
Mach 2 (2000)
Megiddo: The Omega Code 2 (8X Entertainment, 2001)

It Came from Hollywood (Paramount, 1982) features footage of Hedison in *The Fly*.

KATHLEEN HUGHES

It was easy to be bad, to be evil. I loved those parts.

Blonde, busty Kathleen Hughes specialized in villainous vixens and "other woman" roles throughout her movie heyday, the 1950s. This was an unexpected career development for the Hollywood-born actress, who pictured herself playing "innocent" parts, but she quickly got into the sinister swing of things, portraying pulchritudinous predators with panache in a string of movie and TV melodramas. Amidst her "bad girl" roles, she tackled a supporting part in *It Came from Outer Space* (1953), donning a tight-fitting sweater and skirt as the trampy girlfriend of Russell Johnson ("It was in 3-D and I knew I'd get a chance to project more than usual"). In a switch from her usual routine of femme fatale roles, she was the victimized ingenue, menaced by snake woman Faith Domergue, in the supernatural suspenser *Cult of the Cobra* (1955).

The niece of screenwriter F. Hugh Herbert and a cousin of Simone Signoret, Hughes had designs on an acting career right from childhood. Following a stint at Fox (where she played unsubstantial parts), she landed a co-starring role as a conniving coed in star-director Paul Henreid's *For Men Only* (1952), a drama about hazing in college fraternities. Hughes next scored a contract at Universal-International, where she had an opportunity to strut her stuff in yet more wicked roles.

Long married to veteran producer Stanley Rubin (*The Narrow Margin*, *River of No Return*, *Promise Her Anything*), Hughes is still occasionally active in movies and TV and is a popular guest at celebrity autograph shows.

Was it inevitable that you'd become interested in acting, growing up in Hollywood?

I think it *was*. My uncle was F. Hugh Herbert, who wrote [the plays] *The Moon Is Blue*, *For Love or Money*, *Kiss and Tell* and a radio show called *Meet Corliss Archer*. He used to take my two cousins and me on the sets of movies and to the radio broadcasts of *Meet Corliss Archer*, and I spent a lot of time at his house when I was a child, sitting across the table from directors and [other Hollywood types]. I just got interested very, very early.

Who were some of the stars you saw on the sets of these movies?

It's funny, but this is the one picture

that I really, really remember: My uncle took the three of us to Republic Studios, where they were making *Hit Parade of 1941* [1940] with Ann Miller and Patsy Kelly. We were on the set for quite a while and I just thought it was absolutely wonderful, and their names just stuck in my mind even though I wasn't that familiar with them in those days. I've just never forgotten that experience, it just looked like so much fun.

The first studio to place you under contract was Fox. How did you land there?

The bug really got me, I knew that I just *had* to be an actress, when I was about 13 and I went to see a Donald O'Connor picture. I came out of the movie thinking, "Now, *that* is what I have got to do. I just *have* to." So I entered a scholarship contest when I was about 17; this was when the G.I.s were coming back [after the War] and going to school on the G.I. Bill, and they needed girls to play opposite the *guys* in the drama school. All you had to do was send your picture in. So I sent them my picture and I won a scholarship. While I was under scholarship at this place which no longer exists, the Geller Workshop, a talent scout from Fox came and saw me in a play called *Night Over Taos* by Maxwell Anderson. I was really *terrible* in it [*laughs*] — I really think I was awful! And I was *not* feeling well that night, and I had taken a lot of pain killers because I was having *very* bad cramps. In the course of a scene in the first act, I was wearing this beautiful costume, a lace mantilla and everything, but I had to stand at the back of the stage for the whole act. And as the curtains closed after the first act, I passed out! I came to, and of course I then went on for the second act, and I was told that there was a talent scout in the audience and he wanted to *see* me. And, sure enough, he wanted me to come out to Fox and make a test!

I told my uncle F. Hugh, who was under contract to Fox as a writer-director. I told *him* about it and he was sort of astounded, because he thought that I was much too tall for pictures, I was five-foot-nine and he said that was *much* too tall because most of the leading men were short. But he said *he* would make my test — direct it. And he wrote and directed just the *cutest* test — how I wish I could get my hands on it. It was what was called a personality test. He had me sitting at a dressing table and the camera was the mirror, and it looked at first like I was looking into a *smaller* mirror on the dressing table and blowing kisses at it. He was talking to me [from off-camera] and I was answering him, and he said, "Stop *admiring* yourself." I said, "I'm *not* admiring myself, I'm looking at a picture of this wonderful, wonderful man," and I was going on and on. I kept picking up this framed thing and going on and *on* about this wonderful man. And finally at the end, he said, "All right now, this is ridiculous. I want to see who it is that you're admiring and blowing kisses to," and so I turn it around to the camera and it's a picture of [Fox executive] Darryl F. Zanuck [*laughs*]! So I got the contract! But it was *so* cute! And it *must* still be around, because in *one* of the tests that I made while I was under contract, I supported Rock Hudson in *his* screen test —

At Fox?

At Fox! And *that* screen test was shown on AMC recently — they dug it up. He was *nobody* then, he was just one of the actors I did a test with. It was a very, very cute test, written and directed by someone I just adored, Richard Sale, and I gave Rock Hudson his first screen kiss. And the studio looked at it and went [*Hughes makes a disparaging sound*] and they just put it on the shelf. And he then went on to Universal, where he became a big star.

In all your Fox pictures that I've seen, your parts were pretty smallish. Did you play many good roles at Fox?

No, all the good roles were in the *tests*. I made a test with Bob Horton, I made a test with Peter Graves, and did some excellent scenes in the tests. But I made 14 movies at Fox (I was cut out of two or three of them) and it was a learning experience and it was a lot of fun because I worked with a lot of the big stars—I worked with Cornel Wilde and Ida Lupino and Dan Dailey. It was a *lot* of fun.

At what point was your name changed to Kathleen Hughes?

That was at Fox. It was so funny—they were sending some publicity to Europe, and they said, "We've gotta change your name *right* now, because we're sending out this publicity, and you've *got* to have a new name because Betty von Gerkan would just look *terrible* on a marquee!" Little did anybody know that, a couple of years later, Betsy von Furstenberg would come along and be on a marquee [*laughs*]! But in *those* days, whatever they wanted, okay! fine! whatever you want! We had it narrowed down to Kathleen Hughes and Juliet Ames, and I thought Kathleen Hughes sounded a little more *sincere* than Juliet Ames. We had gone through hundreds and hundreds of names, and I don't really know how the Kathleen Hughes name was picked. My mother's name is Kathleen and my uncle was Hugh, but I don't know whether *he* had any input. I just don't remember.

Did you leave Fox before you made For Men Only *for Lippert?*

I had a seven-year Fox contract, but that's with an option every year. At the end of the *third* year, they dropped my option, and I freelanced for nine months. It was during that time that I did *For Men Only*.

Oh, I *loved* that movie. I had always wanted to be another Jeanne Crain, I had *never* thought of myself as a sexpot—never!

Never thought of yourself as a sexpot, or as a "bad girl"?

Never! I had always thought of myself sort of as *Alice in Wonderland*, sort of pure and innocent. When I read for the part in *For Men Only*, they said I would have to cut my hair and become a blonde, and I said *fine*. I mean, in *those* days, I would have *shaved* my head, I would have done *any*thing to get the part—I guess I still *would* [*laughs*]! That was a real "new beginning," when I did *that*.

Was it tough to play a meanie?

Oh, no, it was so *easy*—oh, that was one of the easiest parts I ever played. I don't know why, but it just *was*. It was *so* easy, and I loved every minute of it. Paul Henreid was *the* most wonderful man, I *adored* him, he was so nice to work with. The whole bunch, everybody connected with the picture, was wonderful, it was a very joyful experience.

And then Universal—how did you get your foot in the door there?

Well, I did a lot of television shows while I was freelancing—I used to do *The Alan Young Show*, *The Ed Wynn Show* and all of these shows that were going out live over the air as you did them, which was so scary! Then one day I got a part on *The Frank Sinatra Show*, which they did live at CBS—I had been cast as a sexy nurse in a psychiatrist's office, in a little skit with Frank Sinatra and Leo Durocher. Well, one of Frank Sinatra's best friends, Don McGuire, who died recently [1999], was in the audience and he came backstage after the dress rehearsal and introduced himself, and said that he thought I should be at

Universal, and would I be interested? And I said, "Sure!" [*Laughs*] He asked, "Do you have any film?" and I said, "Well, I just finished a movie called *For Men Only* and I've got a terrific part in it." He told Universal, they sent for the film and they signed me.

And your first part there was Sally and Saint Anne, *if my research is right.*

It is. When I was having my wardrobe fittings for that film (I had a lot of costume changes), the director Rudy Maté came into wardrobe to see all of the changes, to approve them or disapprove them. They would put me in an outfit and he would come in and he'd shake his head from side to side. No matter what I modeled for him, he was shaking his head. And I was thinking, "Gee, I wonder why he doesn't *like* it ... " Well, I found out later that this was a *tic* [*laughs*] — he *loved* the clothes, but he had this tic which caused him to shake his head from side to side!

Then I had a *horrible* experience. Rudy Maté turned me over to an assistant director or a dialogue director — Rudy wanted this guy to coach me on the part. This guy gave me terrible, terrible readings — I just didn't understand why he wanted me to *do* it this way. So we worked on it and then I went back to show Rudy, and Rudy looked at me in *horror* and asked me, "Why are you *doing* it like that?" I looked at the guy who had just *made* me do it that way — I was very shy and I didn't make waves and I didn't "fink" on people. I looked at him, and he just sat there, very blandly, didn't say a word. And I was too shy to say, "Well, *this*

Three-D or not three-D, "Iamazon" Kathleen Hughes (five-feet-nine) always projected nicely on movie screens.

jerk *told* me to do it like that!" *That* was sort of ... unpleasant! But I ended up doing it *my* way, and everything was fine. *Except*, Rudy never *wanted* me in that part, he wanted Barbara Lawrence. He had done a picture with Barbara and that's who he wanted for that part. And it's never pleasant to do a part that you're not "wanted" for.

Even though you only had a small part in It Came from Outer Space, *it was reportedly a "breakthrough" role for you.*

I heard that Universal was going to do their first 3-D movie, *It Came from Outer Space*, so I got hold of the script. I'd already heard that Barbara Rush and Richard Carlson were doing the leads, and so I looked through the script to see if there was anything *I* could play and I found this little part [Jane, Russell Johnson's girlfriend]. I thought that would be fun. So I went to the front office and I said, "*I* want to play that part"—and *they* said, "This role is much too small. You just played a second lead in *Sally and Saint Anne*. You need to do bigger parts." I said, "It's in *3-D*. How can it be too small? It's in *3-D*. Please, please, pleeeease!" I just begged and begged and begged. And then they used me to test the 3-D cameras—because I was so three-dimensional [*laughs*]! They had me in a bathing suit, parading up and down on a little platform—that's how they tested their cameras. (And that's why there's a clip of me at the end of *It Came from Outer Space* in a bathing suit—that was from the camera test. So I was glad that I had done that, because it gave me some extra footage!) Anyway, I finally wore them down and they said, "Well, *all right*, but it's awfully small ... " But *I* was so glad.

It's funny, they did a lot of ad stills after the movie, and you've probably seen the one of me with my hands up, screaming—which of course I didn't do in the movie, in the movie all I did was go to the police station to report my boyfriend Russ Johnson missing. (Russ had also been signed by Universal from *For Men Only*. So the *two* of us were *both* signed from that one movie.) That one shot of me screaming is the picture that will not die [*laughs*]—it is used *every*where! Absolutely everywhere! For two months, it's been in the magazine *The Big Reel* advertising a big [celebrity autograph] show to which I was *not* invited—I wonder if they even know that it's me! And it was in Tower Video a couple of years ago, advertising a huge sale, and it's been used on party invitations and cocktail napkins, it was in *Newsweek* magazine when the comet was coming—it showed me recoiling from a comet [*laughs*]! It goes on and on and on ... and I just *love* it, because it'll *never* die! And that's because I was in *It Came from Outer Space*! I get such a kick out of it, every time it appears somewhere else.

What memories of Richard Carlson and Barbara Rush?

Oh, I've known Barbara for years and I like Barbara very much. I'm a fan of hers, I think she's wonderful. Richard Carlson I had a *crush* on when I was a little girl. When I was a little girl, my uncle once took my two cousins and me over to Richard Carlson's house, and I just thought he was the handsomest, cutest, most wonderful person. And when I did *The Glass Web*, I at first heard that it was going to be Richard Carlson [in the male lead], and I thought, "Oh! How nice! At *last*! A dream come true!" And I was so *disappointed* when the part was given instead to John Forsythe—who turned out to be such a wonderful person. And Richard Carlson was *not* a very nice person! No, he wasn't! Although we didn't work together, I kind of hung around the set of *It Came from Outer Space* to get to know him, because I *had* admired him so much. But the more I got to know him [*sigh*] ... the less I *liked* him!

What did he say or do that turned you off on him?

"The picture that will not die": Kathleen Hughes reacts to off-camera horrors in the popular *It Came from Outer Space* publicity shot.

Oh, he just told terrible stories. I don't want to go into it, but in talking to him, the things that he told I just didn't *like*. They were stories that a not-very-nice person would tell.

About other actors?

Yes, other actors. And I just didn't think it was nice, and it was stuff that I would have just as soon *not* heard.

He was telling you these stories to try to shock you?

No. Just to "entertain" me, I guess.

Any other memories of It Came from Outer Space?

I just know that I loved doing it. And any time it's showing around town, and they're showing it in 3-D, I *always* go. I just love to see it, and I love the audience reaction when I come on the screen — I get a big kick of it. There's *always* a reaction, so I enjoy that.

Did you have any say in the wardrobe you wore in the movie?

No. I *never* had any say in the wardrobe. But I guess that was a pretty good outfit [*laughs*]!

Universal liked to say that It Came from Outer Space *was the picture that launched you. Was that the movie that got your career on a roll?*

I really don't know. If so, I was never aware of it. I think *For Men Only* was the one that really got me noticed.

In a 1954 interview, you said that if you were asked to pose nude, you definitely would think about it.

That's funny, I don't remember ever saying that. Oh, [the publicity people] made up so *much*! Oh!

Were you ever embarrassed by things they made up?

Oh, yes—*terribly* embarrassed. Like once, when [the U.S.] was trying to get the MiG pilots to surrender, the publicity department did this *awful* thing, they said that I was offering myself as a *date* to the first MiG pilot who surrendered [*laughs*]! Oh, I just wanted to *die*—I thought that was horrible! I got a nasty letter from somebody, and I wrote back and I said, "Look, it wasn't *my* idea, it was the publicity department!"

Was that Universal?

Yes.

For Men Only did type you as a "wicked woman" in the movies. If you could have picked your parts, is that the type of role you'd have gone for?

That *was* the kind of role I liked, what I had in *The Glass Web, For Men Only* and *Three Bad Sisters* [1956]. I was *really* bad in *Three Bad Sisters*, and I loved horse-whipping Marla English [Hughes' sister in the movie]. Although I was actually horse-whipping a pillow on the bed, it was still great fun! It was easy to be *bad*, to be *evil*. I *loved* those parts.

You had no desire to change, once you had started playing those parts?

Oh, no! And then I was really terribly miscast in *Cult of the Cobra*. Again, I would never have turned down a picture— [Universal] said, "Do a picture," so I did the picture. But I felt that it was wrong for me. The director [Francis D. Lyon] hated me; I *haaaated* the director. It was a very, very unpleasant experience.

Do you have any idea why Francis Lyon hated you?

No! But, as I say, I *was* miscast, and I think somebody else would have been much better in it. He just didn't like my performance, and I didn't like his direction.

Early on, Universal considered Myrna Hansen and Mala Powers for that part. Maybe he would have preferred one of them.

Oh, yes. But I just never ever wanted to make waves. Whatever they said, "Fine! I'll do it!"

Apart from the fact that he gave you a hard time, was Lyon a good director?

No, I really thought he was a bad director because he would give me direction, that was kind of embarrassing direction, in a loud, clear voice, so that ev-er-y-bod-y on the set would hear. He'd say, "You're being too coy!" and he'd say this so the whole set heard it! I don't think that's very nice. A good director would have taken me aside and told me quietly how he wanted the scene played.

Also, I came down with just horrible intestinal flu a few days into the picture—a kind of intestinal flu where you don't know *which* end is going to erupt first [*laughs*]! I was deathly ill and I was in bed for a couple of days, and they kept calling me and saying, "We *need* you, come back, come back!" I came back, and just by chance I walked past the assistant director's desk and I saw there were notes to the front office or the production office that said I had held up production by coming in late.

By coming in late that very day?

Yes, that very day. They had phoned me and told me to get in as fast as I could, and I said, "Well, I can be there at such-and-such a time, that's the best I can do." And then when I got there, I saw this memo that said I had come in *many* hours late and screwed up *every*thing for them. I didn't say *any*thing about it, as far as I can remember, but I *was* outraged, because I was *so* sick, and I came back before I was totally recovered. And they treated me so badly! I mean, up 'til then I'd always had the big star's dressing room. Well, this was my last Universal film — I think my option had already been dropped — and so I had this crummy little canvas dressing room on the set, and it was freezing. Even though it was on the stage, it was *very* very cold, and there were all these holes in the canvas. I was just treated so badly!

The Production Report you talked about —

I wish I could remember exactly what it said.

You ready to hear it?

Yes!!

Daily Production Report, November 5, 1954 — "Unable to get hold of Kathleen Hughes, who promised to be home all day waiting for her call — "

That's such bullshit, I was in bed!

"Casting unable to get hold of her at noon when she was needed. She called at 2:05."

I was home in bed, *and they didn't call me.* They wrote that in the report to cover up their own mistake. I had been in bed for days! Now, in fairness, those were the days before answering machines and I might have been in the bathroom when they called [*laughs*], because I was spending an awful lot of time in the bathroom. But the bathroom was right next to the bedroom, and I know I would have heard the phone! That's so rotten, and *that* just made it a really, really bad experience. Really the only bad experience I *had*!

I know you didn't work much with Faith Domergue, but any memory of what she was like?

I did work with her and I liked her very much. I thought she was beautiful, I thought she was a very good actress.

None of your Cult of the Cobra *co-stars went on to be movie stars, but they all went on to be big TV stars — Marshall Thompson, David Janssen, Jack Kelly and Richard Long.*

Marshall Thompson I never really knew. I liked David Janssen very much. I didn't know him that well, but we were in classes together at Universal and I thought he was very, very nice. I *loved* Jack Kelly, Jack Kelly was the *best*. He was just a lovely person. I was heartbroken when I heard that he died. I also loved Richard Long. I didn't see *Cult of the Cobra* for many, many years after I made it, because it only played for about a week, and I was out of town at the time. I kind of liked the end of it. I hated all the beginning scenes that I was in, but I sort of enjoyed the later scenes.

You acted a lot throughout the '50s, but after that you worked a lot less. Why was that?

Well, it was different when I was under contract — there was always another picture coming up! I think it's just [the fact that] the older you get, the less they want you.

Showgirl Kathleen watches as Marshall Thompson battles the *Cult of the Cobra* snake with a coat rack.

I found one old publicity blurb that said that you were going to be on TV's Peyton Place *along with your baby.*

Oh, yes! I started working on *Peyton Place*—a good friend of ours, a director, Walter Doniger, was doing a *lot* of *Peyton Place*, so one day I said to him, "I'd sure love to be on *Peyton Place*. I would do *any*thing—I'd do one line just to get on *Peyton Place*." He said, "You *mean* it? You'd do one line?" I said, "Sure! I would just like to be *on* it." Well, wouldn't you know, he gave me one line [*laughs*]. I was playing a nurse, and the line was, "Yes, doctor."

Well, one of the biggies connected with the show said, "You know, you did that tiny part very well. It isn't *easy* to just say, 'Yes, doctor' and look like it's really happening." So that led to more appearances on *Peyton Place*. I started playing a nurse and I *kept* playing a nurse—that's all I ever played on the show! Then I was pregnant [in real life] with my last child and I worked through most of the pregnancy. (My pregnancies never showed—I was thinner when I was pregnant than I am now, which is pretty embarrassing [*laughs*]!) The last two or three months of my pregnancy I was bedridden, so I said, "I can't work any more until after the baby is born." The baby was born, and about a week after he was born they sent me a [*Peyton Place*] script—in it, I was the nurse who took Dorothy Malone to the birthing room, just a few lines. Then, on the very last page of the script, it mentioned a stock shot of a newborn baby crying in the nursery—that was going to be *her* baby. I said, "My God, that fits the description of *my* baby"—it was exactly the right size, sex, color, *every*thing of my baby. So I called 'em and I said yes, of course I could do the part, and I said, "I have a baby that fits the description. Do you *have* to use a stock shot, or can you use a real baby? I'll have to *bring* my baby to the set anyway, 'cause I'm breast-feeding." And they said "Sure!" So they sent someone over to the house to look at the baby and take a picture of him — and he got the job and he worked for a *year* on *Peyton Place*!

Who was on the show more often, you or the baby?

Oh, *he* [*laughs*]! That's my youngest son Michael.

You were in a couple of fairly recent movies — Ironweed *[1987] and* The Couch Trip *[1988] — and you were cut out of both of them!*

That's true! I had the *best* scene in *Ironweed*, it was such fun. And how I loved that director, Hector Babenco, we hit it off so well. Originally I was called to New York to read for the part of Jack Nicholson's wife. Jack had given my name to Casting, as he was familiar with my work — which just blew my mind! Well, I read the book on the plane and I didn't feel that I could play it right. It was the same kind of a thing where I had been so wrong for *Cult of the Cobra* — I felt that I could not do a good job as his wife. But there was this *one* little part referred to in the book as the Hot Lady — she was a real slut who had sex with the trash man, this filthy, disgusting trash man, as he made his rounds! In the picture, Jack Nicholson gets a day's job with the trash man, and the trash man is talking about this "hot lady" who has sex with him and *loves* an audience. He says to Jack Nicholson, "If you *like*, you can come and watch us through the window, because she loves an audience." And so we did the scene and it was wonderful — while I'm having sex, I see Jack Nicholson looking through the window. He's sort of reluctant, he doesn't really *want* to watch — and I smile and I wave at him and continue having sex with this filthy man! I got to see it in dailies *with* Jack Nicholson and *with* Meryl Streep — we were all there. And it was marvelous, I was so thrilled with that scene. Well, the picture was 40 minutes too long, and it was *not* a comedy — and this was a hysterically funny scene which was *really* out of place in this very, very serious movie. So, of course, that was one of the first scenes to go. But, oh, I loved that scene, how I *wished* I could have a copy of it! But I couldn't...

And in *The Couch Trip*, I had, again, a *very*, very funny scene as a Gucci lady, dressed head to toe in Gucci, with Gucci luggage, two poodles with Gucci sweaters and Gucci leashes. But it slowed down Dan Aykroyd's entry into the scene ... and this was another movie that was too long. So they cut it. But it was a wonderful part, and so funny.

And you'd act again today if you were asked?

Oh, yes, yes! I go on interviews all the time, auditions. I went on one for a commercial last week, and the week before I went on one for a TV show called *The King of Queens*. I didn't *get* them — but that's not gonna stop me [*laughs*]! I plan to be in the Players Directory forever, to have an agent forever, and I will act until the day I die!

KATHLEEN HUGHES FILMOGRAPHY

Road House (20th Century–Fox, 1948)
Mr. Belvedere Goes to College (20th Century–Fox, 1949)
Mother Is a Freshman (20th Century–Fox, 1949)
It Happens Every Spring (20th Century–Fox, 1949)
I'll Get By (20th Century–Fox, 1950)
For Heaven's Sake (20th Century–Fox, 1950)

My Blue Heaven (20th Century–Fox, 1950)
Mister 880 (20th Century–Fox, 1950)
No Way Out (20th Century–Fox, 1950)
Where the Sidewalk Ends (20th Century–Fox, 1950)
When Willie Comes Marching Home (20th Century–Fox, 1950)
Take Care of My Little Girl (20th Century–Fox, 1951)
I'll See You in My Dreams (Warners, 1951)
For Men Only (*The Tall Lie*) (Lippert, 1952)
Sally and Saint Anne (Universal, 1952)
It Came from Outer Space (Universal, 1953)
The Glass Web (Universal, 1953)
The Golden Blade (Universal, 1953)
Thy Neighbor's Wife (20th Century–Fox, 1953)
Dawn at Socorro (Universal. 1954)
Cult of the Cobra (Universal, 1955)
Three Bad Sisters (United Artists, 1956)
Unwed Mother (Allied Artists, 1958)
Promise Her Anything (Paramount, 1966)
The President's Analyst (Paramount, 1967)
Pete 'n' Tillie (Universal, 1972)
The Take (Columbia, 1974)
Revenge (Rastar/Columbia, 1990)

Hughes' scenes were cut from *Dancing in the Dark* (20th Century–Fox, 1949), *Ironweed* (HBO/Tri-Star, 1987) and *The Couch Trip* (Orion, 1988).

SUZANNE KAAREN

Sweetest man in the world [Bela Lugosi]. ...We danced the Viennese waltz right on the set there, especially when his wife Lillian wasn't there, because his wife loved to come almost every day and watch everything.

Bela Lugosi was still a major horror star in the 1940s but, ironically, one of his best movie vehicles of that decade was made by one of Hollywood's most *minor* companies. In PRC's *The Devil Bat* (1940), Lugosi starred as a perfume developer who believes he has been cheated by his employers; his mind turning to thoughts of revenge, he creates giant bats and trains them to seek out and kill anyone wearing his new aftershave. The basic idea may have been a bit far-out even by horror standards, but the film's fans dote on Lugosi's sinister performance, the never-to-be-forgotten scenes of the Devil Bat in flight, and the fast-moving "murder-a-reel" plot.

Suzanne Kaaren, prominent on Lugosi's "enemies list," survived the winged monster's attack — and, in real life, has survived nearly all of her *Devil Bat* co-stars. Born on Manhattan's 72nd Street, she worked on stage (and at Radio City Music Hall as a Rockette) prior to her 1934 Hollywood film debut. After a busy ten-year movie career, she married the consummate stage and screen actor Sidney Blackmer (1895–1973) and retired from the picture business.

Now residing several blocks from her birthplace, Kaaren reveals that the man who menaced her so malevolently in *The Devil Bat* was in fact one of her most delightful film co-stars.

Were either of your parents actors?

Oh, no. My father was 50 percent inventor and he did some remarkable things. He was also very deep in real estate. He and my mother were immigrants from Poland and Austria. I was interested [in show biz] from the first time that my father took me to a vaudeville house. They'd play pictures there, and they also had a session where they had vaudeville. We sat up in the balcony so he could smoke. That's how I learned to dance: I would imitate all the steps and so on. I got *very* interested in it, and as I walked down the street, I felt as if

I was on a stage and all the windows were people watching me. At eight years of age, my grandmother took me to see a wonderful Shakespearean actor who had a school of some sort, and I performed Juliet — eight years old [*laughs*]! "Thou knowest the mask of night is on my face, Else would a maiden blush bepaint my cheek, For that which thou hast heard me speak tonight...!"

At eight? That's funny!

I would try anything. I was so accommodating as a child — any question asked, any favor asked, I was ready. I always liked to *do* things for people, always *loved* to extend myself, without remuneration or any reward or anything. It was just loving to please. Maybe it was that "entertainment thing" in me. Later I won drama scholarships and things like that and I studied theater.

And you were one of the original Rockettes.

Yes, at Radio City Music Hall. I was in this play *Americana* — J. P. McEvoy was the producer-director — and when the play was about to close, they were starting the Radio City Music Hall. I worked very hard on a dance routine with another one of the girls in *Americana* in order to get a job at Radio City. The other girls in *Americana* were all very secretly going over there to try out. There's a secrecy [in show biz] but I never learned that until very late in life. Other actors would ask me about my plans and what I was up for, and I always willingly would *tell* them. And then *they* would go to the producer, go to the director, find every way to get in and to be seen and to audition. I was selling myself short. In show business, you keep your damn mouth shut until you sign a contract [*laughs*] — you learn that after a while!

Anyway, I worked on a little routine and I went to the Music Hall and I was chosen. Those who were chosen went over to one side of the stage, the others were eliminated. I was chosen by Russell Market [who had "founded" the dance team in Missouri in 1925]. So I opened at the Music Hall in ... I think it was 1932.

You were there opening night as a Rockette?

Oh, yes! I was there for six months.

How did you break into pictures?

While I was in *Americana*, there was a very, very interesting Italian hair stylist who came to this country and came to Broadway and wanted to choose the five most beautiful women on Broadway. It didn't matter what capacity [they worked in] — if they were on the stage, that was it. And I was chosen in *Americana* and asked to appear in a short. They had a thing called Pathé Newsreel in those days, and I was chosen to be one of the girls in this newsreel short. I did it, and I forgot about the whole experience. But later, when I was at the Music Hall, I was coming out of the elevator and there was the man from Pathé, and on his arm was hanging another girl who had been in the newsreel short. When I came out of the elevator and this man saw me, he said, "My God! It's Suzanne Kaaren!" You'd think the world was coming to an end, he was so excited. He said, "Do you know how long we've been trying to reach you?" I was living in Brooklyn at the time. "Warner Brothers has been looking for you. You get over to Warner Brothers right away." Warner Brothers was located some place on the West Side. So I went right over there because to me it was like a *command* — if they were looking for me, I'd better go and see what they wanted. When I went in, I got the same reception — "[*Gasp*] It's Suzanne Kaaren! The girl with the big eyes!" It was the red carpet treatment — they wanted to put me under contract. So I went and I asked for my release from the Music Hall and I started being "groomed for stardom." That's the way it all started with film.

Once you got to Hollywood, what were your favorite types of pictures?

Every movie was a challenge, it was a different personality, it was a different "life." There was [no genre] in particular that I liked to do. But I did like to ride horses, and I did a Western with Johnny Mack Brown [*Under Cover Man*, 1936].

Were you a good horsewoman?

Oh, pretty good, because he taught me. In the movie, the bad people captured him and threw him in the river, so I got on his horse and I galloped like mad to go for help. The prop truck was maybe a quarter of a mile away, near where the horse was supposed to stop. I kept looking back, and suddenly when I looked in front of me, my God, I was about to go into the truck. I was afraid the horse would go up against the truck and get killed — and I'd get killed too! So I jumped off this horse ... landed on my feet ... fell down ... and my whole chest just caved in, like. My chest was *so* bruised from this fall. Johnny said, "Listen, I'm gonna teach you how to jump off a horse. You *roll*. Don't stand on your feet, you *roll*." I tried it once when I was in California, out in the Valley, when one of my friends had a one-horse farm and he had a horse called Gypsy that was pretty wild. I was out riding Gypsy with a couple of friends and this horse wanted to get back to the stable to get fed,

Suzanne Kaaren mustered up scared expressions for her *Devil Bat* publicity shots, but actually remembers the making of the movie as a joy. (Photofest)

he was hell-bent on that. He got under the low branches of some huge trees, which meant I was about to get knocked off, so I did my little "trick" of jumping off the horse and rolling. And it was just the most wonderful pleasure in the world! That was my experience with jumping off a horse. You live and learn — and you *do* learn so many things being in the theater, being in the movies. It really is an education.

In 1940, you co-starred with Bela Lugosi in The Devil Bat.

They called my agent and they said

they wanted to talk to me about this new picture. Jean Yarbrough directed *The Devil Bat*, and he was someone I had worked for once already, maybe on a Western. Every now and then, directors ask for particular artists because they've worked with 'em before and they think they're pretty good. So anyway, there I was with Lugosi, and he was a *charming* man, dimples in his cheek ... he was a darling! He had the Hungarian accent, of course, and I would imitate him — I imitated many accents. It always intrigued me to talk to people who had accents: No sooner did they turn their backs than I was imitating them, *immediately*. He had fun with me, and he loved to dance the Viennese waltz. We would dance on the set.

What else did you like about Lugosi?

His smile and, like I said, his dimpled cheek. Sweetest man in the world. And he thought that I was terrific, and he enjoyed so much working with me. We danced the Viennese waltz right on the set there, *especially* when his wife Lillian wasn't there, because his wife loved to come almost every day and watch *every*thing. You know ... just come and look at the beautiful actress who's with her husband, and all of that.

So was she there to watch the movie being made — or to keep an eye on him?

She would watch the whole thing! Like I said, dancing the Viennese waltz was something he loved — especially when she wasn't around, when she had to go to the hairdresser, or maybe go to get her "yearly checkup" [*laughs*]. I also remember that *The Devil Bat* had the most beautiful, beautiful set for the Heaths' home. It was great, it photographed beautifully and it was brilliantly, beautifully lighted. They didn't just throw things together, the sets were just lovely. And the clothes that I wore in that picture are not in any way [dated], they're no different from the clothes that women would be wearing now. I watched it last night to refresh my memory before I talked to you, and it was just great. The only thing I [disliked] about the movie — all the scenes of Bela going in and out of those secret doors, in and out of his secret passageways. It was repeated, repeated, repeated, repeated ... !

Would you agree that he is very sinister on-screen in The Devil Bat?

Yes. His eyes would squint and his mouth would droop — it was like making a funny face for a child [*laughs*]! But you *believed* him. The movie was very believable in every way, it was not "hocus pocus." A man named Ray Nielsen from the Memphis Film Festival sent me an 8 × 10 picture of the poster, and it says *Bela Lugosi* — *The Devil Bat* — *With Suzanne Kaaren*, and over to the side it says, "*Sharp Fanged Blood Sucking Death Dives from Midnight Skies!*" [*Laughs*] Isn't that a beauty? Jean Yarbrough's name is down below, and of course a picture of Bela looking very sssssinister! But he was not at all sinister, he was loving, he was a romantic! Did you know he was a romantic? He loved beauty. It was just wonderful.

Your leading man in Devil Bat *was Dave O'Brien.*

I'd worked with him before. Pete Smith shorts, are you familiar with them? They were very funny, and Dave O'Brien was the bumbling idiot in them — he'd climb a ladder and he would fall off and do all these funny things. I did as many as he could get me to play. He was always trying to get me to do *more* of these shorts with him. Once I was on two different pictures at MGM: I was working in some movie, maybe *The Women* [1939], and he said, "Look, if you've got a coupla days off,

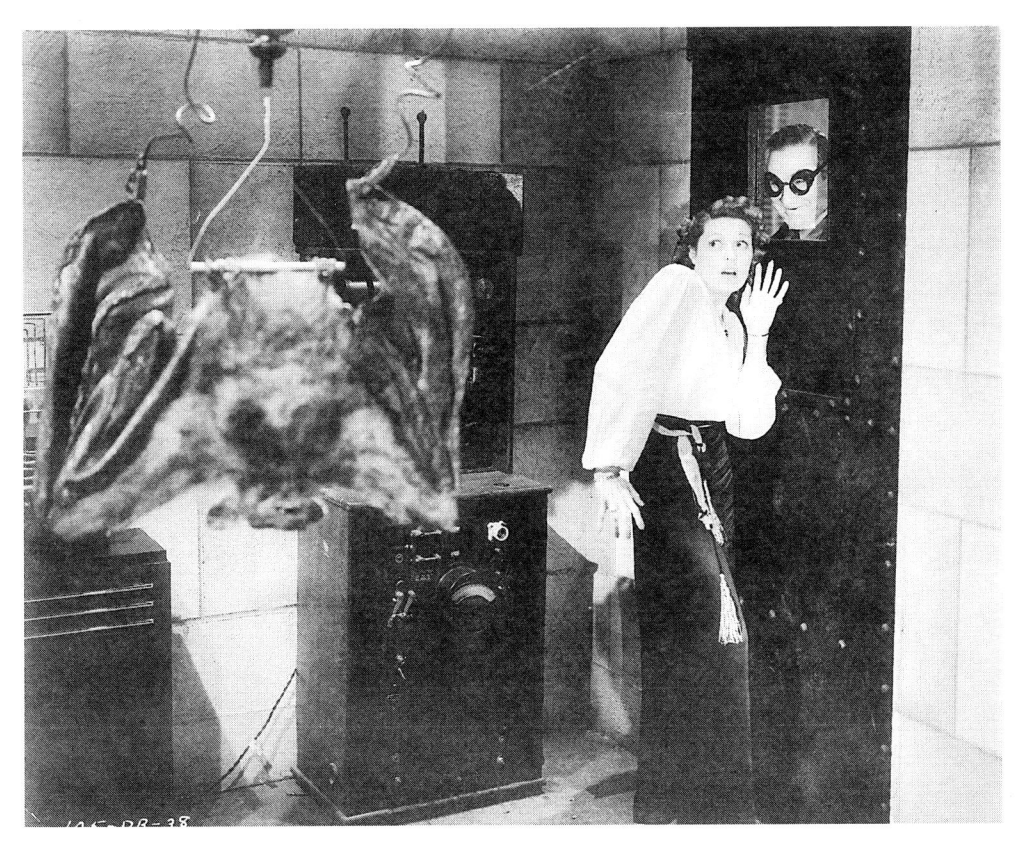

Caught between the Devil (Bat) and the deep-dyed villainy of Bela Lugosi, Kaaren strikes a panic-stricken pose. (Photofest)

would you come and do a short with me?" And I would. He just *loved* to work with me because I "fell into it"—I took on "the essence" of what he wanted me to do. I was one of his favorites.

Do you think maybe he had his eye on you romantically?

This has nothing to do with falling in love or being on the make, it was pure artistry, it was just appreciation of what I had to offer. It was nice talking and working with him again in *The Devil Bat*. And how good he is in the movie! He was a darling. He was a very good friend of [actress] Raquel Torres, and she secretly used to ask me, would I drive past his house? I said, "Darling, he's a married man! It's *shocking*, you mustn't do that, Stephen won't like it!"—her husband Stephen Ames, who had a chair on the stock exchange.

Is it possible it was O'Brien who suggested that you be offered the part in Devil Bat*?*

No, I do think that the *Devil Bat* thing came from Yarbrough. They go into sessions and start thinking about who would be good for this part and that part. Suggestions are made, and they call the various agents. And then the agent calls you and says, "You have an appointment with Bela Lugosi and Jean Yarbrough at such-and-such a studio." By the way, we made *The Devil Bat* at Monogram.

It was a PRC picture, but you're remembering shooting it at Monogram?

Yes, that was the studio where we

worked. PRC must have rented space there. When you worked for Monogram or for PRC, you knew that meant that the picture would be done in a shorter time than if you were working at a major studio like MGM or Paramount or RKO. I worked for *all* of them.

The scenes of the Devil Bat swooping down onto its victims — how was that done?

The Devil Bat was on the top of this great big tall bamboo stick that bent forward and back. Two or three people would hold onto this thing and move it from side to side. It looked very, very real — it was just amazing how well they planned it and how well they did it. Whenever Bela unleashed the Devil Bat, lots of little bats also came out of that damn window of his. But those little ones never came back. What happened to the little bats? Did they go in somebody's chimney [*laughs*]?

Did you ever see Lugosi again after The Devil Bat?

Years later, walking along the street in New York. As I walked down the street, here comes Bela Lugosi. I looked at him and he looked at me, and he said, "I just can't believe this!" He had gotten quite old and he was not very well. He looked haunted. He was ill and walked very slowly, with a cane. He also used a cane in the movie ... I wonder if this could have been an old ailment...

He did have back troubles for a long time, yes.

Well, a couple of times, there he was, on the street.

You got out of the picture business in the mid-1940s.

When I decided that things were looking very bad for the movie business, I wanted to come back to New York and do plays. By then I had gotten secretly married to Sidney Blackmer, my darling, darling angel in Heaven, and I [didn't announce it] because it was none of their damn business what happened in my private life.

What made you think the movie business was in trouble?

They were putting locks on the wardrobe, they were putting locks in the makeup department. If you needed a couple of hairpins, you had to sign a release. It was like they were going broke — there was something wrong.

Was your husband supportive of your continuing acting aspirations?

No. In the back of Sidney's mind, he didn't want me to be a performer any more. Sidney would tell people, "Oh, Suzanne just *loves* being my love, and she wants to retire [from acting]." I mean, at *that* early age? It was crazy, but he would say that to people: "Oh, no, she's not interested." "Ich bin der Herr des Hauses" — that means "I am the lord of the manor" in German [*laughs*].

Everything was fine until Sidney got into this Broadway play *Chicken Every Sunday*. The producer said to me, "I don't want to say anything to Sidney about this, but [actress] Ann Thomas is leaving the play and I want *you*. I think you'd be great in this thing. But don't say anything to Sidney about it yet."

And you still were still interested in acting.

Of *course*! But I did not want to displease him. Well, I had seen *Chicken Every Sunday* a number of times and I knew the part pretty well, and we did a couple of secret rehearsals. Then we bounced this off of Sidney, and he had a fit [*laughs*]! But he wanted to please *me*, too.

Kaaren's main recollection of the screen's blackest villain, Bela Lugosi: "He was a darling."

So you got to do it.

Right. One day he came running over to me because I had done something new and unusual, and the applause and the laughter were so great. He asked, "What was that laugh? What was that long, drawn-out laugh??" He didn't want *any*one to get ahead of the laughs *he* got! If you're really interested in the theater, you realize how important these things are — to get a hand or a laugh, and so on. You're as good in a comedy as the laughter you get, you see! He said, "Look, don't ever put anything in a play without checking with the *star*." [*Laughs*]

I originally met Sidney at a farewell party for a friend of my mother's. I wouldn't give him my telephone number — I said, "I don't give my telephone number to strangers." He said, "But I'd like to call you some time." I said, "Well, if fate means for you to call me and to meet me, perhaps we will. But it will be fate." And I said toodle-oo and off I went! Later, my writer-friend Garrett Fort called me, saying, "Listen, you are driving Sidney Blackmer crazy. He has called me a thousand times. He wants you to go out with him, he wants to know you." I said, "Well, to hell with him. I don't want to meet him, and that's that." I was having a little fun, you see. (And I suppose maybe that's what intrigues a man. You play hard-to-get and he wants to know you all the more.) So one day Sidney called Garrett and he said, "Listen, we have a new Chinese cook. My mother is here from North Carolina, and I want to invite you and Suzanne Kaaren to dinner and meet my charming mother and have this wonderful Chinese cook dinner."

Kaaren nearly becomes victim #5 in a tense scene from ***The Devil Bat***.

And did you go?

Yes, I went, and I met Sidney's mother. She was Southern ... aristocratic ... and she threw her weight around. She said she came to visit Sidney in California to "keep all the bad girls away from him." I was glad to hear that from her, secretly. I said, "You don't have to worry about me because I am not interested in getting married and I am not interested in any romances. I'm here with Garrett, darling Garrett..."

And then of course, you end up marrying Sidney Blackmer.

That's right, in 1943. June 13. We got married in Santa Ana. I was a career girl and held my ground for some time, but Sidney eventually won me over. At the time, I had never seen him in a picture. I didn't go to movies much, until we started dating. Then we went all the time. He was a star, and a brilliant actor. Franchot Tone and others would ask his advice about things when they were on the stage. He studied technique and was someone you could learn a lot from. Such a dear man.

It's so funny — you worked with Bela Lugosi, the star of Dracula *[1931], in The Devil Bat; you worked with Tod Browning, the director of* Dracula, *in* Miracles for Sale *[1939]; and you were a friend of the man who wrote* Dracula, *Garrett Fort.*

[*Gasp*] Garrett! Was it my friend Garrett Fort who wrote *Dracula*?

Yes. And Frankenstein *[1931].*

Honey, he was my dearest, dearest friend. He was in the literary department at Universal Studios and he had a home at Malibu Beach. One day, early on, he came to me and he said, "My mother is in town, visiting me. She came in from New Jersey"—that's where he had his home originally. He said, "I want you to meet her." Well, I met his mother, who was so adorable, and we started going out to different places. I knew all the actors and actresses, and I would regale her with information—"Look, there's Greta Garbo. Ooh, that's Ginger Rogers. Her latest picture was so-and-so and she's now working at Paramount..." The mother stayed on for a long, long time and I would spend weekends at the beach with the mama and Garrett and my little wire-haired terrier. That's how I knew Garrett. But I didn't know that he had written *Dracula*, I *never* have known that! Oh, how wonderful!

What was he like as a person?

Garrett was hard of hearing ... and he sure liked his booze, you know [*laughs*]! But he was a *darling*.

He died of a sleeping pill overdose in 1945. Do you think that was intentional?

I doubt it very much, because he loved life too much. One time Garrett and I were going to some soiree, and there were two girls on a corner in Hollywood. One of them had a brace on her arm because she had broken her arm. So there they were — their car had broken down or run out of gas. I said, "Oh, the poor things!" and he said, "Let's pick 'em up." And so we picked them up and took them along! He was generous and sweet. Oh, no, his death was not intentional, Garrett loved life too much.

After Mr. Blackmer passed away, you did some more movie work right here in New York.

Oh, yes, little bits and things. The reason I took these parts after Sidney died was to get in front of a camera and to see the new ways of directing and photographing, and to be "part of the scene." I did a whole slew of them. I got a good role in *The Cotton Club* [1984] with Richard Gere. Oh, he was naughty, naughty!

To you, or to everybody?

To everyone! I played "the Duchess of Park Avenue," a lady who loved to go out and to go to the Cotton Club. Gere was very cold and he was not a very good actor. [Writer-director] Francis Coppola liked me very much, and we talked about different characters who used to come to the Club, people I had met many years before. He said, "Let her talk, let her talk. I want to hear this." And Gere didn't like that very much. Gere got hold of that picture and re-did the whole thing — before he was through, almost all of [Kaaren's footage] was cut. Gere didn't want anybody's part upstaging his!

What do you think of modern movies?

I think we leave very little to the imagination in films today, with this tremendous outburst of personal exhibition. I mean, if you have to take all your clothes off, what are you gonna do *next*, take your arm off in front of a camera? Well, they even do *that* on [TV's] *ER*, with the blood all over. It's ghastly!

Not like The Devil Bat!

The Devil Bat was just wonderful, I enjoyed it *very* much. Remember the scenes where Bela Lugosi gives the young men aftershave, and then tells them "Goooooodbye…!" I used to do that to him on the set. When we broke and were ready to leave for the day, he'd look at me and I'd look at him and I would say, "Gooooooodbye…!" [*Laughs*] That was so funny in the movie, that "Goooooodbye" — that was really very good. You knew, when Bela said it to someone, "Oh-oh. That guy's going to *get* it!" [*Laughs*]

SUZANNE KAAREN FILMOGRAPHY

Sleepers East (Fox, 1934)
I Believed in You (Fox, 1934)
Bottoms Up (Fox, 1934)
3 on a Honeymoon (Fox, 1934)
Wild Gold (Fox, 1934)
Strangers All (RKO, 1935)
Women Must Dress (Monogram, 1935)
The Affair of Susan (Universal, 1935)
The Big Broadcast of 1936 (Paramount, 1935)
Under Cover Man (Supreme/Republic, 1936)
Disorder in the Court (Columbia short, 1936)
Wives Never Know (Paramount, 1936)
The Great Ziegfeld (MGM, 1936)
The White Legion (*Angels in White*) (Grand National, 1936)
Angel (Paramount, 1937)
Sing While You're Able (Ambassador Pictures, 1937)
A Million to One (*Speed to Spare; Olympic Champ*) (Puritan Pictures, 1937)
Rhythm in the Clouds (Republic, 1937)
When's Your Birthday? (RKO, 1937)
The Wildcatter (Universal, 1937)
Here's Flash Casey (Grand National, 1937)
Romance of Louisiana (Warners/Vitaphone short, 1937)

Phantom Ranger (Monogram, 1938)
Blondes at Work (Warners, 1938)
Trade Winds (United Artists, 1938)
Sweethearts (MGM, 1938)
Miracles for Sale (MGM, 1939)
Pride of the Navy (Republic, 1939)
Mexicali Rose (Republic, 1939)
Yes, We Have No Bonanza (Columbia short, 1939)
Idiot's Delight (MGM, 1939)
The Women (MGM, 1939)
The Devil Bat (PRC, 1940)
City of Chance (20th Century–Fox, 1940)
The Ghost Comes Home (MGM, 1940)
Rags to Riches (Republic, 1941)
Roar of the Press (Monogram, 1941)
I Married an Angel (MGM, 1942)
What's the Matador? (Columbia short, 1942)
Rationing (MGM, 1944)
The Practical Joker (MGM short, 1944)
The Cotton Club (Orion, 1984)
"Crocodile" Dundee II (Paramount, 1988)

DENNY MILLER

*I'm waiting to see [*Tarzan, the Ape Man*] shown on the TV series with the guy and the two robots [*Mystery Science Theater*]! If they haven't had it on there already, they will, and they won't be quiet for one minute!*

Denny Miller has no regrets about playing the title role in MGM's *Tarzan, the Ape Man*—even though Leonard Maltin lists the 1959 movie as a BOMB and Ape Man expert Gabe Essoe, in his book *Tarzan of the Movies*, calls it "Tarzan the Worst."

These are blunt, unkind-sounding assessments, but one of the first people who'd agree with them is Miller, a six-foot-four UCLA star athlete plucked from obscurity and outfitted with the familiar Tarzan loincloth. The Technicolor movie is filled with stock footage from *King Solomon's Mines* (1950) and other oldies (including some in black-and-white!), afflicted with a bongo-heavy jazz score, and packs more phony rear-projection and fake animals than you could shake a spear at. It's an embarrassingly minor footnote to MGM's classic Johnny Weissmuller series, but it gave Miller his start as an actor and, much more recently, has helped advance his new career as a physical educator. He recalled his foray into the foliage with great affection in this recent interview.

Many film reference books list Tarzan *as your first film, omitting* Some Came Running *[1958].*

I was under contract at MGM at the time—it was the tail end of that "stable" system they used to use. I had a very small part in *Some Came Running* with Shirley MacLaine, Dean Martin and Frank Sinatra. I later told people they named the movie after *me*, because I was the only one who "came running"—I came running to tell Dean Martin that somebody was in town to shoot Frank Sinatra! I had rehearsed my one line 7,480 times and I gave it to him in rehearsal, and waited and waited for his response. And he finally looked up and said, "I got lines?" [*Laughs*] He was very relaxed!

The Tarzan film was under the same system: I was just there at MGM. I, as a matter of fact, recommended a friend of mine to play Tarzan, an actor named Bill

Denny Miller dove headlong into campy jungle adventure playing the title role in *Tarzan, the Ape Man*.

Smith. We were both contract players at MGM. Bill was darker-haired and, I thought, was more appropriately built. But MGM didn't seem to think so.

So Tarzan *was your second picture.*

Yes. I had done several TV shows, one with William Bendix, *Life of Riley*, where I played an athlete — which I *was*, at UCLA. Then I did one with Buddy Ebsen called *Northwest Passage*. This was before I went under contract to MGM.

Any idea why MGM thought of you for the Tarzan part?

I was in their stable, so I was cheaper than some of the elephants [*laughs*]. And I was athletic. They tested a bunch of us, and I won. They said that this was going to be an "educated Tarzan" version — it was a remake of the original Johnny Weissmuller one [*Tarzan the Ape Man*, 1932] where he meets Jane [Maureen O'Sullivan] and they run off in the jungle together. On the test, I came out of the jungle and spoke to Joanna Barnes, who had been chosen for Jane — I recited, unexplainably, the 23rd Psalm! That was 20 times more than what I said in the whole film! "Ungawa!" was popular, I remember; it can mean stop, go, turn left, give me a McDonald's burger, whatever.

What other actors were in the running for the Tarzan role?

I don't know who was tested other than, I *think*, Bill Smith. I do know that they also tested different kinds of loincloths, including one that I thought was really outrageous and nice, but it rattled when I walked! It was mainly beads set on leather. It was very colorful, but it didn't make sense because it *did* rattle. So they went back to the original form — well, not the *original* Elmo Lincoln one, the off-the-shoulder leopard skin, but the one that Johnny Weissmuller wore.

But your reaction when MGM began considering you for the role was to try to hand it off to William Smith?

Well, not "hand it off," but I thought that he was better. I've done that through my 42-year career, if I know an actor who seems to be [better suited]. I've been fortunate to play good guys, bad guys, and do along the way a lot of commercials. I was the Brawny Paper Towel giant for about 12 years and the spokesman for Gorton's Fish for eight. A number of the guys I started off with have gone way further than I have, like Clint Eastwood and James Caan, but most of the others have dropped by the wayside. It's an unusual way to make a living, and there are just more actors than there is work. So I've been very lucky. My ex-wife says I have several horseshoes hidden in some orifice of my body [*laughs*], and I don't argue with her!

When you were getting ready to play Tarzan, did they show you any of the old Weissmuller movies?

All of them! Oh, that was one of the most fun things: They'd get a projectionist and I'd go down in the basement, to the projection rooms, and I'd sit there by myself and watch Tarzan movies, all the way back to Elmo Lincoln. Elmo Lincoln really looked the part with the long hair and the big barrel chest. He was not quite as athletic-looking as some who followed, but he was marvelous. So, yes, I watched, oh, *many* of them, if not *all*.

And what were you watching for? What were they hoping you'd "pick up" from seeing these pictures?

I never asked them [*laughs*]. I thought it was entertaining, though, and I probably (by osmosis) got some ideas. In those days, I was a misplaced basketball player, in my own mind, so I just "went to the movies" — it was just *fun*. I was looking at their attire, too.

What was your salary when you were at MGM?

I got 180 a week. More money than I ever thought I'd make.

Was there ever any talk of dyeing your blonde hair for Tarzan?

No.

They liked the idea of a blonde Tarzan.

I guess so. Buster Crabbe [who played Tarzan in the 1933 serial *Tarzan the Fearless*] never dyed *his*. It didn't seem to matter. I wouldn't have stopped them if they *had* wanted to dye it. By the way, my hair wasn't as long as I think it should have been, looking back on it. I think the length of hair should be like Christopher Lambert [in *Greystoke: The Legend of Tarzan, Lord of the Apes*, 1984].

Did you have to have your body shaved?

No, but they did put VO5 hairdressing all over me. They'd grease me up every time — I was very slippery to hold onto. They did that so I'd shine. I also had full body makeup.

Full body makeup and then the VO5 too? How long to clean up at night?

A long time. A loooong, long time…!

What did MGM do to prepare you for the role?

They gave me a gym membership, and I went and worked out. I was always working out at UCLA anyway, so it didn't matter.

There were some funny things that happened during the shooting of it. They were concerned about my feet — running around on the set, indoors or out, there's lots of nails and sharp things. So they took molds of the bottoms of my feet and then they made rubber soles and glued them on my feet. And in the first shot, I swung out over the camera and dropped down from the vine in front of the camera and I *hopped* a little bit. I heard "Cut!" and I looked back, and where I had hopped from, there were my glued soles, three feet behind me [*laughs*]! That's the last time we bothered with *those*. Another time, my stunt double wasn't there and they asked me to swing out from the tree house and be caught by two men on a 30-foot-high stand.

Your tree house was about 30 feet off the floor also?

About. I swung out, and I could tell when I was halfway there that I was gonna hit the top of the platform about chest-high. I got my feet up to save myself and I hit the thing with my feet, and it started to tip. And the two guys who were supposed to catch me were suddenly busy just holding on! I swung back and forth in smaller and smaller arcs and held on until they got a ladder and got me down.

You have *to have a story about your fight with the giant crocodile.*

That was one of the funnier things. Well, first of all, I was told I was gonna do a love scene in the afternoon, so I had spaghetti and meatballs for lunch. Then they said, "We've decided to have a crocodile wrestling scene instead," and I said okay. They had an old mechanical crocodile from Johnny Weissmuller days — it must have been 20, 25 feet long. The machine didn't work, so they put it on a wire and pulled it across the old "Johnny Weissmuller river" on Lot 2 on the back lot of MGM. So I swam and I felt ill and I knew I was going to lose my cookies [because of the big lunch], so I just swam right around the bend, past the crocodile. I could hear everybody yelling, "Where the hell you going? What's going *on*?" I went around the corner and "fed the fish" and came back, and they said, "Oh. Sorry! Well, let's try it again…"

I got out my rubber knife that I was supposed to use to fight the crocodile and I figured, "I'm not feelin' too good, so I'll just go all out." I went down to the bottom of the lagoon, which was only about five feet deep, and I came roarin' up and I landed on the top of the crocodile and I stabbed him a couple times and I thrashed around and everything. Finally I got tired and I stopped and stood up in the water, and when I looked to the shore, people were falling down laughing. I went stumbling to the sidelines, and they told me that when I jumped on the crocodile's head, the thing was so stiff, it tipped up and the tail came out of the water! And then it sunk like a submarine [*laughs*]! They said, "We won't be able to use *that*!"

Several actors have mentioned to me how dirty and awful back lot pools can be. Was MGM's better than most?

Oh, yes. When I was on *Wagon Train* for 110 episodes, I dealt with putting my face in man-made ponds in cow country, and it wasn't good [*laughs*] — you'd call for the nurse right away for mouthwash and eyewash and everything else! So I know exactly what you're talking about.

Your Tarzan was shot entirely at MGM?

Yes.

The producer, Al Zimbalist — was he ever around?

Yes, always. And his son as well [associate producer Donald Zimbalist]. They were small of stature, dressed very nattily in suits and ties all the time, and they walked very similarly. They were always in the background of the goings-on, from the tests on. Joseph Newman, the director, was quite nice and amiable, and Robert Douglas [who played Jane's father] was kind and considerate. Joanna Barnes I've subsequently bumped into on several occasions. Joanna showed up at one of the Dum-Dums [Tarzan fan conventions] in L.A. a couple of years ago and she was *marvelous* and *looked* marvelous, and we got along just famously.

And during the making of the movie, you got along well?

We got along fine, there were no fights or anything. But she just didn't seem to me to be too thrilled with the production of it — she was busy doing crossword puzzles and reading *The Wall Street Journal* and whatever else. (Of course, neither *one* of us knew that they would be using old *King Solomon's Mines* footage in it, and also tinting black-and-white film from old Tarzan movies. It was just bizarre, what they got away with.) In one of the scenes, Joanna wakes up in the tree house and sees me, we tussle and she's frightened of me — and she bit me! She *denies* it, but she bit my knee — not badly, but...! So it got a little more raucous, this tussle, than it was written to be! But [at the Dum-Dum convention], after 38 or 39 years or whatever, we didn't tussle any more — she laughed and giggled, and if she wasn't havin' a good time, she fooled *me*! She said she was thrilled with having been a Jane and was very personable and laughed a lot about the silly things that go on at those get-togethers. So I was probably wrong when I got the impression that she wasn't in favor of playing Jane. Joanna was a Phi Beta Kappa and she has since written a number of novels.

You mentioned that they used a lot of footage from King Solomon's Mines *in your Tarzan. And at the end, when you're riding away from that African village in flames, I think that's actually stock footage of* Rome *burning in* Quo Vadis!

It might be. And in one of the swing-throughs that they lifted from one of the old Tarzans, the guy was on a trapeze. You can see the trapeze!

What do you remember about your other co-star, Cesare Danova?

Cesare Danova, who played the white

Jungle king meets Jordan king: Hussein (ibn Talal) chats up Miller and Joanna Barnes during a production break.

hunter, was a lovely man, but why would they get an Italian to play that part? He had a scene one time where he said, "Whether you're wearing banana leaves or pearls, you'll always be a queen." It came out [*in an Italian accent*], "Whether you're-a wearing banana leaves or-a pearls, you will-a always-a be a queen."

In one scene, there was an elephant lying down with an arrow in its side. They had a trained elephant lying on the ground, and on its side was a rubber socket that flared out so they could glue it on the elephant's side; that way, they could stick the broken arrow in this socket and not hurt the elephant. I was told that, when I pulled out the arrow, I was supposed to press down with the other hand on the flange around the socket so that *that* thing didn't come off too. So I did. Do you know the difference between a cocktail lounge and an elephant fart? One's a barroom and one's a *barrr-rrrroom* [*laughs*]! The elephant farted, but *I* went on with the scene! I turned to Joanna, and Joanna was gone; I turned to Cesare, *Cesare* was gone; I looked around, the guys on the *camera* were gone! And the elephant trainer was already up, prodding the elephant to get him out of the area. We did that one over again, and I didn't press as hard the next time!

Incidentally, some words of advice, if you're ever in a parade on an elephant: They never stay still, even when they're standing in one place, they sway back and forth. And their hair is much like an S.O.S. pad ... bristles. So wear long pants — loincloths don't work!

What about the scene where you fight the leopard?

That was shot on an indoor set. They constructed a 20- or 30-foot screen around it, and had a guy there with a shotgun. And they brought in a leopard that was a house pet — the woman owner of the leopard was there, too. My stuntman hadn't shown up that day for some unexplainable reason, so they asked me to go in there and get up on this tree limb and drop down on top of the leopard as he went by. I said, "I'd like to see the stuntman do it first." The fact that my usual stunt double hadn't shown up that day — *that* made me a little suspicious! So they had another [stuntman], a new one, one I'd never seen before. They dragged a wild live goose on the ground along the path that they wanted the leopard to go, they got the stuntman up there on the tree limb and then they put the leopard in place and let him go. He went exactly where they wanted him to, underneath the limb ... but as soon as the stuntman crouched to jump off, the leopard heard him and was *gone*, out from under that limb. And afterwards, of course, they couldn't get the leopard to go under the limb any more, 'cause he was suspicious. So the stuntman started patting him on the face and batting his paws. They didn't *hit* the leopard because there was a person there from the SPCA. At first it was playing, but then the playing got out of hand, according to the leopard — he'd just had enough of it [*laughs*], and decided to let everybody know it! He got angry and there was a *blur*. The leopard was gone once again, off to a corner of the cage, and there was the stuntman, who had been clawed from his shoulder, down his side, down part of his thigh. So they took him to first aid and they put me in there with a stuffed leopard and a rubber knife and I rolled around and around with the silly thing! The scene was *so* bad that everybody mentions it.

The fight itself is so fast that it's not terrible, it's those awful closeups of the leopard's face that ruin it. You just have to wonder —

You have to wonder who was in charge there.

Yeah, absolutely. If anybody!

I think they fired the producers shortly thereafter. At any rate, they didn't work for MGM any more, I don't think.

Who was your regular stuntman, the guy who didn't show up the day with the leopard?

George Robotham. I don't know the name of the man who took over when

George decided not to show up, when they were bringing in animals George didn't wanna deal with [*laughs*]! George also did some swings over fire in the scene with the idol. They turned the fire up too high and singed the hairs off Cesare Danova's arm — he was trying to protect the stuntwoman who was on the idol *with* him.

For pure phoniness, your underwater scene runs a close second to the stuffed leopard scene.

Oh, yes! We did get into a tank and they filmed us through a porthole, but there were problems getting Joanna down there long enough to shoot, to hold her breath. *Both* of us had trouble just getting down there and in front of the porthole that they had the camera placed outside of. So the scene didn't work. But [*laughs*], why should it be different than any of the *other* scenes? They took that footage of us swimming and superimposed it on prior film taken of hippopotami doing their "ballet." *Tarzan* was a "classic" — I'm waiting to see it shown on the TV series with the guy and the two robots [*Mystery Science Theater*]! If they haven't had it on there already, they *will*, and they won't be quiet for one minute!

You've mentioned a few people's injuries, but none of your own. You didn't get off scot-free, did you?

The time I swung out from the tree house and came back, I got a small cut on my thigh from bangin' back into the tree house. Plus they had a lion cub which was about the size of a St. Bernard, for a scene where I was playing with it. He wandered around in back of me as I was sitting down or hunched down, and he took a swat at my back and got one claw hung up in my skin. They took me to the infirmary and put some disinfectant on it and gave me a tetanus shot and put some collodion on it to seal it — and then we went back and did it again.

The lion cub was just being playful?

Yeah, he wasn't pissed. And then Joanna's bite, and a couple of slaps in the face during rehearsals of the same fight scene. But after one time, I caught her hand before she could get *to* me. She'll deny all that...!

The giant Watusi guy in the movie [Thomas Yangha] — what was his story?

He was a guitar player they found in a cocktail lounge in Los Angeles. Very pleasant. He didn't bring his instruments along to play at any time that I remember [*laughs*], but he was very relaxed. He was about six-foot-nine. The pygmies were all from a gymnastic team at Manual Arts or Jefferson High School in Los Angeles, with skullcaps on.

And they were not pygmies, of course, they were just teenagers.

Right, teenagers. *Agile* teenagers — most of them were athletes, and they could jump and climb walls and everything. They were very good.

And Cheetah?

Cheetah was a kick — he was smarter than *all* of us. One time, though, he bit me on the hand. I was pulling him along and I lifted my hand up, and he was hangin' on by his teeth! Well, the trainer had said, "If he ever bites you, *punch* him," so I punched him between the eyes, in the forehead, to get him off from munchin' on the meaty part of the palm of my hand.

Why did he bite you? For no reason?

It wasn't his fault. I was supposed to be walking away from camera, and he was sent in to grab my hand. After he grabbed

Miller likens the Tarzan yodel to the sound of "a guy being lowered slowly into a bathtub full of ice cubes."

my hand, the trainer called him back *but I held onto him*— they wanted it to look like Cheetah was trying to get me to go in the other direction. Naturally, Cheetah's gonna want to go to the guy who feeds him all the time, and [in order to make the scene work] I wouldn't *let* him go. And that's why he said, "Well, screw *you*, I'll bite your hand." I punched him, and he went up in the rafters of the sound stage and he wouldn't come down. They had to get a BB gun to scare him into comin' back down again. He also got up in a tree one time in a back lot scene and it took a little bit of doing to get him back down.

Some of the jungle scenes were interiors, shot on sound stages.

Oh, yes. The tree house was inside, and also some of the jungle [around it]. On the back lot, over the "Johnny Weissmuller river," there was a phony tree that had a lot of wires holding up a limb — they were hidden, of course, but they were rather sharp and rusty. I was out on the end of this limb and only about 10 or 15 feet above this body of water that was five or six feet deep. It was easier for me to jump off — dive in — than it was to go back [over the branch], I thought, so I dove in after they had told me to go back and *not* dive in. It would have been harder on my bare feet to climb back through the wires and everything. I caught a lot of hell about that, but I explained why I did it — I did it not to piss 'em off or anything, but because I figured it was the lesser of two evils.

Another time, when Joanna and I are floating down the river, they had not warmed up the water. I didn't have anything to do but grunt and splash her, but she had a lot of words to say. But she couldn't say 'em because her teeth chattered, she was so cold. They gave her a half-pint of brandy to warm her up and *that* caused *another* problem, 'cause she wasn't used to drinking. And so we still couldn't do it, not because her teeth were chattering but because her words were slurred [*laughs*]!

Was that in the studio tank?

No, it was in the Johnny Weissmuller river again. It was a cement river, not very long, and it sure was cold!

You started shooting in March. Was the weather a problem for you, you with practically no clothes on?

That time it was, but not afterwards. It was warm enough, and most of it was done inside anyway. King Hussein showed up one day. We were inside, working in the tree house, and here comes this motorcade, King Hussein and about 20 six-foot-four-plus motorcycle cops from L.A. He was a lovely, quiet man, and I was sorry to hear of his recent passing [1999].

On the second day of production, MGM was already announcing that they were going to make a sequel.

Oh, really? They had the rights to do two, I believe, but when they saw the final cut of this, I think they decided not to do it. And that was the end of that. When the movie came out, I naturally didn't go to any of the showings in the Westwood area, where UCLA is located, because of the catcalls and what have you from my teammates!

Where did you *see* Tarzan? *At the studio, or in a real theater?*

I think it was in a real theater. I broke into a sweat when a few of the catcalls came out ... but there weren't very many people *in* there [*laughs*]! There were a *bunch* of empty seats — more than there were with fannies in 'em!

I used to get very uneasy when I watched myself. I got hung up on my physicality — I would say, "Oh my God, I don't walk like *that, do* I?" I'd have the same reaction when I'd watch film of a UCLA basketball game. *Now* I can watch and be amused, and think back and see the difference between what *I* thought was going on visually, outside of me, and what was going on emotionally, *inside* of me. There was always a difference — to *me,* anyway.

I'm assuming the box office wasn't great on your Tarzan.

Still loinin': Miller and a Cheetah stand-in in a recent shot.

I don't know, I've never heard a report on it, but I would be very surprised if it *was*. But then, it was only a six-week thing, so I don't think they spent a great deal of money on it. For years there's been a book out called *Tarzan of the Movies* ...

I love it.

And I'm in the chapter called "Tarzan the Worst."

I'm afraid I knew that too!

But, whether I'm "worst" or not, it's nice to be *first* at worst: Since the Bo Derek remake [1981's *Tarzan, the Ape Man*, with Miles O'Keeffe as Tarzan], I'm only *second-*

worst by some people's standards. I've been moved down (or up!) a notch, I'm not quite sure!

Now, I don't think that chapter says that you were *the worst—*

No, it didn't. Gabe Essoe was a friend before he wrote the book and, no, he didn't say that. But I've always used it to get a chuckle!

How many of the "old" Tarzans are left these days? Do you happen to know offhand?

Bruce Bennett is still around; Gordon Scott; Ron Ely, who was Tarzan on television; Mike Henry, who was a Ram linebacker…

Ron Ely and Mike Henry don't seem to be in any hurry to—pardon the pun—swing down Memory Lane.

No, they don't, they've taken it negatively and said that it's not been good for their careers one way or another. Recently, Ron has kind of come out—he's writing now, and I think he uses it to promote his books. All the Tarzans got together one time on *The Mike Douglas Show* years ago—well, not *all*, but seven of us showed up for that, out at the Animal Farm, just north of San Diego. Johnny, myself, Gordon Scott, Jock Mahoney…. Anyway, seven of us were there, and also Totie Fields, dressed in a loincloth over-the-shoulder-type thing. They tried to get her on an elephant, and she said she was afraid of heights, so she walked in holding a small elephant by the tail. Which was appropriate, for her size!

So who is *the best Tarzan?*

I think the most impressive *film* I saw was *Greystoke* with Christopher Lambert. It looked like they spent the most money on it and it was the most authentic-looking. I think, if Johnny Weissmuller had been in *Greystoke*, that would have been my favorite. Although I think Christopher is a good actor, I didn't think he was big enough for the part—big enough *physically*. But he was marvelous, his eyes and his facial expressions and all that. But because I "grew up" with Johnny Weissmuller and he did (by far) more than any of the others, I liked him the most. Gordon Scott did six or seven and rode on rhinoceroses and giraffes and stuff, and *they* were good films too. So I guess I have three favorites: The movie *Greystoke* and Christopher facially; and otherwise, acting-wise, Johnny Weissmuller because I "grew up" with him, and Gordon because of the quality of his films and the brute strength of him.

By the way, the best person I've ever heard do the "call" [the "Tarzan yodel"] was Danton Burroughs, the grandson of Edgar Rice. He does the call best—even better than Carol Burnett [*laughs*]! I've heard Johnny Weissmuller's son say that his father did it all in his films, but I think they "sweetened" it with several instruments, and raised the recording a couple of octaves by speeding it up and re-recording it. Johnny Weissmuller would do it anywhere and everywhere. The best of all, as I said, is Danton Burroughs; second is Carol Burnett; and third is any guy being lowered slowly into a bathtub full of ice cubes [*laughs*]! It's a rather painful sound…!

Did you ever try it, while you were making your movie?

MGM gave me a recording of it and I practiced it. I was living at the beach, Malibu, and so at night I would go down and scream at the ocean. They had me do it every time it was called for in the script, but then they removed 'em because mine sounded like a turkey being killed or something! They took mine out and laid in the other one [Weissmuller's].

What other roles have you enjoyed playing?

I've done a few things that I was proud of — I did a series with Juliet Prowse for 26 episodes, a half-hour sitcom called *Mona McCluskey*, and I've been in a few movies that were interesting. I was directed in his first directorial position by Sidney Poitier in *Buck and the Preacher* [1972] with Harry Belafonte, quite an interesting film. It was written by a black man and it was partially true, it was about slaves who (when they were freed) formed wagon trains and moved west. Cameron Mitchell headed a gang of whites hired by the plantation owners to turn them back and I played a really ugly redneck character.

What unexpected benefits — if any!— have you reaped from playing Tarzan?

It's helped me a great deal in ways that I didn't see it would: I have a degree in physical education from UCLA, where my father was the chairman of the department and on President Kennedy's and Eisenhower's Council for Fitness. I have been in favor of exercise and I'm following in the footsteps of Buster Crabbe, who wrote a book called *Buster Crabbe's Arthritis Exercise Book* [1980] waaay before the medical profession was recommending exercise for arthritis. I corresponded with Buster; he had many pool classes in the Scottsdale, Arizona, area. I have, among other things, my own little gym — I've converted a barn in my backyard and I've taught fitness for 10 or 12 years in Ojai, California. And I distribute a pamphlet with the same name as a little book that I'm writing on fitness for people over 50, *Me Tarzan, You Train*.

[Laughs] That's brilliant! What is a "pool class"?

A pool exercise class is one that you do exercise in water, in a four-foot level. You don't have to swim to get good exercise in a pool. That's what Buster Crabbe would teach. I also taught it at spas, and I've been teaching for the arthritis program at the Annenberg Center for Health Sciences at Eisenhower Hospital in Rancho Mirage, near where I live. I have been teaching there for five years, mainly to people who have chronic pain from arthritis and are sent by their doctors, either to take pool class or to take some sort of land-based exercise class. [Patients can] keep their range of motion by stretching and exercising, arthritis swelling goes down, pain is lessened — all kinds of good things. Having been in the role of Tarzan — the notoriety gets people's attention. You have an advantage over other physical educators in that people listen to you because the role of Tarzan seems to be one of an active person and a fit person.

Making that movie was like going to the circus, it was like *being in* the circus, getting to ride on elephants and playing with chimpanzees and lion cubs. I was like a kid at the circus, it was delightful to me. It's really been one of the joys of my acting career. I think that Tarzan was one of the real good guys. He was on the side of right, he was clean-living, he was respectful of women and animals and all of nature. It was a great opportunity.

DENNY MILLER FILMOGRAPHY

Some Came Running (MGM, 1958)
Tarzan, the Ape Man (MGM, 1959)
Love in a Goldfish Bowl (Paramount, 1961)
Doomsday Machine (Filmways/First Leisure, 1967)
The Party (United Artists, 1968)
Making It (20th Century–Fox, 1971)
Buck and the Preacher (Columbia, 1972)
The Gravy Train (*The Dion Brothers*) (Columbia, 1974)
The Island at the Top of the World (Buena Vista, 1974)
The Norseman (AIP, 1978)
Caboblanco (Avco Embassy, 1981)
Circle of Power (*Mystique*) (1983)

DAN O'HERLIHY

I think I've that great Irish sense of privacy that some Irish have, so I didn't want to "play myself." I always wanted sort of extraordinary character roles.

In the early days of his career, Dan O'Herlihy once quipped that in England, they referred to him as "the celebrated 'American' actor" and in America as "that distinguished 'English' actor."

The nationality is wrong in both instances, but the adjectives entirely appropriate. O'Herlihy actually hails from Wexford, Ireland, and graduated from the National University of Ireland with a degree in architecture. He chose acting over this profession, playing some of his first roles at the famed Abbey Theatre and the Gate Theatre.

In 1946, O'Herlihy made his motion picture debut in *Odd Man Out* for director Carol Reed, and in 1954 he received a Best Actor Academy Award nomination for his title role performance in director Luis Buñuel's *The Adventures of Robinson Crusoe*. Now a veteran of over 30 films, O'Herlihy saw the Cold War get catastrophically hot in *Invasion USA* (1952) and *Fail-Safe* (1964), tackled a dual role in the psychological chiller *The Cabinet of Caligari* (1962), donned an iguana mask for the interstellar adventure *The Last Starfighter* (1984) and played the CEO known as "the Old Man" in the *RoboCop* series.

When you were studying law and architecture, were you serious about it, or did you have a suspicion that acting might be in your future?

Oh, no, I had no suspicion. I think the first play I ever saw, I saw when I was about 22 — I never went to a play before that. But when I was at the National University of Ireland in Dublin, for fun I joined the dramatic society and won an amateur award. The judge was the director of the Abbey Theatre, the best director they ever had, and he offered me a part. I played some parts in the Abbey, and with *that* behind me I went on to other theaters, the Gate and so on and so forth. *And* I continued with the architecture. (I went into architecture in the first place because I didn't know *what* I wanted to do.) By the time I graduated as an architect, I had been playing leading roles in the theater in Ireland because [World War II] was on and the foreign companies couldn't come in to play in Dublin. Various companies started up but there weren't enough young leading men, so I became a young leading man fairly fast — myself and Edward Mulhare. I don't think I was particularly good, but I *was* playing leads and attracting some attention. Then I was noticed in England, apparently, and I got a good role in *Odd Man Out* [1947]. That started me off in films. I was working as an architect in the afternoons by this time, and in the theater at night. I then gave up the architecture and came to Hollywood.

Did you just "pick up" and move to Hollywood, or did you get an invitation?

I got an invitation from an agent, Charles Feldman — he was the head of Famous Artists, an agency. They took me over here. Orson Welles was a client of Feldman's, and Feldman mentioned me to him and Orson said, "*I* know of him," 'cause Orson had of course started in Dublin, with the Gate Theatre. Orson asked to see me, and I was put into … that play, the name of which you're not supposed to mention [the 1948 film *Macbeth*]. I played Macduff, and Orson played the *other* part [Macbeth]. Orson had heard I was an architect as well, and he said, "Look, I've designed the main set, Duncan's castle. But there are *so* many other sets and costumes and so on, maybe you could help. See if you can come up with a design for the scene where Macduff is told by the messenger that his wife and children are dead." So I came up with the top of a mountain and I duplicated the Cross of Cong, a well-known ninth- or tenth-century Christian cross with tremendous carving and so on. The actual Cross of Cong is only like six feet, but the copy that we used was, I'd say, 20 feet. Orson got wildly excited and *did* it — it's *in* the movie. (I got no credit, of course. Orson always took every credit conceivable!) So then he asked, "What will we do to establish the forces of *good* in this war between the forces of good and evil?" (Orson's group was the evil, and my group was the good — I was trying to put Malcolm [Roddy McDowall] on the throne.) I said, "Well, give them helmets of the period, and put the Cross of Cong on the top of each one." So they did that, and then Orson asked, "Okay, now, what sign for *my* side?" I said, "V." He asked, "V? For what?" I said, "*Evil*"— it was suggestive of evil. He said, "Good, good!" and he put *that* in [on Macbeth's men's shields]. I got no credit, but I did all that.

How was work on a Welles movie different from other movies?

It was fun and a *joke*!

Was he frustrated to be working at a small studio like Republic?

I think he enjoyed himself thoroughly, he always did. And I think he made the most *of* it.

Is it true that you got your role in The Adventures of Robinson Crusoe *because the producers were thinking of Orson Welles and watched* Macbeth *— and saw you?*

Yes, that's true. Luis Buñuel had already said, "I don't want to see Orson, I don't think he's right for it. He's probably too fat anyway." But then they looked at *Macbeth* anyway, and at the end they all turned and looked at Buñuel, and [producer Oscar] Dancigers said, "Well, how 'bout Orson?" And Buñuel then said, "No, no, no. The man who played Macduff. *That's* my man." And that's how I got it.

You also got into TV very early.

Peggy Webber was an actress who started a dramatic company and did a live half-hour show every week on KFI, one of the first TV stations. Her series, which she

He's in his seventh decade as a film-TV actor, but Dan O'Herlihy says he still thinks of himself as an architect first; "the other thing [acting] is secondary."

wrote, produced and directed, was called *Treasures of Literature*— they were famous short stories. I played the lead in many of them. I was paid $25 a show, so this was early on, obviously!

The first time you dabbled in sci-fi was in Invasion USA *for producer Albert Zugsmith.*

I had done a picture just before that Zugsmith was associated with in some way, *Sword of Venus* [1953] with Robert Clarke. I was a very good-looking young man, and [producers] kept trying to put me into leading roles. But I think I've that great Irish sense of privacy that some Irish have, so I didn't want to "play myself." I always wanted sort of extraordinary character roles. I wanted to play the old man in *Sword of Venus*, the old Baron Danglars. I told the producers that I wanted to do that. I wasn't yet 30, but I made up as an elderly gentleman and walked in, in costume.

Did you do your own makeup?

Oh, yes. Don't forget I was an actor on stage, doing makeup of course. I said, "I've come to play Danglars." They looked at me and they didn't recognize me right away — I'm very good at that sort of thing. Then they *did*, and [co-producer] Jack Pollexfen said, "Well, by God, you *can* do it!" So I got the part. And from *that* I went into *Invasion USA*.

You had good billing and a pivotal part in Invasion USA, *even though you were only in at the beginning and the end.*

Ah, yes. I was "new" and I was doing some showy work, *like* Baron Danglars. They were B pictures, of course, but I was doing some showy work and people were beginning to notice me. I had a sort of small, *prestigious* name by then, so Pollexfen and company and Zugsmith wanted to use me, and *did*, in *Sword of Venus*. Then Zugsmith had me in *Invasion USA*.

You employed an unusual accent in Invasion USA.

I think it may have been a Cork accent. Just to make it different.

In the movie, you hypnotize several people into thinking that Russia is attacking the U.S., dropping atom bombs.

Later on, I was a wild liberal and I spent some time in Russia. Later on, I would have disapproved of that [plot] — that was too right-wing. Of course, *I* wasn't right-wing. But I never questioned a script, I just looked at the part.

Albert Zugsmith was the producer of *Invasion USA*. Later, when he was out at Universal, Zugsmith offered me *The Incredible Shrinking Man* [1957]. That was after I was nominated for an Oscar for *Crusoe*. I read the script and I got angry. In *The Incredible Shrinking Man*, there's nobody else in the picture because he shrinks *so* small that he can only see the toe of somebody's boot. It was real Hollywood thinking: I was nominated for playing Crusoe, who's alone all the time except for Friday, and now they've got another "alone" character. I was *not* going to become The Man Who Does the Alone Pictures. And I refused. They came back, and I refused and refused ... and so everybody got angry! I went to Ireland to get away from them — I went up into the country, to a farm that an uncle of mine ran. As soon as I got there, he said, "Somebody from Hollywood has been trying to call you. His name is ... let me see ... Zoogsmith!" [*Laughs*] I said, "Oh, I, I, I, I see ... no, I, I *won't* call him back." Universal then came into it, and offered me a three-picture deal if I'd do it. I was stupid, I said no ... so they made it without me. *That* was a moment that I should have grabbed and taken because I think, with that picture on *top* of the others, I would have moved up some. Of course, I *had* moved up with *Crusoe* ... but I didn't want to succeed *Crusoe* with *The Incredible Shrinking Man*, I didn't feel right about that.

A dozen years after Invasion USA, *you were in another Cold War-atom bomb picture,* Fail-Safe.

There was a very good agent, a *wonderful* agent who I called and told I had done a TV show, one of those "doctor" TV

"It could never happen *here*": Manhattanites line up to see their own city being attacked from the skies in O'Herlihy's first Cold War melodrama.

shows, *Ben Casey* I think. It was a very romantic role of a man whose face had been destroyed. She showed that to [director] Sidney Lumet, and I was offered the part in *Fail-Safe*. I got first billing — with [Walter] Matthau behind me [*laughs*]! And Larry Hagman behind *him*!

And Henry Fonda behind you.

Well, Fonda wasn't really behind me, he had "special billing" at the end. That was an interesting film — *I* enjoyed it, anyway. Sidney Lumet was extremely clever. But one thing I *didn't* enjoy, I thought he over-rehearsed it. Rehearsing went too long; *my* taste in acting is more spontaneous. When you over-rehearse, you end up *copying* spontaneity instead of *being* spontaneous. *I* like to work with more spontaneity than to be very rehearsed. But that was a minor thing. From the point of view of doing his pictures fast and well, Lumet was good.

Did you think the plot of Fail-Safe *was plausible?*

Plausible? I guess so. But at that stage, I wasn't terribly politically oriented, as I *have* been in the years since. The story of *Fail-Safe* seemed to make *some* sense, because after all it did point out that the Russians were not to blame for this, it was the *Americans*. I seem to remember there was some conversation about the fact that there was too much hysterical anti-Russianism going around in the world, politically, and that *Fail-Safe* did a little *good* that way. It made you think a little bit.

The world teetered again at the brink of atomic destruction in the classic *Fail-Safe*, with O'Herlihy top-billed.

Did you happen to catch the recent, live George Clooney TV remake of Fail-Safe?

No, I didn't. Very good actors, all of them, but the casting, in my opinion, was "off." So I didn't watch it.

In the early 1960s you starred in a remake of one of the pioneering German horror films, The Cabinet of Caligari.

I had worked in TV for Roger Kay [producer-director of *Caligari*]. He was a very clever man, but *I* thought he said everything twice or three times. He was too wordy. And I had a fight with him. Of course, I was in no position to fight anybody, I wasn't a commercial star or what have you. But I had a fight with him about *that*, I said, "Look, you have a very academic sense of English, and your script is too academic. The story is very good, I *love* it. But—I hope you don't mind my saying so—it's over-written. It goes on for*ever* on points. If everybody would just stop talking and *do* something, it might be better!" [*Laughs*] I told him, "I can't play this. That's impossible." And Kay said, "Okay, you don't *have* to. You're fired." He threw me out, he said, "You're out of the picture." And I said, "Okay"—which he didn't expect me to say! And I left. So then later he called me up and apologized and said he would try to edit it down and so on.

And did he edit it?

He made a pretense of editing it. But when I was actually playing it, I left out every third sentence, I think [*laughs*].

Actually, the writer of Caligari *was Robert Bloch...*

Was it Robert Bloch? Oh, no, no, no, no. *No*, no. It was Roger Kay. Robert Bloch wouldn't have written anything the way this script was written. It was too wordy, and it was obviously written by a foreigner. Unless Robert Bloch wrote an original, and Roger Kay rewrote it completely.

Bloch gets the screen credit. And in his autobiography, he goes on and on about his problems with Kay on that picture.

Well, then, Roger Kay took the script over. *That* would have been why Kay was so angry with me when I said, "It's too wordy, too foreign."

What other memories of the shooting of the movie?

I've had a bad back ever since I was about 17, and it was at its worst then. When my back started acting up (as it did, constantly), I was sent down to a place in Westwood and they tried to help me. They were going to give me heat treatments: They had me lying on my face and put a very hot, wet thing on my back. After a few days of this, my back was vastly improved. It was called a Hydrocolator — you boiled it in water and then put about six thicknesses of towels on the back of the patient and then put the Hydrocolator on top of them. It emitted little streams of wet heat which went into you and which did help. So I bought one, and while shooting *Caligari*, I asked them to boil it up every day. But it was *so* painful to get up. I said, "Can I play Caligari sitting down?" I did get up to play the *other* role [Dr. Paul], but *just* for the shot. And I'd play Caligari sitting down — and I found my back was even *more* painful sitting down! But I think it was disguised pretty well.

How is your back today?

For about the next two years, whenever my back got bad, I immediately put the Hydrocolator on. For the last 35 years, I've had no trouble. I can have a tricky back, but no pain — not really what you'd call pain. It has vastly improved.

Reportedly Dolores Michaels was the first choice for the female lead in Caligari.

Really? I never heard that. Dolores Michaels... I seem to remember the name, but I can't place her. Glynis Johns got the part, and I got to know her during that. A lovely actress, as you know. Estelle Winwood, who was also in it, was very old, and very good.

Were you the first choice to play Caligari?

So far as I know.

What was Roger Kay like in general? Did you get along with him?

Oh, yes, yes, yes. I knew Kay very well, I'd worked a lot with him and we were social friends because I liked talking to him. He and his wife Paulette would come to our house and have a meal with us, and we'd go to theirs. It was quite a close friendship, because I was fond of him. But he had an enormous ambition and an enormous ego which got in his way, and in the end he had to leave Hollywood because of that.

Kay told The New York Times *that for* Caligari *he made up a color chart on graph paper, with each space representing one minute and the color in the square indicating what the audience should be feel-*

The two faces of O'Herlihy — as the benign Dr. Paul (left) and the creepy Dr. Caligari (right) in the psychological shocker *The Cabinet of Caligari*. (Photofest)

ing at that minute. Was Kay kidding, or would he do things like that?

I never saw that article, but it *sounds* like Kay [*laughs*]!

Did you ever meet the producer, Robert Lippert?

I don't think I did. I was a B picture star in a B picture. *But*—I didn't think that *was* a B picture, but that it had far more individuality than one would expect in (say) *Invasion USA* or *Sword of Venus*. It had a sense of quality.

I interviewed one of Lippert's screenwriters, and he recalled visiting Roger Kay's office during the making of Caligari. *He said Kay was disheveled, and he suspected that Kay had just been in a fistfight with one of his cast members.*

I don't believe it. Roger would have *fled*. He was too heavy, and a little awkward.

Well, I pressed and pressed this writer, and finally he said that he thinks the guy who beat up Kay ... was you.

Oh! [*Laughs*] Oh, no! The only fight I had with Kay was when I was fighting with him about his writing — and he fired me. I told him, "You can't write anything with simplicity," and that's when he really went mad and raved with anger at me. But he never touched me, nor would I have touched *him*. I was being polite all the time, I said, "I'm trying to *help* you!" I told him, "You are not *naturally* an English speaker. You were a French speaker in *Egypt*, where you grew up, and it shows in the way you write dialogue." I think he realized I *was* trying to help the picture, actually, but he was offended and he said, "I don't think we can continue together," and I said, "Well, if you can't, you can't," and I left. Then he asked me back. The next day's rehearsal, he called up and said, "Why aren't you *here*?" [*Laughs*] Do you know whatever happened to Roger Kay?

No, I don't.

I don't either. He was Egyptian-born, but he went to Paris afterwards, after working in Hollywood. He *fled* to Paris [*laughs*]—he couldn't get work here, I don't think. That's the last I heard.

Were audiences not supposed to realize that one actor was playing both Caligari and Dr. Paul?

I don't know. I hoped that maybe they wouldn't, which is why I made Caligari have a Cork accent. I made Caligari play with a Cork accent and I had Dr. Paul play with a "normal" accent, an accent that would be accepted as American, I think. And, of course, the makeup was utterly different.

I'm afraid I'm enough of a fan of yours that I knew immediately that it was you in both parts.

I would expect that. But with the average audience, they might not all have known. I would imagine they would after they'd listened and watched for half an hour.

Did you ever see the silent Caligari?

With Veidt? Yes I did. I was bored by it [*laughs*]! By the way, a well-known psychologist, I can't remember his name, was terribly impressed with my performance in *Caligari*. He was originally an American, went to England for years, married the actress Joyce Howard and then came back here, and they lived close to us. He saw *Caligari* and he asked four or five other psychologists to look at it. And they were so impressed! Afterwards they said to me, "You really must be one of the most brilliant actors in the country. How on Earth did you work that attitude out?" I said, "I *didn't*. I just *did* it. And I don't think it's all that brilliant." They said, "Oh, it was, it was!" And the one psychologist, my neighbor, kept saying, "I can't understand how an actor could have played these *two* roles. The psychology is so different," etc., etc., etc., and he kept harping at it. He asked, "How did you come to the conclusion of so-and-so?" "How is it that you came to do *this*?" "How is it that you came to do *that*?" So I lost allll respect for psychologists [*laughs*]! I *did*, I lost all respect for them. This famous psychologist sort of fell down at my feet for my doing a *very* ordinary job of acting. He thought my performance was quite extraordinary, he said he'd never come across anything like it. He didn't know what he was talking about. I thought, "He must be an idiot!"

Some of my past interviewees have talked a little about you and some of the pictures you were in. Would you have any interest in reading some of this stuff?

Yeah, sure. I've retired, I don't care what they say [*laughs*]! I was always anti-establishment, and of course I had to leave the country not too long after I was sort of responsible for bringing to a head the government's suit against MCA [the worldwide talent agency that had acquired Universal]. The government closed MCA down, and I was the principal one [responsible] there. So, from then on, agents from the top level would never touch me. Jack Warner once called me a Communist. Which wasn't so [*laughs*]—I wasn't one! Nevertheless, work closed down and I went to Ireland for five years. I've told you the story of my closing down MCA, haven't I?

No, you haven't.

Oh! It was the reason I had to leave the country later. It all started in the early 1960s. I was with MCA, and it was several years since I'd been Oscar-nominated for *Crusoe*. The agent who represented me there—I won't use *his* name even though

O'Herlihy tackled a dual role in the 1962 remake of the silent horror classic.

he's dead, because his family's still alive. I'll call him Mervyn. Anyway, he called me up and said, "Hey, baby, this is Mervyn. They're going to make a picture about that guy who discovered China, Marco Polo. We're going down to the big projection room in Beverly Hills underneath MCA, and [MCA executive] Taft Schreiber will be there, *and* the producer of the picture, and we're going to show them your movie that you got nominated for, *Swiss Family Robinson*." I said, "You mean *Robinson Crusoe*." He said, "Yeah, yeah, whatever" [*laughs*].

I went down that night, and Mervyn said, "Sorry, baby, they didn't think you were right for Marco Polo, but Taft Schreiber has a great idea. We will do a series on *Robinson Crusoe*. And of course, with you getting nominated for that role, it'll go together fast. It'll be very good for you and for us." Then he added that his brother would be producing. Well, his brother was a hack television producer — I knew that. I said, "Well, no, no, no, I've *done Crusoe*, I don't want to do it again." He said, "Oh, come on, don't be silly. Gimme a reason." I didn't want to give him the reason that his hack brother was going to produce, but that *was* the reason; I had done *Crusoe* for Luis Buñuel and I didn't want to go from Luis Buñuel to a hack Hollywood producer-director. So I said no.

Several weeks after that, I read in the trades that MCA was going to produce for Universal *The Adventures of Robinson Crusoe* with Dan O'Herlihy, who had been nominated for that role, etc., etc. So I called Mervyn up and I said, "Don't put that out. I told you I wouldn't do it." He said, "Oh, come on, baby," and I said, "No, I *mean* it." Some time passed — a couple months — and I wasn't getting *any* work. This was four years after my nomination. I called Mervyn up and he said, "Sorry, baby, but nobody in Hollywood will touch you with a 40-foot pole. But I can put you into something that'll make you a millionaire." I said, "You mean *Crusoe*?" and he said, "Yeah!" I said, "Well, *don't*. I won't do it."

Did they give up at that point?

No! Some time later, Mervyn called me up and said, "[Producer] Jennings Lang wants to talk to you." So I came down and met with Jennings Lang and Mervyn, and Mervyn said, "Here are the first six *Crusoe* scripts. My brother wrote every one of them. There they are, take 'em and look at 'em. This'll be a big success." I said, "No, I will *not* take them and look at them, I told you I would *not* do this series under any circumstances *whatsoever*. Not for a million a week." Mervyn jumped to his feet and started to shout at me, and Jennings Lang, I'll never forget, said, "Mervyn, *sit down*! Don't ever forget, the agency is the servant of the client." I tried to keep a straight face when I heard *that* one!

A little time later, I ran into a producer who was a social friend of mine, a man who was working at Universal. He said, "Pity I couldn't get you for that movie last month." "*What* movie?" I asked, and he told me. I said, "Did they tell you I wasn't available? Because if they *did*, they broke the law." He said, "No, they asked twice your going money." Of course, that knocked me out [of the running for that movie part]. MCA wanted to keep me unemployed so that I'd do the series. A little time later than *that*, a young MCA agent, a fellow who had blacked the eye of one of the higher agents and been fired, called me up and he said, "I'm going to tell you something that, if you quote me on it, I'll deny it." I said,

"Okay ... " He said, "Taft Schreiber passed a memo down about you. I memorized it at the time. It said, 'Put O'Herlihy on ice until he agrees to do the series.'"

I've heard that the people at MCA used to do business like that.

So I fired MCA, because under the Screen Actors Guild contract, you can break any contract with any agent if you haven't worked for three months. I'd been out of work for *four* months, so I sent them a telegram saying, "Under the appropriate clause six of our contract, you no longer represent me." And the shit hit the fan: They called me and started to scream at me and so on and so forth.

What was your reaction to that?

At that time, the *Los Angeles Mirror* was attacking MCA because it had bought Universal and was now both agent *and* employer. The *Mirror* asked, "How can they be on both sides? How can MCA make pictures and then *sell* the talent to themselves?" The *Mirror* was attacking MCA very hard. Well, I was so angry with MCA after they'd called me and yelled at me that I called the *Mirror* and I said, "You've been talking about restraint of trade and what have you with MCA. Well, here's a story for you ... " And the story I just told *you* appeared on page one of the *Mirror* with my picture! Well, a great silence then descended [*laughs*]!

At least you've retained a sense of humor about this!

Yes, as you can see! Well, about six months after I left the agency, there was a knock on the door — this would have been about '61, the Kennedys were in and Robert Kennedy was the attorney general. At my door there was a neat little man who said, "Dan O'Herlihy?" I said "Yes?" And he said, "Subpoena," and he handed it to

Dan O'Herlihy's Oscar nomination for *Robinson Crusoe* led — indirectly, and years later — to the dissolution of the world's largest talent agency and the actor's own self-exile.

me! It was a subpoena to appear, to give evidence in court downtown *against* MCA. I was the first witness on the stand. To my astonishment, the T-men or the G-men, T-men probably, had really gone into *every*thing at MCA and they came up with *seven memos* about me. The first one from Taft Schreiber was "Put O'Herlihy on ice until he agrees to do the series," which of course I knew about, but I didn't know about the other six. And a week later I was down there, I can't remember why, and I was talking to Bobby Kennedy's next-in-command and he said, "MCA has lost." I asked, "What's going to happen?" He said, "Next week they'll be given three days to close down worldwide." And that was the end of MCA as an agency.

And the repercussions later? You mentioned that you had to leave the country for five years.

My reputation just grew and grew from the MCA days on. Everything slowed up, because of how I had behaved towards one of the big "powers" in this country. None of the bigger agencies would touch me, they'd say, "Oh, he's trouble." Finally I moved to Ireland, from about 1970 to '75. I remember some people there asking, "Are you going to *stay* here in Ireland?" and I said, "No, no, I'll go back to Hollywood in five years." They asked, "Five years? How did you pick that [figure]?" And I said, "Because most of the ones who are responsible for my condition over there will be *dead* by then!" [*Laughs*] So I went back and they *were* dead, most of them!

You came back in 1975 because...

Because I was beginning to get work back here again.

You mentioned a few minutes ago that

Jack Warner thought you were a Communist when you weren't.

When I was doing *Home Before Dark* [1958] at Warners for [producer-director] Mervyn LeRoy, LeRoy kept talking about [J. Edgar] Hoover—his dear friend Hoover. I made no comment, and he said, "You look like you don't like Mr. Hoover." And I said, "Well, as a matter of fact, I don't." He said, "He's one of the great patriots of this country," and I said, "Well ... okay ... " He asked, "What do *you* think of him?" I said, "Well, I think he's one of the great *traitors* to this country." He hit the roof [*laughs*]. This is the sort of trouble I always got into with my tongue. Mervyn LeRoy, Jack Warner's ex-son-in-law, told Jack Warner that, and of course Warner thought I was a Communist because I said that.

In a 1965 interview, you mentioned that you were up for a part on Lost in Space.

Yes, I was, and I turned it down. It was the lead, the father of the family, as I remember. After MCA had been closed down by *me*, people from MCA had gone and formed another agency and they started to put together *Lost in Space* for me.

Why did you turn it down?

Well, I didn't want to *do* it. I read the script and didn't think much of it. But then, if *I* liked the script, that was a guarantee that it would not be successful! The general American public, which would provide a very large audience, is not very educated. Not that *Lost in Space* was an educated thing—it *wasn't*! So I did think it might be successful, yes. But I didn't do it.

You've also been in some comparatively recent horror and sci-fi movies. Halloween III *[1983]—what did you think of that?*

Whenever I use a Cork accent, I'm having a good time, and I used a Cork accent in that. I thoroughly enjoyed the role, but I didn't think it was much of a picture, no.

RoboCop *[1987]?*

Well, the first one was a very good movie. I didn't have too much to do in it, but I liked the part. The second one [*RoboCop 2*, 1990], I *loved* the part, but it wasn't as *good* a movie. The third movie [*RoboCop 3*, 1993], they took it for granted I'd do it, and I refused. Because it wasn't the same producer. The third movie was made by two different guys. They arrived up at the house and invited themselves to lunch to persuade me, and of course I realized why: Peter Weller [RoboCop in the first two movies] decided he wasn't going to do the third. [Co-star] Nancy Allen *was* in *3* but she was killed off on page 27. So they *needed* me as the "connection" to the previous two movies—I could see that that was why they wanted me. Then I read the script, and I thought it was *awful*! So I refused to do it.

You played an "iguana man" in the space adventure The Last Starfighter.

Those sort of exaggerated roles, I love to do. I didn't use a Cork accent with *him* [*laughs*], but what I *did* do was, they made the mask for me and I said, "When [the iguana] mask is fresh, I can *make* it smile if I stretch my lips inside *very* far—the lips stretch half as much on the mask. And if I raise my eyebrows *very* high, the eyebrows on the mask do raise slightly. I can make the face alive—but the mask hardens after 24 hours." They asked, "Well, what can we do?" and I said, "Make the mask fresh every night, so that it will last during the following day." We shot for five, six weeks, so they had to make 30 masks—they had to make one every night.

I remember one day I went up to

Robert Preston, I had the mask on, and I stretched out my hand and I said, "Hello, delighted to meet you. I'm Dan O'Herlihy." And he said, "Oh, for God's sake, you don't have to tell me, Dan, I'd know you *any*where!" [*Laughs*]

You mentioned to me a while back that you're retired—so why am I still seeing you every time I turn the TV on?

I *had* retired. I was offered TV shows, but in my seventies, I didn't want to work eight days in a mediocre television show and get paid even *good* TV money. So I kept turning them down. I did do two over the last eight years, but that's *all* I did, and then I said, "No more, no more." My agent was growing unenthusiastic, so I went to an agent who understood what I wanted and I said, "I only want to work one day in a week." On *The Rat Pack* [the 1998 TV movie], he insisted on that. They crammed it down into one day, which of course was very hard on me. But it worked all right.

I long ago lost track of how many interviews I've done, but it might be around 400. And I think you're only the second actor ever to tell me that he was really enjoying being retired and that he was turning down jobs.

Well, don't forget I *am* an architect. I was a "semi-pro" in Ireland when I was in my twenties, and I'm still a semi-pro. I found myself doing movies here and making a lot of money—comparatively speaking, a lot of money—and I couldn't get out of it if I *wanted* to. And I did want to, quite a few times. I got nominated, and after I was nominated I got more and more bored with what I was doing. If I was paid to do a job, I was very conscientious. If it was a part I loved, that's different. *Then* I loved the part and did it with great fun. But I've never thought of myself as an actor first.

I've thought of myself as I did in Ireland— I'm an architect or designer first, and the other thing is secondary.

DAN O'HERLIHY FILMOGRAPHY

Odd Man Out (Universal, 1947)
Hungry Hill (Universal, 1947)
Kidnapped (Monogram, 1948)
Larceny (Universal, 1948)
Macbeth (Republic, 1948)
The Iroquois Trail (United Artists, 1950)
The Highwayman (Allied Artists, 1951)
Soldiers Three (MGM, 1951)
The Desert Fox (20th Century–Fox, 1951)
The Blue Veil (RKO, 1951)
Actors and Sin (United Artists, 1952)
At Sword's Point (RKO, 1952)
Invasion USA (Columbia, 1952)
Operation Secret (Warners, 1952)
Sword of Venus (RKO, 1953)
The Adventures of Robinson Crusoe (*Robinson Crusoe*) (United Artists, 1954)
Bengal Brigade (*Bengal Rifles*) (Universal, 1954)
The Black Shield of Falworth (Universal, 1954)
Hunters of the Deep (narrator; DCA, 1954)
The Purple Mask (Universal, 1955)
The Virgin Queen (20th Century–Fox, 1955)
City After Midnight (RKO, 1957)
Home Before Dark (Warners, 1958)
Imitation of Life (Universal, 1959)
The Young Land (Columbia, 1959)
One Foot in Hell (20th Century–Fox, 1960)
Night Fighters (United Artists, 1960)
King of the Roaring 20's—The Story of Arnold Rothstein (Allied Artists, 1961)
The Cabinet of Caligari (20th Century–Fox, 1962)
Fail-Safe (Columbia, 1964)
100 Rifles (20th Century–Fox, 1969)
The Big Cube (Warners, 1969)
Waterloo (Paramount, 1970)
The Carey Treatment (MGM, 1972)
The Tamarind Seed (Avco Embassy, 1974)
MacArthur (Universal, 1977)
Halloween III: Season of the Witch (Universal, 1983)
The Last Starfighter (Universal, 1984)
The Whoopee Boys (Paramount, 1986)
RoboCop (Orion, 1987)
The Dead (Vestron, 1987)
RoboCop 2 (Orion, 1990)

KATE PHILLIPS

[The Blob] came out just at the right time. …Until that time, the monsters [in '50s monster movies] had been mechanical things or giants. There hadn't been anything nearly like The Blob. *The timing was perfect.*

One of the most original movie monsters of the 1950s, the Blob was a baseball-sized glob of footloose (albeit foot-*less*) protoplasm that arrived from outer space and, indulging its appetite for human flesh, grew until it threatened an entire town. In 1957, this basic idea was presented to the moviemaking ministers of Valley Forge Films, a commune in rural Chester Springs, Pennsylvania, that specialized in shorts and TV programming with religious themes. The filmmakers agreed to produce the sci-fi thriller and worked on the story, but needed a professional screenwriter to give some form to their story of an amorphous monster. They turned to veteran radio and TV writer Kate Phillips.

Born in Pine Bluff, Arkansas, the future *Blob* writer (real name: Mary Katherine Linaker) was educated at a private school in Connecticut and later attended New York University. While living in New York, she became interested in the stage and began attending the American Academy of Dramatic Arts. Her work in several small Broadway roles brought her to the attention of screen scouts and she was signed for movie work. She appeared under the name Kay Linaker in many films of the 1930s and '40s, including *Young Mr. Lincoln*, *Drums Along the Mohawk*, a quartet of Charlie Chans and James Whale's final two films. Meeting and marrying singer-turned-writer Howard Phillips, she relocated to the East and began writing for television (her husband became an NBC executive). And in 1957, while Phillips was bouncing a newborn daughter on her knee in her Long Island, New York, home, *The Blob* took shape in her mind…

Why did you leave acting in the mid-40s and move to New York?

I wanted to make a viable contribution to the War effort. Since I was not a singer or dancer, I couldn't go with the USO troupe, so I joined American Red Cross. I was a hospital recreation worker and I worked in psychiatric hospitals. On a weekend I went to New York and met

Howard Phillips. It was kind of a whirlwind courtship, and we got married. He was in the Air Force when we met. Before that, he had been a big band singer; he had his own radio shows on CBS and NBC, he'd been Andre Kostelanetz's soloist and he had been Ray Noble's soloist. But while he was in the Air Force, he started doing some writing for magazines like *Esquire*, *The New Yorker* and *True*. He didn't want to go back into the music business, and I didn't want to go back into acting, so we decided we would just write together. We first wrote [for the radio series] *Our Gal Sunday* and *Ma Perkins* and we got paid $20 a script. They gave you the story, they gave you the characters, and all *you* had to do was write the dialogue. It was like taking money under false pretenses! We progressed from those to the *big* radio shows like *Masterpiece Theatre* and *Cavalcade of America*. Then we heard about this thing called television, which of course wasn't gonna be a success because the box was too expensive.

Kate Phillips (a.k.a. Kay Linaker) modeling the latest fashions back in her acting heyday. (Photofest)

What were your first TV assignments?

We wrote four or five *Ford Theatre*s. For an hour adaptation of a play that had been done on Broadway, *Ford Theatre* paid a hundred dollars. It was live TV, one set, done *in* a theater in Manhattan. We had three cameras, but only one was mobile.

Your husband got in on the ground floor of NBC-TV in the early days of television.

Gen. Sarnoff decided that he had better take a step into national television before CBS did, so he gave it to his son Bob Sarnoff and said, "*You* do it." So Bob Sarnoff hired seven other people to head up NBC National Television, the whole thing, and my husband was one of them. He was in charge of program procurement, which meant the writing department. It was unbelievable, how he worked. He took the 6:30 train into New York in the morning, usually came home on the eight o'clock train which didn't get in 'til about 9:15, and he would have his dinner and he was reading scripts all while he was having his dinner. He had two readers working for him but he didn't think it was right to accept the verdict of a reader, particularly if it was a no. And of course if it was a yes, he *had* to read it. So that meant he read everything that came through. Of these seven people who were the original group at NBC, there was one heart attack, two nervous breakdowns, one bleeding ulcers, one suicide. And one who was emotionally totally unstrung. (He got to the point where we tried very hard to get him into an institution because he did sort-of strange things like ... like leaving his apartment without his trousers on. And was *convinced* he was totally dressed.) I remember one night I sat up in bed and Howard was walking the floor. It was about three-thirty in the morning and he was walking the floor with a script in his hand, and he was stumbling, he was so tired. It was really a man-killing operation.

Meanwhile, you were still writing for TV.

I was still operating on my own, writing [the series] Mama and The Goldbergs—*both* of them! They were in competition with one another, but nobody minded that I was doing both. I was very busy and everything was going along fine. About that time, Howard and I went down to an International Christian Leadership meeting in Washington because one of the backers of the movement was from Islip [Long Island] and was a good friend of ours—that's how we happened to get interested in it. I believe that year it was held at the Hilton, because Conrad Hilton was very interested in International Christian Leadership. All of a sudden a chap came up to me in the hotel and said that somebody had suggested that he talk to me because I was a writer. He asked me if I knew about film and I said, "Yes, I do." He said, "Well, we are gonna do a picture and I would like to have you be part of the picture." His name was "Shorty" Yeaworth.

Irvin S. Yeaworth, who directed The Blob.

Yep. He was at the conference because his little film company down in Pennsylvania was making "how-to-teach-Sunday-school" films, 15-, 20-minute films, for Christian education purposes—they were shown at the ICL meeting. He was an ordained congregational minister, as was the chap who was with him, [writer] Theodore Simonson. "Shorty" told me that somebody was going to give 'em the money to make a full-length science fiction film and they had $60,000 and they were going to make it in color. He asked, "Would you be interested in doing something with it?" Well, under these conditions, you don't say, "No, I'm not interested"—I said, "Why, yes, I think that would be fine" and gave him my telephone number and thought I'd never hear from him again.

I was very pregnant at the time. My baby was born, and when she was three months old, I got a phone call one day saying, "This is 'Shorty' Yeaworth"—he and Simonson were on their way up from Pennsylvania to Long Island. Not "We'd *like* to come up" but "We're on our way," so I couldn't say, "Don't bother" [*laughs*]!

Now the story becomes a little interesting. They arrived, and they told me a little bit of a story about a thing that comes from outer space. There was very little else. They showed me a beautiful leather-bound loose-leaf book and said, "Everything you need is in here." Now remember, I am a professional writer. When you say something like that to me, I immediately think that you have a whole script. Then they opened a two-pound coffee can and out came this ... thing. They poured it out onto my coffee table, which was made of half a tree on wagon spokes. This thing climbed up over a stack of magazines; it divided and went around a pipe smoker's ashtray; went on down, went over some more books; and then Simonson was at the end of the table to catch it in the empty can. And it went right into the can. I said to myself, "It has no moving parts, no electrical charges. This is a wonderful, wonderful monster!"

Was the table tilted at all?

No, no, it just moved all of its own accord. It climbed up over the magazines and whatnot and it changed shape — it was really exciting.

And that was your introduction to the Blob.

That's right. They were calling their production *The Molten Monster*— that was the original title. So we chatted a little bit longer, and they asked if I would do the script. "There's everything here that you need," they said again, indicating the loose-leaf book. I said fine, gathering that what they needed was some kind of a pulling-together and some kind of a rewrite. I asked, "When do you need this?" and they said, "In two weeks." Mind you, I had not looked in the book. Then they talked about the fee, they said, "We'll send you a check for $125. You will do it on speculation, with ten percent of the gross." I said fine.

They left, I fed the baby, changed her, and looked in the book. In the book, there were a few little sketchy things about a storyline. There were lists of places where they could shoot — a school, a diner, a market. There was a list of places where they could rent equipment. Then there were lists of people in town who would play parts, and a letter or some kind of a statement saying that the police department had assured them their cooperation. And that's all! So I took what was there and wove it together into the script.

When you were writing The Blob, *did your husband do any writing or make any suggestions?*

No, he didn't. He walked by and said, "*You* did it. *You* agreed. It's your baby!"

[Laughs] Why did he say that? Were you having a hard time with it?

No, I wasn't, but my daughter Gina was three months old at this time and she was kind of colicky, and at night she used to be quite noisy. I had a nest of little end tables and one was a perfect height for putting a little typewriter on. I would go downstairs and sit in this Victorian living room chair that gave me nice support, at this end table, with her on my knee, and bounce my knees up and down. The vibration and the sound of the typewriter would lull her to sleep. I would put her over in her tiny little crib and keep on working. Howard was very sweet, he'd stop and say, "How'd it go today?" and I would say "All right" or "I didn't get as much done as I thought," or whatever. But that was his only interest!

How long did it take you to finish it?

I mailed them the script in two weeks. Another ten days or so went by, and they mailed me a check for $125. Then I didn't hear from them. Meanwhile, my husband was telling his friends at NBC how stupid I was, and all agreed that I was very stupid.

Why were you stupid?

Because I did it for such a little amount of money. And because I didn't do it through the Writers Guild — which *was* stupid. The head of talent there at NBC was a man named Martin Begley — he is young Begley's [Ed Begley, Jr.'s] uncle. Marty called me one day and said, "I just saw a young man who would be great in your show. This is a most unusual young

Phillips wrote *The Blob* without ever having seen a science fiction movie ("Look, Mary Shelley didn't know what *she* was doing either!").

man," and he kept on about this young actor. He said, "I'm enthusiastic and excited. I saw him last night — he's taking Tony Franciosa's part in *A Hatful of Rain* on Broadway. You've really got to come in and see him 'cause he is *perfect* for your show." I said, "But ... I don't have anything to do with *that* part of it [the casting]." Marty said, "Kate, it's a great opportunity for you to do some good for somebody. I'll leave the tickets for you at the box office and I'll tell Howard to meet you at the station ... " I didn't really want to see *Hatful of Rain*, I had already seen it in Philadelphia and thought it was a good show, and I didn't see any reason to subject myself to it again [*laughs*]. But I took the train and went in and Howard and I went to see the show. After the very first scene, Howard and I looked at one another and he said, "Marty's right." And I said, "Yes. He usually is!" I didn't go backstage to see this young actor Steve McQueen, I stayed out of it. I just called down to "Shorty" in Pennsylvania and I said, "This guy is really stupendous. Grab him." And so they did.

Did you ever hear from Yeaworth or any of the other Chester Springs people after that?

Yes, a little more time went by, and they called and asked if I could come down to Pennsylvania so we could have a meeting. I got my daughter's godmother, a real Auntie Mame character, to come down with me and my daughter — we drove down to Pennsylvania and she took over as the nanny while I went in and we talked. I don't know how "Shorty" "promoted" this, but he did: They had a kind of a commune there and they lived in this big old house.

They owned an entire pre–Revolutionary War village there.

His house was a lovely Revolutionary house. It had been restored very nicely, but the floors still leaned in all directions and the place was very sparsely furnished. I walked in, and there at the table sat a guy who had on a silk suit ... his shirt had his monogram embroidered on it ... he had dark hair. He was very smooth, very sleek, and he was picking his teeth with a gold toothpick. *That* was the producer [Jack H. Harris]. So there we were, "Shorty" and Simonson and his nibs [Harris]. The only other people I saw aside from those three men were "Shorty's" wife Jean, who served sort of a vegetarian lunch and then wasn't around very much, and a couple of other people who kind of walked through. But we were busy, and nobody stopped for socializing. So we started; I read the script aloud.

Was it still "your" script?

There had been no changes made in it. I was reading the script, and all of a sudden I came to the line where the character of Steve says, "I looked down and there was this ... blob." At that point, Harris opened his mouth for the first time and said, "*That's* the title. *The Blob.*" And everybody just said "Yes, my lord" sort of things. We continued to go through the script, and at a couple of points Harris said, "Why is it done *that* way?" I said, "'Cause all you've got is a few pounds of liquid glass. What you have to do is show the reaction of people to this thing, you can't show it in action *unless* you are showing it in action *with* a model." And after a pause he said, "Oh. Yeah. That makes sense." Mr. Harris was much impressed with that.

When you suggested using miniatures, that was the first time they thought about that?

Yes.

Did you read the whole script aloud?

We didn't finish because it was getting dark and it was getting late, and the baby was getting fussy. I said, "I think we've done everything that we need to do today. If you need anything more, let me know." And so I departed, back to Long Island.

Simonson gets co-credit for the screenplay. Did he do enough to deserve it?

Well, what *he* wrote suggested what *I* wrote. It gave me the stepping stones. A couple of places, the ideas that they had for storylines I felt I couldn't follow. They wanted to have a lot of "bad" teenage acting-up. The only thing that I left in was a very small amount of the backwards drag race.

You made the kids a lot more clean-cut?

Yes. Kids have been treated badly enough in films. I really think that there are so many more good kids than bad kids. It gets worse all the time. What the media are doing to the minds of young people is absolutely criminal. I work with youngsters now [Phillips is a teacher at New Hampshire's Keene State College], and they have a very bad habit of saying, "I'll kill him ... I'll kill him ... " I asked a youngster one day, "Have you ever killed anything?" This boy looked at me and he said, " ... A cockroach." I said, "Have you ever, say, caught a mouse in a trap and then taken the mouse out and killed it?" He said [*appalled*], "Oh, no!" I said, "Then just please remember that what you are saying may get somebody *else* to feel more violently about something. And you may inadvertently, by your actions, cause some people to pull another Columbine."

Was it you who came up with the idea that the Blob can't tolerate cold?

I don't remember. But the Blob had to respond to *something*. There's the sequence where the Blob is in the supermarket, going down one aisle, and the boy and girl [McQueen and Aneta Corsaut] get in the walk-in refrigerator and shut the door.

In the supermarket freezer scene, McQueen and Corsaut are about to discover that Blobs like it hot.

The Blob comes up to the door (knowing where they are) and starts to squeeze under, but the moment it hits the cold it draws back. That was the way we established that the Blob couldn't stand the cold. When you do that kind of [foreshadowing], you don't want the whole audience to "get it" right at once [to know too soon that cold will be the Blob's eventual undoing]. I tried to do it in such a way that it wouldn't be like sending up a flare on a dark night. When you're writing something, you don't put it on so heavy that your audience says, "Yeah, yeah, I already know this." What you do is you *suggest* something, and let the audience respond. That's the whole secret: To get your audience to the point where they participate. You ask people who have seen lots and lots of films, "What is the sexiest scene you ever saw?" and they will tell you that the sexiest scene they ever saw was the beach scene in *From Here to Eternity* [1953]. What you *see* in that are two people [Burt Lancaster and Deborah Kerr] who are swept up in a real current of passion. You do not see any nudity, you do not see him moving on top of her, you don't see anything like that. But the audience is able to identify with these people, and *that's* the whole trick, having the audience have a part in the movie.

Not enough horror and science fiction

moviemakers realize that sometimes less is more.

Oh, there's one scene in *The Blob* that people tell me is the scariest scene they ever saw. That is when Steve McQueen is walking around the side of the house of the doctor [Stephen Chase]. As he does, he looks up at a window and sees the Venetian blinds jumping around and the slats all change direction. People say to me that seeing the doctor all draped with the Blob was terrible. But you *never* see the doctor draped with the Blob. You see Steve reacting to what *he* sees through the blinds.

And you did it that way because…

Because I have always been convinced that if you have a big fire, you don't stay on the fire, what you do is cut to people watching the fire. Because, after all, how much emotion can there be in a fire [*laughs*]? So that was what I did with that.

Somehow I can't picture you watching a bunch of teenage monster movies back in the '50s as you were preparing to write The Blob.

I never did. I don't think I had seen a monster movie — not since *Frankenstein* [1931].

So you wrote one without ever having seen one.

Look, Mary Shelley didn't know what *she* was doing either [*laughs*]!

When the movie was shooting, did they bother to invite you down there?

My husband and I had moved to California by that time.

So you don't know anything about the shooting.

Well, yes I do. My husband had a cousin in Boston who had a son, Philip Epstein. Philip went to Amherst University and did a play there, he was extremely good in it and the theater bug bit him. So, instead of going to graduate school, he announced that he was going to go into theater. (His mother and stepfather just hit the roof!) About that time, *The Blob* was going to be made, so I called "Shorty" and said, "I have somebody for one particular part" [one of the teenagers]. I asked "Shorty" if he would use Philip, and he said sure. Of course, all that Philip got for it was his board and room — nothin' else. Not cent one! Not even his train fare from Boston down there. But he went, and I knew it was either gonna kill him or cure him. And it worked.

It cured him.

It cured him [*laughs*] — he came back and went to Columbia and got his graduate degree in international banking, and he did well enough in it to retire at 50. So, you see, much *good* came out of this picture! Well, according to Philip, they didn't know *what* the hell they were doing. The best explanation of them is what Harry Truman once said about himself: He said, "I was playing piano in a whorehouse and didn't know what was going on upstairs." [*Laughs*] "Shorty" didn't know from nothin' — the only thing they had done were these little Sunday school films. I don't know who the cameraman was on the thing, but he didn't know how to call the shots — that's what Philip told me. Philip said that the person who made suggestions about calling shots was Steve. Steve would walk up to 'em and say, "Hey, don't do it that way, do it *this* way…"; "Don't move the camera around — let the actors come in and out, let *them* be the action." They really didn't know.

Did you get ten percent of the gross?

Once they sold *The Blob* to Paramount,

I decided I would call Valley Forge Films and find out about my ten percent. When I got them on the phone, I talked to a man who had sort of a business manager deal with the company. I told him I had been promised ten percent and he said, "Oh, all that doesn't matter. It's not in writing, we don't have to honor that contract." I said fine and I hung up, and I went out to the Writers Guild. As I stepped in the door, the girl standing behind the counter said, "Kate, please, turn around and leave. You have *not* been here." They had seen the film and she knew what I was there for. I said, "What are you talking about?" She said, "You didn't do what you were supposed to do. You didn't notify the Guild that you were doing a screenplay on speculation. There *is* a penalty for that, and you *don't* want to get mixed up in it." So I said, "No, I don't." About that time, Steve McQueen had come out to the Coast and he was seeing a young lady, and that young lady happened to be Howard's cousin [*laughs*]! So one day in Schwab's Drug Store we met one another and I said something to him about *The Blob*. He looked at me and said, "My God. You're the writer." I said, "Yes, I am." Then he said, "And you're in the same boat I am." Because *he* had not notified the Screen Actors Guild, and *they* had the same policy as the Writers Guild! So neither one of us could do anything. After that, every once in a while we would meet and one of us would say, "Have you...?" and we'd both shake our heads [*laughs*]! But the thing about it was, *I* got a screen credit and *he* got a career. And if that's the way the cookie was supposed to crumble, that's the way it did.

So $125 was all that you ever got for writing The Blob.

That's right.

When I interviewed Yeaworth, he told me that all you did script-wise was "help give it some polish."

Well, what else *could* he say? I really feel very sorry for him. He should have gone to Las Vegas and been a front man [*laughs*].

Do you remember where you saw The Blob *for the first time?*

Yeah, it was either at the Pantages Theater or some other theater in Hollywood. I saw it with Howard's mother and his aunt — his Aunt Leah was the [ex-wife] of writer Borden Chase and had worked with Borden.

Why didn't your husband go?

He had something else he had to do. He said, "If you *want* me to go, I'll —" I said, "No. Uhn-uh. It's not important enough." Because I didn't think it was! So Howard's mother and his Aunt Leah and I went to see it. Leah was not very polite about other people's writing — if she thought it stunk, she'd say so [*laughs*]. Well, as we were coming out of the theater, she said, "You know, that is an extremely good, workmanlike job."

Talking about the writing?

Talking about the film. She was a very talented woman, a fine technician, so I thought that was a great compliment. But *I* didn't think the film was too sharp ... !

Well, let's start off with what you did *like about it.*

There were a couple of things that I liked very much, such as the opening scene of [McQueen and Corsaut] in the car. I was impressed with the good taste [the filmmakers] showed — they were not slobbering all over one another. She was played all the way through the movie as the typical ingenue, *so* sweet and *so* nice — but back in that era, if they'd had a real slobbery love scene at the beginning, *that* would have immediately marked her as a barroom girl. The scene was tastefully done and they were both *very* very good. I think there were only four professional actors in *The Blob*—there was the beautiful young lady [Aneta Corsaut], the old man [Olin Howlin], the doctor [Stephen Chase] and Steve. But there were not too many places where I said "ow" or "oh no." To this day, I'm not ashamed of it.

Did you think McQueen was too old for the part?

No, I didn't. He was older than the other guys and he was *written in* as older.

So what were some of the parts where you went "ow" or "oh no"?

The panicking people running out of the movie theater—that was just horrible. They had many, many, many too many people for that small town. And I will *not* take any credit at all for the big question mark at the end of the picture. I *will* not! It was "Shorty's" idea to have the big question mark.

And the Blob effects?

I thought they were very good, considering that this was done with two pounds of liquid glass—you have to bear that in mind!

Did you see the 1988 remake?

No. I just had no interest in it.

What accounts for the box office success of The Blob?

It came out just at the right time. There hadn't been anything quite like it. Until that time, the monsters [in '50s monster movies] had been mechanical things or giants. There hadn't been anything nearly like *The Blob*. The timing was perfect—they fell into a tub of butter with it. I'm very glad for them. As for [being underpaid], as far as I was concerned, and as far as Steve was concerned, it was all right with us if that's how they wanted to play. It was *their* problem, not ours.

I told Yeaworth that you say you were cheated, and he told me that "everybody got paid what they were supposed to get paid."

I guess when something like this happens, you have to believe your own lies. I'm really very sorry for him, because if he had handled himself differently, his whole career would have been different. If he had said [about his inexperience at making a feature film], "Look, I don't know very much but, by God, I'm gonna learn," and *if* they had not shortchanged people, he would have been able to follow *The Blob* up with enough low-budget pictures in that same area to become the king of the walk.

When was the last time you saw The Blob? *Do you show it to your classes?*

When I was teaching at Queens University in Canada, I showed it to my writing class up there. Then when we were starting the film department at Keene State College, we needed to get some money in for the film society and we decided to run a double-bill of *The Blob* and one of the pictures I acted in, and have me there to answer questions. The first picture we showed was *The Blob*, and then I talked about it. Then we showed a picture called *The Girl from Mandalay* [1936] which I had the lead in, with Conrad Nagel as the fellow I fell in love with. My daughter Gina and her husband were sitting in the back of the theater with *my* husband. In the opening scene of *Girl from Mandalay* I danced with Conrad, and there was nothing but a

Phillips won't accept the blame for *The Blob*'s hokey "question mark" ending.

On her eightieth birthday, Phillips (right) went up in a hot air balloon with her grandsons and their other grandmother (left).

little music and looking-from-one-to-the-other. All of a sudden, in this quiet moment, Gina said, "My God ... he was almost my *father*!" Because I was engaged to Conrad Nagel [*laughs*] — on *three* different occasions!

Actually, my grandsons have a great deal of fun with the fact that I was an actress and that I wrote *The Blob*. The youngest one is just 13, and he had to write an article on somebody, a little essay. He wrote an essay on his nana: "I have a different nana than most people do...." He wrote about some of the things I did, and at the end he wrote, "I have to remember that she was an actress in Hollywood, and she also wrote *The Blob*." Well, all the kids said, "Awww, come on, you're telling a big lie!" and he said, "No, I'm not!" It got to such a pitch that his teacher called his mother and said, "This essay that Matthew wrote — is it true?" and she said, "Yes, I'm afraid it is!" [*Laughs*] And the *next* thing that happened was that Matthew said to me, "Nana, if I get permission, will you come to school and talk?" I said I'd be glad to. So I went over and the whole eighth grade — allll of the eighth grade — was gathered together and I talked about what it was like to have a life in an industry like the motion picture industry. Then I answered some questions. We had a *wonderful* time, and I got letters from the teachers thanking me for coming and asking if I would do that same kind of thing again some time. This was just this year [2000].

What are you teaching now?

I teach screenwriting and public speaking, and also courses in film classics and creative drama. I also teach a course in acting for the screen.

You're 86. Why are you doing all this at your age?

Well, my husband once said that if, when you retire, you do not have a demanding schedule for yourself, retirement is the first step to the cemetery. I think it's so true! And I have a lot of fun on my birthdays because I do something special every birthday: On my eightieth birthday, I went up in a hot air balloon with my three grandsons and their other grandmother. We had a lovely trip. Then on my 86th birthday, I jumped out of an airplane — and that was fun! Recently I had to promise my 14-year-old grandson that, when he is 20, I will do a parachute jump with him.

KAY LINAKER–KATE PHILLIPS FILMOGRAPHY

As Kay Linaker
The Murder of Dr. Harrigan (Warners, 1936)
Crack-Up (20th Century–Fox, 1936)
Road Gang (Warners, 1936)
Easy Money (Chesterfield, 1936)
The Girl From Mandalay (Republic, 1936)
The Outer Gate (*Behind Prison Bars*; *Beyond Prison Gates*) (Monogram, 1937)
Black Aces (Universal, 1937)
Charlie Chan at Monte Carlo (20th Century–Fox, 1937)
I Am a Criminal (Monogram, 1938)
The Last Warning (Universal, 1938)
Personal Secretary (*The Comet*) (Universal, 1938)
Trade Winds (United Artists, 1938)
Man About Town (Paramount, 1939)
Young Mr. Lincoln (20th Century–Fox, 1939)
Charlie Chan in Reno (20th Century–Fox, 1939)
Charlie Chan at Treasure Island (20th Century–Fox, 1939)
Drums Along the Mohawk (20th Century–Fox, 1939)
Girl from Rio (Monogram, 1939)
Heaven With a Barbed Wire Fence (20th Century–Fox, 1939)
Elsa Maxwell's Hotel for Women (20th Century–Fox, 1939)
The Invisible Woman (Universal, 1940)
Buck Benny Rides Again (Paramount, 1940)
Green Hell (Universal, 1940)
Hidden Enemy (Monogram, 1940)
Charlie Chan's Murder Cruise (20th Century–Fox, 1940)
Free, Blonde and 21 (20th Century–Fox, 1940)
Kitty Foyle (RKO, 1940)
Mystery Sea Raider (Paramount, 1940)
Sandy Is a Lady (Universal, 1940)
Blood and Sand (20th Century–Fox, 1941)
Blossoms in the Dust (MGM, 1941)
Charlie Chan in Rio (20th Century–Fox, 1941)
Glamour Boy (Paramount, 1941)
Married Bachelor (MGM, 1941)
Moon Over Her Shoulder (20th Century–Fox, 1941)
Private Nurse (20th Century–Fox, 1941)
They Dare Not Love (Columbia, 1941)
Remember the Day (20th Century–Fox, 1941)
Men of Texas (Universal, 1942)
A Close Call for Ellery Queen (Columbia, 1942)
The Night Before the Divorce (20th Century–Fox, 1942)
Orchestra Wives (20th Century–Fox, 1942)
War Dogs (*Pride of the Army*; *Unsung Heroes*) (Monogram, 1942)
Pittsburgh (Universal, 1942)
The More the Merrier (Columbia, 1943)
Two Weeks to Live (RKO, 1943)
Cinderella Swings It (RKO, 1943)
Happy Go Lucky (Paramount, 1943)
Let's Face It (Paramount, 1943)
Wintertime (20th Century–Fox, 1943)
Here Come the Waves (Paramount, 1944)
Laura (20th Century–Fox, 1944)
Lady in the Dark (Paramount, 1944)
Men on Her Mind (PRC, 1944)
Bring on the Girls (Paramount, 1945)

As Kate Phillips
The Blob (screenplay only; Paramount, 1958)

KASEY ROGERS

[Two Lost Worlds] ultimately became quite a cult-type film.... Think about it — we had the dinosaurs, we had the volcanoes erupting, we had the big-masted ships firing in battles at sea, we had everything!

She packed enough capable performances (and exciting times) into her acting life for *two* people, so perhaps it's appropriate that many movie buffs think that she *is* two people: They know her as Laura Elliott, Paramount contractee of the early 1950s, and also as Kasey Rogers, prolific TV actress (*Peyton Place*, *Bewitched*, scores of Westerns), and don't realize that the "two" are actually one and the same. She was menaced by dinosaurs in the low-cost fantasy epic *Two Lost Worlds* (1950) and stalked by psycho Robert Walker in Alfred Hitchcock's suspense masterpiece *Strangers on a Train* (1951), but she embarked on some of her favorite adventures *between* takes, tomboyish-ly scaling the masts of sound stage sailing ships and running with stuntmen along the top of a moving train. (And for "relaxation" between acting jobs, she took up motocross!)

Hailing from Morehouse, Missouri, she was born Imogene Rogers and moved with her family to California at age two and a half. She got the nickname Casey when her neighborhood playmates discovered how well she handled a baseball bat ("I could hit a baseball farther than anybody in grammar school except Robert Lewis — he and I were always the opposing captains of the sixth grade baseball teams!"); she later changed the C in Casey to a K. Twice-married and the mother of four (and a grandmother), Rogers has in recent years turned her talents to writing and development, including the proposed new TV series *Son of a Witch*.

When did you get your start on the stage?

When I was about eight! I started piano lessons at seven and accordion about ten, but in between there my mother paid to have me take what they then called elocution lessons — enunciation and pronunciation — and I did little monologues. I think my mother, God love her soul, was a frustrated actress all of her life. *She* never attempted anything, but I think that she just liked the glamour and that sort of thing. Maybe her influence pointed me in that direction, although it certainly didn't take much pointing because I loved every *bit* of it. I did little plays, and I always had the lead, even then! Then I did the lead in my junior high school play and the lead in my high school play. So I always loved acting, right from the beginning.

At what point did you set your sights on getting into the movies?

It sort of happened accidentally. I was 20 years old and had just gotten married—I got married when I was 19, which was really dumb. It was a wartime thing. And at 20, an agent from MCA saw me in Beverly Hills or Hollywood or some place, and wanted to represent me.

He saw you in a play?

No. I can't say I was sitting on a drugstore fountain stool or anything like that [*laughs*]—he just spotted me ... *some* place. Whether it was a restaurant or walking down the street or whatever, I don't remember the exact situation. And I *was* with my husband, and so it was okay that he approached me. In those days, you were very leery. *I* didn't know Hollywood, I didn't know anything *about* it.

I went over with my young husband because [*laughs*]—because I was afraid to go to "a Hollywood agent's office"! And of course it was only the biggest agency in town. But then I discovered I was going to have a baby, so I didn't go back. After the baby was born, however, I thought, "Hmmm ... I wonder if they're still interested..." I called the agent and he said, "Yes, by all means," so I went in. They took me to Paramount and I auditioned in a scene there. They liked it, and so I did a screen test. And they liked *that* and signed me and I went into the lead in *Special Agent* [1949], like, the next week [*laughs*]! So I didn't have to go through the "struggling actress" bit.

Do you remember what your screen test was?

I *used* to know. It was with George Reeves, who was TV's Superman, of course. *Oh!* It was *Voice of the Turtle*, it was a scene from *Voice of the Turtle*. My *God*, I can still remember that [*laughs*]! I worked on that scene with the coach and with George. God, I thought I was not going to be able to remember that!

I've talked to other actors and actresses who went through Paramount, and they all tell me horror stories about a room called "The Fishbowl."

[*Laughs*] Oh, yes! Yes indeed! You're one of the few people who know about the Fishbowl, eh? What that *was* was a room that had couches and chairs and lamps and a piano and light switches, a totally furnished, lovely room. *Except* that one wall was double-glass, the entire wall, and you could not see out through it. On the other side of that glass were two rows of seats and an intercom thing. That's where the coach would sit, that's where (if you were doing a class) the other students would sit, that's where the casting director would sit, or the producers, or the director...! The only terribly intimidating thing was that you could not see through that glass—and *they* were looking at *you*! It took some getting used to!

Your side of the glass—was it a mirror, or just dark?

Just dark—a mirror would have been too distracting for the scene. I do think it served the purpose of making you learn to concentrate on what you were doing, like you would in front of a camera. You had to get rid of your consciousness of self and learn to be natural in a very *un*natural environment.

Did you object when Paramount changed your name to Laura Elliott?

Oh, no, I thought it was very glamorous and "very Hollywood" and all that sort of thing! But then after five years I got tired of it and I went back to my own name. So almost all of my films are Laura Elliott, and all of my television is Kasey Rogers. It's like two different actresses, and very *very* few people in this entire world associate the two.

Do you have any anecdotes that go along with your tiny part in Samson and Delilah *[1949]?*

Just [Cecil B.] DeMille—*he* was wonderful. I had, I think, only one or two lines, but they were in big closeup, *gorgeous* big closeups, me and an actor. DeMille took like half a day to shoot those two lines—he was on this big boom, the big arm that goes up and down with the camera. He was clear up in the air and we were up on the second level of the Coliseum—oh, it was such a production to get those two lines! Incredible! But I knew Mr. DeMille quite well at Paramount. He was intimidating to many people, but he was always very kind to me. So I liked him very much.

How did you know him? Just from seeing him around the lot?

Yes. In fact, I had auditioned for a different role, I auditioned for the role of Miriam in *Samson and Delilah*. I actually did a screen test, but he told me later, "You're too pretty and you're too young." [Olive Deering played Miriam in the movie.]

Well, if you had to lose out on the role, that's an explanation you could live with!

Yeah, yep ... but I would rather have done the *role* [*laughs*]! But that was good of him. I'd see him around, and you could go up and talk to him on the lot or in the commissary, or whatever. He always had an entourage around, and he had on the leather riding boots and the jodhpurs and the crop—he cut quite a figure!

If you can remember that your screen test was Voice of the Turtle, *I'll bet you can remember your line from* Samson and Delilah.

Um ... okay, let's see ... I turned to this fellow and said, referring to Delilah, something like, "Why don't you look at *me* like that?" And *he* said, "Because she's *Delilah*." And I pouted and turned away [*laughs*]! That's as near as I remember! And I had a long-stemmed rose in hand.

What is it like to work at a studio where you can have the lead in a movie one day, and the next day you're an uncredited bit player in a different movie?

Sometimes it was frustrating. It was especially frustrating after *Strangers on a Train*. That was on loanout to Warner Brothers, and there I worked with Hitchcock in this wonderful film. I had writeups which said ... I'm not bragging, but one of 'em, *Variety* or somebody, said, "brilliant performance." And I go back to Paramount, and the next thing they had me doing was color tests, holding up swatches of material for the camera crew to test their new film with! And I'd think, "Jeez, was it for nothing?" [*laughs*]—it was very frustrating. But then I *did* get some other pictures at Paramount, and so it worked out okay.

On loanout from Paramount you got top billing in an adventure-fantasy called Two Lost Worlds.

It *was* a loanout, and it was my third film. Interestingly enough, that was James Arness' first film—it was my understanding, when we were shooting it, that that

They came from the stock footage library — the pirate battles and prehistoric monsters of *Two Lost Worlds*.

was his first film. Of course, *I* was "the old pro," 'cause that was my *third* film [*laughs*]! [*Two Lost Worlds* was Arness' first starring role, but *not* his first film.] That film ultimately became quite a cult-type film, which *I* didn't know for years — I thought, "Oh, who would ever remember *that*?" But then I had various friends saying, "Are you kidding? That's a cult film!" Think about it — we had the dinosaurs, we had the volcanoes erupting, we had the big-masted ships firing in battles at sea, we had *every*thing!

It may have all been stock footage, but you had it all!

We had it all. The volcanoes and dinosaurs were from *One Million B.C.* [1940]. It was fun — well, it was sorta fun.

We worked in Red Rock Canyon out here in California, it's on the way to the desert, and Red Rock Canyon is solid rock. And the floor is sharp little rocks, like a half-an-inch, triangular-type, sharp rock. In this one sequence, I had to run to a pool of water — we were dying of thirst and then we saw the water, so we ran and got down on our knees and drank the water. Talk about pain! It hurt! I was barefooted. They tried taping the bottoms of my feet, but it wouldn't stay on. So you just had to go through with it, just do it. It was uncomfortable, to say the least!

Any memories of the people who made Two Lost Worlds? *Producer Boris Petroff?*

His little girl [Gloria Petroff] played my little sister in the movie. And there was

Years before TV stardom in *Gunsmoke*, James Arness clinches with his first big-screen leading lady (Kasey Rogers) in *Two Lost Worlds*.

a funny story which I was told, that when James Arness met Boris Petroff for the first time, Arness' agents told him, "Now sit down — and *don't stand up!* No matter what you do, don't stand up!" Because he would have towered over Petroff — and sometimes, if you're too tall, that's not good. So he sat through the whole entire interview, and he got the role.

I also remember that I used to love to go climb the riggings of the ships on the sound stage — at lunchtime, I'd climb up the riggings and see what it felt like up there. That was fun.

How high were they?

High [*laughs*]!

Were you still in costume?

No, no, you'd take the costumes off for lunch, and then get back in 'em later. Another thing I remember which is kinda funny: There was a certain period of time when it was *extremely* hot on the sound stage — so hot! And I had this one scene leaning over the railing of the ship. I had my costume on top and my *shorts* from the waist down, because it was so hot [*laughs*]! But you couldn't see that, 'cause that was behind the railing.

My interviewees tell me they sensed that James Arness was never comfortable being an actor. Did you see any of that, did you find him at all "different" from the average actor?

I didn't think so. I thought he was a very nice man — just very, very tall! I'm five-five and he was six-six. I remember at the end of the movie there's a shot of two people standing with their backs to the camera, and I thought, "Who's that little girl?" And it was *me* standing beside him [*laughs*]!

You also had love scenes with Arness. Is it tough to do romantic scenes with people you've perhaps just met?

Yes and no. You learn to look at it very professionally. I did a love scene with Charlton Heston in some of his first tests, and I hardly knew him except through rehearsals. But I remember the crew saying, "Wow, that was really a hot love scene!"— implying, like, "What's going *on* here??" Well ... nothing. Hel-lo! [*Laughs*] We were working, is all. Especially if you're with a professional actor, you know you're both doing a job. And you can finish kissing and say, "Oh. Thank you. What's next? Where's my lunch?"— whatever [*laughs*]!

There was a romantic triangle in that movie — you and James Arness and an actor named Bill Kennedy.

He was always trying to upstage me [*laughs*]! Oh, dear, I hope he doesn't read this! One time he had his arm around me as we were watching the volcano or something, and he tried to bury my face into his shoulder! There were a couple of situations like that, and that's all I remember of him. That's where I learned about upstaging — and how to protect yourself.

Back at Paramount, you had just the tiniest little part in When Worlds Collide.

At that time at Paramount, there was a thing called the Golden Circle — a dozen contract people, all of us very young, who Paramount was, quote, grooming for stardom. A whole bunch of the Golden Circle group was in *When Worlds Collide* [Barbara Rush, Peter Hanson, Judith Ames *et al.*] but while they were shooting, I was in Sonora, doing the second lead in *Silver City* [1951]. We got off location and came back to the studio, for just the last two or three days of filming on *When Worlds Collide*, and I was just kind of thrown in. I think the only thing I did was walk down some airplane steps [playing a stewardess]— that's all I can remember doing! But [producer] George Pal was very lovely — he gave all of the kids, *all* of us, beautiful gold charms with an inscription about the film. I got one, too, even though — you know, what did I *do*? Nothing. There was another member of the Golden Circle in *Silver City*, Michael Moore, a nice-looking guy who played the heavy, and he and I just got in on the last two days of *When Worlds Collide*.

The Golden Circle was very interesting. Actually, it was the *second* Golden Circle — there was a Golden Circle probably a dozen years before, and from that came a number of well-known stars. The year before Paramount revived the Golden Circle, I was the only young actress under contract to Paramount. So they decided [to re-start the Golden Circle] and they signed the others. It was a neat thing, because now we had all these guys and girls to do scenes with and become friends with, we did a lot of promotions and we all worked together in *A Place in the Sun* [1951]. Again I don't think I had a line to say and I don't remember what we did [*laughs*]— we were all at this resort, around a swimming pool. But we got to work in movies with George Stevens and Frank Capra and C. B. DeMille — you name 'em! It was an incredible training ground.

When Paramount finally did give you a few more co-starring roles, they were in Westerns like Silver City *and* Denver and Rio Grande *[1952].*

Denver and Rio Grande was filmed outside of Durango, Colorado. We stayed in Durango, then took those little narrow gauge track trains for an hour every day up into the mountains. I told you I was a tomboy: At night, coming in after work, I'd get up on top of the train cars with the stuntmen and run along and jump the cars. Oh, [producer] Nat Holt would have killed me if he'd seen me up there!

Who were a few of the stuntmen?

A fellow who Yvonne DeCarlo ultimately married, Bob Morgan; Leo McMahon, Harvey Parry ... they were all just great.

And who was the instigator? Did they get you up there, or did they follow you?

No, *they* did it. And so, if they did it, then *I* had to do it. I said to myself, "Okay. I can do that"—and did! We pulled another terrible joke on Nat Holt: We were back here at the studio and I was not working one day. They were going to have a great big barroom brawl that day, all the stuntmen and [stars] Eddie O'Brien and Sterling Hayden and all the guys. So I came in very early in the morning and I had the makeup guys make me up like a *guy*. They put this brown makeup on, and whiskers, and my long blond hair was all tucked up under a cowboy hat. And I've got on men's cowboy clothes and things.

I set this up with Bob Morgan: I went onto the saloon set and sat down at one of the tables. (You never realize how small you are as a woman until you put on men's clothing. *Then*, all of a sudden, they're all towering over you [*laughs*]!) We waited 'til the dress rehearsal. Eddie O'Brien came in the one door and Sterling Hayden came in the other, and they started talking and yelling back and forth. Finally *I* stood up and I said something like, "*You* can't say that to *him*!" Bob Morgan hauled off and threw a punch, and I threw a punch back at him, and he did a flip back over a table.

I started to run around, and then two stuntmen jumped up and they held me back—everybody in the room, their jaws were dropping, like, "What's happening? *What's happening*?" They were holding me back, holding onto this wild man, and my hat fell off and all the blond hair fell down. I think it took 30 seconds before anybody finally realized what was going on, and then they started laughing. Nat Holt was one of the people whose chin dropped—he was like, "What is this going on on my set??" [*Laughs*] We created this whole fight sequence which didn't hurt [the studio], it didn't cost them very much money, and they didn't get too mad at me. And it *was* funny!

How many people were in on it?

Probably a half a dozen of the stuntmen is all. The two guys that had to grab my arms and Bob and maybe one or two others. But we had a whole saloon full of people and crew and Eddie and Sterling Hayden who didn't know what was happening!

Denver and Rio Grande *also had a tremendous head-on train wreck. Were you around for that?*

I was. It was *very* spectacular. They brought 150 members of the press up there to photograph and witness it, but the day the press people were there, the weather did not permit filming. So a number of them had to leave, and the scene was filmed the next day. We were all many hundreds of feet back from the actual impact. What I remember are the engineers—some of these little guys with white hair had driven those trains for 50 years! They started the two trains on the same track, coming toward each other, far apart. The trains got up to six or ten miles an hour and the engineers had the controls locked down, and then they jumped out.

The trains picked up speed, picked up speed, until they crashed into each other. And they had rigged it with some dynamite and stuff, to make it *really* explode. Those little engineers had tears rolling down their cheeks—oh, it was so sad to see them, they were so emotional. They were holding it in, but the tears were there. The impact threw pieces, *huge* pieces of metal as far away as *we* were, hundreds of feet. And when the smoke finally cleared, here were these two engines *still standing*. Still standing, just like, "*We* won."

Strangers on a Train. *Even though you don't have the biggest part in the world, that's the first thing all my friends thought of when I said I'd be interviewing you.*

Strangers on a Train—oh, my favorite, of course [*laughs*]. No, it *wasn't* the biggest role, but it was certainly memorable, and that's what counts. I had heard about the role from another actress, *months* before. The actress was Jean Ruth, a young contract player at Paramount—she came from musical comedy. She said, oh! it was perfect for her, and she'd auditioned for it. And I thought, "Well, she and I are *such* different types that there's no way it would be right for me," so I didn't think anything more about the role. She and I looked nothing alike, our personalities were nothing alike, so I thought, "If it's right for her, it's *not* right for me!"

I guess they were searching, searching, searching [for the right actress], and my agent called one day—this is like three or four months later. He said, "Laura, you have an interview over at Warner Brothers on this Hitchcock picture." I said, "Well ... I don't think I'm *right* for that," and he said, "Go. Just go to the interview." So I went over there and I read the scene and I thought, "*Oh*, my *God*, it's *wonderful!*" [*Laughs*]

Was it the scene in the record store?

Yeah. Well, that's the only big dialogue scene there *was*. I just lovvvved the scene, so I auditioned and the casting directors loved it. So, after they'd interviewed girls for months, they finally screen-tested six of us girls in one day. I had not even met Hitchcock, had no direction from him, so what we brought to the role that day, each of us, was what *we* brought to the role, you know? I tested, and I got the role. Just as simple as that! I was thrilled.

Was Farley Granger in the test with you?

No. I've forgotten who was in the test. Forgotten totally!

And when you finally did work with Hitchcock...?

I must say Hitchcock really didn't give me a lot of directorial stuff about the character, just ... "Play it as you played it" and "Walk *here*" and "Go *there*." That was pretty much it.

In the movie, Pat Hitchcock reminds Robert Walker of you. Besides the glasses, was anything done to make the two of you look a bit more alike?

No, I don't think we were made-up to look like each other at all. The only similarity, basically, *was* the glasses. There were six pair that were made up—two pair had clear lenses, two pair had medium prescriptions in them, and two pair were so thick that I literally could not see the blur of my hand passing in front of my eyes. *I could not see through them.* If you can imagine this, all I could see was just a little bit out of the sides, on either side. And that was the pair Hitchcock wanted me to wear, because in reverse, they made the eyes look very small—very "pig-eyed," as he called it. Therefore, I did the entire film without being able to see. I could not see Farley Granger's face when I looked at him;

Bitchy Miriam (Rogers) meets her end at the strangling hands of Bruno Antony (Robert Walker) in the suspense classic *Strangers on a Train*.

I could not see the merry-go-round when I was trying to jump on [*laughs*] — I could not see! And Hitchcock insisted that I wear those glasses even in the long, long shots, out of doors. Which was pretty strange!

Any idea why he insisted on that?

There could have been the possibility that somebody could forget and I'd be wearing the clear glass when we went to closeup — if that had happened, then suddenly I'd have a different look entirely. Look at the picture again: In the record store, when I'm ringing up the cash register sale, I can't see the cash register. When I'm running after Farley as he's leaving the store, when I'm saying, "You can't toss me aside like that," I could not see him. Watch for my hand running along the counter — the reason I did that is because when my hand came to the end of the counter, I knew I had hit my mark, and that's where I stopped. In my scenes with my two young boyfriends [Tommy Farrell, Rolland Morris], you'll see they'll always offer their hands, or I'll take their hands. Up and down the bus steps, on and off the carousel — because I couldn't see anything.

So you had them helping you.

Yes, and Bob Walker. Bob Walker was wonderful because in real life he *wore* thick lenses like that — but he didn't in the film. So he always said, "It's the blind leading the blind!" [*Laughs*]

Did you like Hitchcock?

Oh, yes. He had a wry sense of humor, and you never wanted to cross him or to be a smart-ass, 'cause he could just *cut* you down. So you were pretty respectful of Mr. Hitchcock!

That was his rep, or you saw him do that?

He could do it with a *smile*. And his wit was just rapier-sharp. He was brilliant — he did some wonderful, wonderful things. I'm just so thrilled that I was lucky enough to *be* in one of his films.

Remember when Miriam is choked and her glasses fall to the ground? The camera shoots into one of the lenses and you see the strangulation taking place and she's sinking lower, lower, lower, and then Bob Walker stands back up — all in the reflection. Well, of course, we shot the exterior things out at the park, but then one day they had me come in, onto an empty sound stage. Hitchcock had this big, round, like two-and-a-half, three-foot diameter, concave-type mirror sitting on the concrete floor of the sound stage. The camera was on one side, shooting down at the mirror, and Hitchcock said, "Now go to the other side of it and turn your back." I did, and my reflection was now in the mirror. He said, "Now, Laura, I want you to float to the floor. Float backwards to the floor." Like I was doing the limbo, bending backwards under a stick. He said, "Float to the floor," and I said, "Yes, Mr. Hitchcock."

"Okay, roll 'em," he said, and I started leaning back and back and back. But you can only get so far until, suddenly, THUNK — you drop two feet to this concrete floor! He'd say, "Cut! Laura ... fllloat to the floor." [*In a despairing voice:*] "Yes, Mr. Hitchcock." And we'd do it again and I'd get just-so-far, and go THUNK on the cement floor. *Seven* takes — but on the seventh take, I literally fllloated all the way to the floor. And he said [*imitating Hitchcock*], "Cut. Next shot." [*Laughs*] That was it! I don't know *how* I did it, and I've never tried it since! But it shows what you *can* do when somebody insists — you can do things that you had no idea you could do.

And that seventh take is what we see in the reflection in the glasses in the movie?

That's what you see. And furthermore, Robert Walker was not there; the tree branches were not there; *all* of that stuff you see surrounding me wasn't there. That shot is studied at UCLA and USC, in their film schools, to this day, and *I* don't have an explanation for how he did it. I should go to school and find out how it was shot [*laughs*]!

What memories of Robert Walker and Farley Granger?

I adored Robert Walker. He was very quiet, very much a gentleman, verrry talented. He was just brilliant. Farley Granger was ... handsome. He was the 8 × 10 glossy, you know what I mean [*laughs*]? But he did fine. He was in a *couple* of Hitchcock films — you can't be *all* bad and be in a Hitchcock film, you know. Robert Walker and Farley Granger and the two actors who played my boyfriends were the only people I really worked with in the whole movie.

Strangers on a Train *didn't do your career any immediate good...*

No, and that was rather a shame. I had the feeling that no one at Paramount watched the film [*laughs*]. It would have been nice if *some*body had been a *little* bit impressed, or something! But I just think they didn't even see the film. Therefore you have nobody "pushing" you publicity-wise or putting blurbs in the trades or anything of that sort.

One thing was kind of fun: When it was in release, I went on a junket full of stars. We traveled on this big bus and we were raising money, or we were doing *some*thing like that. We were going through Oklahoma and various places and of course at the various places everybody is introduced to the audience by an emcee. Well, they would introduce Laura Elliott and everybody would give me a very polite little who-the-heck-is-*she*? round of applause. Finally one time I said to the emcee, "You know, I've got a picture out right now." He said, "Oh? What is it? Let me announce it." I told him, and he said, "Oh my God!" So the next time he announced me, he said, "This is Laura Elliott, who in *Strangers on a Train* was ... Miriam." And everybody [*Rogers gasps*]—*big* gasp! They all recognized the character, and they'd look at me with these wide eyes, like, "Oh! You *horrible* girl!" [*Laughs*] And then *great* applause, a wonderful reaction! It was funny.

Oh, you've got me *going* on this now! My little niece Harlene, she was turning 16 and she was taking a bunch of her girlfriends to see her auntie in this film, *Strangers on a Train*...

This is when the picture was new?

Yes, when it was just out. They're all sitting there in the dark theater watching the movie and I come on, being the "sweet" person I was in that picture. And they were all asking Harlene, "Is *that* your aunt? Is *that* your aunt?" But Harlene told 'em [*stuttering*], "No—no—I—I—I don't *know* that woman! I've never seen her before!" She would not admit to it!

And you enjoyed playing a meanie? You certainly excelled at it!

Oh! *Love* it! Are you kidding!

After you left Paramount, you changed your name back to Kasey Rogers. Did that create problems? Was it like starting from scratch again?

In retrospect it sounds really dumb, but it didn't seem to hurt because I went right into television. In those days, people kinda looked down their noses at television but I had a young son to support and I was a divorced single parent, so I did television. It was a fairly smooth transition.

You acted in lots of TV Westerns — including one where you were almost hanged.

I don't remember which TV series that was, but it was a half-hour series and I was in a Western girl's costume, and I was going to be hanged. You know how you go up stairs and you're about six feet high on a platform? They ran a big plank out from the platform and balanced it on barrels at the far end, and had a scaffolding up above with three nooses hanging down.

There were two older bit player-types and me waiting to be hanged. We walked out there, the one guy and then I'm in the middle and then the next guy, and they placed the nooses around our necks. Now, milling about are cowboys on horses—one kick of that barrel and down we'd all come! We're standing there ready to shoot when suddenly the gentleman next to me — his eyes got big as saucers. I asked, "What is it? What's the matter?" His hands were tied so he motioned with a movement of his head, a "look behind you"-type movement. I turned around to look and I saw guys tying and nailing down the far ends of each of the noose ropes. The nooses were already around our necks, and our hands were tied behind us. If a horse had kicked over a barrel, they'd have had three hung actors—there's nothing we could have done. The other two actors were afraid to say anything, so I spoke up—I said, "Please! Undo that!" They did, and then it was okay. So they weren't exactly thinking — sometimes you have to watch out for yourself.

In addition to all the chances you took in

your movies and TV shows, you were also a real-life motorcyclist.

I *love* motorcycles—I raced 'em for eight years or something.

How in the world did that start?

My little son Mike was nine years old and he came home one day and he said he wanted to motorcycle. "You want to *what*?!" [*laughs*]—what did *I* know about motorcycles? Nothing. Anyway, I got him a little mini-bike, a mini-motorcycle—those things are powerful as can be, you just don't realize. I got on a 50 cc and immediately ran into a chain link fence! At any rate, Mike learned to ride in the Encino hills and became very good. (I didn't even know he should have a helmet—I was very uninformed!) He wanted to race minicycles, and it fell to me to take him out to Indian Dunes to race. I remember the first time I went out to Indian Dunes, about a 600-acre motorcycle park. I thought, "Oh, my God, it's dirty, it's loud, it's muddy, it's dusty"—and then I learned to love it [*laughs*]! At first we went every Sunday to ride, and it didn't take very long before I was unhappy sitting and watching. So I got a racing bike too. Then I learned to ride on the regular motocross tracks with all the teenage boys. They had a Friday night race for the minicycles also, so we would go Friday night *and* Saturday night. And that's how I got into motorcycles, because Mike wanted to race and he happened to be very, very good—he became one of the top five or six minicycle racers in the United States. We ultimately raced in Texas and Florida and Missouri and all over the United States.

How old was he at this point?

Nine or ten. They have all different categories, from beginning to expert. My son used to race with Jeff Ward—Jeff rode for Honda when he was a youngster, but he turned pro when he was 17 or 18 and at some point became what they call a "factory rider" for Kawasaki. My son raced him, and they would dice it out all the time. Sometimes Mike would win, sometimes Jeff would win. But that's how I got into it—and then of course found that I loved it. I learned to ride motocross sitting on the start line with all the teenage boys. You rev on the line, dump a clutch and grab a handful!

[Laughs] You're going to have to translate some of that for me!

You rev on the line—in other words, you're revving your bike, getting the RPMs up. "Dump your clutch" means you put it into gear. And when you "grab a handful," you twist the accelerator on the right handle. Then you haul ass, trying to get the hole shot in the first corner!

I read in one of your earlier interviews that you used to see Steve McQueen at the track.

Steve McQueen was a wonderful rider. He raced the six-day international trials in Europe, and they pick only about six or eight riders to go over there and compete in that. You don't get picked because you're Steve McQueen, you get picked because you're *good*. He raced a lot and his two children [son Chad and daughter Terry] raced minicycles with my son. Terry passed away a few years ago, unfortunately. We knew each other on the track, and—it was funny—one day Steve walked up to me and his TV series *Wanted: Dead or Alive* came up. I said, "Yeah, Steve, I did a couple of those with you." He *looked* at me and he said, "*You're* an actress? You did shows with me?" "Yes, Steve, I did!"

One day I was riding the track, practicing, and I had on white leathers and a white racing jersey and white helmet and black boots. But in those days, we didn't even have chest protectors or shoulder protectors or *any*thing. I was out there play-riding, practicing, and I heard this big bike come up behind me. When you hear that and you know they're coming fast, you just "hold the line"—that means, you just go straight ahead and let 'em go around any way they want to. So this big bike went around me, and then the rider gassed it, he twisted the throttle. The tires are called knobbies 'cause they have big thick one-inch tread for traction—and they also pick up every rock, and shoot 'em back [at the rider behind]. I was just showered with all these rocks hitting me—they're peltin' your chest, because (as I said) there were no chest protectors in those days. At any rate, I finished that lap and I pulled off because I thought I'd like to catch my breath. Steve came up and, "Oh, my God, Kasey, I'm so sorry! I didn't know it was a girl! I didn't know it was *you*!" [*Laughs*]

What kind of bike did you have?

Usually a 125 cc Honda. Loved, just *loved* racing. I ultimately put on the International Women's Motorcycle Championship for four years. I was the entrepreneur, I organized it and presented it. I had a race director who ran the races, but I was the one who did the advertising and the publicity and got the prizes to be given to the winners and all of that sort of thing. We had two hard days of racing—we had the Grand Prix one day and motocross the next. The Grand Prix is a very long race—I've run hundred-mile Grand Prixs—and motocross is tighter and harder, but shorter loops. They really had to ride hard and, boy, those girls were wonderful. We'd have 300 girls from all over the United States come. *Very* family-oriented, all of this—no Hell's Angels stuff. I wrote the motorcycling column for the [Los Angeles] *Herald Examiner* for four years, and a lot of feature stories for motorcycling magazines.

How did you land your role as the wife of Mr. Tate [David White] on Bewitched?

Again, very easy. (I've had such incredible luck!) First of all, *Bewitched* and *Peyton Place* started the very same year, and I started on *Peyton Place*, playing Julie Anderson, Barbara Parkins' mother. It was a great experience. We were shooting two and three episodes a week, and I left the show on episode 252. We did that all in, like, a little over two years. And *Peyton Place* was in the Top Ten, *if* not number one—I've forgotten the exact ratings, but it was just a hot show and great recognition. I left the show and, I think within the month, I met with the people on *Bewitched* and I was hired. And that was that! I didn't have to read, I didn't have to do *any*thing. I think it was all because of the *Peyton Place* exposure.

You took over from an actress named Irene Vernon. Do you happen to know why she left the show?

I don't know the exact reason, but I know that *she* was gone and I was just lucky enough to get the role. (We were very different types.) I did talk to her on the phone in recent years, and it was cute: I called her one day and I asked, "Is this Louise Tate?" She said, "Well ... uh ... yesss..." I said, "Well, *this* is Louise Tate..." [*Laughs*] And so we had a cute conversation—she appreciated that. She has since passed away.

A question I'm sure Bewitched *fans have frequently asked you—which of the two Dicks did you like best?*

No, no, no, you didn't phrase that properly. You're supposed to say, "Which of the two Darrins did you like best?"

With TV husband Larry Tate (David White) in a *Bewitched* publicity pose.

[*Pause*] *Okay ... which of the two Darrins did you like best?*

Dick. [*Laughs*] See, if you don't set it up right, I can't say it!

I adored Dick York, he was just brilliant, great comedic timing and a rubber face and a lovely person. Unfortunately, his health and back and things caused him to have to leave the show. And Dick Sargent came in, a totally different type of Darrin, brought different qualities to it and was a lovely person. But I can't play favorites.

And Elizabeth Montgomery was a great pro, just a professional girl, great sense of humor. She *should* have won an Emmy — she was nominated various times and didn't win it, but she should have, she deserved it. And of course a great dramatic actress as well. She had done dramatic things before, and then after.

What is Kasey Rogers doing these days?

Kasey Rogers these days has a writing partner, a young man from Atlanta named Mark Wood. At one point I said to him, "If you come to California, to Hollywood, I'll put you up for a coupla weeks." He's been here eight years [*laughs*] — talk about the Man Who Came to Dinner! We've just become the best of friends, he's like my "youngest child," and we write together. We had tried very hard to get a spinoff of *Bewitched* on, called *Bewitched Again*. Columbia Sony wants to do a feature film, they've wanted to for ten years and they don't have a script yet. But they won't let *any*body do a series. If we had Elizabeth, we'd have a series, but she didn't want to … and she's gone now. So we said, "Okay. Goodbye," and we wrote our *own* series, called *Son of a Witch* [*laughs*]. It's the same genre as *Bewitched* but it is *not Bewitched*, *we* own it, *we* created it, and there are people interested in purchasing it at this point. We hope to do either a movie-of-the-week or a film, and then have it go to series. That's one of the projects that's near and dear to our hearts, and one that we hope goes. We've written other things together and of course we're pushing those as well. So I've been doing a lot of writing, as you can see.

Now an author, Rogers' newest (with co-writer Mark Wood) is the bewitching book **Halloween Crafts: Eerily Elegant Decor.**

What if anything would you change about the way your acting career panned out?

I wouldn't change it. The only thing that was frustrating was, *between* jobs you think you'll never work again. Or you *know* you'll never work again, that no one will remember you! But I think, especially for a woman, it was an incredible career. My second marriage [to a public relations man, now deceased] was a wonderful marriage, and I had four wonderful children. I still *have* them, thank God! They're grown now, and I have grandchildren. I got to travel the world with my husband and I worked *with* him, I did writing with him. I had *time* for all this. See, if you're *the* lead in a TV series, the time demands are very extreme. But when you're not the lead, when you're supporting — my God, most of my time was spent at home with my kids and entertaining and doing things with my husband. And when I got to go to work, it was like a vacation. So it was a wonderful career for a woman, and I have thoroughly enjoyed it. I've enjoyed the creative aspects and the creative people who you meet and work with.

KASEY ROGERS FILMOGRAPHY

As Laura Elliott
Special Agent (Paramount, 1949)
Top o' the Morning (Paramount, 1949)
The Great Gatsby (Paramount, 1949)
Samson and Delilah (Paramount, 1949)
Chicago Deadline (Paramount, 1949)
The File on Thelma Jordon (*Thelma Jordon*) (Paramount, 1949)
Two Lost Worlds (Eagle-Lion, 1950)
Girls' School (Columbia, 1950)
Riding High (Paramount, 1950)
Paid in Full (Paramount, 1950)
Union Station (Paramount, 1950)
Dark City (Paramount, 1950)
No Man of Her Own (Paramount, 1950)
My Favorite Spy (Paramount, 1951)
Here Comes the Groom (Paramount, 1951)
A Place in the Sun (Paramount, 1951)
The Mating Season (Paramount, 1951)
When Worlds Collide (Paramount, 1951)
Silver City (*High Vermilion*) (Paramount, 1951)
Strangers on a Train (Warners, 1951)
Something to Live For (Paramount, 1952)
Denver and Rio Grande (Paramount, 1952)
Jamaica Run (Paramount, 1953)
About Mrs. Leslie (Paramount, 1954)
The French Line (RKO, 1954)
The McConnell Story (Warners, 1955)

As Kasey Rogers
The Gunfight at Dodge City (United Artists, 1959)
Ask Any Girl (MGM, 1959)
Naked Flame (Headliner, 1963)
Lost Flight (Universal, 1970)

A clip of Rogers in a TV episode is seen in *The Green Mile* (Warners, 1999).

JACQUELINE SCOTT

William Castle would talk [about Macabre *on TV] and there'd be nurses at the theaters and everybody would be insured against death by fright. Then they would release* Macabre *all over that area…. And when people went and weren't scared, they jerked it out fast and then went somewhere on the* other *end of the country and started promoting it all over again!*

One of the big box office horror hits of the 1950s was William Castle's *Macabre*, the Abominable Showman's first venture into the genre. Based on the mystery novel *The Marble Forest*, the movie came complete with a typically outrageous Castle gimmick: Audiences were insured against death by fright. Chances of a fatality were slim; the dark, downbeat movie, about a small town doctor (William Prince) notified that his young daughter has just been abducted and buried alive, lacked the potent shock effects of later Castle extravaganzas. (*Macabre* is, however, currently slated to be remade by Robert Zemeckis on a multi-million dollar scale.) Castle's premiere shocker was also the film debut of a young New York stage actress who met her future husband on the set and has remained in Hollywood to this day: Jacqueline Scott.

Born in Sikeston, Missouri, Scott admits that acting was all she ever wanted to do. She appeared in school plays and, immediately after her high school graduation, began working in St. Louis repertory theater. The auburn-haired teenage actress next relocated to New York, appearing on the Broadway stage and on live TV (she was a ghost in an *Omnibus* version of "The Turn of the Screw" with Geraldine Page). In 1957, Castle spotted her on TV and sought her out for the co-starring role (opposite Prince and Christine White) in *Macabre*.

Scott's roster of credits also includes multiple episodes of *Gunsmoke*, *The FBI*, *Perry Mason* and *The Outer Limits*, a recurring role on *The Fugitive* (as Richard Kimble's loyal sister) and—on the big screen—the notorious Florida-made *Empire of the Ants* (1977), writer-producer-director Bert I. Gordon's saga of tiger-sized, mind-controlling swamp ants.

I made all the rounds in New York

and I studied at the American Theater Wing. Then I thought, "This is ridiculous, I'm never going to be able to [become an actress]," and I went to Hunter College — I thought I wanted to be a teacher. I said I was going to stay out of the drama department there, but of course I didn't. I was in plays there, and an agent saw me and set me up for a Broadway play called *The Wooden Dish* [1955] with Louis Calhern. I was hired for the ingenue lead. Then I went into *Inherit the Wind* with Paul Muni — I played Rachel, the fiancée of the man on trial [Karl Light].

Did you also do TV in New York?

Yes, lots of live TV. I think the first one I did was with a Hungarian accent. My mother was a wreck, she thought, "She'll *never* be able to keep talking like that!"

Then I went out into summer stock again. Everybody said, "No, no! You've done all this television and you've done Broadway. You shouldn't leave New York, you shouldn't go into stock." I said, "I still have a lot to learn. I'm not gonna sit here all summer doin' nothin'." So I went out to Worthington, Ohio, a place called the Playhouse on the Green. I was there five weeks and we did *Anastasia*, *Bus Stop*, *Charley's Aunt* and a wonderful little play called *Anniversary Waltz*. While I was there in Ohio, my agent called and said someone wanted me for a movie. I just died laughing — I thought it was the funniest thing I ever heard. I asked, "Who do you think they meant?" — I thought they'd made a mistake. He said, "No, no, they mean *you*!" Someone had seen me on a live television show out of New York and wanted me for the movie. And that's when I came out to do *Macabre*.

Do you happen to know who it was that saw you on that TV show? Was it Castle himself?

Mm-hmm. He saw me on an *Armstrong Circle Theatre* and he contacted my agent and brought me out. I had never done a film. I'd done *one* filmed television show, I think the series was called *Navy Log*, and the next piece of *film* I did was *Macabre*.

Did you go right from Ohio to California to make the picture?

No, I went back home to Missouri, and went to California from there. An agent — not *my* agent, but a William Morris agent picked me up at the airport. While we were making the movie, I stayed at first at the Hollywood Knickerbocker on Hollywood Boulevard, and then they moved me to the Chateau Marmont. All the busboys and the waiters at the Knickerbocker were very worried about me, and telling me to be very, very careful whenever I went some place else. They were worried about me in this big bad town — they knew I was pretty dumb [*laughs*]! Somehow they had figured that out!

Was Macabre *your first time ever out in California?*

Yeah.

How did you feel, starting your "Hollywood career" with a low-budget horror movie?

Well, going into it, I thought I wouldn't like it. And I *didn't* like it ... I just thought it was silly! But I liked [the experience] fine. We shot it in, I think, seven days and they made it for $100,000. Maybe less, maybe 90-something.

Macabre *was based on a book. Did you bother to read it?*

I didn't know until this moment that it *was* based on a book!

What did you think of William Castle?

As I recall, I really didn't have that much to *do* with him. Since he was the director, it seems kinda funny to *say* it, "I didn't have much to *do* with him," but it's true. He was more of a camera director, and he didn't give me a lot of personal direction. So I worked on it the same way I would a theater piece. I'd worked with Uta Hagen in New York, so I just "broke down" the scenes in *Macabre* the same way I would if I were doing a play. I was pretty much able to look after and take care of my*self*.

Macabre *was shot at the Ziv studios.*

Right, and on location in Chino, California. The graveyard scenes were shot on a sound stage and they brought in trucks and trucks and trucks of dirt. For the rainstorm scenes, there were pipes overhead dripping water down onto us ... and pretty soon we were sloshing around through mud. On the last day of the shoot, we shot 17 hours — they were gonna finish that movie or know the reason why! We were on the graveyard set and I was off-camera, back behind all these trees, and I got stuck in the mud straddling a log. I had tried to step over it and I got stuck there. I had one shoe on either side of the log, stuck in the mud — and couldn't move [*laughs*]! Nobody could see me, I was back there all by myself, and I couldn't make my entrance 'cause I was trapped across this log! I got *so* tickled — I got absolutely hysterical laughing. I *know* that Bill Castle said, "*Don't* go near her," that they really thought I'd snapped! They wouldn't let anybody come and help me [*laughs*]! Like in so many horrible situations, you do one of two things: You either laugh or you go crazy. I usually laugh.

Did you think a horror movie would at least be a good opportunity for a beginning movie actress?

No, I just thought it was something I *should* do. I really didn't want to be in the movies, I had absolutely no desire. If I hadn't met my future husband during the making of *Macabre*, I don't think I would have stayed here at all. I met my husband Gene Lesser on the set of *Macabre*. He was a magazine feature photographer, and I kept hiding from him. I didn't want him to think I was flirting with him 'cause he was so *cuuute*! So he had a hard time getting pictures of me [*laughs*]! *Macabre* was shot in 1957 and we got married in 1958.

Any nervousness about starring in your very first movie, or did you go in there with a lot of confidence?

I was too dumb to be scared [*laughs*]. The same thing went for my early days in New York — my mother and I were just too dumb to be afraid. I'd grown up in this little tiny town in southern Missouri, never been to a city in my life, but my mother and I thought I'd be just fine in New York! We thought, "Oh, it's just another town. You just have to mind your business and behave yourself."

You do a lot of screaming in Macabre. *How does an actress psyche herself up for that?*

Well ... just remember all the people that you don't like [*laughs*]! I'll tell you the truth, screaming in *Macabre* was quite an art for me because my father would never let me scream as a kid. I really couldn't scream when I was frightened until one time when I was babysitting in New York. I was still a kid myself and I was babysitting somebody's baby. I was walking past a long hallway within the apartment, and I looked down that hall and I saw the back of a man's coat going into the bathroom. Well, I let out a scream you could have heard 20 blocks away, I guess because I was responsible for the baby. Turned out to be my boyfriend who had come over. That's

William Prince and Jacqueline Scott embark on a grave undertaking in William Castle's 1958 shocker *Macabre*.

the first time I'd ever been able to scream. So for me to be able to scream in *Macabre* was *probably* the biggest accomplishment in the entire picture!

Do any *of your scenes stand out in your mind?*

No, they don't. The only thing that I remember is that I *didn't* get any help acting-wise, Bill Castle never said two words to me. But because of the training that I had had in New York, I was able to handle it. I knew *nothing* about film but, as I mentioned before, I set up all the scenes exactly as Uta Hagen taught me to break down a script for the theater.

According to one trade paper item, Macabre *was shot on closed sets.*

They weren't closed sets. I remember my friend Susan Oliver coming over.

Any memory of Castle's partner Robb White?

He also wrote *Macabre*. I remember him very vaguely. The one who I remember the most, and who was just *so* nice, was Howard Koch, one of the producers. I was around him more, and for some reason I drove to an airport with him to pick up William Prince, who came in from New York to do the picture. Howard Koch was a very nice man and he made you feel comfortable and very welcome. I always liked him. I'll tell you *one* funny story: There was another redhead in the picture, Susan Morrow, and then there was another producer, Aubrey Schenck. (I hesitate to say

Co-starring in her very first movie, Scott felt no jitters — but only because "I was too dumb to be scared!"

his name on the set because I didn't know if it was pronounced Shenk or Skenk and I knew whichever one I chose was gonna be the wrong one.) I'm sitting there one day with Aubrey Schenck and Howard Koch, and Susan Morrow was shooting a scene. Schenck is sitting there and he's watching Susan Morrow and he says, "I'll never understand this business. Look at that girl, she's just gorgeous. And you get in the dailies and she's nuthin'." I'm sitting right beside him, and then he points to *me* and he says, "And *this* one looks like nuthin', but you get her on the film and she's dynamite!" [*Laughs*] I'm sitting there and I said to myself, "I thought I looked pretty cute ... !"

Castle brought you and William Prince, and maybe even Christine White, in from New York. Why didn't he want Hollywood actors in Macabre?

That was at a time when they *loved* New York actors. It was right around then that Joanne Woodward was up for the Academy Award for *The Three Faces of Eve* [1957]; Paul Newman, who also had come in from New York, was big; and there was also Brando, of course, and some others. It was *that* period. The only one that I really remember from that company was Chris White. She was *sooo* beautiful, oh, she was the prettiest thing. And a good actress—a *wonderful* actress. I remained friends with her for quite a period. She was a really nice, fun person.

Do you remember how much you were paid?

I think I got $750 a week, *if* I got that. We used to do leads on those live television shows for $350.

You watched Macabre *again just the other night. What's your unvarnished opinion of the movie?*

Well, it's just a ridiculous picture. It was a terrible picture, a terrible script. I didn't think the *actors* were so terrible, I just think they had nothing to work with. But I don't like scary pictures—I really didn't even want to do *Macabre*. But everybody said, "Oh, you'll go to California and you'll move up…," so I went ahead and I did it. But I'm not a good judge of that kind of movie. Even if I'm *in* 'em, I don't like 'em! But, listen—William Castle sold it, and that was great!

Who came off the best in the movie?

Oh, I don't know … I think *I* came off as well as anybody. Actually, I thought the guy playing the undertaker [Jonathan Kidd] was wonderful in it, really, really good. He came to see me in a play I did recently here, it was very sweet of him.

Castle reportedly shot two different Macabre *endings to submit to exhibitors. Do you remember shooting two different endings?*

Nope. Bill Castle was very canny p.r.- wise and promotion-wise, maybe that's why he [made that claim]. You know how he promoted *Macabre*, don't you? He would go into a certain area, say Atlanta, with the picture, and he'd do allll the local talk shows. They would talk about the fact that he was about to bring in *Macabre* and there'd be nurses at the theaters and everybody would be insured against death by fright. Then they would release *Macabre* all over that area, in that major city and all the little towns around. And when people went and weren't scared, they jerked it out fast and then went somewhere on the *other* end of the country and started promoting it all over again [*laughs*]! I am told that is the way he sold that movie. And they made $2 million on it!

On TV, you and Cliff Robertson starred in the pilot episode of The Outer Limits.

I had worked for [*Outer Limits* producer] Leslie Stevens before—I did an episode of his series *Stoney Burke*, a show about a professional rodeo rider [Jack Lord]. After that, Leslie called me in to do *The Outer Limits*. I did the *Outer Limits* pilot ["The Galaxy Being"] with Cliff Robertson. Cliff and I were in two TV pilots together, and they both sold. One was *The Outer Limits* and the other one was *The Wide Country* with Earl Holliman and Andy Prine—Cliff and I did that before *The Outer Limits*. Cliff was fine to work with.

According to an Outer Limits *book, Robertson's dialogue in that episode was so technical, he needed cue cards.*

I don't think that's true. I *will* tell this story, and Cliff can call me and raise hell with me. Here's the way *I* remember it: Cliff *may* have had cue cards, but if he did, it was just for meanness. *He* wanted to rewrite the script. Leslie Stevens had written it—and Leslie was *not* going to have him rewrite it. And so Cliff would blow

"Rain" soaked the *Macabre* graveyard set until Scott was mired in mud. (Left to right: Jonathan Kidd, Jim Backus, Scott, William Prince.)

take after take after take, acting like he couldn't remember the words—which of *course* he could. But Leslie would just sit there and say *cut* and then say, "Take 18" or whatever the hell it was [*laughs*]! *That's* what I remember from that situation, I don't remember Cliff having to have cue cards. There was nothin' wrong with his memory!

Also, if Cliff didn't like a take, he'd just *blow* it. It was really something to see him and Leslie Stevens lock horns—it was two monumental egos that were not gonna let go. And I think Leslie won out! Leslie was a nice man, by the way, I liked Leslie. He would always sit on a camel saddle—he had a camel saddle on a tall stool or something, and he'd sit up high on that.

Did you ever get to see the Galaxy Being in person?

That was an outlandishly expensive pilot, and they had a second unit shooting all the special effects stuff with the monster. The monster was played by a guy named William Douglas, Supreme Court Justice Douglas' son. William was a mime and he had studied in Paris. That's why Leslie wanted him, because Leslie felt that William would have an "awareness of his body." William lived down the hill from me in Laurel Canyon in Hollywood. We would just pass one another on the street or in the studio or whatever, but I didn't really know him and I was not around when the second unit was shooting his scenes as the Galaxy Being. That pilot, as I said, was just unheard-of, it was so expensive. I think I'm right that it cost $250,000. But people make more money than that being an extra on *Friends* now [*laughs*]!

What do you think of sci-fi?

I'm not a big science fiction buff. I'm a people person. But I saw the episode when it ran, and I thought it was real good. I thought it was a good series.

There's a scene in the episode where a bullet strikes the doorway that your character is standing in.

I did so many stupid things in my career. I mean, I was so damn dumb, I'd just do *any*thing until I got smarter. The things I did with fire, it's a miracle I'm alive. In that *Outer Limits* scene with the gunshot, I got something in my eye in that shot. If I'd had to work one more day, I wouldn't have been able to do it — a piece of *some*thing went in my eye and it was really hurting. The makeup man said, "You know what you do about that? You rub it with a gold ring." There again, I said, "Oh. Okay!" I come from the Ozarks, where we bury sticks to get rid of warts, so of course it made sense to me to put a gold ring across my eye [*laughs*]! So he rubbed that ring across there. That was my last day of shooting, *fortunately*, because the next day my eye — literally — looked like a ping pong ball. I think when the makeup man rubbed me with that ring, all that infection just spread clear through my whole eye!

You were also in a second Outer Limits *episode, "Counterweight."*

I could hardly breathe when I did that one. I was five and a half months pregnant, and for some reason I had myself wardrobed in a straight skirt with a wide belt. My eyes were practically popping out [*laughs*]! My pal Sandy Kenyon was also in it, and he told me later that he kept looking at me — my body — and he thought, "Jacquie's really lettin' herself go!" He didn't know I was pregnant — nobody did! It was *so* uncomfortable!

In the "expanded" European version of Steven Spielberg's Duel *[1971], you had a small part as Dennis Weaver's wife.*

I was only on that one day. This is kind of a funny story. *Duel* was originally shot as a 90-minute movie of the week, but it was such a big hit they wanted to add scenes for a European release as a feature. On *The Fugitive* [the TV series], I had played David Janssen's sister and I was always talking to him on the phone. One of the producers of *The Fugitive*, George Eckstein, also produced *Duel*, and to expand *Duel* for Europe, they wanted to add a scene of Dennis Weaver having a phone conversation with his wife. And, since I used to do the phone conversations on *The Fugitive* all the time, *they* thought of a phone conversation and they thought, "Oh, Jacquie Scott does phone conversations!" [*Laughs*] I would not have done a part that small, but they said it would *never* be shown in this country. Now, of course, *that's* the version of *Duel* that's on all the time — my God, it's on more than *Seinfeld*. It's become a *big* cult picture!

Did Spielberg direct your scene?

Yes. I'm sometimes asked, "How did you feel working with a director that young?" And I say, "Well, as long as they know what they're doing, *I* don't care how old they are." When I first saw him, he looked to me like he was about 18 years old and weighed about 135 pounds dripping wet [*laughs*]! Here came this child toward me, in cowboy boots and cowboy hat. Another director who was like that was Randal Kleiser. I walked on the set and here's Randal with his little Dutch boy haircut and shorts and sneakers. I thought he was playing my son, but, no, he was the director!

One movie scene that really shocked me when I first saw it was the scene of you shooting the policeman in the face at the beginning of Charley Varrick *[1973].*

We had to do take after take after take, I just couldn't do it. There was not even a blank in that gun. I was in the driver's seat of that car and, off-camera, there was a guy in the back seat, a guy who was a perfect shot, shooting a blood pellet at that policeman's forehead. I guess it was just psychological; holding a real gun and pulling the trigger with the gun pointed at another human being's face is a traumatic thing. It took me about five takes. I was scared to death pulling that trigger.

Do you remember that I rolled down the car window as the policeman was walking up to the car? Before we shot that scene, I thought to myself, "Now, if this were really *my* car, I wouldn't have to look down at the buttons to see how to roll down the window." So we did a take: The policeman started coming toward the car, I looked at him *very* cool and calm and I moved my hand over to push the button to roll the window down. I didn't look down at the buttons. And one of the back windows rolled down [*laughs*]. We did it again, and a window on the *other* side rolled down! Don Siegel directed that movie, and Don Siegel was the funniest man in the world. We had a lot of laughs with that one.

That was a great scene, followed by a great car chase.

All those big car crashes had been scheduled initially for a Saturday, but [because it was being shot in a Nevada town], Don Siegel changed it to during the week because he was afraid that on a Saturday, all the children would show up to watch. Don figured that if he did it during the week, children would be in school and they wouldn't be around. People, even people in the business, will get right on top of stunts, which I have *never* understood.

Word gets around when you're gonna do scenes like that, and mobs of people will show up and they want to stand right up close and watch. Me, *I* was a quarter of a mile away, up on a hill [*laughs*]! Just because they're stunts doesn't mean they're not dangerous. In a scene like that, the stunt people hate more to play people standing on the street than being in the car that's going to be crashed. If you're standing on the street when those cars crash, glass and metal and tires and every other damn thing can fly in a million different directions.

You were also in two episodes of the Planet of the Apes *TV series.*

I played apes in both of those. I got hysterical when they sent me the first script—I just laughed 'til I was sick. I had gotten typecast into Westerns and I had a terrible time getting out of 'em. Then I get this script for *Planet of the Apes* and it reads, "The two astronauts come over the hill and see a little farmhouse..." And I said, "Oh my God, I'm gonna be a farm ape!" [*Laughs*] I was gonna do a Western ape!

How long did the makeup take?

It takes about four hours to put all the makeup appliances on, and your first instinct is to pull your face and get 'em loose. They had the funniest makeup man in the world working on 'em—and the *finest* makeup man, because all that hair around the mask has to be laid on by hand. I *loved* acting in 'em. You had to find ways to express yourself with your body, because you don't have your face.

And another thing: People will come on the set and they'll touch you and pull on you, just like you're an animal. You'd be walking across the lot for lunch or something, and tourists would just slam on the brakes, jump out of cars and take pictures with you. They don't *talk* to you a lot, 'cause they think you're an animal [*laughs*]. Roddy McDowall said that's where he really learned to hate people! And you *never* get used to it — I mean, you still inside feel like yourself, and you'll walk past a mirror and you go, "AUUUUGHH!" And when you eat, you have to eat in *front* of a mirror, because you have no sense of where your mouth is. You have to sit in front of a mirror and open your mouth and lay the food in there.

That series didn't last very long, did it?

20th Century–Fox only made 13 of them 'cause they were very expensive to make. Oh, that was the stupidest decision in the world because those shows will last forever. There's nothing in 'em but monkeys and humans in rags, there's nothing in 'em to "date" 'em.

You worked for Bert I. Gordon in a sci-fi movie made in Florida, Empire of the Ants.

My agent sent me up for it. I knew people who had worked in the Florida Everglades, so I told Bert Gordon right up front, "I ain't gettin' in no water with no alligators." [*Laughs*] He said, "Oh, no, no, no. There will be ropes and nets [to protect the actors from gators] and there'll be doubles and there'll be no problem." Well, of course, we get there — no ropes, no nets, no doubles, no *nothin'*! So, if you'll notice, in the scene where our rowboat capsizes, there are six people in the boat and only five fall out!

You refused to get in the water.

No way. Well, for *another* thing, we had on these high boots. If I had fallen out of the boat and they'd filled with water, I'd have been in trouble. I'm not a swimmer. I mean, I can swim in somebody's *pool*, but if I had fallen into that water and the boots had filled with water, I would have drowned. They did one take of me on the bank, hanging onto branches or something, and Robert Lansing rescuing me. I was spitting and spewing as though I'd *been* in that water. Later, we go to see the dailies, and here's this shot of me spitting and screaming and carrying on. The special effects man says to my husband — my husband came down there for awhile — he says to Gene, "Gene, don't ever let her take a bath by herself!" [*Laughs*] I didn't look like I was "water-safe" at all, under any circumstances!

What kind of weather did you have during the filming?

Robert Lansing and I were walking on the beach when we first got there and this awful storm blew up. And after that, it was just freezing cold and pouring rain. In Florida! All the restaurants had to get out coat racks and hat trees and every other damn thing, they had no closets or anything for coats 'cause it was always hot down there. But when *we* were there, it was just freezing cold. And we had all been wardrobed in cotton so we wouldn't be *hot*!

Where did you stay?

We were in a place called Stuart, Florida, and then we were in Belle Glade, which at that time had the highest crime rate of any place in the United States. One night my two sons, about seven and nine, were sitting in the restaurant having dinner with me and the property guy. All of a sudden, shots were fired in the bar and people came barreling and crashing out of there. The property guy yanked me and my sons under the table. He was the only smart one in the whole room. People were running around screaming and yelling, and we were sitting quietly under a table!

The other women in the movie, Joan

Scott (right, with Lonny Chapman) thought the *Planet of the Apes* TV series would provide a break from a run of Western roles — but she had a surprise in store for her.

Collins and Pamela Shoop — how well did they cope?

They were *much* better than I was, they did lots of terrible things that I refused to do. They were much nicer people than I was [*laughs*]! Oh, both Joanie and Pamela, their legs were all cut from getting in the water. There were all kinds of branches and weeds in that water in the Everglades, all kinds of weird plants and stuff, and so their legs were all cut. But not *my* legs, 'cause I didn't *do* anything. I were skeered [scared]!

Memories of Joan Collins in Empire?

Joanie is fabulous, I just adored her. I think anyone who really gets to know her finds that she's really a marvelous person.

Scott, John David Carson, Joan Collins, Robert Lansing and Pamela Shoop on the lookout for the next production hardship on the Florida-made *Empire of the Ants*.

And she's so beautiful. She's always got that makeup piled on three inches thick, but she doesn't need it. She's just a natural beauty, she really is.

We had these five o'clock in the morning calls and then we'd sit in trailers alllll day long. And we *might* do one drive-through, and we might *not*. It was like a concentration camp! One day I'm in my trailer and I hear this weeeeping and sobbing. It was coming from Joanie's trailer. So I go over there and she's saying, "Look at me! This is not the face I came here with! These are not the hands I came here with!"—and, indeed, she was right! My God, her cuticle was all chewed up, it was just awful. She really *didn't* look so hot that day! So I went over to Robert's trailer and he was in a deep drunk sleep [*laughs*]. I said, "Robert, Joanie's crying. What are we gonna do?" He reached over and he said, "Here's a box of candy, take it and give it to her." So I took her the candy and she kinda calmed down. Oh, it was horrible!

You're startin' to convince me.

My God, it was just a nightmare. It was crazy. In the swamp scenes, we had garbage bags wrapped around our legs. Because you'd take a step in those Everglades swamps and you didn't know where your foot was gonna stop. You could take a step and all of a sudden sink right up to your knees. So they would tie those black trash bags around our legs.

One on each leg.

Yes—fortunately! They didn't just give us one apiece [*laughs*]! And I'm surprised they didn't! I never laughed so much in my life. I mean, it was so horrible, you had to laugh or you would have died. There was an oatmeal factory in that same area, so we all had to walk around in sunglasses when we were outside 'cause this stuff, like oatmeal flakes, flew around in the air. We had to wear sunglasses all day long or it'd get in your eyes. And the smell — if you've ever been around a sugar refinery, you will never ever forget it as long as you live. The worst smell in the world!

It smelled terrible inside or outside the refinery?

Both! You could smell it for miles — you could practically smell it all the way to Kentucky [*laughs*]! We went in the sugar refinery and Bert Gordon had us going up and down these steep iron steps, *open* steps. He would want us to *run* up and down 'em. Well, of course we weren't *about* to run up or down 'em, 'cause we would have fallen into a sugar vat [*laughs*]! It was *so* horrible, you can't imagine how bad it was.

What was Bert Gordon like in general?

He would be very pleasant and very nice, and really never understand why anybody was upset at the end of the day. At the end of each day, he was just ready to get all cleaned up and have a nice dinner, and some people were ready to *kill* him [*laughs*]! He was just in his own world. There were trees and then there was water and then there were the actors, and there were tables and chairs, and it was all the same to Bert Gordon! He cut himself or scratched himself or some damn thing one day, and he was very upset. And I said, "I wouldn't say anything to Joanie about that if I were you."

Because she was so beat-up?

That's right. Bert started carrying on, and I said he should keep it under his hat! John David Carson was in the movie too, and he would do *every*thing 'cause his father [Kit Carson] had been a stuntman. He just loved doin' all that stuff — and he did *really* dangerous things. He was adorable.

In the Empire of the Ants *press material, Gordon said he shot the picture in sequence. That way, he said, if an actor got hurt, they could put a bandage on him and it would still be logical.*

He *would* think of that! Well, *I* got hurt on it, come to think of it — I pulled a muscle in my leg and I could hardly walk. They had a doctor there, and every day he would wrap my leg like they do football players. It was so tight, I couldn't believe that was good for me — I thought, "My God, that's gonna cut off the circulation!" It would just make me cry, it was so tight. We were out in the middle of nowhere and I kept saying, "Get me some Ben-Gay." "Oh, no," they told me, "you can't use Ben-Gay." No, I had to soak in a warm bath four times a day. I'd be up at three o'clock in the morning, soaking it, because soaking relaxed the muscle, I guess. You can shoot six days a week [instead of five] when you're on location. Well, as soon as Sunday came, I said, "Somebody get me into town, to a drug store." I got some Ben-Gay and put it on my leg, and that was the end of it. But when I got back home, I told my own doctor what had happened and he said, "Oh, no, you can't use Ben-Gay, you shouldn't have done that." It's horse liniment, I don't know why not! I *still* don't know what the problem with Ben-Gay was.

Snakes? Insects?

No snakes, thank God. I might've gone home if I'd have seen a snake [*laughs*]! The insects were terrible, but that's all *over* Florida. One day I got in a car that had been sitting there all day, I figured I'd get in there and sit down and rest, and oh my God! There are insects called no-see-'ems — you can't see 'em, these little bugs, but they'll get allll over you! Anybody who's ever been to Florida will know what I'm talking about. Oh, don't talk to me about bugs!

When everything was said and done, did the cast have any close calls with alligators or any other critters?

No, not that I know of. There were Teamsters there, supposedly to shoot the alligators if they got too close, but we never did get attacked [by gators], thank God.

Did you see the movie when it came out?

Yes, and it was fun to see because we had all laughed so hard. We were all great pals. It was a very congenial group of actors, we all got along well. Under the circumstances, we'd had as good a time together as was humanly possibly!

Jacqueline Scott today.

Any closing comments or thoughts about your Hollywood years?

I think that if I hadn't met my husband on *Macabre*, I wouldn't have stayed here. I *love* the theater. I was very, very lucky, I did an awful lot of television and I had a lot of good parts out here ... but I *still* love the theater first. I'm just now back from Provincetown, Massachusetts, where I did Provincetown Repertory this summer. It went fabulously, I just loved it. And it's a repertory group, and so I will be going back next year. It was a huge success and they're buying a new theater for us. I love to work on the stage, I just lovvvve it, so it's just a storybook situation.

JACQUELINE SCOTT FILMOGRAPHY

Macabre (Allied Artists, 1958)
House of Women (Warners, 1962)
Firecreek (Warners, 1968)
Death of a Gunfighter (Universal, 1969)
Charley Varrick (Universal, 1973)
Empire of the Ants (AIP, 1977)
Telefon (United Artists, 1977)
Jinxed! (MGM/United Artists, 1982)

WARREN STEVENS

No, I don't think [sci-fi fans are] screwy. Maybe a little strange!

The *only* veteran of an outer space classic of the 1950s (*Forbidden Planet*) *and* an episode of *Star Trek*, Warren Stevens was born in Clark's Summit, Pennsylvania, and joined the Navy at age 17. His interest in acting was piqued while he was attending Annapolis, and this resulted in 12 weeks of summer stock in Virginia. His friends Gregory Peck and Kenneth Tobey later arranged interviews for Stevens at the renowned Neighborhood Playhouse in New York City.

Following Air Force service as a pilot during World War II, Stevens began concentrating on his acting career, working in radio and summer stock and joining New York's Actors Studio. His break came via a key role in Broadway's *Detective Story*, which in turn led to offers from Hollywood studios and a contract with 20th Century–Fox. In the half-century since his movie debut, he has acted in dozens of features and untold hundreds of TV episodes, from *Forbidden Planet* and the *Terminator*-like *Cyborg 2087* to small-screen SF fare like *The Outer Limits*, *Star Trek*, *The Twilight Zone* (both incarnations) and, back at Fox, the Irwin Allen series *Voyage to the Bottom of the Sea*.

You were active on TV before you got into the movies, correct?

Yes, in New York, in the old Dumont Studios, which were down in Wanamaker's basement. It was pretty primitive. I did what I think was the *very* first soap opera on television — this was back in 1947, I guess. It was called *Highway to the Stars*, and 15 minutes once a week was all it was. I remember one incident where one of the big overhead lamps *exploded* and showered glass all over us as we were playing the scene! But this was live TV, so we just kept going.

You were also in early TV series like Suspense *and* Actors Studio. *Were those also out of New York?*

Oh, yes. That was early live stuff too, '48 and '49. I did all the big live shows like *Studio One* and *Philco TV Playhouse* — all of 'em. On *Actors Studio* we did *The Tell Tale Heart*, and I think we won the Peabody Award for that one! Russell Collins was in it, and Jimmy Whitmore. That was all, just the three of us; I think Marty Ritt directed it but I'm not quite sure. It was a good story and a good script. I played the storyteller.

From Wanamaker's basement to Hollywood: Warren Stevens recalls his TV-movie career.

You were a member of the Actors Studio in New York at that time.

Correct, a charter member. The Actors Studio was started by Elia Kazan, Bobby Lewis and Cheryl Crawford, who was a producer. They were all members of the Group Theater earlier, and they recognized the need for a professional workshop in the theater, and that's how they started it in '47. There were two groups in the Actors Studio. One was run by Elia Kazan — that was the one I was in — and the other group was run by Bobby Lewis. It was a professional workshop for actors: Brando was in it, Karl Malden, Monty Clift, lots of talent in there. I also did the first play ever done on Broadway for the Actors Studio, *Sundown Beach*, which Kazan directed.

And then the Actors Studio branched out into TV.

Well [*laughs*] ... work is work! Donald Davis and his wife ran a company called World Video and the Actors Studio had a deal with them, and we did the TV show every week.

How did you come out to Hollywood?

I had been in a hit play for a while, *Detective Story*, and several of the studios evinced interest in me. So I chose one of them, Fox, and I did a test for them in New York. It was a scene from a play, and I did it with Kim Stanley, who had agreed to work with me on it. We did it and a couple of weeks later, by golly, Fox said okay! And so I went to Fox under a seven-year contract. I came out here in 1950 to 13th Century–Fox.

[Laughs] Why do you call it that? Just because it was so long ago?

I have my reasons.

And you don't care to share them?

No. It doesn't matter. Anyway, I did my penance there for two years — I did eight or nine pictures. The first one I was *ever* in was a picture called *Follow the Sun* [1951], the story of Ben Hogan the golfer. You have to look fast — I was the sports announcer. And then there were several more before I left in 1952 to freelance.

The atmosphere at Fox — what was that like? Being around a lot of top Hollywood stars — did that mean anything to you, a stage actor?

Oh, sure! I knew them very well. It was "part of my plan," when I was a kid, to be an actor. So my "plan" worked out okay, I was very happy to be there and mingle with those people and work with them.

When I interviewed actress Merry Anders, she told me about a Fox movie that never got finished. A movie called First of April, *about talking animals, with you starring as the voice of a race horse.*

That was a marvelous script. I can remember a great deal of it because I always wanted to get the rights to it and do it myself. With today's technology, they could very easily do it. In the story, First of April was the first offspring of a mare named April — they called him Firstie. We were going to put human voices over animals "speaking." But at that time, I guess it was too difficult technically.

So it would have been a Mr. Ed *type of movie.*

Wellll, yeah, but it was a *great* story. All of the animals were understandable; when *humans* spoke in the picture, it was all gibberish. It was a well-conceived thing. They had, of course, the chance to do English horses and South American horses, all with those accents—

Merry Anders says she played a French poodle.

Yes, there *was* a French poodle, and also a bulldog — the bulldog was Firstie's buddy. I wish it could have gotten made, I always thought that was a great story.

So you recorded all the voices —

And that's about as far as it got.

Gorilla at Large, *one of your freelance jobs, wasn't a great picture, but it certainly has a terrific cast.*

We shot most of it down in Long Beach, which had an amusement park then (I don't think it's there any more). We had the use of the amusement park from midnight, after they closed, all through the rest of the night *and* the morning. We were there for about a week. I enjoyed working on it with Lee Cobb and Anne Bancroft and all those folks. It was in 3-D originally, but they later took that away and made it "regular." I've seen it on the tube a couple of times.

Lee J. Cobb played a police detective and you played his partner.

He and I had pretty good rapport, we worked good together because we had mutual friends back in New York, in the theater. I had met him in New York, when he was doing *Death of a Salesman*, and of course we both knew Kazan quite well. It was the first time I had met Lee Marvin, and we eventually did some other things.

Any memory of getting the role of "Doc" Ostrow in Forbidden Planet?

I had done a movie in Italy called *The Barefoot Contessa* [1954] and it had just premiered while I was in Mexico doing *another* movie. So when I came back from Mexico, everybody had seen *The Barefoot Contessa* and I got a call from Metro and, with my agent, I went out there to meet the producer Nicky Nayfack. That was it — they wanted me for the movie. Nicky was marvelous. Kind of laid-back, and he enjoyed actors—he liked to be around us. It was a fun thing to do for 12 weeks. [Leslie] Nielsen and Jack Kelly and I played three-handed hearts all the time, when we were waiting for the next setup. I think they took me for ... a *bunch* [*laughs*]!

I've been on the sets of a couple new science fiction movies, and I'm always disappointed—they never look very large or elaborate "in person." What is your memory of the Forbidden Planet *sets? Impressive?*

Oh, *yeah*! As far as size and everything was concerned, it was the most elaborate that I had been on up 'til that time.

In any movie.

Yeah. Well, because of the nature of the piece. They had one entire sound stage with a huge cyclorama all the way around it, for the landing site on the planet. To be on that set was pretty breathtaking. The [interior] spaceship sets and Morbius' laboratory were also very impressive. And we had Robby the Robot, with Frankie Darro inside of that. But we had no monster to work with—the monster was thrown in later by the special effects people. All we had to do was stand there and aim the ray guns at it. And nothing came out of the ray guns either—it was *all* put in later! We were reacting to *nothing*! Even the people that got thrown around by the monster [James Drury and Robert Dix] were being "thrown around" by *nothing*. Until we saw the finished product, we had no idea what was throwing them around.

Before Forbidden Planet, *most "Hollywood sci-fi" was low-budget movies and TV kid shows. Who did you think the "target audience" for* Forbidden Planet *was?*

I never even thought about it. Hey, work is work! And I'm sure *none* of us had any idea that it would become the so-called cult classic that it *has* become.

Everybody I've talked to about Forbidden Planet *has nothing to say about the director, Fred Wilcox. Can you break my losing streak?*

Well, he was very laid-back, that's all I can say. He was a gentle man, and never got excited and was never forceful in any way about what he wanted. He let us pretty much alone. He had figured out *all* of this stuff ahead of time [coordinating actors and special effects]—things the actors didn't know anything about. So I give him great credit.

Memories of some of the stars of that movie? Walter Pidgeon?

Oh, he was a *love* to work with—he was one of my heroes from 'way back anyway. So that part of "my plan" worked out, to get to work with him. Anne Francis is someone I can't say enough nice things about, she was terrific. And still *is*. She was marvelous to work with, and just to *be* with, because she was nice. I did see her periodically after that, and then not for years. But I just saw her last November down in Orlando, Florida, at a *Forbidden Planet* convention. Leslie Nielsen in those days was *very* serious—oh, yes! We were *all* very serious then.

Do you remember where you saw it for the first time, and what your reaction was?

It was some place in Westwood, a preview. My agent, who incidentally was Leslie Nielsen's agent also, and his then-wife and I all went to this preview. That was the first time I saw it. I went in there wondering how the monster scenes turned out, the scenes where we were shooting *at* nothing, *with* nothing. So I was very interested to see how *that* worked out! We didn't know what to expect. And I don't

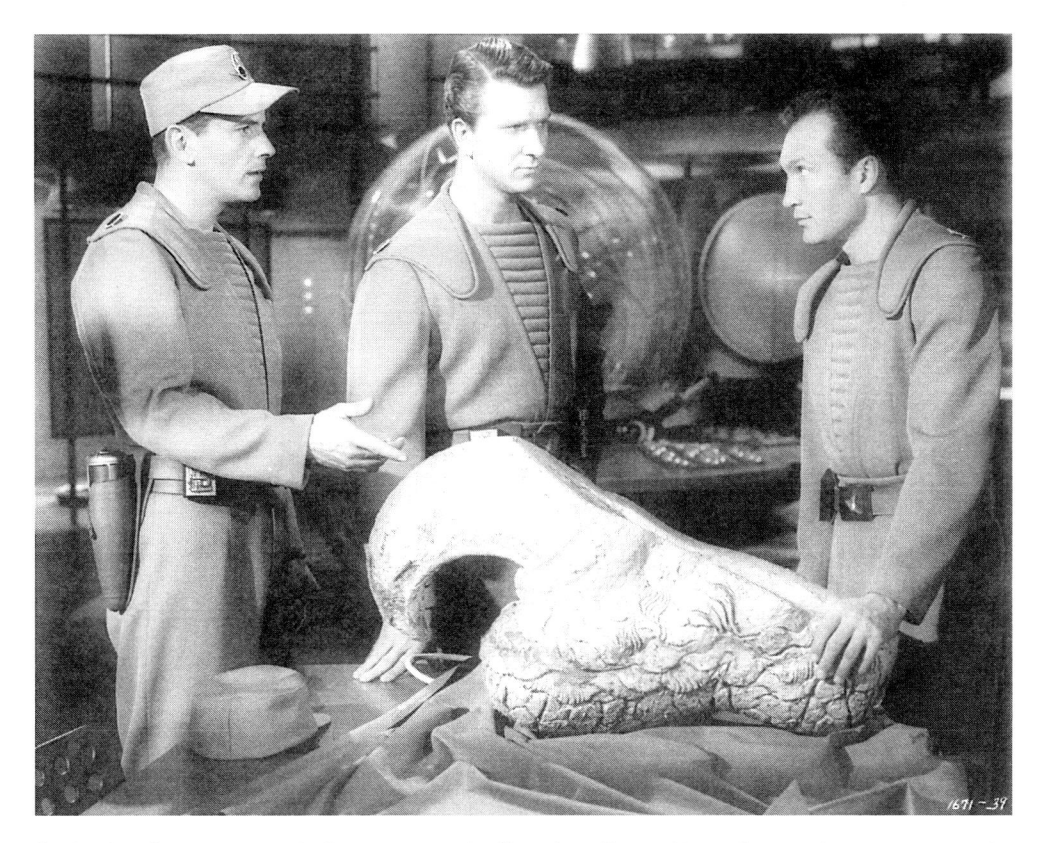

"I think we're gonna need a bigger spaceship": Jack Kelly, Leslie Nielsen and Stevens gauge the size of the *Forbidden Planet*'s marauding monster from its plaster cast.

know anything about the audience's reaction at that first showing because we left pretty hurriedly afterwards. To tell you the truth, I don't remember my *own* first reaction; I don't think I *had* any great gut reaction about the thing at all. We just hoped that it would be a success, that's all.

It sure was a success. It's still getting you invited to conventions 40 years later!

It's a whole new audience, generation-wise, that's come along now. That's probably the movie I'm asked about the most.

What recollections of your episode of Twilight Zone *["Dead Man's Shoes"], directed by Montgomery Pittman?*

Pittman said, "Listen, I don't know *how* you should play this. You're on your own!" [*Laughs*] So that was it, I was on my own! I played a bum who put on the shoes of a dead gangster and then "became" the gangster.

When an actor reads a script and figures out how he'd like to play his part, then gets to the set, does he really want to have a director now to be telling him how he should do his job?

I think it *should* be a joint effort, with suggestions from both parties kind of melding into something that comes out right. So I never forgot Pittman saying to me, "*I* don't know what to tell ya!" I met Rod Serling—not on that show, but I had met him before. He smoked far too much, but otherwise he was a very personable guy. Years later I was in [the 1980s *Twilight Zone*], and in my episode of *that* I worked

The only gal on Altair-4 (and in the *Forbidden Planet* cast), Anne Francis is quite popular with fellow players Leslie Nielsen, Jack Kelly, Morgan Jones and Stevens.

with Ken Tobey, who I'd first met at the Barter Theater in 1940. We've been friends ever since, so that was kind of fun.

Don't take this the wrong way, but I "buy" you as a bad guy quicker than I "buy" you as a good guy. Which do you prefer playing?

That's not a good question, really. I think, first of all, that bad guys are the better parts. *Everybody* has to go through that bad guy phase; all the so-called leading man play bad guys first, they always *have*. I think my record goes probably about 50-50 between the good guys and the bad guys, and it doesn't make any difference to me because, as I say, work is work.

Another series you were in a couple times was Alfred Hitchcock Presents, *with both of your episodes directed by Robert Stevens.*

The *Hitchcock* shows were fun to do. I had worked with Robert Stevens in New York in one of those live shows back there, and ... he was *nervous*, that's about all I can say [*laughs*]! *But*, he got the work done. I had met Alfred Hitchcock before *and after* I did *Alfred Hitchcock Presents*—he wasn't involved on that show, really, it was Joan Harrison and Norman Lloyd. I was interviewed by Hitchcock for one of his films, *North by Northwest* [1959]. He knew my work—or *said* he did. That's exactly what he said, he said, "I'm familiar with Mr. Stevens' work" ... which I took very badly, because I didn't get the part [*laughs*]!

How about The Outer Limits?

"Keeper of the Purple Twilight"—that's another one where the director [Charles Haas] said, "I can't tell ya how to do this, you have to do it yourself." I remember *that* very well, that he couldn't help me either!

What do you think of science fiction movies and TV shows? Do you ever get the idea that people who like science fiction are ... screwy?

No, I don't think they're screwy. Maybe a little *strange*! But working in science fiction doesn't bother me, not if the script is good. That's the secret of *any* film or play: If the script is good, you can go to work. If the script is nonsensical, then you feel that maybe you shouldn't do it.

Speaking of nonsensical scripts, what were your impressions of Cyborg 2087?

By and large it wasn't a bad picture, as I recall, given the premise—which *was* pretty outlandish. But it had some awful good people in it. I had known Mike Rennie from way back in Fox days, and we used to play cards together—poker and stuff. I thought Mike was a super guy, I liked him and we got along very well. Wendell Corey I had known from New York, and "Dobie" Carey [Harry Carey, Jr.] was also in it. I'd known him and his mother [actress Olive Carey] and his aunt and the whole bunch of them from years back.

Cyborg *was one of Wendell Corey's last pictures. Did he seem to be ailing?*

No, he didn't. But he couldn't stop *talking*! He was a recovering alcoholic, and I guess talking was a replacement for *drinking*, because he went on and on and *on* and on. It was a sad thing for me to see Wendell come down to something [like *Cyborg 2087*], because he was an excellent, excellent actor. He was *never* a bad actor—he wasn't bad in *this*! But he couldn't get a job, I guess because of the reputation that he had acquired while he was *really* drinking. He *wasn't* drinking on these last things ... but he couldn't stop talking!

You were also on various Irwin Allen science fiction TV series.

I got along with Irwin pretty well, and I guess he liked my work because I *was* on several of them. The Time Tunnel, Land of the Giants—I think I did *two* of those. And then of course Voyage [to the Bottom of the Sea]. Dick Basehart was a very close friend of mine. We were both at Fox at the same time, and before that, back in New York, we lived on the same street in Greenwich Village, Perry Street. He was married to Valentina Cortese [1951-60], and then she left him—she went off to Italy and took their son with her. One day I found Dick on the street, wandering around—he didn't know *where* he was going [*laughs*]! So I took him in and found him an apartment next to mine over on Olympic Boulevard in West Beverly Hills. For months, he had a standing phone call in to Italy, but she never answered it. He was *very* upset about the whole thing. But we had a marvelous apartment: We had adjoining apartments, so we opened it up and we had a *big* one! Dick and I got along very well; we took a nice trip to Mexico one time, one weekend, and I was his only witness when it finally came down to [getting] his divorce from Valentina in Santa Monica Court. He had to give her a whole *bunch* of stuff, I think. And I introduced him to his *next* wife, Diana Lotery. She had had a very small part in a picture I was doing in England, because her father was a distributor of films there.

Years after Forbidden Planet, *you went back into space on* Star Trek.

I was doing a *Bonanza* for Marc

Daniels, who was directing, and at one point during the last couple of days on the *Bonanza* I asked, "Where are you doing next, Marc?" He said, "I have to go to Paramount and do one of those *Star Trek* things." I said, "They *owe* me one over there"—and it was true, I forget *why* but they *did* owe me a show at Paramount. Well, we finish the *Bonanza* and about a week later I get a call from Paramount: Marc was gonna do this thing, and that's how I did the *Star Trek*, because he remembered that they "owed" me one.

Both Leslie Nielsen and Jack Kelly had love scenes with Anne Francis in Forbidden Planet—*and you didn't—so it was nice to finally see you get a very similar one with Barbara Bouchet on* Star Trek.

We were rehearsing one of the kiss scenes, where she was explaining to me about how humans apologize or something like that. In the rehearsal we kissed, and Marc Daniels yelled, "Close yer mouth!" And I remember saying, "Hey, it's only a rehearsal!" [*Laughs*]

Star Trek, *like* Forbidden Planet, *has certainly remained popular.*

Star Trek has become a lot larger than it was then, let's put it that way. Back then, people weren't dying to watch it every week.

And actors weren't dying to be in it.

Right. I met Gene Roddenberry, but that's all; he kept hands-off of the show, I think, and he didn't pal around on the set as far as I can remember. The show went very smoothly.

What were some of your most rewarding experiences in movies or TV?

The Richard Boone Show [the 1963-64 repertory theater-like anthology TV series]. Boone and I had worked together quite a bit: We were both at Fox and we were great friends, and we organized a workshop along the lines of the Actors Studio. We'd both gone to the Neighborhood Playhouse earlier, in New York, and then I was in the Actors Studios. He came out to Fox a few months before I did, and then found ourselves both at the same studio and they wouldn't let either one of us in their acting classes for the new stars and starlets! They thought we might be disruptive or something, and that we didn't *need* it—that was their attitude. So while we were still at Fox, we decided to start our own workshop. Later we got Jimmy Whitmore in it, so the three of us ran this workshop. We got together in various places—places we could get for nothing, mostly —and then we got a place at the Brentwood Country Mart. Whitmore organized that one, and we did have to pay for *that*. The three of us assumed all of the expenses and we "screened" everybody in it. The premise of the workshop was to have a place where actors could "stretch" and not be in danger of losing any employment by experimenting. We had a whole bunch of people, we "screened" everybody—we even screened Gary Cooper [*laughs*]! Pat Neal was in our group, and therefore *he* wanted to be a part of it.

Because they were an "item" at the time.

I know. I'll never forget, the three of us—almost beginners in the business—we *interviewed* Mr. Cooper, to see if he was *fit* to be in our group [*laughs*]! Anyway, he came and he *worked*—all because of her, I'm sure. We met once a week and people did scenes, and then we'd critique the scenes. We didn't charge anything, this was actors getting together to "stretch." We did two or three plays that got presented to the public, and we did a couple of short films. Then I guess it kind of petered out for a while. But one of the things that we agreed upon was, if ever any one of

Left: Despite *Star Trek*'s current cult status, Stevens (seen here as "Rojan" in the episode "By Any Other Name") is quick to point out that it was no hit on its original run. *Right:* Stevens is today a favorite at sci-fi–themed cons and autograph shows.

us really hit it big, we would try to do the same thing commercially. So when Boone hit it with his *Have Gun Will Travel* TV series, he sold the idea of *The Richard Boone Show* to the network, so we *did* get to do it commercially. We thought we were doing pretty good, until we found out we were cancelled by reading it in *Variety* on the set! But I did some of my best work there because ... I was *allowed* to do it.

And were most of the regulars on The Richard Boone Show *part of your original group?*

No, that's not the way it worked out; I was the only one, actually. But all of the people who were in the network show were people Boone and I had known and worked with before. Of course, both of us knew Harry Morgan very well, and *my* favorite person in the whole bunch was Jeanette Nolan. God, she was marvelous! So that's how that series got started, the idea of the *Boone Show* came out of our workshop.

And do you feel that you've fulfilled your "plan" during your 50 years in Hollywood?

Well, let's put it this way: Like the man says, "Life is a journey ... and I'm still enjoying the ride!"

WARREN STEVENS FILMOGRAPHY

Follow the Sun (20th Century–Fox, 1951)
The Frogmen (20th Century–Fox, 1951)
Mr. Belvedere Rings the Bell (20th Century–Fox, 1951)
Deadline — U.S.A. (20th Century–Fox, 1952)
Phone Call from a Stranger (20th Century–Fox, 1952)
O. Henry's Full House (20th Century–Fox, 1952)
Wait Till the Sun Shines, Nellie (20th Century–Fox, 1952)
Red Skies of Montana (*Smoke Jumpers*) (20th Century–Fox, 1952)
The I Don't Care Girl (20th Century–Fox, 1953)

Shark River (United Artists, 1953)
The Barefoot Contessa (United Artists, 1954)
Black Tuesday (United Artists, 1954)
Gorilla at Large (20th Century–Fox, 1954)
Women's Prison (Columbia, 1955)
Duel on the Mississippi (Columbia, 1955)
The Man from Bitter Ridge (Universal, 1955)
Robbers' Roost (United Artists, 1955)
On the Threshold of Space (20th Century–Fox, 1956)
Forbidden Planet (MGM, 1956)
Accused of Murder (Republic, 1956)
The Price of Fear (Universal, 1956)
Intent to Kill (20th Century–Fox, 1958)
The Case Against Brooklyn (Columbia, 1958)
Hot Spell (Paramount, 1958)
Man or Gun (Republic, 1958)
No Name on the Bullet (Universal, 1959)
Stagecoach to Dancers' Rock (Universal, 1962)
Belle Sommers (Columbia, 1962)
Forty Pounds of Trouble (Universal, 1963)
Gunpoint (Universal, 1966)
Madame X (Universal, 1966)
An American Dream (*See You in Hell, Darling*) (Warners, 1966)
Cyborg 2087 (United Pictures Corp., 1966)
The Sweet Ride (20th Century–Fox, 1968)
Madigan (Universal, 1968)
The Student Body (Surrogate, 1976)
Stroker Ace (Universal/Warners, 1983)

LYN THOMAS

We made all kinds of obscene remarks about the "Blood Rust" when we were shooting [Space Master X-7], because it looked so awful. The special effects men were trying so hard to make it look scary, and all we came out with were sexual innuendoes!

During the "monster movie boom" of the 1950s, scores of actresses co-starred in these science fiction adventures, generally in the most conventional types of roles (lady scientist, shrinking violet, etc.). The low-budget *Space Master X-7* (1958) featured an unusual menace: "Blood Rust," live mold from outer space which can multiply Blob-like until it devours all living matter on Earth. And leading lady Lyn Thomas had a unique starring role, as a space scientist's estranged wife, briefly coming in contact with the mold — and unknowingly spreading its deadly spores in her travels, like an atomic-age Typhoid Mary.

Indiana-born, Thomas (real name: Jacqueline Thomas) came out to Hollywood in the late '40s, working under contract to Eagle Lion, Hal Wallis Productions and 20th Century–Fox and yet never catching the proverbial brass ring. Throughout the 1950s, she appeared in many Westerns, TV series (including *The Abbott and Costello Show*, *Adventures of Superman*, *The Millionaire*, *Dragnet* and *General Electric Theatre*) and *Space Master X-7*, her one SF credit. Throughout the decade she also frequently appeared on TV commercials and billboards.

In 1960, Thomas played her final screen role (opposite a 350-pound lion) and then "got married, married, married." Now living at a California golf club with her husband of 21 years ("That's a record"), the happily retired Thomas has become a popular guest at Western cons where she reminisces about the life and career she swears she would never live over.

According to Space Master *publicity, you once intended to be a psychologist.*

Right. While I was working in pictures, I went to night school for seven years, and I did get my degree in psychology. I thought, "This modeling and acting's all right, but I really want to be a doctor." I knew I wasn't gonna make *that*, so I got my degree in psychology, and I did spend some time at the Veterans Hospital in Westwood here in California. And I found out I wasn't very *good* at it [*laughs*]! I got too involved, and you can*not* become subjective. And I was. I couldn't be objective enough. This was probably in the middle to late '50s.

Around the time of Space Master X-7.

Right. Whenever I had free time, I'd go out there. I was strictly volunteering at the Hospital, to see whether I really could *go* into a practice. I found out I couldn't.

You were in several Robert Lippert movies in the late 1950s, starting with Space Master. *How did that association begin?*

Well, he kinda *liked* me [*laughs*] — we can leave it at that! And so, whenever he got a chance, he would shove me in as his leading lady. Fortunately, most of the time I didn't disappoint.

You're implying you were his girlfriend...?

Well, kind of ... but he was *married*. They were *all* married, for cryin' out loud — the only one I went out with who *wasn't* married was Howard Hughes. He was *very* strange! I don't know how it happened, whether *he* had seen me somewhere or if one of his right-hand men had, but he wanted to test me for a movie. So my agent took me over and Hughes looked at me. Of course, I'm not endowed like Jane Russell, not by any means. So he spent a whole month having a corset made, and a costume made, and I made a *wonderful* test, *I* thought, with Ava Gardner. Billy Wilder directed, and Ava Gardner was an absolute doll, very helpful. She was a treasure, I *really* liked her. And we made a very nice test, really very good. I hate to sound egotistical, but it *was*.

Then we were gonna talk about contracts. Johnny Maschio was a big guy at Warner Brothers and also a big friend of Hughes, and Johnny took me out to one of Howard Hughes' houses to meet Hughes for dinner — Hughes had a lot of houses up in Bel-Air and Beverly Hills. Then, of course, Johnny left. I had met Hughes before that, in his office, and he really did wear a rope belt and tennis shoes. I met him again that night up at the house and he had his rope belt and his tennis shoes [*laughs*], but *very* neat and clean — he was *not* dirty, like I understand he became later in life. We had dinner in front of the fireplace, he had a houseboy to serve the dinner, and then he said, "Well, now it's time." I asked, "It's time for what?" He said, "Well, it's time to go to bed." "Well," I said, "I think you better call a cab." He said, "You gotta be kidding! After I spent all this money and everything?" I said, "You never told me this was part of the contract!" So Johnny Maschio came over and took me home! And my screen test sat on the floor in Hughes' projection room at RKO for over a *year*. My agent and I tried *so* hard to get it to use for other prospective jobs, but Hughes would *not* let it go, he was very vindictive. The "if you don't go to bed with *me*, why, you're gonna be blackballed in this town!" thing. So it sat on the floor for over a year.

Did you ever get your hands on it?

Yes, I finally got it, probably in the late '50s or early '60s. But those were the days when they made film with a separate soundtrack, and eventually in my moves (I moved a lot), I lost the soundtrack. But I still had the 35mm film, which I lugged around for *years*. Finally I took it to a friend at Republic to have it transferred to tape, and they rushed and threw it in water because, they said, "My God, that's nitrate film, and it's so old, it's ready to explode!" I said, "I've been carting it around for years and it hasn't exploded yet!" But it was too late, it was gone. I was furious. They said there was no way they could put it through *any* machinery at all, it would have exploded.

Was the scene you did with Ava Gardner from some movie?

It was a scene from the movie that I was *supposed* to do with Ava Gardner [*My Forbidden Past*, 1951], and the thing was all set, but I wouldn't go to bed! Janis Carter got the part. Well, [sleeping with producers] *was* part of it, and I didn't *do* it. (I was kinda dumb.) That seemed to be kinda "my problem": I wouldn't go to bed with Hal Wallis and I was under contract to him for six months. I wouldn't go to bed with *him*—he chased me around the desk a lot. I wasn't gonna go to bed with those funny old, fat, *ugly* fellows [*laughs*]! And I didn't!

But...didn't you just tell me you were Bob Lippert's girlfriend?

I played footsie with him—but no bedtime!

Back to Space Master—*what memories do you have of landing that role?*

Same fellow, Bob Lippert—that's why I got the job! I think one of the most interesting things was that I had to wear a brunette wig after I supposedly dyed my hair in the movie. I'm sitting on the set and my own agent came in and asked me where I was [*laughs*]! I said, "You dingdong, it's *me*!" and he said, "Oh, that's not *bad*, we oughta promote you as a brunette sometimes." I said, "No way. I'm *not* dyeing my hair"—at that point I was a natural

Lyn Thomas never attained stardom, perhaps because she wouldn't go the "casting couch" route ("I was kinda dumb").

blonde—"and I'm *not* gonna run around wearin' this damn wig." It was a pistol to put that thing on every day and go to work. And also, another thing, I *walked* a lot in that movie—I walked allll over the railroad station, and I spent half the movie in telephone booths trying to make phone calls [*laughs*]! I did wear my own wardrobe. In most of those pictures in those days, you wore your own clothes if they were appropriate. I happen to have had an extensive wardrobe, because I love clothes. In fact, I still have some clothes I think I wore in those years [*laughs*]. If you keep things long enough, they "come back"!

You did a lot of location shooting in Space Master, *unusual for a low-budget picture.*

Yes, we did, we spent a lot of time in downtown L.A. and, like I said, I walked a lot. The train station was Union Station, which is a beautiful edifice, gorgeous. The airport I think was in Burbank.

How did they shoot those scenes? Was there a hidden camera, or were the people around you extras?

They were extras. The interiors of the airplane, of course, were shot on a set, in an airplane mock-up.

What was Bill Williams like?

I worked very little with Bill in that picture, but I had worked with him many times and I knew him and Barbara [Williams' actress-wife Barbara Hale] very well. They were just delightful people, a great couple. And the same thing with Steve Brodie — he was a dingdong, *always* playing jokes. In those days, you *could* play jokes and you could screw up a scene, and the shoemaker who owned the production company would run down and scream at you, "You're holding up production!" One time Steve Brodie and I were in Mexico City; he was shooting on one picture and I was shooting in another, we ran into each other and I said, "Come up to the room, we'll have a drink." He came up to the room and *five* minutes later the manager was at the door — no men were allowed in the women's rooms at that time. (This was the '50s.) I said, "This is my brother," and the manager said, "It doesn't make any difference, you can't have a man in your room." And so Steve left, and then he came up the back fire stairwell and came right back to the room [*laughs*]! I thought that was so *stupid* [of the manager], 'cause Steve and I never had a sexual relationship at all, we were just very good friends, playing jokes and doing silly things. "Don't worry," he said, "I'll come up the fire escape"— and he did!

What about Paul Frees, who played your husband in Space Master? *You had a good dramatic scene with him.*

He was kinda strange, kinda like a Method actor. He was nice, but not the type that was fun and jolly to be around — he had to "concentrate" on the part. And Moe Howard of the Three Stooges was in that, too, playing my cab driver. I really don't remember that much about him, though, because it was just a one-day shoot with him.

How fast was Space Master *made?*

Oh, golly, I think we made that in ten or 12 days. You worked long hours in those days and you got a lot of "Golden Time"— anything after eight hours was double-time and after 12 hours was "*Golden Time.*" I was lucky if I got four or five hours sleep in between each day. That was the way with *all* the B pictures in those days, they were shot *so* fast, and late into the night. Ed Bernds, the director, was a doll even though he was under a lot of pressure. They had to get *so* many scenes, *so* fast, we had to shoot x-number of pages every day. And if we didn't, somebody above screamed and hollered. There were lots of times Ed Bernds had to print things that he wasn't happy with because of the time element. But he was a really neat guy.

And the producer, Bernard Glasser?

Had a little problem with him ... he was the one who was *pushin'* all the time. "Oh, that take was great. Print it." Ed Bernds would say, "Hey, it wasn't that good...," because he'd want another take, but Bernie would say again, "*Print* it!" So that's what would happen, they'd "*print* it"! And you hoped that in the editing, they could make it look good.

In the movie, a police sketch artist draws a

Thomas' rocky marriage to cold-fish scientist Paul Frees becomes the *least* of her troubles after he unleashes the Blood Rust in *Space Master X-7*.

sketch of you. Did you think it was a good likeness?

Oh, I think it was excellent, because they used my photograph [to copy it from]! And there's one scene in *Space Master* where I had a beret kind of sideways on my head, and I wore my own suede coat. One day years later, my present husband brought home a copy of *The Wall Street Journal*, and there was that picture of me in that outfit! I said, "My God, that's *me*!" and he said, "I *thought* it looked like you!" I took him out to my guest house, and that photo from *Space Master* is on the wall out there. They had used it in conjunction with some article in *The Wall Street Journal*—I forget what the article was about, but it had nothing to do *Space Master X-7*. Kiddingly I said to my husband, "I better call 'em and say, 'Hey, you owe me some money. You didn't get my permission,'" and my husband (who's a bean counter) said, "Well, you *should*." I said, "Bill, that's so stupid. I've never heard anything so ridiculous, that I would *sue* 50 years after the fact!"

You just saw Space Master *again. What do you think of the movie?*

I thought it was kinda way-out, with all that "Blood Rust" stuff bubbling around. Of course we made all kinds of obscene remarks about the "Blood Rust" when we were shooting the picture, because it looked *so* awful. The special effects men were trying so hard to make it look scary, and all we came out with were sexual innuendoes [*laughs*]! It looked a *lot* better in the movie than on the set; on the set, it was really gross.

How old were you when you first thought about becoming an actress?

I don't think I ever *decided*, I think it was just *thrust* upon me. My mother entered me in a "Gerber Baby" contest, and I was a Gerber baby when I was not quite a year old. It escalated from there into modeling and then into the local children's theater and then the adult theater, and then into stock. A talent scout from Metro-Goldwyn-Mayer caught one of my shows, *Kiss and Tell*, and said, "Cap your teeth and come to California!"—and I did!

Kiss and Tell *was in Indiana?*

We took the shows all around, Indiana, Ohio and Illinois. I don't know where the show he saw was.

You've acted in movies under two or three different names.

When I was under contract to Hal Wallis, he said my real name, Jacqueline, was too long for the marquee. Of course, they've got nine *million* names that long *now*, but he said I could either be Lyn or Gwen. I don't like Gwen, so I took Lyn because it's *kinda* like the last half of my name, except I wanted it spelled L-y-n, which it is. My family still call me "Jack"—my father called me Jack 'til the day he died.

What type of picture did you most enjoy making?

They never let me do what I wanted to do: I wanted to be a comedienne. I wanted to do the Doris Day–Mary Tyler Moore type of thing. That's what I did on the stage, I was always in comedies. I'd go on interviews for comedy things and the guy would say, "Oh, no, you're not the type." I said, "What 'type' is a comedienne?" "Why, they're funny-lookin'. You're too pretty." I always thought, if they ever would have let me be a comedienne, I would have been great. But they never did. And this is why now they want me at all these Western film festivals, they say, "You're so *funny*. We gotta have you back, you're *funny*!" Even though I'm gonna be 70 in November [1999], I haven't figured out yet what I'm gonna be when I grow up!

That's how I feel sometimes.

And you're not even close—what *are* you?

Forty-one.

Oh, you're a *baby*. God, I wouldn't go back and do all that again, never, never.

You'd never want to live your life over?

No! Because I'd do the same dumb things I did before. I don't think you ever *learn*. People always say, "I'd do it differently"—but you know you really wouldn't. Because the circumstances would not be like they are today, they'd be the same as they were *then*. I've already told God, "I am *not* coming back, because I've done it and I'm finished!" [*Laughs*]

According to The Hollywood Reporter, *you and Bill Williams were scheduled to attend the world premiere of* Space Master *in Florida, and then visit Cape Canaveral.*

Oh, my God, no. Oh, my Lord! I've never *been* to Cape Canaveral! Isn't it amazing what they can make the public believe?

Bernie Glasser told me that Space Master *made a lot of money because 20th Century–Fox double-billed it with* The Fly. Space Master *rode on the wings of* The Fly *and made a lot of money.*

Those were the days when you'd go to the movies and go [*Thomas lets out a long groan*] when the second feature came on [*laughs*]! And half the people would leave!

Did you go see your B movies when they'd play in a theater?

The original theatrical posters offered no hint of the actual, Earthbound, *Blob*-like plotline of *Space Master X-7*.

Lyn Thomas ("69 and three-quarters of a year old!") at a 1999 Western film festival.

Of course! Oh, of course — listen, I'm an egomaniac, just like all actors and actresses. And if they tell you they're not, they're lying. They're *lying*. It's the same thing when they say, "I never watch my old movies when they come on television." They're the first ones sitting there, all set to record it on video [*laughs*]! I don't know of anyone I've ever associated with who didn't want to see [themselves]. And then you watch yourself and think, "Oh, you dummy, why did you do *that*?" or "Why did you *turn* there?" I had a very bad habit of biting my lower lip. Whenever I was supposed to be concerned, I'd bite my lower lip. I said to myself, "Lyn, you gotta stop *doing* that!" — but I would do it unconsciously. And for a long time, I had "the blinkies" — I would blink when I would talk. The director would say, "Can you do that without blinking?" It was because of my eyesight, I didn't see well, and of course in those days I didn't have contacts. That's why I kept blinking. Then on the second take I would go into this god-awful stare, and they'd say, "*Now* do it without the stare!" [*Laughs*]

What was the best part you ever had in a movie?

Oh, good Lord, they were all so awful, *so* many of those low-budget B pictures I did. However, one I did do with Steve Brodie was about fighter pilots, *Here Come the Jets* [1959]. That was fairly decent, that worked out fairly well.

You have fond memories of your career?

I wouldn't have missed it for anything.

But you also wouldn't do it again *for anything!*

Oh, no. I'm going down to Wilcox, Arizona, for a Rex Allen Western festival, and I told 'em, "I'm gonna tell you right now, I don't sing any more, I don't dance any more, and I *don't* ride a horse!" And I hope I *never* have to ride a horse again!

Most everybody at these festivals sell their pictures; I *give* mine away. I just cannot ask somebody to pay five dollars. Some of these people ask $15! To which *I* say, "*Why?* I'm just happy somebody *remembers* me!"

LYN THOMAS FILMOGRAPHY

Stage Struck (Monogram, 1948)
The Accused (Paramount, 1948)
Home in San Antone (Columbia, 1949)
Black Midnight (Monogram, 1949)
Cheaper by the Dozen (20th Century–Fox, 1950)
Kill the Umpire (Columbia, 1950)
The Petty Girl (*Girl of the Year*) (Columbia, 1950)
Big Timber (*Tall Timber*) (Monogram, 1950)
Covered Wagon Raid (Republic, 1950)
The Missourians (Republic, 1950)
Triple Trouble (Monogram, 1950)
That's My Boy (Paramount, 1951)
Wedding Yells (Columbia short, 1951)
Strop, Look and Listen (Columbia short, 1952)
Blades of the Musketeers (Howco, 1953)
Red River Shore (Republic, 1953)
Witness to Murder (United Artists, 1954)
Rock Around the Clock (Columbia, 1956)
Space Master X-7 (20th Century–Fox, 1958)
Frontier Gun (20th Century–Fox, 1958)
Teacher's Pet (Paramount, 1958)
Alaska Passage (20th Century–Fox, 1959)
Arson for Hire (Allied Artists, 1959)
Here Come the Jets (20th Century–Fox, 1959)
Three Came to Kill (United Artists, 1960)
Noose for a Gunman (United Artists, 1960)

Thomas' footage was cut from *Love in the Afternoon* (Allied Artists, 1957).

DARLENE TOMPKINS

The mutants taught me how to play cribbage! I'd never played cribbage before; I played chess and other games, but never cribbage. So they taught me that, and I really enjoyed them!

In the year 2024, the Earth is a desolate wasteland, devastated by cosmic radiation that pierced our damaged ozone layer. Man has been evacuated to Mars. Those few humans who remain, "first-stage mutants," live in an underground city.

The Texas-made *Beyond the Time Barrier* featured this fanciful premise (now *less* fanciful than it used to be, given recent speculation about the ozone layer and interstellar flight). Independently made in 1959, directed by Edgar G. Ulmer and starring Robert Clarke as a twentieth-century Air Force test pilot who passes through a time warp into this bleak futureworld, the movie co-stars Darlene Tompkins as Trirene, the mute, telepathic Princess of the subterranean "Citadel."

Chicago-born Tompkins came from a "show biz family," with relatives who worked in vaudeville and in plays. (Tompkins' three-years-younger *aunt* is actress Beverly [*Old Yeller*] Washburn.) A beauty contest victory opened some Hollywood doors for Tompkins, who began appearing in commercials, co-starring in *Time Barrier* (at age 18) and appearing in TV series and additional features, including Elvis Presley's *Blue Hawaii* (1961). Marriage and motherhood derailed Tompkins' screen career, but she managed to return in the 1970s to work as an extra, a stand-in and stuntwoman(!), occasionally stunt-doubling on *Charlie's Angels* (for Cheryl Ladd) and in other TV series and movies.

Leslie Parrish and Yvette Mimieux were both interviewed for the part of Princess Trirene, before either of 'em was anybody.

I didn't know that, I just know that they had a *lot* of people come in. I had an agent at that time and he had heard about the movie, and he sent me on an interview. I was really excited about it. The audition was in an office; a lot of the studios had little teeny offices, and you'd go in and read. The day I auditioned, it was Robert Clarke and Edgar Ulmer — just the two of them.

How do you audition for a mute part like that?

That's right, in that case, there *were* no lines, so they would tell me things that would happen. I would have to stare out into space like I was looking at somebody, or act as if I saw somebody fall down, or saw somebody crying, or I had to look like I was in love — or whatever. Well, they called me back and I got the part. I was real lucky. That was very nice.

Were you still living at home at the time?

Yes. In fact, my mother went with me to Texas when we made the movie.

Beyond the Time Barrier *was shot in about ten days, in the abandoned buildings where the Texas Centennial was held in the 1930s.*

It was very, very desolate — those buildings looked to me like airplane hangars. We had Sunday off, and that one Sunday we could go into Dallas if we wanted. Well, I had never been there, and so a couple of people and I got in a station wagon and went into Dallas, to just walk around downtown Dallas, maybe stop and get a sandwich or something, walk through a store and then come back. We were all in Levis because we were out in the middle of nowhere. (None of us had anything *but* Levis.) And I want to tell you, I never realized how "dressy" that town was at that time! To see six people walking down the street together in Levis — everybody would stop and stare. *Everybody*! And we're thinking, "What's the problem? Why are all these people turning around?" and then one of the people I was with turned around and said, "Oh my God, we're in *Dallas*! We should be *dressed*!" We ate at a hamburger stand, because we were afraid to try to go into any restaurant — we thought we wouldn't be allowed in! "If they're looking at us like *this*, we don't *dare* go in a restaurant!"

Who was with you that day?

Just the crew, and one young man who was "Mr. Texas," a real good-looking, dark-haired guy. In the movie, he played one of the guards. Muscles — a lllllot of muscles! And they looked good on him, *really* good. They got him [for the movie] because of that. He was just a nice, nice guy.

Memories of Edgar Ulmer?

Edgar Ulmer sort of stayed to himself; most of the time, my direction really didn't come from him, it came from Robert Clarke. The love scenes, the kissing scenes and everything. Edgar Ulmer's daughter Arianné [who played a villainous scientist in the movie] was very nice, and Vladimir Sokoloff [playing Tompkins' grandfather "The Supreme," head of the futuristic city] was very charming, very soft-spoken. He acted like he *was* my grandfather, he really did. He took care of me and would want to pat me on the shoulder and talk real soft to me. A very gentle person. One of the things that I've been asked a lot, and I really wish I knew: On the Supreme's table, are those really bowling balls? [*Laughs*] I always thought they were, but I can't swear to it.

And Robert Clarke, who you say directed you?

That's right, Edgar Ulmer didn't do that much to direct me, I felt that Robert Clarke did. That was surprising to me. Robert was such a gentleman, he *never* lost his cool, always nice, never raised his voice, just a wonderful human being. There was only one time I ever saw him upset, and I felt so bad about it. Remember the scene where Princess Trirene is shot? Because it was a black-and-white movie, they used chocolate syrup for the blood. So on my outfit was chocolate syrup. And they said, for the scene where Robert carries my body, "Just hang like dead weight. Throw your arms out, and

Sexy Darlene Tompkins parlayed some beauty contest victories into a brief but colorful movie-TV career.

just be as dead weight as you can be." He was in the flight uniform that he had rented, the real-life flight uniform — expensive. *Very* expensive. He was carrying me in that, and I'm dead as a mackerel. Edgar said *cut*, and as soon as he said *cut*, the first thing I thought of was to sit up and put my arms around Robert so he could lower my legs. I reached up, and I got chocolate on his outfit. And he said, "Ohhh, no, no!" He set me down real gently and again, "Ohhh, no, no," and he just shook his head and walked away. And I thought, "My God, I feel so bad." He never said another word to me again about that, never brought it up or anything, and I kept wanting to ask him, "*Did you get the chocolate out?*" [*Laughs*] But I didn't have the nerve — I thought, "Oh God, don't ask, don't ask!" — I didn't dare. I was afraid he'd say, "*No, it's there for life!*" so I figured I'd better not say anything and hope everybody forgot!

The makeup man on the movie was an old-timer named Jack Pierce.

Oh, I remember Jack Pierce — he's the one who did *Frankenstein* [1931]. I remember him very, very serious, and sooo glad that he was working. And everybody treated him with so much respect. He really had "quite the name," him and Vladimir Sokoloff. These two gentlemen were just idolized, they were wonderful, wonderful people.

How do you know Pierce was "glad to be working"? Did he come out and say so?

What I meant was, he was just so intent and *happy* about it. I don't think I've ever seen anyone so happy to be doing that craft. He really loved it, he gave me the im-

Tompkins, third from left in a Sacramento "Maid of Cotton" beauty contest, faced stiff competition from Raquel Tejada (later Raquel Welch, fourth from right).

pression that this was the most important thing that there was, that this was so phenomenally important to him. As opposed to other makeup people I have worked with, people who treat each new assignment as "just another job," he was really wonderful.

And he was your makeup man?

Yes, he was, and I was thrilled. On that picture, I had one of the best makeup men and one of the worst hairdressers—on the same show [*laughs*]! Oh, she was a disaster! I had long hair and a ponytail, and they said to the hairdresser, "Add a little fall [fake hair] to the ponytail, to give it length. We want it up high, not down at the nape of her neck." She was behind me working and she picked up a scissors, and I thought she was just trimming the fake hair. Well, that night I found out what she had done: Because I had so much hair, *long* hair, she didn't know how to wrap it all together, so she parted my hair and then cut a lot of it right off! It was like a hole in the back of my head, a two-inch circle that was just stubble! Oh, God, it was bad, it was just a mess. After that, when anybody did my hair, I'd say, "Can I watch?" [*Laughs*] "I wanna see how it's done!"

Do you happen to remember how much you were paid?

$350 a week. And I'll tell you another thing I'll bet you don't know: The mutants taught me how to play cribbage [*laughs*]! I'd never played cribbage before; I played chess and other games, but never cribbage.

So they taught me that, and I really enjoyed them!

You were asked to do a nude swimming pool scene in Time Barrier.

They saved that scene for last, and since they didn't have any access to an indoor pool, they were going to do it at night, right at the motel we were staying at. It *had* to be done at night because it was supposed to look like the pool was in the underground city. The motel was a two-story and it was shaped like a U. One end of the U was a restaurant, and in the middle of the U was the courtyard with the pool. Well, they asked me if I would do it nude, and I said, no, I wouldn't, I don't do nudes. But I said I'd wear a flesh-colored or pink bathing suit, because as long as *I* knew I was covered, I didn't care. They said okay. So they put a pink bathing suit on me.

I was upstairs in my motel room, getting ready for makeup and everything, and all of a sudden someone opened the door and yelled, "Fire!" and we all ran out. What happened was, in the restaurant, the flue over the stove caught fire. And, because the motel was connected to the restaurant, when the restaurant caught fire, smoke went through all the air ducts—smoke came in everywhere. We were all outside, all watching, and a couple things happened that I thought were funny. One thing was, Texas was a "dry" state; I don't know if it still is, but at *that* time it was, so the people would bring their own set-ups. This man and his wife had gone into the restaurant and he brought his own set-up and they were having dinner ... the place caught on fire ... and he grabbed his *bottle* and ran out. He left his *wife* [*laughs*]! I don't know if they're still married after that! I thought that was kind of funny!

This was the last night of the shoot on *Time Barrier*, and *The Amazing Transparent Man* [1960] was going to start shooting in the next day or two.* One woman who was going to be in *Amazing Transparent Man*, I don't know her name [presumably Marguerite Chapman, the movie's co-star], was sitting in her room under one of those old hair dryers—you know those old "space age" hair dryers that's like a big cone on your head? She had the rollers and everything, and she didn't have any clothes on. Someone opened up the door and yelled to her "Fire!" but all *she* saw was this man charging in. Under that hair dryer, she couldn't *hear* anything! So she jumped up and ran out, naked. So *he* grabbed the mink coat that she had laying on the bed, and he *chased* her with her mink coat! Oh, God, that was funny—I really enjoyed that!

How much of the motel burned that night?

I don't think *any* of it did, except for the flue. Being that the fire was in the kitchen, the smoke went through every single bit of the motel, through the air ducts. But the actual fire, I believe, was contained in the kitchen. Thank God nobody got hurt.

So, obviously, you didn't shoot your supposedly-nude scene that night.

That's right, they didn't film it. A month or two later, after we had all returned home from Texas, Robert Clarke called me and said, "We're gonna shoot again. We have enough time and we wanna shoot [the swimming scene]." I said that sounded great. They were going to shoot it in the pool at Robert's home in North Hollywood, in his backyard, again at night because it was supposed to look like the pool was indoors. So I go over to Robert's house

---

*Ulmer and his crew shot Beyond the Time Barrier *and* The Amazing Transparent Man *back-to-back in Texas.*

Tompkins and her mutant admirers, between cribbage sessions on the set of *Beyond the Time Barrier*.

and I've got my bathing suit on and my Levis over my bathing suit.

I came into the house, and he had a piano in one of the rooms. I walked in and there was this lady sitting there at the piano bench, and she had a ponytail like mine. I said hello and the lady turned around ... and it was *me*. I almost fell over! It absolutely took my breath away — I was staring at *myself*. I just stood there! And she looked at me and *she* didn't say anything either! She just stared at me and I stared at her! I was just dumbfounded. Robert Clarke came in and he explained: He said he called around to some photographers telling them that he needed a double for me, a girl who did nudes, a girl who was five-foot-three, 105 pounds, etc. Well, he called Peter Gowland [a Hollywood photographer known for his "nudes"] and mentioned my name, and Peter said, "Oh, *I* know Darlene. No problem!" He had been a judge at a couple of beauty contests that I was in.

He was able to supply a girl who looked exactly like you, because he knew *you.*

That's right, Peter matched me *perfectly* because he knew me, I had worked for him.

When you swam, you had a flesh-colored bathing suit?

That's correct, a strapless pink bathing suit. But it didn't make any difference, 'cause they only did head shots with me. I went out and did the swimming scene — I did like an Australian crawl, and then came to the end of the pool where you

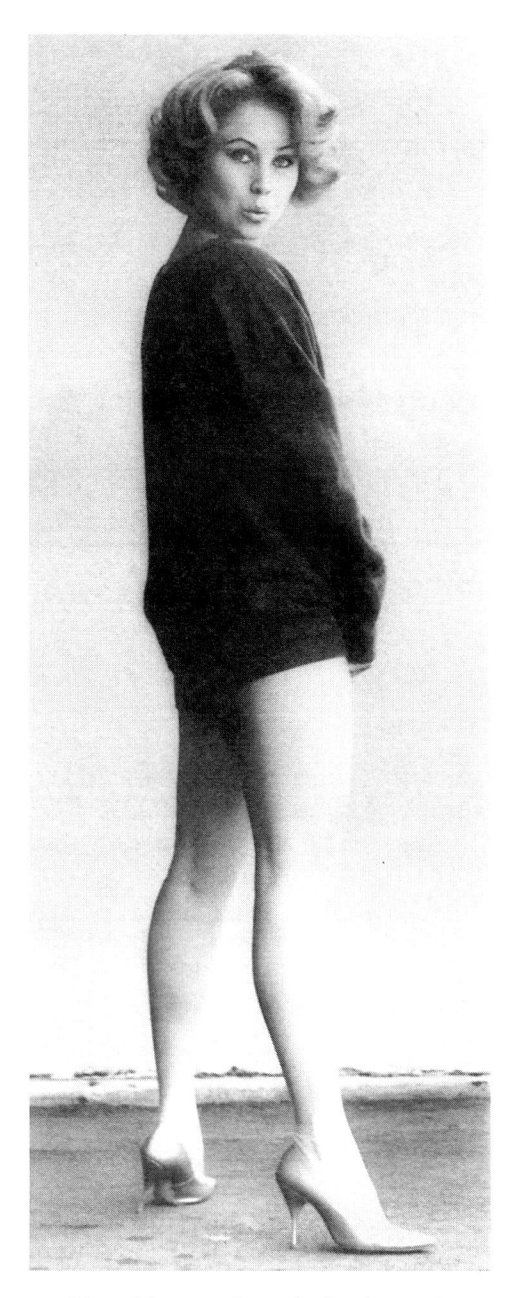

Tompkins, nearly ready for the pool.

18, and he came home from wherever he'd been all day. And his mother said [*excitedly*], "Stop! Stop! You go *right* to your bedroom!" [*Laughs*]

Because the naked girl was swimming outside in their pool?

Right! The mother said, "You go *directly* to bed!" and the kid didn't know what was happening — he turned to her and went, "Huh?? What??" And again: "You go directly to your bedroom!" And he had to go right to his room — the mother told him, "Stay in there. Stay in there." They were very much family-oriented people, very gracious, very wonderful — a real class act — and [the nude swimmer] just "wasn't her thing" [*laughs*]!

Do you recall seeing Time Barrier *the first time?*

It was playing at a theater in Van Nuys, and my mother and I went down and she took a picture of my name up on the marquee! And the first time I saw it was there. My reaction to myself? It was really a surprise — I was so glad that I hadn't had any opportunity to see dailies during the making of the movie. On future movies I didn't *want* to see dailies until after every single thing that I did in that movie was over with. Other people can look at dailies and see "the whole picture," but I'd keep looking at *me*, it was hard to look at anybody else in the scene. And I'd keep saying, "Oh my gosh, I should do *this*" or "I should do *that*," because seeing myself would make me so self-conscious.

Did you ever see the foreign version with the nude swim?

No, and I've never even *talked* to anyone who saw it. I've gotten fan mail from it, people saying it was great or they loved it. If they *only* knew ... [*Laughs*]

go up the steps. When I started climbing out of the pool, they shot my head and then they cut it. Then it was *her* turn to do it nude, and I went in the house.

By the way, after I did *my* swimming, Robert Clarke's stepson came home. He was a young boy at that time, probably 17,

Did you ever work with Clarke again?

The only other time I got to work with him was on [the TV series] *Dynasty*.

How friendly did you get with Elvis on Blue Hawaii [1961]?

I was his good buddy. I remember he had a penthouse at the hotel, the Reef in Oahu, Hawaii, and he had guards so that no one could get up there. I can't remember how many floors there were in this hotel, I think it was like 11, and one day some teenage girls managed to get up to the roof, and then from the roof they jumped down onto his balcony. If they had slipped, it would have been 11 floors down. Unbelievable!

Elvis was really nice. We had dinner and he pushed the potatoes away and I asked, "Don't you *like* potatoes, Elvis?" He said, "Oh, I love 'em, I really, really *love* potatoes, they're my favorite thing. But … I don't wanna get fat." For him to be so worried about getting fat, and then to have that [getting fat] happen to him — oh, dear! But things were different in those days, almost everybody took diet pills, or Valium, or whatever. Nobody knew that you could get addicted to them. A man in Elvis' position could get prescriptions from *any*body, and people wouldn't ask, "What *else* are you taking?" He just didn't know, and I think it was very sad.

Why did you leave the business?

The disappointments were a little bit hard for me, and I began to think, "Well, maybe this isn't meant to be." Like, I was set to do *CinderFella* [1960], and the day before I would have shot my scene, they called and told me Jerry Lewis had had a heart attack while running up some stairs. So I wasn't in *CinderFella*. On *A Guide for the Married Man* [1967], I was in a scene where Walter Matthau sees a girl walking and he flirts with her. The scene was shot, but it was cut out — they shot it again, this time using one of the female leads instead. Then when I did *Grandpa Was a Cop*, a TV pilot, what happened was kind of sad: The pilot got rave reviews, and four sponsors were fighting to do it. Everything was great, and I was told to go out and buy my Cadillac. And then all of a sudden, bang! they couldn't find a time slot for it. I really was disappointed when *that* didn't air. I was the granddaughter, Joe E. Brown was Grandpa and Dick Foran was his son, my father. Then there would be me and a young boy. It was a cute show, really nice. I think that was my first *major* disappointment, because I really thought that that was gonna go. *Every*body did — it was a disappointment for everybody who worked on it.

So I had a couple of disappointments, and then I got married, and the gentleman that I married — well, it was hard for me to go on interviews and stuff, because [actors and actresses] are always having to do love scenes with other actors who you've only just met that morning! It became a little difficult. So I got married and had my two sons, and then unfortunately I got a divorce. At that time, I was 33, and there really isn't much call for a 33-year-old ingenue. And I had to support my family.

I'm very, very happy with what I did. I think I should have put more effort into it while I was raising my kids. I thought I could raise my children and then I could come back and I could work. But it isn't that way. You can't be gone in that kind of a business for ten years, you can't leave at 23 and come back at 33, you can't. But that hadn't occurred to me. When I came back at 33, I had to go behind-the-scenes and do things. I made a good living doing it, but it was not the same.

Nowadays you do the occasional "celebrity autograph" show.

I'll tell you one of the things that was a little scary for me about that: Remember Vivien Leigh, *Gone with the Wind* [1939]? Well, Vivien Leigh in the early '60s went to

Tompkins (second from left) as part of "The King's" court.

a theater down South where they were showing *Gone with the Wind*. She came, and one of the ushers looked around and said, "Where *is* she? Where *is* she? Where's Vivien Leigh?"—with her standing or sitting right there! He had seen the movie, and he thought she was gonna be the same age as she was in the movie. So when I recently started going to some of these signings around the country, I thought, "People are gonna see these pictures of me"—a lot of my pictures are in bathing suits—"and they're gonna think that I'm supposed to be this girl ... but that was 30 years ago!" It was kind of hard for me at first to *do* the signings. But then when I went on 'em, I found that people are really, really nice, and they *know* that time goes by. The people are just wonderful and they make me quite comfortable—but at first, after I read that thing about Vivien Leigh, I *was* a little worried to go out in public. I thought people were going to expect a teenager!

You got special "and introducing" billing in Time Barrier. *Were you harboring hopes that this would be your "big break"?*

Actually, I did—I really did. *Beyond the Time Barrier* was the first thing that I had done, and I was star-struck. I'd only done a couple commercials before, and I was really hoping that something would work out, because I *loved* the industry. There was nothing like it, everybody was so happy to be there and they were having fun and they were makin' money doing what they really loved. It's both the hardest and the best of jobs.

DARLENE TOMPKINS FILMOGRAPHY

Beyond the Time Barrier (AIP, 1960)
Wake Me When It's Over (20th Century–Fox, 1960)
Blue Hawaii (Paramount, 1961)
The Ladies' Man (Paramount, 1961)
My Six Loves (Paramount, 1963)
Fun in Acapulco (Paramount, 1963)

As a child, Tompkins was the stand-in for Lori Lee Michel in *The Snake Pit* (20th Century–Fox, 1948). Tompkins' scene was cut from *A Guide for the Married Man* (20th Century–Fox, 1967). She has worked as an extra, stand-in and stuntwoman in more recent TV series and features.

INDEX

Numbers in *italics* refer to photographs.

Abbott, George 114
Abbott and Costello Meet Frankenstein (1948) 144, 146
The Abbott and Costello Show (TV) 287
The Abdication (1974) 77
Ackerman, Forrest J 136
Actors Studio (TV) 277
Adams, Maude 10
Adams, Neile 84
Adams, Nick 95, *101*
Adler, Buddy 169, 171
Adler, Jay 124
Adler, Stella 111, 120–21
The Adventures of Frank Merriwell (radio) 135
The Adventures of Jim Bowie (TV) 114–15
The Adventures of Ozzie & Harriet (TV) 102, 107, *108*
The Adventures of Rin Tin Tin (TV) 99
The Adventures of Robinson Crusoe (1952) 220, 221, 223, 228, 229, *231*
Adventures of Superman (TV) 24, 287
Advise and Consent (stage) 127
Afraid to Talk (1932) 125
The African Queen (1951) 27
Agar, John 130
Ailey, Alvin 60
The Alan Young Show (TV) 188
Alda, Alan 6
Alda, Robert 6, *7*
Alexander, Ruth 138
Alfred Hitchcock Presents (TV) 282
All Quiet on the Western Front (1930) 44
Allen, Irwin 167, 178, *180*, 182–83, 277, 283
Allen, Nancy 232

Allen, Woody 65
Alvin, John 1–14, *3, 5, 7, 10, 12*
The Amazing Transparent Man (1960) 300
Americana (stage) 198
Ames, Judith 252
Ames, Stephen 201
Anastasia (stage) 264
Anders, Merry 279
Anders, Rudolph 162
Anderson, Judith 16
Anderson, Maxwell 187
Andy Hardy Gets Spring Fever (1939) 128
Ann-Margret 169
Annie (stage) 63
Anniversary Waltz (stage) 264
Antosiewicz, John vii–viii
Apache Woman (1955) 133, 137
Arden, Arianné *see* Ulmer, Arianné
Arkoff, Hilda 135
Arkoff, Samuel Z. 44, 123, 129, 133, 134, 135, 136, 138, 140, 141
Arms, Russell 2
Armstrong Circle Theatre (TV) 264
Arness, James 249–50, 251–52, *251*
Arnold, Edward 124, 125, 126, 127
Arnold, Tom 109
Around the World in 80 Days (1956) 99
Arsenic and Old Lace (stage) 148
Ashe, Eve Brent *see* Brent, Eve
Ashe, Michael 27, 32, 33–34
Aten, Larry 40, 42, *43*
The Atomic Submarine (1959) 141
Aykroyd, Dan 194
Babenco, Hector 194
Bacharach, Burt 91

Back from the Dead (1957) 122
Back to Methuselah (stage) 120
Backus, Jim 269
Bailey, David viii
Ballad of the Sad Café (stage) 59, 62, 65
Bancroft, Anne 279
The Barefoot Contessa (1954) 279
Barnes, Joanna 209, 211, *212*, 213, 214, 216
Barnett, Buddy viii
Barrymore, Ethel 8
Barrymore, John 2, 19–20
Basehart, Richard 174, 182–83, 283
Bat Masterson (TV) 25
Baumann, Marty viii
Baxley, Barbara 118
Baxter, Anne 175
Beach Girls and the Monster (1965) 99, 102–06, *105, 106, 107*
The Beast of Yucca Flats (1961) 37, 38–44, *39, 41, 43*, 45–46
The Beast with a Million Eyes (1955) 82
The Beast with Five Fingers (1947) 1, 4–7, *7*
Beginning of the End (1957) 20
Begley, Ed, Jr. 237
Begley, Martin 237–38
Belafonte, Harry 219
Bellamy, Ralph 159
Ben-Hur (1959) 99
Bendix, William 208
Bennet, Spencer Gordon 138, 141
Bennett, Bruce 218
Benton, Doug 57
Berman, Israel M. 124
Bernds, Edward 290
Bernstein, Morey 122
Bert, Flo 135
The Best Man (stage) 127

305

Beware! The Blob see *Son of Blob*
Bewitched (TV) 247, 259–61, *260*
Beyond the Time Barrier (1960) 296–303, *301*, 304
Bid Time Return (novel) 9, 10
Bielema, Linda 40
The Big Valley (TV) 24, 51
Bigfoot (1970) 40
Black, John D. F. 15–23
The Black Sleep (1956) 21
Blackmer, Sidney 197, 202–04, 205
Blaisdell, Paul 136
Blake, Robert 139
Bleifer, John 124
Blithe Spirit (stage) 110
The Blob (1958) 79, 80–94, *83*, *85*, *88*, 96–98, 234, 236–43, *238*, *240*, 244
The Blob (1988) 94, 243
Bloch, Robert 226
Blood and Sand (1941) 167–68
Blood and Sand (proposed 1950s remake) 168
Blue Hawaii (1961) 296, 303, 304
Bohus, Ted viii
Bonanza (TV) 283–84
Bond, Ward 54–56
Boone, Richard 284, 285
The Bottom of the Bottle (1956) 164–65
Bouchet, Barbara 284
The Bounty Killer (1965) 57, 138
Brahm, John 56
The Brain Eaters (1958) vii
BrainWaves (1982) 33
Brando, Marlon 268, 278
Breaking Away (1979) 32
Brendel, El 134–35
Brent, Eve 24–36, *26*, *28*, *30*, *31*, *34*
Brent, Romney 148
The Bride and the Beast (1958) 24, 122
Broderick, Jimmy 60
Brodie, Steve 290, 294
Bromiley, Dorothy 48
Brooks, Conrad *39*
Brown, Gilmor 34
Brown, James H. 57, 58
Brown, Joe E. 303
Brown, Johnny Mack 199
Browning, Tod 204
Brunas, John viii
Brunas, Mike viii
Buck and the Preacher (1972) 219
Buferd, Marilyn *16*
Buñuel, Luis 220, 221, 229
Burn 'Em Up Barnes (1934) 132
Burnett, Carol 218
Burroughs, Danton 218
Burroughs, Edgar Rice 27, 218
Burton, Richard 74

Bus Stop (stage) 264
Buss, Gottfried 87
Buster Crabbe's Arthritis Exercise Book (book) 219
Byrnes, Edd 139
Caan, James 209
The Cabinet of Caligari (1962) 220, 225–28, *227*, *229*
The Cabinet of Dr. Caligari (1919) 225, 228
Cagle, John 38
Cahn, Edward L. 122, 123–25, 128, 129–30, 134, 136, 138, 139, 140, *140*, 141
Caillou, Alan 56
Calhern, Louis 264
Callahan, Mushy 4
Cameron, Bruce 9
Campbell, Jack 5
Capucine 169
Cardoza, Anthony 37–46, *41*
Cardwell, James 5
Carey, Harry 124, 283
Carey, Harry, Jr. 283
Carey, Olive 283
Carlson, Richard 190–91
Carmichael, Ralph 91
Carradine, John 15, *16*, 18–20, 21, 126–27
Carré, Bart 136–37, 138, 141
Carson, Jack 164
Carson, John David *274*, 275
Carson, Kit 275
Carter, Janis 289
Casey, Sue 104
Castle, Peggie 164
Castle, William 47, 51–52, 54, 55, 263, 264–65, 266, 267, 268
The Cat and the Canary (1927) 132
Cavalcade of America (radio) 235
Cavett, Dick 63, 65
Chaney, Lon 113
Chaplin, Charlie 13
Chaplin, Sydney 13
Chapman, Lonny *273*
Chapman, Marguerite 300
Charley Varrick (1973) 271
Charley's Aunt (stage) 264
Charlie's Angels (TV) 296
Charnin, Marty 63
Chase, Borden 242
Chase, Stephen 241, 243
Chicken Every Sunday (stage) 202–03
Christopher, Dennis 32
CinderFella (1960) 303
Cinefantastique (magazine) vii
Clarke, Robert viii, 222, 296, 297–98, 300, 301, 302, 303
Clavell, Holly 171
Clavell, James 169, 170, 171

Clavell, Michaela 171
Claxton, William F. 57
Clement, Kevin viii
Clift, Montgomery 106, 278
Climax (TV) 1, 7–8
Clooney, George 225
The Clutching Hand (1936) 132
Cobb, Edmund 130
Cobb, Lee J. 279
Cocchi, John viii
Collins, Joan 47, 272–74, *274*, 275
Collins, Russell 277
Conan Doyle, Arthur 178
Connell, W. Merle 18
Connery, Sean 9
Connors, Mike 130, 133, 134
Conrad, Robert 70–71, 109, 117, 182
Conried, Hans 51
Conway, Tom 127, 132, 133, *142*
The Cool and the Crazy (1958) 123
Cooper, Gary 284
Coppola, Francis Ford 205
Corey, Wendell 283
Corman, Roger 82, 123, 137
The Corpse Vanishes (1942) 130
Corrigan, Ray "Crash" 99–102, *101*, 103, 107
Corsaut, Aneta 82, 84, *85*, 86, 89, 90, 240, *240*, 242–43
Cortese, Valentina 283
Cosby, Bill 65
Cotten, Joseph 164
The Cotton Club (1984) 205
The Couch (1962) 9
The Couch Trip (1988) 194
Crabbe, Buster 210, 219
Crane, Richard 8
Crawford, Cheryl 278
Creature of Destruction (1967 TV movie) 141
Cregar, Laird 2
Crime and Punishment (1935) 125
Cronenberg, David 181
Crosby, Floyd 137
Crowley, Kathleen 119
Cult of the Cobra (1955) 186, 192–93, *194*, 195
Cummings, Bob 31
Cunha, Richard E. 153
Curse of the Faceless Man (1958) 122
Curtis, Jamie Lee 13
Cyborg 2087 (1966) 277, 283
Dailey, Dan 188
Dalton, Audrey 47–58, *49*, *50*, *52*, *53*, *55*, *57*, 138
Damato, Glenn viii
Dancigers, Oscar 221
Daniels, Marc 283–84

Danova, Cesare 211, 213, 214
Dantine, Helmut 2, 6
Darabont, Frank 33, 34–35, *34*
The Dark Tower (stage) 127
Darro, Frankie 280
Darrow, Barbara 51
Darwell, Jane 124
Daves, Delmer 12
Davies, Marion 9
Davis, Bette 134, 179
Day the World Ended (1956) 136
Dead Ringers (1988) 181
Death of a Salesman (stage) 279
DeCarlo, Yvonne 253
Deering, Olive 249
DeMille, Cecil B. 127, 249
Dennis, Geoffrey *see* Black, John D. F.
Denver and Rio Grande (1952) 252–54
Derek, Bo 217
Desert Sands (1955) 127
The Desperados Are in Town (1956) 164
Destination Tokyo (1943) 1
Detective Story (stage) 16, 22, 277, 278
The Devil Bat (1940) 197, 199–202, *199, 201, 203, 204, 204*, 205
Devon, Richard *57*
Dingle, Charles *7*
A Distant Thunder (1978) 96
Dix, Robert 280
Dr. Christian (TV) 25
Dr. Jekyll and Mr. Hyde (1931) 169
Dr. Jekyll and Mr. Hyde (1941) 169
Domergue, Faith 186, 193
Doniger, Walter 194
Doppelt, Jack 124
Dorin, Phoebe 59–78, *61, 66, 73*
Doughten, Russ 79–98, *81, 92, 97*
Douglas, Robert 211
Douglas, William 269
Douglas, William O. 269
Downs, Cathy *126*, 130, 140
Downs, Hugh 2
Dracula (1931) 146, 204
Dracula (stage) 144–45, 148
Dragnet (TV) 35, 38, 287
Drum Beat (1954) 48
Drums Along the Mohawk (1939) 234
Drury, James 280
Dubov, Paul 136
Duel (1971) 270
Duffy, Henry 3
Duggan, Tom 107–09
Dukesbery, Jack viii
Dullea, Keir 33

Duncan, Michael Clarke 35
Dunn, Michael 59, 60–69, *65*, 70, 71–72, 73–77, *73*, 117
Dunning, Patty 95, 96
DuPont, Elaine 99–109, *101, 105, 106, 107, 108*
Durante, Jimmy 11
Durocher, Leo 188
Duryea, Dan 138
Dynasty (TV) 303
Earle, Edward 132
Eastwood, Clint 209
Ebsen, Buddy 208
Eckstein, George 270
The Ed Wynn Show (TV) 188
Eden, Barbara 25, 164
Edmiston, Walker 104, 105
Edwards, Penny 8
Elan, Joan 48
Ellenstein, Robert 74, 110–21, *113, 116, 118, 120*
Elliott, Laura *see* Rogers, Kasey
Ellison, Harlan viii
Ely, Ron 218
Empire of the Ants (1977) 263, 272–76, *274*
The Enemy Below (1957) 167, 170, 182
English, Marla 123, 127–28, 129–30, *131*, 134, 192
Ephron, Henry 168
Epstein, Philip 241
Erdman, Richard 5
Erwin, Bill 12
Essoe, Gabe 207, 218
Evans, Robert 169
Fade to Black (1980) 24, 32
Fail-Safe (1964) 220, 223–25, *225*
Fail-Safe (2000 TV movie) 225
Fairbanks, Douglas 160
The Falcon Takes Over (1942) 128
Fangoria (magazine) vii
Farnum, Franklyn *133*
Farrell, Henry 94
Farrell, Tommy 255
The FBI (TV) 263
Feldman, Charles 221
Felsen, Henry 94–95
Felton, Norman 111, 113, 114, 119
Fever Heat (1968) 94–95
Fields, Totie 218
The Fiend Who Walked the West (1958) 169
Fiend Without a Face (1958) 148
The Fifth Season (stage) 30
The Fighting Sullivans see The Sullivans
Finley, Mari 128
Finn, Mali 33
Finney, Albert 74
First of April (unmade movie) 279

Fitzgerald, Michael viii
Five Fingers (TV) 167, 178, 182
Flaherty, Robert 137
Flesh and the Spur (1957) 123, 128, 130
Fletcher, Bramwell 114
Florian (1940) 128
Flowers, Bess *133*
"The Fly" (story) 167, 169–70
The Fly (1958) 167, 168–77, *170, 172, 173, 175, 177*, 182, 183, 292
The Fly (1986) 181
The Fly Papers (2000 TV documentary) 183
Follow the Sun (1951) 279
Fonda, Henry 111–12, 224
For Love or Money (stage) 186
For Men Only (1952) 186, 188, 189, 190, 192
Foran, Dick 110, 303
Forbes, Scott 114, 115
Forbidden Planet (1956) 277, 279–81, *281, 282*
Ford Theatre (TV) 235
Forsythe, John 190
Fort, Garrett 203, 204–05
Forty Guns (1957) 24, 25
The Four Horsemen of the Apocalypse (1921) 132
Franciosa, Tony 238
Francis, Alan 40
Francis, Anne viii, 280, *282*
Francis, Barbara 40
Francis, Coleman 37, 38, 40, 42, 43, 44, 45
Francis, Ronald 40
The Frank Sinatra Show (TV) 188
Franke, Anthony 82–83
Frankenstein (1931) 204, 241, 298
Franklin, Mike 21
Frees, Paul 290, *291*
French, Susan 12
Fright (1957) 122
Frith, Christopher viii
From Here to Eternity (1953) 106–07, 240
Frye, William 57
The Fugitive (TV) 263, 270
Fuller, Lance 25, 133–34
Fuller, Sam 24
Fun in Acalpulco 304
Gardner, Arthur 50
Gardner, Ava 168, 288, 289
Gardner, Joan 105
Gargan, William 159
Garner, James 162, 164
Garrison, Michael 57, 69, 70, 71
The Gay Divorcee (1934) 135
General Electric Theatre (TV) 287
Gere, Richard 205
Ghost of Dragstrip Hollow (1959) 99, 102, *103*

Gibson, Mimi *52*
Gilbert, Helen 128–29, *129*, 138
Gilling, John 146
Gingold, Michael viii
The Girl from Mandalay (1936) 243–45
Girls in Prison (1956) 123, 124, 125, 128, 130, 138
The Girls of Pleasure Island (1953) 47, 48
The Glass Web (1953) 190, 192
Glasser, Bernard 290, 292
Glen or Glenda (1953) 144
Gobel, George 30
The Goldbergs (TV) 236
Goldblum, Jeff 181
Gone with the Wind (1939) 303
Gordon, Alex 57, 122–43, *126*, 148, 149, 150
Gordon, Bert I. 263, 272, 275
Gordon, Richard 124, 125, 127, 144–52, *145, 148, 151*
Gorilla at Large (1954) 279
Gowland, Peter 301
Graham, Billy 92
Grandpa Was a Cop (TV pilot) 303
Granger, Farley 254, 255, 256
Grant, Cary 119, *120*
Grass, Gunter 65
Graves, Peter 188
The Green Mile (1999) 24, 33–35, *34*
Greenstreet, Sydney 4, 5
Greenwood, Charlotte 3
Greer, Dabbs 24, 33, 34, *34*, 35
Greystoke: The Legend of Tarzan, Lord of the Apes (1984) 210, 218
Griffin, Tod 153–66, *154, 156, 158, 161, 163, 165*
Grip of the Strangler see *The Haunted Strangler*
A Guide for the Married Man (1967) 303, 304
Gun Girls (1956) 24
Gunsmoke (TV) 99, 263
Haas, Charles 283
Hagen, Uta 167, 177, 265, 266
Hagman, Larry 224
Hale, Barbara 290
Hale, Creighton 132
Hall, Jon 102–04, 107
Halloween III: Season of the Witch (1983) 232
Hamilton, George 120
Hamlisch, Marvin 71
Hampton, Orville H. 141
Hansen, Myrna 192
Hanson, Peter 252
Harris, Cynthia 60
Harris, Jack H. 80, 81, 82, 85, 89, 91, 93–94, 150, 239

Harrison, Joan 282
Hart, Judith 124, 139
Hatfield, Hurd 114
A Hatful of Rain (stage) 84, 238
Hathaway, Henry 165
Hatton, Raymond 130, 132
The Haunted Strangler (1958) 148
Have Gun Will Travel (TV) 99, 285
Havens, Richie 65
Havoc, June 13
Hayden, Sean *12*
Hayden, Sterling 253
Hayes, Allison *16*
Hayward, Susan 134
Hayworth, Rita 168
He Fell Down Dead (novel) 6
Healey, Myron 18, 19
Hearst, William Randolph 9
Hedison, Al see Hedison, David
Hedison, David 167–85, *170, 172, 173, 175, 177, 179, 180, 184*
Hedren, Tippi 9
The Hellcats (1967) 44
Henreid, Paul 4, 186, 188
Henry, Mike 218
Hepburn, Audrey 143
Hepburn, Katharine 27
Herbert, Charles 174
Herbert, F. Hugh 186, 187
Here Come the Jets (1959) 294
Heston, Charlton 252
Highway Patrol (TV) 25
Highway to the Stars (TV) 277
Hilton, Conrad 236
Hit Parade of 1941 (1940) 187
Hitchcock, Alfred 9, 111, 119, 247, 254, 255–56, 282
Hitchcock, Pat 254
Hogan, Ben 279
Hole, William 102
Holland, Richard 156, *158*
Holliman, Earl 268
Holmes, Stuart 132, *133*
Holt, Nat 253
Holt, Tim 50
Home Before Dark (1958) 232
Homolka, Oscar 52
Hoover, J. Edgar 232
Hopper, William 111
Horton, Robert 188
The Hostage (1968) 94
Hot Rod (novel) 94
Hot Rod Gang (1958) 136
How to Marry a Millionaire (1953) 107
How to Marry a Millionaire (TV) 164
Howard, Joyce 228
Howard, Moe 290
Howlin, Olin 86, 90, 243
Hudson, Rock 187

Hughes, Howard 288
Hughes, Kathleen 186–96, *189, 191, 194*
Humberstone, H. Bruce 25
The Hunchback of Notre Dame (1923) 113
The Hunchback of Notre Dame (1939) 113, 115
The Hurricane (1937) 103
Hush...Hush Sweet Charlotte (1964) 94
Hussein (ibn Talal) *212*, 216
Huston, Walter 124
Hyman, Eliot 149
I Dream of Jeannie (TV) 25
I Was a Teenage Werewolf (1957) 122
Image of the Beast (1980) 96, *97*
The Impossible Years (stage) 30
The Incredible Shrinking Man (1957) 223
Indusi, Joe viii
Inescort, Frieda 132–33
Inherit the Wind (stage) 264
Invasion USA (1952) 220, 222–23, *224*, 227
The Invisible Man (audiobook) 117
Irons, Jeremy 181
Ironweed (1987) 194
It Came from Outer Space (1953) 186, 190–92, *191*
It! The Terror from Beyond Space (1958) 100
I've Lived Before (1956) 122
Jailhouse Rock (1957) 107
Janis, Edward 105
Janssen, David 193, 270
Jarmyn, Jil 25
Jenks, Frank 130
Jet Attack (1958) 140–41
Johns, Glynis 226
Johnson, Carl Tor 40, 41
Johnson, Greta 41
Johnson, Russell 186, 190
Johnson, Tor 19, 21, 22, 37, 38, *39*, 40–42, 43, *43*, 44
Johnson, Van 164
Jones, Morgan *282*
Journey into Freedom (1957) 24
Journey to the Center of the Earth (1959) 179
Joyce, Brenda 27
Kaaren, Suzanne 197–206, *199, 201, 203, 204*
Kane, Joe viii
Karatnytsky, Christine viii
Karloff, Boris 24, 47, 56, 57, 100
Karloff, Evelyn 56, 57
Karlson, Karl 87
Katzman, Sam 141
Kay, Roger 225–28
Kaye, Mary Ellen 124

Kazan, Elia 278, 279
Keatan, A. Harry 15
Kelly, Jack 193, 280, *281, 282*
Kelly, Patsy 187
Kennedy, Bill 252
Kennedy, Burt 54–55
Kennedy, John F. 63
Kennedy, Robert 230
Kenyon, Neal 63
Kenyon, Sandy 270
Kerr, Deborah 240
Kidd, Jonathan 268, *269*
Kiel, Richard 71
Kilgallen, Dorothy 113
King, Andrea 5, 6
King, Arthur 82
King, Stephen 33
The King of Queens (TV) 195
King Robot (unmade movie) 150
King Solomon's Mines (1950) 207, 211
Kinsella, Walter 159
Kiss and Tell (stage) 186, 292
Kleiser, Randal 270
Knight, Marcia 42, 43
Koch, Howard W. 266, 267
Kogan, Alexander viii
Kolchak: The Night Stalker (TV) 8–9
Kostelanetz, Andre 235
Kramer, Stanley 59
Labansat, Bob 40
Ladd, Cheryl 296
Lambert, Christopher 210, 218
Lancaster, Burt 240
Land of the Giants (TV) 283
Landau, Martin 119, *120*
Lang, Jennings 230
Langelaan, George 167
Lansing, Robert 272, 274, *274*
LaRue, Jack 41–42
The Last Starfighter (1984) 220, 232–33
Laughter in Hell (1933) 124
Laughton, Charles 113, 114, 115
Laven, Arthur 50, 51
Law and Order (1932) 124
Lawrence, Barbara 189–90
Leigh, Vivien 303
Lerner, Alan Jay 13
LeRoy, Mervyn 232
Lesser, Gene 265, 272, 276
Lesser, Sol 25, 29–30
Lessing, Arnold 105
Levy, Jules V. 50, 51
Lewis, Harry 2
Lewis, Jean Ann *see* Brent, Eve
Lewis, Jerry 107, 159, 303
Lewis, Ronald 52, *55*
Life (magazine) 62, 111, 112
The Life of Riley (TV) 208
The Life of the Party (stage) 3, 13

The Life Stories of Lucan and McShane (book) 147
Light, Karl 264
Linaker, Kay *see* Phillips, Kate
Lincoln, Elmo 209
Lippert, Robert L. 227, 288, 289
Lipton, Celia 114
Lloyd, Norman 282
Lockhart, Gene 126
Loewe, Frederick 13
Lommel, Ulli 33
Long, Richard 193
Lord, Jack 268
Loren, Sophia 168
Lorre, Peter 4, 5–6, 125, 183
Lost in Space (TV) 183, 232
The Lost World (novel) 178
The Lost World (1960) 167, 178–82, *179, 180*, 183–84
Lotery, Diana 283
Love at First Bite (1979) 119–20
Loving You (1957) 107
Lucan, Arthur 144, 146–47, 148
Lugosi, Bela 130, 144, 145–47, *145*, 148, *148*, 149, 150, *151*, 152, 199, 200, *201*, 202, *203*, 205
Lugosi, Lillian 144, 145, 146, 147, 149, 200
Lumet, Sidney 112, 224
Lupino, Ida 188
Lyon, Francis D. 192
Ma Perkins (radio) 235
Macabre (1958) 263, 264–68, *266, 267, 269*, 276
Macbeth (1948) 221
MacDonald, Kenneth 132
Mackaill, Dorothy 132
MacLaine, Shirley 207
Magers, Boyd viii
Mahoney, Jock 218
Main Street After Dark (1944) 125
Major V, the Daring Leader of the Underground (radio) 2
Makelim, Hal 125
Malden, Karl 278
Malone, Dorothy 194
Maltin, Leonard 207
Mama (TV) 236
Man Against Crime (TV) 159
Man Beast (1956) vii
The Man from U.N.C.L.E. (TV) 118–19
Man of Conflict (1953) 125
Mank, Greg viii
Mann, Jane 18, 21
The Marble Forest (novel) 263, 264
March, Fredric 169
Marco, Paul viii
Marcus, Vitina *179*
Market, Russell 198

Marnie (1964) 9
The Marriage-Go-Round (stage) 31
Marsh, Mae 124
Marshall, Herbert 174, *177*, 181
Martin, Dean 107, 159, 207
Martin, Ross 70–71, 73, 117
Martin Kane, Private Eye (TV) 159
Martucci, Mark viii
Marvin, Lee 279
Marx, Groucho 101, 183
Maschio, Johnny 288
Mason, Buddy 135
Masterpiece Theatre (radio) 235
Maté, Rudolph 189–90
Matheson, Richard 9, 10
Matthau, Walter 13, 224, 303
Mature, Victor 2
Maugham, W. Somerset 13
Maverick (TV) 164
May, Bob 183
The Maze (1953) vii
McCalla, Irish 8, 153, 162–63, *163*
McDonald, Frank 141
McDonnell, Dave viii
McDowall, Roddy 61–63, 221, 272
McEvoy, J. P. 198
McGavin, Darren 9
McGuire, Don 188–89
McKinney, Austin 43
McMahon, Leo 253
McQueen, Chad 258
McQueen, Steve 79, 82, 83–85, *85*, 86–87, 89, 92, 238, 239–40, *240*, 241, 242, 243, 258–59
McQueen, Terry 258
McShane, Kitty 147, 149
Medea (stage) 116
Meet Corliss Archer (radio) 186
Mellor, Douglas 40
Michaels, Dolores 226
Middleton, Wallace 127
The Mike Douglas Show (TV) 69, 218
Miles, Jim 40
Miles, Vera 27
Miller, Ann 187
Miller, Denny 207–19, *208, 212, 215,* 217
Miller, Scott *see* Miller, Denny
Millgate, Irvine H. 81–82
The Millionaire (TV) 164, 287
The Milton Berle Show (TV) 148
Mimieux, Yvette 296
Minter, George 144, 145–46, 147, 148, 149, 150
Miracles for Sale (1939) 204
Missing Women (1951) eight
Mr. and Mrs. North (stage) 111
Mr. Sardonicus (1961) 47, 51–54, *53, 55*

Mr. Skeffington (1944) 179
Mitchell, Cameron 219
Mitchell, Thomas 7, 115
Mitchum, Robert 167
Mix, Tom 132
Mona McCluskey (TV) 219
Monroe, Marilyn 107
Monster from the Surf see *Beach Girls and the Monster*
The Monster That Challenged the World (1957) 47, 49–51, *52*
Montgomery, Elizabeth 261
Montgomery, Ray 2
Montgomery, Robert 111, 114
A Month in the Country (stage) 167, 177, 179
The Moon Is Blue (stage) 186
Moore, Michael 252
Moore, Roger 182
Moore, Terry 182
Morgan, Bob 253
Morgan, Dennis 12
Morgan, Harry 285
Morris, Chester 122, 123, *126*, 127, 132, 138, 143
Morris, Rolland 255
Morrison, John 40
Morrow, Susan 266–67
Mother Riley Meets the Vampire (1952) 144, 145–52, *145, 148, 151*
Mulhall, Jack 132
Mulhare, Edward 221
Muni, Paul 264
Murphy, Barry viii
My Cousin Rachel (1952) 48
My Forbidden Past (1951) 289
My Pal, the King (1932) 132
My Son, the Vampire see *Mother Riley Meets the Vampire*
Mystery Science Theater (TV) 45
Nagel, Conrad 243–45
Naish, J. Carrol 6–7, *7*
The Narrow Margin (1952) 186
Navy Log (TV) 264
Nayfack, Nicholas 279–80
Neal, Patricia 284
Nealand, Dick 48
Nelson, Lori 136
Nelson, Ozzie 107
Nelson, Ricky *108*
Nero, Franco 185
Neumann, Kurt 171, 174, 176, *177*
Newland, John 8, 117, 118
Newman, Joseph 211
Newman, Paul 84, 267
Nicholson, Jack 194
Nicholson, James H. 123–24, 127, 129, 133, 135, 136, 138, 140, 141
Nielsen, Leslie 280, *281, 282*
Nielsen, Ray viii, 200
Night of the Ghouls (1958) 38

Night Over Taos (stage) 187
Night Train to Mundo Fine (1966) 44
Nimoy, Leonard 110, 115–17
Noble, Ray 235
Nolan, Jeanette 285
North by Northwest (1959) 119, 282
Northern Pursuit (1943) 4
Northwest Passage (TV) 208
Novak, Eva *133*
Nye, Ben 169
Oates, Warren 57
Objective, Burma! (1945) 1
O'Bradovich, Bill 113
O'Brien, Dave 200–01
O'Brien, Edmond 253
O'Brien, Pat 124
O'Connell, Brian viii
O'Connor, Donald 187
Odd Man Out (1947) 220, 221
Offerman, George, Jr. 5
O'Herlihy, Dan 220–33, *222, 225, 227, 231*
O'Keeffe, Miles 217
Old Mother Riley's New Venture (1949) 149
Old Yeller (1957) 296
Oliphant, Jim 38, 40
Oliver, Susan 266
Omega Code (1999) 185
Omega Code 2 (2001) 185
Omnibus (TV) 112, 117, 263
One Million B.C. (1940) 250
One Step Beyond (TV) 1, 8, 110, 117–18, *118*
Operation Neptune (TV) 153, 155–59, *158*
Oscar Wilde (stage) 2
O'Sullivan, Maureen 29, 209
Our Gal Sunday (radio) 235
The Outer Limits (TV) 263, 268–70, 277, 282–83
Owens, Patricia 171, 174, 176, *177*, 181
Page, Geraldine 263
Pal, George 252
Palance, Jack 160
Papp, Joe 177
Parker, Eleanor 2, 12
Parkins, Barbara 259
Parrish, Leslie 296
Parry, Harvey 253
Pascaretti, Clint A.P. viii
Pascaretti, Erin Ray viii
Pascaretti, Rufus viii
Pascaretti, Tigger viii
Patri, Dan viii
Paul, Louis viii
Payton, Lee *88*
Peck, Gregory 178, 277
Penn, Arthur 111
Perdue, Virginia 6

Perfect Family (1992 TV movie) 77
Perry Mason (TV) 111, 263
Peters, Brooke L. *see* Petroff, Boris
Petroff, Boris 15, 16, 18–19, 20, 21, 250–51
Petroff, Gloria 250
Peyton Place (TV) 194–95, 247, 259
Philco TV Playhouse (TV) 277
Phillips, Howard 234–36, 237, 238, 242, 246
Phillips, Kate 82, 85, 89, 90, 234–46, *235, 245*
Phipps, William viii
Photon (magazine) vii
Pickford, Mary 160
The Pickwick Papers (1954) 125
Pidgeon, Walter 280
Pierce, Jack P. 298–99
Piscator, Erwin 111
Pittman, Montgomery 281
A Place in the Sun (1951) 252
Planet of the Apes (TV) 271–72, 273
Playboy (magazine) 169
Poitier, Sidney 219
Pollack, Sydney 176
Pollexfen, Jack 223
Power, Tyrone 167, 168
Powers, Mala 192
Presley, Elvis 107, 128, 296, 303, *304*
Preston, Robert 233
Price, Vincent 174, *177*, 181
Prince, William 263, 266, *266*, 267, *269*
Principe, George 38, 40
Prine, Andrew 268
The Prodigal Planet (1983) 96
Promise Her Anything (1966) 186
Provost, Jeanne viii
Provost, Oconee viii
Prowse, Juliet 219
Quo Vadis (1951) 211
Rain (stage) 13
Rains, Claude 19, 178, 179–81
Randell, Ron 127
The Rat Pack (1998 TV movie) 233
Raymond, Gene 30
The Rebel (TV) 95
Redgrave, Michael 167
Reed, Carol 220
Reed, Donna 106
Reeve, Christopher 1, *10*, 11, 12
Reeves, George 248
Reform School Girl (1957) 123, 139
Rennie, Michael 178, 283
Requiem for a Gunfighter (1965) 138
Return of the Fly (1959) 171, 177

Rhoden, Elmar, Jr. 123
Rhodes, Erik 135
Rhodes, Gary viii
The Richard Boone Show (TV) 284, 285
Ridgely, John 2
Ritt, Martin 277
River of No Return (1954) 186
Rivers, Joan 63, 65
Road to Paradise (1930) 132
Robards, Jason 74
Robert Montgomery Presents (TV) 110, 111–15, *113*, 117, 118, 119
Robertson, Cliff 109, 268–69
Robeson, Paul 111
RoboCop (1987) 232
RoboCop 2 (1990) 232
RoboCop 3 (1993) 232
Robotham, George 213, 214
Rocky Jones, Space Ranger (TV) 1, 8
Roddenberry, Gene 115–16, 284
Rogers, Kasey 247–62, *251, 255, 260, 261*
Rogue Cop (1954) 110, 112, 119
Rolfe, Guy 53–54, *53*
Roman, Ruth 164–65
Rooney, Mickey 128, 132
Rosenstein, Sophie 3
Roth, Gene 162, 164, *165*
Rubin, Richard M. 138
Rubin, Stanley 186
Runaway Daughters (1956) 123, 124, 128
Runser, Mary viii
Rush, Barbara 190, 252
Rusoff, Lou 123, 134, 135–36
Ruth, Jean 254
Ryan, Edward 5
Rydell, Mark 176
The Saint (TV) 182
St. John, Jill 178, *180*
Sale, Richard 187
Sally and Saint Anne (1952) 189–90
Samson and Delilah (1949) 249
Sanders, George 181
Sargent, Dick 259–60
Sarnoff, Bob 235
Sarnoff, David 235
Schallert, William 13
Schary, Dore 112
Schenck, Aubrey 109, 266–67
Schreiber, Else 178
Schreiber, Taft 229, 230, 231
Scott, Gordon 24, 25–27, 29, 30, *30, 31*, 218
Scott, Jacqueline 263–76, *266, 269, 273, 274, 276*
Scrivani, Rich viii
The Search for Bridey Murphy (book) 122

The Search for Bridey Murphy (1956) 122
The Secret of Dr. Kildare (1939) 128
Sen Yung, Victor *161*, 162
Serling, Rod 281
Seymour, Jane 11, 12
Shadow of a Woman (1946) 6
Shake, Rattle and Rock (1956) 123
Shane (1953) 160
Shauer, Melville 128
Shaw, George Bernard 120
Shayne, Bette 8
Shayne, Robert 8
Shayne, Stephanie 8
The She-Creature (1956) 122–43, *126, 129, 131, 133, 135, 137, 140, 142*
She Demons (1958) 153, 160–64, *161, 163, 165*
She Devil (1957) 164
Sheena, Queen of the Jungle (TV) 8, 153
Shepard, Bill 11
Shield for Murder (1954) 127
Ship of Fools (1965) 59, 62, 64
Shoop, Pamela 273, *274*
Siegel, Don 271
Signoret, Simone 186
Silver City (1951) 252
Simonson, Theodore 82, 93, 236–37, 239
Sinatra, Frank 188, 207
Sinclair, Mary 114
Siodmak, Curt 4
Skelton, Red 155
Skouras, Spyros 44
The Skydivers (1963) 44
Sloane, Bart 87
Small, Edward 141
Smalls, Charlie 64
Smith, William 207–08, 209
Sofaer, Abraham 56
Softness, John 63, 76, 77
Sohl, Jerry 9
Sokoloff, Vladimir 297, 298
Some Came Running (1958) 207
Somebody Up There Likes Me (1956) 84
Somewhere in Time (1980) 1, 9–12, *10, 12*
Son of Blob (1972) 93–94
The Son of Robin Hood (1959) 171, 176
Space Master X-7 (1958) 287, 288, 289–91, *291*, 292, *293*
Spalding, Tom 80, 86, 87, 93
Spangler, Vincent 80, 86, 87, 90, 93
Special Agent (1949) 248
Spielberg, Steven 270
Stafford, Bing 40
Stafford, Graham 40

Stanley, Kim 278
Star Trek (TV) 15, 115–16, 277, 283–84, *285*
Star Trek: The Next Generation (TV) 110, 117
Star Trek III: The Search for Spock (1984) 115, 116
Star Trek IV: The Voyage Home (1986) 110, 115, *116*
Starrett, Charles 132
Steinmetz, Charles Proteus 65
Sterling, Robert 182
Stevens, Leslie 268–69
Stevens, Onslow 9
Stevens, Robert 282
Stevens, Stella 169
Stevens, Warren 277–86, *278, 281, 282, 285*
Stewart, James 110
Stoianovich, Christian 77, 78
Stoney Burke (TV) 268
Strangers on a Train (1951) 247, 249, 254–57, *255*
Streep, Meryl 195
Strosnider, Lee 43
Studio One (TV) 277
Submarine Seahawk (1959) 141
The Sullivans (1944) 1, 4, 5, 7
The Sun Also Rises (1957) 168
Sundown Beach (stage) 278
Suspense (TV) 148, 277
Sword of Venus (1953) 222–23, 227
Szwarc, Jeannot 9, 10, 11, 12
Tales from the Crypt (TV) 24
Tales of Wells Fargo (TV) 99
Tarzan and the Trappers (1966 compilation) 30, 31–32
Tarzan of the Movies (book) 207, 217–18
Tarzan the Ape Man (1932) 209
Tarzan, the Ape Man (1959) 207–18, *208, 212, 215*, 219
Tarzan, the Ape Man (1981) 217–18
Tarzan the Fearless (1933) 210
Tarzan's Fight for Life (1958) 24, 25–30, *28, 30*, 31–32, *31*
Taylor, Robert 112
Teenage Diary 94
The Ten Commandments (1956) 126
The Texas School of the Air (radio) 24
There's No Business Like Show Business (1954) 107
A Thief in the Night (1972) 95–96
The Thing from Another World (1951) 82
This Island Earth (1955) 133
This Time for Keeps (1947) 11
Thomas, Ann 202

Thomas, Lyn 287–95, *289, 291,* 294
Thompson, Marshall 193, *194*
Three Bad Sisters (1956) 192
The Three Faces of Eve (1957) 267
The Three Stooges 100, 290
Three Strangers (1946) 4–5
Thriller (TV) 47, 56–57, 110, 118–19
Tighe, Virginia 122
The Time Machine (audiobook) 116–17
The Time Tunnel (TV) 283
Timpone, Tony viii
The Tin Drum (1979) 62, 65
Titanic (1953) 47, 48–49, *50*
Titanic (1997) 47, 48–49
Tobacco Road (stage) 19
Tobey, Kenneth 277, 282
The Today Show (TV) 69
The Tom Duggan Show (TV) 107
Tomorrow Is Forever (1946) 111
Tompkins, Darlene 296–305, *298, 299, 301, 302, 304*
Tone, Franchot 204
Top Hat (1935) 135
Torres, Raquel 104, 201
Toulouse-Lautrec, Henri de 65, 68
Tracy, Spencer 169
Treasures of Literature (TV) 221–22
Turner, Lana 32
Twilight of Honor (1963) 95
The Twilight Zone (TV) 277, 281–82
Twin Peaks (TV) 24
Two by Saroyan (stage) 60
Two Lost Worlds (1950) 247, 249–52, *250, 251*
Ullmann, Liv 77
Ulmer, Arianné 297
Ulmer, Edgar G. 296, 297, 298, 300
The Undead (1957) 122
Under Cover Man (1936) 199
The Underwater City (1962) 141
The Unearthly (1957) 15–23, *16, 17, 20*
Valdes, David 33, 34
Valentino, Rudolph 132

Vampire Over London see *Mother Riley Meets the Vampire*
Van Dyke, Vonda 94
Vaughn, Robert 118–19
Veidt, Conrad 228
The Veil (TV) 24
Venora, Diane 185
Vernon, Irene 259
The Very Thought of You (1944) 12
Vicker, Angus see Felsen, Henry
Voodoo Woman (1957) 128, 136
Voyage to the Bottom of the Sea (1961) 182
Voyage to the Bottom of the Sea (TV) 167, 168, 174, 181, 182–83, *184*, 277, 283
Wagner, Robert 47, *50*
Wagon Train (TV) 54–56, 211
Walker, Robert 247, 254, 255, *255*, 256
Wallis, Hal B. 289, 292
Wallman, Jan 64, 69
Walters, Luana 130–31, 138
Wanted: Dead or Alive (TV) 92
Warner, Jack L. 228, 232
Washburn, Beverly 296
Weaver, Dennis 270
Webb, Jack 35, 38
Webber, Diane *184*
Webber, Peggy 221–22
Weissmuller, Johnny 103, 207, 209, 218
Welch, Raquel *299*
Weller, Peter 232
Welles, Orson 111, 127, 221
Wells, H.G. 116
West, Frederick 136–38
West Point (TV) 25
Whale, James 234
What Ever Happened to Baby Jane? (novel) 94
When Worlds Collide (1951) 252
Where Love Has Gone (1964) 134
White, Christine 263, 267, 268
White, David 259, *260*
White, James Gordon 44
White, Robb 266
Whitmore, James 277, 284
The Wide Country (TV) 268
Wilcox, Fred McLeod 280
A Wild Irish Night see *Old Mother Riley's New Venture*

The Wild Wild West (TV) 57, 59, 69–76, *73*, 110, 117
Wilde, Cornel 188
Wilder, Billy 288
Williams, Adam 119, *120*
Williams, Bill 290, 292
Williams, Esther 11
Williams, Grant 9
Williams, Wade viii
Winchell, Walter 32
Winwood, Estelle 226
The Wiz (stage) 64
The Women (1939) 200
Wood, Edward D., Jr. 37–38, 45, 144
Wood, Mark 261
The Wooden Dish (1955) 264
Woodward, Joanne 267
Worley, Jo Anne 63
Worlock, Frederick 114
The Wrong Man (1957) 57, 111–12
Yangha, Thomas 214
Yarbrough, Jean 200, 201
Yeaworth, Irvin S. 81, 82, 83–84, 86–87, 90, 91, *92*, 93, 236–37, 238–39, 241, 242, 243
Yeaworth, Jean 82, 239
York, Dick 259–60
York, Michael 185
You Are There (TV) 112
You Bet Your Life (TV) 101
You Can't Take It with You (stage) 10
Young, Gig 2
Young, Loretta 57, 132
The Young Lions (1958) 112
Young Mr. Lincoln (1939) 234
You're Never Too Young (1955) 107
Zanuck, Darryl F. 187
Zemeckis, Robert 263
Zigmond, Jerry 123
Zimbalist, Al 211
Zimbalist, Donald 211
Zimmerman, Vernon 32
Zinnemann, Fred 106
Zucco, George 125–26
Zucco, Stella 125
Zugsmith, Albert 222, 223